S0-AWL-462

AUSTRALIA
• AT COST •

A TRAVELLER'S GUIDE TO MAJOR TOWNS AND CITIES

Patricia Daum

LITTLE HILLS PRESS

ACKNOWLEDGEMENTS
Thanks to the co-operation of the Tourist Commissions of the Federal and State Governments of Australia, the National Roads and Motorist Association (N.R.M.A.), and the Shire Councils this book has become a reality. My thanks also go to Fay Smith and Charles Burfitt for their input.

Photographs by Eduard Domin
Designed by Richard Hassall
Typeset by Deblaere Typesetting Pty Ltd
Printed in Singapore by Kyodo-Shing Loong Printing Industries (Pte) Limited

© Little Hills Press, 1987

Little Hills Press
34 Bromham Road, Bedford MK40 2QD
United Kingdom

Regent House, 37-43 Alexander St.,
Crows Nest. NSW, 2065. Australia

ISBN. 0 949773 67 0

All rights reserved. No part of this publication may be reproduced, stored in a retrieval system, or transmitted in any form or by any means, electronic, mechanical, photocopying, recording or otherwise, without the prior permission in writing of the publishers.

DISCLAIMER
Whilst all care has been taken by the publisher and author to ensure that the information is accurate and up to date, the publisher does not take responsibility for the information published herein. The recommendations are those of the Author, and as things get better or worse, places close and others open up some elements in the book may be inaccurate when you get there. Please write and tell us about it so we can update in subsequent editions.

ABBREVIATIONS

C – Celsius.
m – metre
km – kilometre
ha – hectare
kg – kilogram
Hwy – highway
RO – room only
B&Lt.B – bed and light breakfast
B&B – Bed and breakfast
ppn – Per Person Night
Ph – telephone
TAA – Australian Airlines.

CONVERSION

1m = 3.28 feet
1km = 0.62 miles
1kg = 2.20 pounds
1ha = 2.47 acres
1 sq.km = 0.386 sq. miles
0 deg.C = 32.4 deg. Fahrenheit

CONTENTS

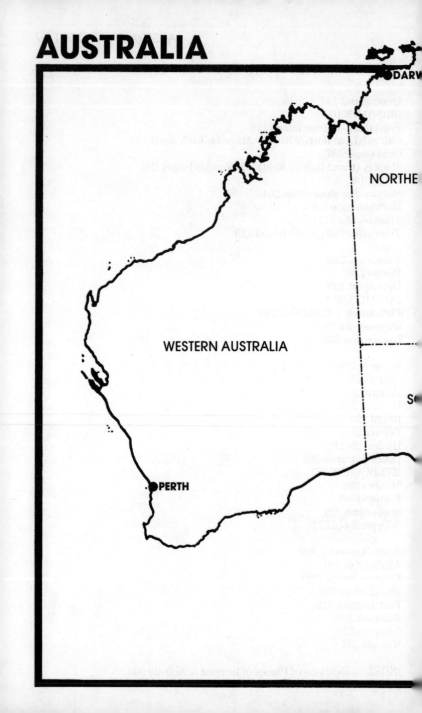

INTRODUCTION

Like the English, Australians call 'gas', petrol; 'fries', chips; but they do have McDonalds, Pizza Hut, Kentucky Fried. The country is a strange blend of United States consumerism and English social structure. The legal system, public service and government structure is English based, but the social environment is heavily influenced by US media and movies. California has a lot in common with Australia's east coast.

SOME HISTORY

This land measuring 7,682,300 square kilometres was settled by aboriginals around 20,000 years ago. There were between 300,000 and 500,000 when the European settlers arrived in 1788. Captain Arthur Phillip, was assigned the task of transporting 564 male and 192 female convicts to the shores of the new colony of New South Wales, previously known as New Holland and earlier The Great South Land of the Holy Spirit. The use of Australia as a penal settlement was as a direct result of the American War of Independence, however, by the early 1830s all convict transportation had ceased.

In the 1850s, the discovery of gold, brought a huge influx of migrants in search of their fortune. Australia's population increased from a little over 400,000 to more than a million in 10 years. Today the population is in excess of 16 million.

Australians fought in Word War I and II, Korea and Vietnam. The nation has lost over 100,000 in War this century. Of these, 60,000 were lost in the first world war.

The political make up of the country is that of a federation of states. Federation took place on 1st January, 1901. Since that time Australia has started to play a much greater role in world affairs.

THE PEOPLE

During the 1950s and 60s it provided assisted passage to people wishing to migrate from Europe and the United States, however, it was not until the late 1960s that restricted entry to Australia from Asia was eased. In the last 40 years Australian society has undergone a tremendous change with now one in four people being a migrant or child of a migrant.

Australia since the 1970s has become aware of its presence in Southeast Asia. The countries of the region are starting to have more of an impact on Australian life. The new migrants are Asian, and the society reflects this blend of European and Asian.

The vast majority of Australians belong to the Christian Churches. Anglicans are in the majority and 25% of the population are Roman Catholic reflecting the influence of Irish and Italian migration.

85% of the population live in urban areas. The East coast of Australia is the most populous because of the fertile plain east of the Great Dividing Range. The major cities are the state capitals, and the most populous state is New South Wales with almost 6 million people, followed by Victoria with 4.5 million people.

THE LAND

Australia is the flattest continent and the driest: 60% of the country is arid, receiving less than 400 millimetres per year. Its size gives it a varied climate but one without great extremes. Slightly more than half of Queensland, a third of Western Australia and 80 % of the Northern Territory lie within the tropical zone. The climate of the towns is covered so you will know what to expect, for example, if you decide to go to Townsville in December (it will be wet).

Central and southern Queensland are subtropical, with the warm temperate regions being in New South Wales, South Australia and Western Australia. The coolest areas are Victoria, southwest Western Australia and Tasmania.

The Vegetation is almost entirely evergreen with over 550 different species of eucalypts and 700 species of acacias. Its fauna consists of reptiles, such as the freshwater crocodile, the frill-necked lizard (360 species of lizard); Mammals, such as the platypus and the echidna (the only egg laying mammals). Most, such as the kangaroo and koala, are marsupials.

SPORT

Sport is an Australian addiction. In the summer, Cricket is the major sport, however, tennis, baseball, field hockey, netball and athletics (track and field) are popular and in the winter months, football of various codes (rugby, rubgy league, Australian Rules, soccer) take over.

TRAVEL GUIDELINES

GETTING TO AUSTRALIA

For travellers to Australia a valid passport is required and visitors of all nationalities (except New Zealand) must obtain a visa before arrival. These are available at Australian embassies, High Commission and consular offices listed in the local telephone directory.

CURRENCY

The Australian Currency is decimal, with the dollar as the basic unit. Notes come in colourful array of $100, $50, $20, $10, $5, and $2 demoninations, with minted coins for lesser amounts including the gold $1 coin. There is no limit to personal funds when entering the country and visitors may leave with whatever they brought in, but with no more than $5,000 in notes and coins of Australian Currency. Currency exchange facilites are available at international airports, and most banks and large hotels.

SEEING AUSTRALIA

Most of the roads on the eastern seaboard are sealed and the major cities are linked by four-lane expressways or excellent highways. Australians drive on the left hand side of the road like the British and Japanese. The infrastructure and the services in the country are those of an advanced western nation. As outlined in the book in detail, you can see Australia by rail, motoring by bus or car (all the well known car rental companies are in major cities) or by flying. A comprehensive network of domestic and international air services has been developed, with one of the best safety records in the world.

ACCOMMODATION

Australia has well-developed hotel and motel accommodation in cities, resorts and rural areas. A typical room is usually spotlessly clean, and has air-conditioning, a private bathroom, tea and coffee making facilities, a telephone, television, and a small refrigerator. Because of the climate, many hotels and motels have small outdoor swimming pools.

Although the rooms are often the same, there is a difference between a hotel and a motel in Australia. A hotel must have a public bar among its facilities; motels often provide a bar for paying guests and invited friends, although they are not obliged to do this. Most hotels and motels have a dining room or restaurant.

Premier class hotels include names familiar throughout the world – Hilton, Sheraton, Regent International, Hyatt and Intercontinental can all be found in Australia's major cities.

Motels have generally been developed to meet the needs of travelling motorists and are located in cities, towns and resorts, and along major highways. Youth Hostels offer an inexpensive alternative to budget conscious travellers in most parts of the country. Membership of the International or Australian Youth Hostel Federation is required. Most towns and holiday resorts have caravan parks and camping grounds with shower and toilet facilities, at very reasonable rates.

CONCESSIONAL AIRFARES:

Ansett Kangaroo Airpass – $500 for 6,000km or $800 for 10,000km. Certain stopover conditions apply. Students over 15 and under 19, enrolled at a secondary education establishment, receive a 50% reduction while students under 26 receive a 25% reduction. Standby Fares – save 20% Flexi-Fares – save 45% and Apex Fares – save 35%.

Australian Airlines has an Air Pass which costs –

$540 for up to 6,000 km minimum 2 stopovers and a maximum of 3

$860 for up to 10,000 km minimum 3 stopovers and a maximum of 7

You must stay away at least 10 nights and the journey must not take longer than 42 nights, and at least 4 nights must be spent in a town which is not a capital city.

Air NSW has a Take off 35 fare which saves 35% but is for a min. of 7 days stay, and must be paid for at least 30 days in advance. Also special return excursion fares between Sydney & Melbourne, Sydney & Brisbane and Melbourne and Hobart. They also have standby fares and a red centre circle fare $504.90.

EXPRESS COACH SPECIAL FARES:

The three major Australian bus companies sell bus passes for unlimited travel on their routes for a certain number of days. If you intend to travel exclusively by bus, these offer considerable savings.

Ansett Pioneer has the Aussiepass. There are 4 types:

the 15 day pass for $285 adults and children under 15 $238

the 21 day pass for $375 adults and children under 15 $310

the 30 day pass for $495 adults and children under 15 $418

the 60 day pass for $690 adults and children under 15 $540.

Greyhound has the Bus Pass and again there are 4 types:

the 14 day pass for $275 adults and children under 15 $220

the 21 day pass for $375 adults and children under 15 $300

the 30 day pass for $499 adults and children under 15 $399

the 60 day pass for $735 adults and children under 15 $588

Deluxe has the Koala Pass – the 10 day pass for $199 adults (passengers from overseas only)

the 14 day pass for $270 adults

the 22 day pass for $370 adults

the 32 day pass for $449 adults

the 62 day pass for $690 adults

the 90 day pass for $990 adults.

For example if you were to travel from Sydney to Cairns, across to Mt. Isa and down to Alice Springs, then to Adelaide and back to Sydney, the usual fare would be $418.90, if you purchased a 21 day Bus Pass for $375 you would have saved $43 or about 10%.

There is one big advantage with a bus pass, and that is it enables you to overcome some rather annoying Government Rules and Regulations, particularly in New South Wales. The Government, in its wisdom, tries to protect its railways and does not permit the interstate buses to carry passengers unless their final destination is interstate. This restriction has been partly lifted for a six month's trial period along the coast of NSW, and hopefully it will not be reintroduced.

Tassie Pass: Unlimited travel on the Tasmanian Red Line coaches (Aussie-pass and Bus Pass accepted) – 7 days $53, 14 days $66.

Westrail Pass: Unlimited travel on Westrail coach and rail services in W.A. – 14 days $140, 30 days $220 and 90 days $600.

RAIL PASSES:

Queensland: 14 days $152, 21 days $184, 1 month $231.

New South Wales: Nurail Pass $110 per person for 14 consecutive days of unlimited travel. Weekly Rover Travel Pass $22.50 per person. Quarterly and Yearly Rover Tickets are available. Day Rover ticket $5.50.

Good travelling and we hope you enjoy the stay.

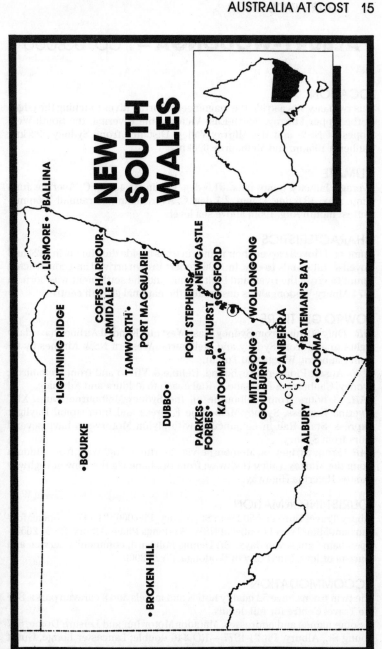

ALBURY-WODONGA – Pop. 55,000

LOCATION
This twin city sits astride the magnificent Murray River touching the edges of the Upper Murray, North-East Victoria, the Riverina, the South-West Slopes of NSW and the Murray Valley. Distance from: Sydney 592 km; Canberra 195km; and Melbourne 300km.

CLIMATE
Average January temp. max. 31.5 deg. C min. 15.4 deg. C; Average June temp. max. 13.6 deg. C min. 2.4 deg. C. Average annual rainfall 796mm – wettest month Aug. 195m above sea level.

CHARACTERISTICS
Hume and Hovell carved their names in trees beside the Murray in 1824 and Hovell's still stands to-day. In 1836 Robert Brown arrived and constructed a punt to cross the river, and built an inn, and the settlement was born. In 1974 Albury-Wodonga was designated the national growth centre.

HOW TO GET THERE
AIR.   Only 50 mins from Sydney. East-West and Kendell Airlines have daily flights to and from Sydney and Melbourne. Western NSW Airlines fly to/from Canberra, Wagga and Tumut.
BUS.   Ansett Pioneer, Greyhound, Deluxe & VIP to and from Melbourne, Sydney, Canberra & Brisbane. V/Rail coach to Mildura and Adelaide.
RAIL.   3 hours from Melbourne on the Sydney/Melbourne route. XPT Riverina Express, Sydney/Melbourne Express and Intercapital Daylight Express. State Rail in conjunction with Mylon Motorways have several tours from Sydney.
CAR.   From Sydney or Melbourne via the Hume Highway; from Mildura along the Murray Valley Highway; from Brisbane via the Newell Highway and the Riverina Highway.

TOURIST INFORMATION
Albury Travel Bureau, 550 Dean St., Albury, Ph (060) 21 1477 – open Mon-Sun 9am-5pm. Travel Centre of NSW, Wodonga Place, Albury, Ph 21 2655 – Open 9am-5pm seven days. Mr. Dennis Millward, community service and tourism officer, Rural City of Wodonga, Ph 24 2000.

ACCOMMODATION
The twin towns have 52 quality hotels and motels and 9 caravan parks. See the Travel Centre for full details.
   Some names and addresses: Matador Motor Inn and Leisure Dome, 617 Young St., Albury, Ph 21 1877 – RO $46 double; Lancaster Lodge, Guest House, 473 Young St., Albury, Ph 21 3127 – BB $30 double; The Terminus

Thredbo Creek, New South Wales

Hotel, 417 Dean St., Ph 21 3166 – B&B family rooms fr $35, Doubles fr. $26. Stagecoach Motel, Melbourne Rd., Wodonga, Ph 24 3044 – RO $42-48; Golden Fleece Bunkhouse Motel, 180 Melbourne Rd., Wodonga, Ph 24 2219 - RO $30-32 double; Trek 31 Tourist Park, Cnr. Hume Hwy & Catherine Cresc, Albury North, Ph 25 4355, – sites $8-10 double; Wodonga Drive-Inn Caravan Park, Melbourne Rd., Ph 24 2598 – site $6.50 double – overnite vans $15.50-20.

EATING OUT
Just a few names and addresses: The Saucery, 454 Dean St., Albury, Ph 21 1002 for fine foods and fine wines; The Albion Hotel, Dean St., Ph 21 3377 is open 7 days for breakfast, lunch and tea; Pete's Pizza, 1079 Mate St., North Albury, Ph 25 2900; Albury's Food Complex, 272 Dean St., Albury, Ph 21 4491; The Curry Kitchen, 36 High St., Wodonga, Ph 24 2243 for curries and an extensive Australian menu. For fast service try Ollie's Family Restaurant, High St., Wodonga.

POINTS OF INTEREST
If you will be in Albury-Wodonga on a Wednesday then contact the Tourist Bureau on 21 1477, and reserve your seat on the Development Corporation's free guided bus tour. You will see town planning at its best, and business and factory projects like Uncle Ben's, Borg-Warner, Sanyo, Moore Paragon, Lee Jeans and the ANM Paper Mill.

` The Albury Regional Museum, Australia Park is definitely worth a visit – open 10.30 am to 4.30pm daily, and the Albury Regional Art Centre has permanent and changing exhibitions – open from 11am daily. The Royal Australian Army Ordnance Corp Museum, 31 Supply Battalion, Gaza Ridge Barracks, Bandiana, displays military vehicles. At Albury Pottery you can take a self-guiding tour and watch the potters at work – open daily.

The old iron Waterwheel beside the Hume Highway in Albury was used for gold mining, and later to power chaffcutting and milking machines. Albury-Wodonga has its own Cobb & Co coach. It is a replica of the original coaches.

For aquatic sports, head for Lake Hume only 12km upstream from town. It has 320km of shoreline, and is ideal for sailing, swimming, water skiing, canoeing, windsurfing, pedal boating, a trout farm (open 9am-5pm seven days) and fishing. If you intend to fish then make sure you have both an NSW and Vic Fishing License. The Wymah ferry links NSW with Vic and is operated by friendly folk. At Dora Dora there is 130 year old hotel, which is more like an entertainment centre than a pub.

Albury-Wodonga's latest attraction is a new paddlesteamer modelled on the former PS Cumbeeroona. It is a wood-fired steamer and will operate daily from October to April (water level permitting). Cruises will last for about an hour morning and afternoon, with a longer luncheon cruise from 12-2pm with a boxed lunch available.

There is a lovely Riverbank Walk at Albury (museum has leaflets). The 7.5km marked trails from Nail Can Hill go along the river, over Monument

Hill and past old gold diggings - maps can be obtained from the Travel Centre.

If you have time then a visit to the Flying Fruit Fly Circus is a must – for bookings and details Ph 21 7433.

FACILITIES

The Wodonga Entertainment Centre, Hume Hwy, has dodge 'ems, pinball machines, etc. Indoor cricket, indoor tennis, roller skating, ten pin bowling, swimming, waterslide, grass skiing at Inverlock Lakeside Ski Park about 32km from Albury, lawn bowls (14 licensed clubs), snow skiing (Mt. Buffalo Mt. Hotham, Mt. Beauty, Falls Creek), and fossicking (try Beechworth). Bike riding is popular and there are safe cycle tracks through cities and towns. Rutherglen's hot air balloon operates from behind the Stanton and Kileen winery from March to November – bookings through the Travel Bureau. You can hire canoes and have water skiing tuition on Lake Hume. If you feel like getting away from it all then Trains'n Trecks in Morgan Country have donkeys for trekking and children's rides. Gelanglo Park, Lavington and Tooma Ranch, Tallangatta have horse riding facilities. Regular horse racing meetings are held in Albury/Wodonga.

FESTIVAL

Wheelbarrow Race from Beechworth Post Office is the highlight of their Sports Day held each New Year's Day for over a century.

OUTLYING ATTRACTIONS

BEECHWORTH is known as Victoria's best preserved gold town, and it is well worth a visit. It has over 130 classified buildings dating from the Gold Rush of the 1850's. An excellent booklet 'A Guide to Historic Beechworth' is available from the tourist information centre. Beechworth is the centre of a fruit growing area. At High Grove Berries you can pick your own berries in December and January seven days a week from 10am-5pm.

YACKANDANDAH is the Strawberry Capital of Victoria. Allan's Flat Strawberry Farm also makes strawberry wine! Yackandandah has been classified by the National Trust and contains some impressive buildings. Cottage crafts are a feature of the Workshop.

The N.E. WINE GROWING AREA around Rutherglen is rich in history as well as wine. The town sprang up virtually overnight when gold was discovered in what's now the main street. The first vines were planted in 1851 by three Germans, and today there are 26 wineries in the area. Most are open from 9am-5pm Mon-Fri and some are open on Sat & Sun as well. On the long weekend in June a 'Winery Walkabout' is held. It provides a blend of information and informality on the Walkabout with music, tastings of special wine releases and a colonial dinner.

The 'famous' bushranger 'Mad Dog' Morgan roamed around Culcairn in what is known today as Morgan Country. Visit the arts and crafts centre at Culcairn and the Zion Lutheran Church at Walla Walla, and picnic at Morgan's Lookout.

WANGARATTA'S Drage Airworld Museum is an unusual undertaking. It has been developed around antique and historic planes, and many aviation enthusiasts come here for a flight in a vintage machine. The Cathedral in the town has some fine stained glass windows.

ARMIDALE – Pop. 18,900

LOCATION:
New England Tablelands which are part of the Great Dividing Range which stretches from around Newcastle to the Queensland Border. Distance from: Sydney 563km; Melbourne 1,268km; Brisbane 464km; Adelaide 1,636km.

CLIMATE:
Average temperatures: January max 26.6 deg. C – min. 13.5 deg C; June max. 13.9 deg. C – min. 1.7 deg. C.; Average annual rainfall 795mm; 1000m above sea level; Has definite seasons and occasional snowfalls in winter.

CHARACTERISTICS:
Principal town of the area and site of the New England University. District produces fine merino wool, wheat and fruit.

TOURIST INFORMATION:
135 Rusden Street, Tel. (067) 72866. Hours: Mon-Fri 8.30am-5pm.

HOW TO GET THERE:
AIR.   East-West have twice daily flights to Sydney and flights to Tamworth. Eastern Airlines have daily flights to/from Brisbane and on Saturdays and Sundays to the Gold Coast.
BUS.   Ansett-Pioneer, Deluxe and Greyhound buses stop at Armidale on their Sydney/Brisbane or Melbourne/Brisbane services. Deluxe also stop on their Brisbane/Adelaide direct service travelling via Ballina. The usual restrictions apply i.e. you must have an Australia wide bus pass or have travelled interstate by public transport. There is also a service to/from Coffs Harbour and Port Macquarie.
RAIL.   On the Sydney/Brisbane line. The XPT does the run on Mon, Wed & Fri and takes appox. 8 hours, and other days there is a normal service. Coaches travel to Uralla, Tamworth, Guyra, Glen Innes and Tenterfield.
CAR.   From Sydney – via the New England Highway from Newcastle. From Melbourne – via either the Princes or Hume Highways to Sydney or via the Newell Highway to Tamworth and then the New England Highway. From Brisbane – via the Pacific Highway and then either Route 78 from Coffs Harbour, the Gwydir Highway from Grafton, the Oxley Highway from Port Macquarie or the Bruxner Highway from Ballina.

ACCOMMODATION:

16 motels, 3 hotels, 3 caravan parks – contact the Tourist Information office for a comprehensive list. A few examples: Cattleman's Motor Inn, 31 Marsh St., ph 72 7788 – RO $44 double; Rose Villa, New England H'way, Ph 72 3872 – RO $28-32 double; Tattersalls Hotel, 174 Beardy St., ph 72 2247 RO $24 double; Pembroke Caravan and Leisure Park, Cnr. Grafton & Cooks Rds., ph 72 6470 – Site $6 for 2, overnite vans or cabins $16-25 double. Youth Hostel also in the park – 20 beds $5.50 ea.

EATING OUT:

As usual you will find a lot of places to eat in the main street and the licensed clubs welcome visitors. The Cattleman's Motor Inn, 31 Marsh St, Ph 72 7788, has a la carte menu and you can select your wine from the public wine racks. The Moore Park Motor Inn, New England Highway, Ph 72 2358, also has a licensed restaurant and cocktail bar which is open seven days. Mama Rosa's Pizza Palour, K-Mart Plaza, Beardy St., Ph 72 5326 is open 7 days and also has a dial a pizza service. Big Rooster is also in K-Marta Plaza, Ph 72 7193. Jessie's Restaurant, 113A Jessie St., Ph 72 6333 is open for lunch Tues-Fri and for dinner Thurs, Fri & Sat. The Turkish Delight Restaurant, 211 Beardy St., Ph 72 7355 is open for Lunch Tues-Fri and for dinner Mon-Sat. Squids Seafood, Moore St., Ph 72 1910 has fish'n chips Armidale style and is open Mon-Sat 10am-7pm

POINTS OF INTEREST:

Central Park is attractive in all seasons and contains a tourist directory, rotunda, a memorial fountain and picnic facilities. There is also a signposted Tourist Drive which takes in the main attractions.

The University of New England, off Queen Elizabeth Drive, 5km north-west of centre, Ph 73 333, has 5 faculties and is open for inspection 9am-5pm daily. It features Booloominbah, an historic house and a deer and kangaroo park.

The College of Advanced Education, cnr. Mossman & Dangar Sts., 72 2271, is built on the site of the old Armidale Gaol and is open Mon-Fri 9am-5pm. The Education Museum at rear, is a re-creation of a mid-Victorian school – Ph 73 4211 for inspections.

The Folk Museum, Cnr. Rusden and Faulkner Sts., Ph 72 8666 ext. 236, is classified by the National Trust and has displays of early transport, lighting, handicrafts etc. – open daily 1-4pm.

The New England Regional Art Museum, Kentucky St., ph 72 86666 houses the famous Hinton, Armidale City and Coventry Collections- Mon-Sat 10am-5pm, Sun 1am-5pm.

The Berry Patch on the New England Highway towards the airport, Ph 72 5972, is the largest hydroponic berry farm in Australia. They specialise in pies and strudels using a wide variety of berries – open daily 8.30am-6pm.

From Apex Lookout you can obtain a view of the whole city.

St. Mary's Roman Catholic cathedral, Dangar St. near Central Park, built in Gothic Revival style has a fine spire, marble sanctuary and flemish

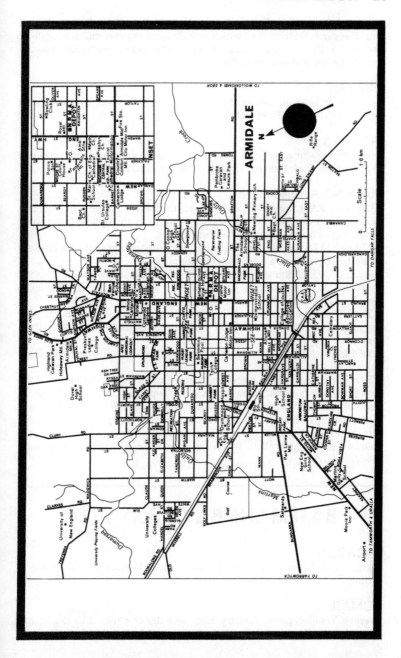

bondwork – open 7am-6pm daily. Nearby is St. Peter's Anglican cathedral (cnr. Dangar & Rusden Sts.) which is built in an entirely different style. It also has an Ecclesiastical Museum with exhibits not only relating to the church itself but also to Armidale.

FESTIVALS:

Woolexpo is held annualy in March and the Arts Festival, lasting about a week, is held biennially in October.

FACILITIES:

Bowls, trout fishing, golf, squash, swimming pool, and tennis. Bicycles can be hired from Jock Bullens, 114 Marsh St., Ph 72 3718.

OUTLYING ATTRACTIONS:

DANGAR'S FALLS and Lagoon, 22km south, feature a large rock pool and many species of birds. Dumaresq Dam 8km from town, boat ramp (only non-powered boats permitted) and swimming.

EBOR FALLS, 74km east, is another delightful picnic spot. The falls are divided into two with a total drop of 115m.

HILLGROVE, 27km east, is an old goldfield ghost town with uncanny reminders of its vibrant and colourful past. The Musuem, Ph. 67 1159, is open Wed 2-5pm and weekends 10am-5pm but closes for lunch.

The L.P. Dutton Trout Hatchery, 70km from Armidale on the Serpentine River, has guided tours, a visitors' centre and displays – open daily 9am-4pm.

WOLLOMOMBI FALLS, 40km east of Armidale, are the highest falls in Australia with a drop of 460m.

For Rockhounds and Gemfossickers: The area has numerous little pockets which contain Sapphires, Zircons, Topaz, Diamonds, Gold, Silver, Tin, Jelly Beans, Quartz, Smokey Quartz, Grass Stone, Agate, Rhodorite, Tourmaline, Petrified Wood and almost anything else you can think of. A comprehensive booklet entitled 'The Fossickers Way' is available from the Tourist Centre. Inverell to the north-west is one of the more popular fossicking towns.

BATEMANS BAY – Pop. 9,000

LOCATION:

On the Clyde River Estuary at the foot of Clyde Mountain 306km south of Sydney.

CLIMATE:

Average Temperatures: January max. 23.4 deg.C – min. 15.7 deg.C; July max. 15.9 deg.C – min. 5.7 deg.C.; Average annual rainfall 916mm; Hours of

Sunshine: Summer 7, Autumn 6, Winter 6 and Spring 6.

CHARACTERISTICS:
Weekend and holiday retreat for people from Canberra. It is an unusual place in that the regulars from Canberra think its a superb place with clean water, and fantastic fishing, and it does have all the facilities one expects at a beach resort, but its all very understated. It is the only place where the commercial fishing trawlers are permitted to sell their catch direct to the public and the general atmosphere is very friendly. Strangers smile and say hello in the street.

HOW TO GET THERE:
AIR. Hazelton fly to Moruya.
BUS. Ansett Pioneer, Deluxe and Greyhound all stop on their Sydney/Melbourne route and Murrays Express Coach has a service from Canberra.
RAIL. to Nowra with connecting coach.
CAR. Via the Princes Highway 279km from Sydney and 769km Melbourne.

TOURIST INFORMATION:
Bateman's Bay Tourist Centre, Princes Highway, Ph (044) 72 6990 – open daily 9am-9pm.

ACCOMMODATION:
Some names and addresses: Argyle Terrace Motel, 32 Beach Rd., Ph 72 5022 – RO $44 double; Batemans Bay Bridge, 29 Clyde St., Ph 72 6344 – RO $40-48; Clyderiver Lodge, 3 Clyde St., Ph 72 6444 – RO $42 double; Reef Motor Inn, 27 Clyde St., Ph 71 6000 – RO $45 double. Coach House Caravan Park, Beach Road, Ph 72 4392 – site $7 double – on site vans $16-35 daily; Riverside Van Village, Wharf Rd., Ph 72 4048 – sites $9 double – onsite vans $16-36 daily.

EATING OUT:
The Archorage Restaurant has a Blackboard Menu of fresh local fish and changes daily – Ph 726 333; Rafters BYO Restaurant, 28 Beach Rd., Ph 724 288 is open for dinner from 6pm – children's menu; Lum's Court Chinese Restaurant is open daily for lunch and dinner (next to the Post Office), 9 Orient Street, Ph 724 982; Bang Bang Chinese Restaurant, Bateman's Bay Bowling Club, Princes Highway, Ph 725 700 – closed Mondays and Smorgasbord every Friday 5.30-7.00pm $6.50.

POINTS OF INTEREST.
The population increases to approx. 90,000 during the peak holiday season from about mid-December to mid-February. Bateman's Bay has 16 golden beaches, some with sheltered calm waters, other with waves rolling in from the Pacific to tempt the board riders.

The Clyde River is navigable for 51km from Bateman's Bay up into the hills with regular cruises on modern tour boats going to past Nilligen, an old steamer centre or you can hire your own, if you prefer to be away from the madding crowd. Much of the surrounding land is a wildlife sanctuary and tame kangaroos and wallabies will nibble food from your fingers at Pebbly Beach.

Bateman's Bay Shell Museum, Beach Road, Bateman's Bay, Ph 724 648 is open 9am-5pm daily.

Batehaven Birdland is a sanctuary with a train running through it – open daily 9am-4pm except public holidays.

Nelligen Rock and Mineral Display open Thursdays, Friday and Saturday 10am-6pm.

Mogo Goldfields Park, 15km south of Bateman's Bay, is open seven days with tours at 11am and 2pm – you can pan for gold and visit an old gold mine.

FESTIVALS:
The Neptune Festival is held each November.

FACILITIES:
Boat, catamaran and sailboard hire, golf, tennis, and lawn bowls. Tenpin Bowling at Bay Twilight Bowl & Leisure Centre, Gregory Street – open 7 days 9am to Midnight.

OUTLYING ATTRACTIONS:
South of Bateman's Bay:
MORUYA, 6km from the mouth of the Moruya River, has some fine old buildings. The Wesleyan Church was built in 1864 of local granite. Moruya airport is on the northern headland of the river entrance. South Moruya has a fine surf beach and there are boats for hire at Tuross Lake which has a number of good boat ramps but care must be exercised if venturing 'outside', as the sandbar passage can be dangerous.

NAROOMA on the estuary of the winding Wagonga River is another popular fishing resort. It has excellent beaches in both directions and a narrow channel which leads to the small harbour. Montague Island, 8km offshore, is a flora and fauna reserve and its waters are well known for their game fish. It is also the half way point for the yachts in the Sydney to Hobart Race. Youth Hostel: The Lakes Leathercraft Barn, RMB 80A Old Highway, Ph (044) 76 2824 – $7ppn.

BERMAGUI is the mecca for big game fishing in New South Wales and was made famous in the 1930's by the novelist, Zane Grey. To-day a big fishing fleet operates out of Bermagui and game fisherman from all over come for the sport between November and May.

BEGA, 170km south of Bateman's Bay, is the commercial centre of this district which is famous for its cheese. The Bega Co-operative on the northern side of the river, is open for inspection Mon-Fri. The Bega Museum, Cnr. Auckland & Bega Sts. is open 11.30am-4.30pm Mon-Friday and 9.30am-12.30pm Saturdays. 23km north of Bega on the Princes Highway is Brogo Valley's Rotolactor which is open to the public 7 days a week from 2-5pm – milking is at 3pm. Youth Hostel, Kirland Cresc., Ph (0649) 2 3103 – $6ppn.

MERIMBULA is a flourishing resort on Lake Merimbula which is actually not a lake at all but the wide entrance of the river. Oyster leases take up 660ha upstream and nearly 4,000 bags are harvested every year. The Magic Mountain Recreation Park, Tura Road has a super mountain slide, 2 heated waterslides, a prehistoric world, mini golf course aand huge playground. Merimbula also has an airport.

EDEN, the main port of the south coast, is built on the crest of a peninsula and overlooks Snug Cove which shelters a large fishing fleet. The beauty of the coastline attracts many holidaymakers. North of the town is a reserve which contains the famous Red Cliffs.

North of Bateman's Bay:

ULLADULLA, 122km north, is another popular holiday resort. It's major tourist attraction is Rowens Funland, a family entertainment centre which is open Saturdays 9.30am-10.30pm and Sundays 12 noon-5pm. Magnificent views of the coastline can be obtained from the lighthouse on Wardens Head. Ulladulla has a sailboard school and seven day scuba diving courses.

Mollymook, Lake Conjola and Swan Lake are all popular family holiday spots.

Next is St. Georges Basin with Sussex Inlet on the ocean. The Basin has every kind of water sport from sailing to water skiing in sheltered bays with caravan parks scattered around the water's edge.

Just north is an even larger bay, JERVIS BAY, which, apart from the Naval College has a few popular holiday spots. Green Patch where the parakeets come to feed, is a popular camping place but it is essential to book as it's usually full. Huskisson is another sleepy place with a good camping ground right on the beach and river. It is another popular scuba diving spot and boats go out regularly to take divers to some of the best spots. They also run diving courses. Nearby Vicentia Beach is known as a nudist beach.

BATHURST – Pop. 24,500

LOCATION:
On the fertile western slopes of the Great Dividing Range 208km west of Sydney.

CLIMATE:
Average Temperatures: January max. 26.6 – min. 13.4 deg. C.; July max. 11.2 deg. C. – min. -0.6 deg. C; Average annual rainfall 629mm; Drizzle rain in winter and storms in Summer.

CHARACTERISTICS:
Australia's oldest inland city and centre of a large grain and pastoral district with many historic and distinctive buildings. When gold was discovered in the hills around Bathurst many towns such as Hill End,

Sofala, and Hargraves sprung up. Most of them have either disappeared or are ghost towns.

HOW TO GET THERE:

AIR.   East Coast Airlines have several flights daily to/from Sydney.

BUS.   Ansett Pioneer stop at Bathurst on their Melbourne/Gold Coast/ Brisbane run. Greyhound stop there on their Sydney/Melbourne (Hume & Great Western Highways) run and their Sydney/Adelaide run. Deluxe also stop there on their Sydney Adelaide run as do VIP.

RAIL.   There is an XPT Service from Sydney to Bathurst & Orange.

Car.   From Sydney: via the Great Western Highway or via the Kurrajong Road through Bilpin and Bell to Lithgow; From Melbourne: Via the Hume Highway to Seymour and thence the Goulburn Valley Highway to Tocumwal and then the Newell Highway to West Wyalong. From Adelaide: Via the Sturt Highway through Renmark and Mildura to Hay then via the Mid Western Highway to West Wyalong or via the Barrier Highway through Broken Hill to Nyngan and thence via the Mitchell Highway. From Brisbane: Via the Cuinningham Highway to Warwick and Goondiwindi, thence via the Newell Highway through Moree to Dubbo, or via the New England Highway from Warwick to Tamworth and Coonabarabran via the Oxley Highway and thence via the Newell Highway to Dubbo.

TOURIST INFORMATION:

Bathurst and District Tourism Management Committee, Court House, Russell St., Ph (063) 33 6288 – open Mon-Fri 9am-4.30pm & weekends 10am-4pm.

ACCOMMODATION:

8 motels, 2 hotel/motels, 2 hotels and one caravan park. See the Tourist Information Office for details.

Some names & addresses: Coachman's Inn Motel, cnr. Gt Western Hwy & Littlebourne St., Ph 31 4855 – RO $44 double; Abercrombie Flag Inn Motel, 362 Stewart St., Ph 31 1077 – RO $42; Capri Homestead Motel, 357 Stewart St., Ph 31 2966 – RO $45; The Kelso, Sydney Rd, Kelso, Ph 31 6675 – RO $30-32 double; Bathurst Caravan Park, Sydney Road, Kelso, Ph 31 8286 – sites $8.50-11.50 – onsite vans $24 double. Youth Hostel at Orange 55km away, Pinnacle Rd., Orange, Ph (063) 65 3349 – $6 ppn.

POINTS OF INTEREST:

The Tourist Information Office has trained guides available to provide a commentary on historic buildings in Bathurst for coaches, and makes brochures available to individuals.

Some of the historic buildings are:

The Victorian Renaissance Court House with its double-storey portico and large octagonal central dome faces Kings Square. It has two wings and the verandahed wing was built as a telegraph office.

Abercrombie House, built in the 1870's. and classified by the National Trust – open for inspection on Wednesdays at 3pm.

Ben Chifley's Cottage, the home of this former Prime Minister, is open Mon-Sat 2-4pm & Sun 10am-12noon. The engine that he drove is on display at the Bathurst Railway Station.

Old Government House, behind No. 1 George St – open Sundays 2-4pm. Where Macquarie stayed during his farewell visit to Bathurst in 1821.

Miss Trail's House, Russell Street, is also a National Trust property and is open Sundays 11am-4.30pm.

The Holy Trinity Church at Kelso was completed in 1835 and is the oldest consecrated Anglican church in Australia.

St. Michael and St. Johns Catholic Cathedral was completed in 1861. St. Stanislaus' College has taken pupils since 1873 and is Australia's oldest Catholic Boarding School.

The Historical Museum in the east wing of the Court House is open weekdays 9am-4.30pm, Saturdays 9.30am-4.30pm & Sundays 10am-4pm. The Regional Art Gallery is open 10am-4pm weekdays and from 1pm on weekends.

Outside the Visitors Centre is Victors' Walk. Brass plaques have been embedded in chequerboard concrete to commemorate winners of the James Hardie 1000.

At Mt. Panorama is the Motor Racing Circuit which is used for the James Hardie 1000 and the Easter Bike Races. Part of it is public road which is closed off during the races. Nearby is the Sir Joseph Banks Nature Reserve which has koalas, kangaroos and wallabies in a 41hectare park – open Friday-Tues 9am-4pm. Also at Mt. Panorama is the Gold Diggings at Karingal Village. It is a reconstruction of a gold mining area – individual tuition in gold panning is available – Ph 31 3319 for further information.

The Bathurst Sheep & Cattle Drove, Rossmore Park, Limekilns Rd., Kelso is only an 8min drive from the centre of town. There you can milk a cow or sit back in air-conditioned comfort and enjoy an 80 min show during which a sheep will be shorn and the wool classed. If it's fine you can see a sheep dog in action.

FESTIVALS:

The James Hardie 1000 is held during the October long weekend and the Motor Cycle Races at Easter at the Mt. Panorama Circuit.

FACILITIES:

An olympic swimming pool and water slide – open from 10am-7.30pm daily and 6.30am-8am weekdays as well. All the usual sporting facilities you would expect in a large town including lawn bowls, golf course, tennis courts, and squash courts.

OUTLYING ATTRACTIONS:

ORANGE. 55km from Bathurst, produces 10% of Australia's apples as well as cherries and other stone fruit, on the rich volcanic soil slopes of Mt. Canobolas. The upper slopes of the extinct volcano are a flora and fauna reserve with picnic areas and walking trails. There is a lake in the crater and canoeing, sailing and fishing are popular. The Ophir gold find gave the early settlement a firm foundation and it has grown into the largest town in the district. Bowen Terrace is a perfect and rare example of its period. The row of ironwork-decorated houses was built in 1876 by the owner of the first tannery. Endsleigh House, built in 1858, is thought to be the oldest house. The golf club is housed in the 1876 Duntryleague mansion. A.J. (Banjo) Paterson, perhaps Australia's most popular poet and writer, was born along the Ophir road in 1864 and an obelisk marks the spot. It is inscribed with a verse from 'Clancy of the Overflow'.

OPHIR, approx. 40km from Orange. Here gold was first discovered in Australia in 1851. 5ozs. were washed from Summer Creek. To-day the area is a reserve and trails lead to old tunnels, sluices and other relics among the hills. The reserve is popular with fossickers.

Abercrombie Caves, 72km from Bathurst on the Goulburn Road, is one of the smaller but most spectacular limestone cave systems in Australia. The Reserve has a camping/caravan park with picnic facilities. Cave inspection times are 10am, 11am, 2.30pm and 4.00pm daily – Ph (063) 68 8603.

SOFALA, amongst the steep hills of the Turon valley, is one of the old gold rush towns. It has a quaint store and some faded old-time buildings. The Royal Hotel is the only hotel remaining of the 40 which were operating during the gold rush era.

HILL END, 84km from Bathurst, has been declared an historic site and is administered by the Parks and Wildlife Service. They publish an excellent information sheet 'Exploring Hill End Historic Site' which has a map on one side and an excellent walking tour on the other. Only a small community remains to-day but miners dug up 701,000 ounces of gold here. Panning and fossicking are still popular and gold pans may be hired at the Vistors' Centre.

MUDGEE, 69km north of Hill End, is the second oldest town west of the Blue Mountains and was laid out in 1838. A score of handsome buildings, classified by the National Trust, dot the town, the oldest being the Catholic presbytery built in 1852. The Church, St. Marys, was commenced 5 years later and has an exceptional iron screen, and stencilled decorations. The Court House, St. John the Baptist's Church, the Police Station and Post Office were all built in the early 1860's. The Colonial Inn Museum, Market St is open 2-5pm Saturdays, 10am-5pm school and public holidays and Sundays. Mudgee is renowned for its honey and visitors are able to watch honey processing at two factories. There are 18 wineries in the district. All of them are open for cellar door sales. For further information contact the Tourist Information Centre, 64 Market St., Ph (063) 72 1944. The town is well known for its fine wines and is gaining fame for its beautiful rose gardens. The town holds a Days of Wine and Roses Festival at the end of September/ beginning October each year.

GULGONG, 29km from Mudgee, is 'The Town on the Ten Dollar Note'. It has narrow streets which wind between quaint clapboard and iron buildings, complete with verandahs and iron lace. The Pioneers Museum in Medley Street covers an acre and includes an astonishing array of

Australiana. The Henry Lawson Art Gallery is open during school holidays. The Phonograph Parlour, 69 Lee St, has recorded sound equipment dating back to 1898. Gold is still found around Gulgong and panning is popular.

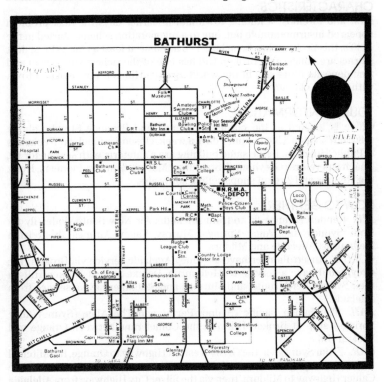

BROKEN HILL – Pop. 27,000

LOCATION:

Lies in the Barrier ranges in outback NSW near the SA border. It is a long way from anywhere, Sydney is 1170km away, Melbourne 882km and Adelaide 510km.

CLIMATE:

It is 304m above sea level and has an average rainfall of 235mm which is spread fairly evenly throughout the year, with the greatest fall usually in June. As a rule the temperature only climbs above 38 deg C 8 or 9 times a year. Maximum summer temperatures are generally in the low 30s but this causes little discomfort due to the low humidity, but the nights are cold throughout the year. The winter months of May, June and July can be quite cold.

CHARACTERISTICS:

First and foremost a mining town and in earlier days the dust problem appeared insurmountable but, due to a regeneration scheme started in the 1930's, this problem has been largely overcome at least as far as local dust storms are concerned. Broken Hill has one of the richest silver, lead and zinc deposits of its size in the world. Broken Hill is a very isolated town with a harsh climate.

TOURIST INFORMATION:

Office is located at the corner of Blende and Bromide Streets, phone (080) 6077. Open 8.30am-5pm 7 days a week, closed for lunch on Weekends & Public Holidays. In the same building are a cafeteria with seating for 60, Coach Operators (Greyhound, Stateliner, Murton & Ansett Pioneer), Hertz Car Rentals and 2 retail shops selling souvenirs.

HOW TO GET THERE:

AIR. Kendell Airlines fly to/from Adelaide; Air New South Wales fly to/from Sydney and Alice Springs; Murray Valley Airlines fly to/from Melbourne, Adelaide and Mildura.

COACH. Ansett Pioneer have a Sydney/Adelaide service via Broken Hill; Greyhound have a service to Melbourne; Deluxe stop at Broken Hill on their Sydney/Perth route; and Murtons and Stateliner have a service from Adelaide.

RAIL. The Indian Pacific (Sydney/Perth) and The Alice (Sydney/Alice Springs) stop at Broken Hill and the Comet runs between Orange and Broken Hill.

CAR. From Sydney via the Great Western Highway to Orange, the Mitchell Highway to Nyngan and then the Barrier Highway; from Melbourne via the Calder Highway to Mildura, then via the Silver City Highway; from Adelaide via National Route 32.

ACCOMMODATION:

11 Motels, 2 Hotel/Motels, 7 hotels, 2 Caravan /Camping Parks and a Youth Hostel.

Some names & addresses: Broken Hill Overlander Motel Inn, 142 Iodide St., Ph 88 2566 – RO $45-50 double; Mine Host Motel, 120 Argent St., Ph 6627 – RO $50 double; Miners Lamp Motor Inn, 357 Cobalt St., Ph 88 4122 – RO $45; Royal Exchange Hotel, Cnr. Argent & Chloride Sts., Ph 2308 – RO $24-26 double; Theatre Royal Hotel, 347 Argent St., Ph 3318 – RO $22 double; Tourist Lodge Guest House, 100 Argent St., Ph 88 2086 – RO $24 double; Broken Hill Caravan Park, Rakow St., Ph 3841 – sites $4 double – onsite vans $16-23 double; Lake View Caravan Park, 1 Mann St., Ph 88 2250 – sites $7 double – onsite vans $16 double – cabins $25; Youth Hostel: Tourist Lodge, a private guesthouse, 100 Argent St., Ph 88 2086 – $7 ppn.

EATING OUT:

10 Restaurants, 15 Cafes, 7 Clubs and 3 hotels serving meals.

Some names and addresses: Pagoda Chinese Restaurant, 357 Cobalt St., PH 3695; Oceania Chinese Rest., 432 Argent St., Ph 3695; David & Maryanne's Coffee House and Pancake Kitchen, Cnr. Argent & Oxide Sts., Ph 88129; Silver City Workingmen's Club, 402 Argent St., Ph 5337; Silver City Pizza Bar, 322 Argent St., Ph 2664.

POINTS OF INTEREST:

Mine Tours: Interesting and informative inspections of the surface workings of North Mine are conducted every afternoon Mon-Fri. Contact Visitors' Information Centre. NB. solid footwear must be worn. If you want an underground tour there are two possibilities: Departs Mon-Fri 10.30am & Sat 2pm NB. no children under 12; or the Daydream Mine near Silverton 3/4hrs drive – no age limit.

Broken Hill has 2 Tourist Drives: Silver Arrow Tour 1 or 2 – maps are available from the Information Centre. Walking Tours depart from the Information Centre and are approx. one and a half hours in duration and leave Mon-Fri 10.30am and Sun 10.30am & 2.30pm. The Sundown Nature Trail situated in the rocky Sundown Hills on the northern edge of the city Common, winds through the countryside for 2.8km and affords the visitor an opportunity to examine the sparse vegitation close up – takes approx. one and a half hours and is at its best just before sunset or just after sunrise.

For tours of the Royal Flying Doctor Base book at Silver City Travel. The School of the Air is open week days but bookings must be made at the Tourist Centre.

At the Gladstone Mining Museum, cnr. South & Morish Sts you can see life size replicas of current and old-time mining procedures. The Sulphide Street Station Railway Museum diagonally opposite the Tourist & Travellers' Centre has a large display of old railway machinery.

Broken Hill has more than fifteen Art Galleries open for public viewing. Some names and addresses: The Boken Hill City Art Gallery in the Civic Centre, Chloride Street, is open Mon-Sat 9am-4pm with guided tours on Tues, Wed, Thurs, Fri & Sat at 11.30am; Pro Hart Gallery, 108 Wyman St. is open Mon-Sat 9.30am-5pm; Hoppy Hopgood's Gallery, 589 Fisher St. is open daily from 9am.

FACILITIES:

Car Hire: Avis, Ph 7532; Budget Ph 88 1928; and Hertz Ph 2719; Taxi services: City Radio Cabs Ph 2555 and Radio Taxis Ph 2222. There are 2 Laundromats, and 3 Council run libraries; Royal Automobile Association of SA Office, 261 Argent Street, phone 2414; 3 swimming pools (one heated), golf, horse riding, lawn bowls, indoor cricket, squash and tennis.

OUTLYING ATTRACTIONS:

At MENINDEE, 110km south-east of Broken Hill there are a series of natural lakes stretching 50km above and 35 km below the town of

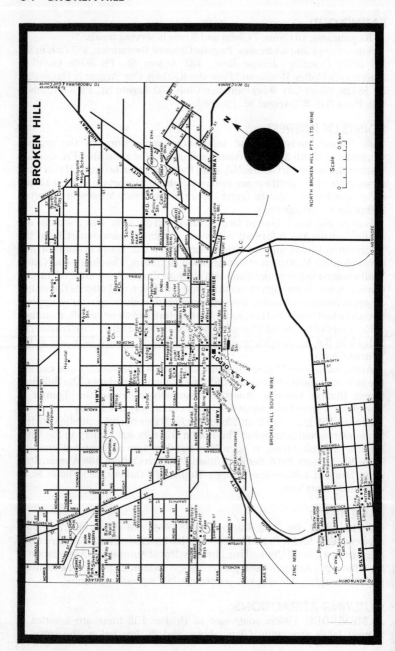

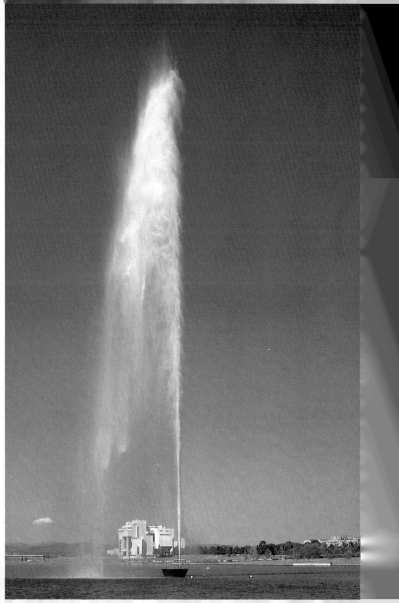

Rural scene – Victoria

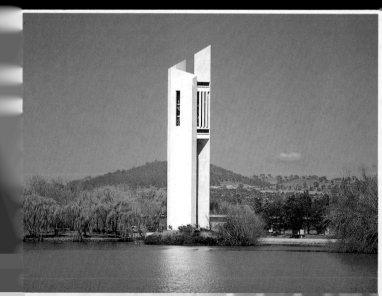

Menindee and areas have been developed for caravan parks, weekend cottages, speedboats, water skiing, sailing, safe swimming and good fishing. The Kinchega National Park, on the western bank of the Darling River adjacent to Menindee, is a significant example of one of the major landscape categories of the arid and semi-arid regions of NSW.

SILVERTON, 25km north-west of Broken Hill, along a sealed road, was once a thriving community of over 3,000 but is now a ghost town where many films or parts of films have been shot e.g. A Town Like Alice, Mad Max II, Razorback and several commercials and documentaries. The Silverton War Memorial Youth Camp can accommodate 52 people in 7 rooms. Enquiries to The Secretary;, PO Box 3, Broken Hill or phone 3006.

The Sturt National Park starts just north of Tibooburra which is 337 km north of Broken Hill and reaches to the where the NSW, Qld & SA borders meet. At the three-state corner the dingo fence can been seen. It is part of the 'longest fence in the world'.

The well-known opal field and township of WHITE CLIFFS is 295km north-east of Broken Hill. There you can try your luck at fossicking, see the supurb opalised Plesiosaur skeleton and dugouts where many of the residents live. Facilities include a Caravan Park and Hotel, general store and cafe.

FOSSICKER'S LICENCES are available from the Tourist Information Office in Broken Hill or at Post Offices in outlying towns – cost $2.50 single or $5.00 family.

FISHING LICENCES are required if you wish to fish in the area. They are available at Courtesy Corner, Cnr Menindee Rd & Argent St.

CANBERRA – Pop. 250,000

LOCATION:
In the southern tablelands of NSW 100km from the coast and 300km from Sydney; 654km from Melbourne; 1,654 from Brisbane and 1,201km from Adelaide.

CLIMATE:
Average summer temp: max. 27 deg C, min. 13min.; average winter temp max. 12 deg C, min. 1 deg C. Annual average rainfall 52mm. City centre is 580m above sea level while much of the surrounding country is 900m above sea level. Enjoys more sunshine than most Australian cities.

CHARACTERISTICS:
The National capital. The site for Canberra was chosen by ballot in 1908 from 23 other sites, and an international competition to design the capital was won by the American architect, Walter Burley Griffin. The Commonwealth Parliament did not sit in Canberra until 1927, when the provisional

Parliament House was opened. A new Parliament House is now under construction, and is due to be completed in 1988 in time for the Bi-centenial celebrations.

HOW TO GET THERE:

Air. 30 minute flight from Sydney, 60 minutes from Melbourne and 45 mins from Albury – daily flights (Australian Airlines, Ansett, East West, Western NSW Airlines and Air NSW). Also some direct flights from Brisbane and Adelaide. Hazelton Air Services fly to/from Dubbo and Orange and Eastern Airlines fly to/from Newcastle. Levers Coach Line meet the planes at 9.45am and 4.45pm only, every day.

BUS. Daily services to Sydney and Melbourne. Less frequent services to Adelaide, Brisbane, Wollongong, Cooma, Yass, Batemans Bay and Orange. Greyhound, Deluxe, Levers, Murrays Transborder and other interstate services (with the exception of Ansett-Pioneer) leave from the Coach Passenger Terminal as well as the airport bus and the Canberra Explorer Bus.

RAIL. Daily services from Sydney including XPT and from Melbourne with coach connection from Yass.

CAR. Via the Hume Highway from Sydney or Melbourne. Approx. 4 hours from Sydney and 9 hours from Melbourne.

TOURIST INFORMATION:

The Jolimont Tourist Centre (including theatrette showing Canberra films) Northbourne Ave, Ph (062) 45 6464. Open Mon-Fri 8.30am-5.15pm and 9-11.30am Sats. The Visitor Information Centre, Northbourne Ave (just south of the junction of Federal and Barton Highways). Open daily 9am-5pm except Christmas Day. To see what's happening in Canberra look for the giant computer screen at the cnr. Northbourne Ave and Alinga St. Canberra also has a Hire-A-Guide service which operates 7 days a week and can be contacted on (062) 49 7978. They are available to individuals or coach parties.

ACCOMMODATION:

For full details contact the Tourist Information Office or the Canberra Accommodation Centre, 30 National Circuit, Forrest, Ph (062) 95 3433.

A few names and addresses: Hostels: The Canberra Youth Hostel is at Dryanda St., O'Connor, Ph 48 9759 – $7 single.; YWCA, 2 Mort St., Ph 47 3033 – only females $13.00 for a twin rooms or dorms at $10; Ainslie Village, Quick St., Ainslie, Ph 48 6931 sometimes takes in travellers. $10 a night, $35 a week plus $10 for linen. Meals are very cheap. Guest Houses: Chelsea Lodge, 526 Northbourne Ave., Ph 48 0655 charges $18 single for B & B or $26 for a double; Blue & White Lodge, 524 Northbourne Ave., Ph 48 0498 – $28 double B&B; Motels range in price from around RO $132 double to about RO $40 double. e.g. Noahs Lakeside International, London Circuit, Ph 47 6244, RO $132 double; Acacia Motor Lodge, 65 Ainslie Ave., Ph 49 6955 Bed and Lt. Breakfast $49.50 double; Gunthers Lodge, Cotter Rd., Curtin, Ph

81 5499 RO $40 double. South Side Motor Park, Canmberra Ave., Ph
80 6176., sites $6.50 double – cabins $24 double – chalets $30 double.

EATING OUT:

Canberra eateries cater for all tastes and pockets. As in other cities, the
Clubs offer good value for money, and welcome visitors. For example the
Canberra Labour Club, Chandler St., Belconnen, Ph 51 5522 has special
lunches every Monday and Tuesday for $2.50 and Sunday Hot Roasts for
lunch and dinner for $6.00. The Downer Olympic Soccer Club, Hawdon St.,
Dickson (off Antill St.), Ph 48 5959 has lunches for $2.40 Mon-Fri. A few
restaurants – The Acropolis, 35 East Row, Civic, serves main courses from
around $5.00 and you chose from a display. The High Court Cafe serves
lunches from 12-2pm daily 7 days a week and homemade cakes and scones
for morning and afternoon tea. The Bunga Raya Restaurant, 25 Colbee
Court, Phillip, Ph 81 1351 serves Malaysian food and accepts Bankcard,
American Express, Visa and Mastercard.

LOCAL TRANSPORT:

Canberra has a good bus service. For detailed information visit the kiosk at
the corner of Alinga St and East Row, which is open Mon-Sat 6am-11pm
and 9am-6pm Sun. The flat fare is 70 cents, or 60cents before 6am and after
9pm weekdays and all day Sats, and only 10 cents on Sundays. Day Tripper
tickets cost $2.60 for unlimited use. There is also a Canberra Explorer bus
which costs $7 per day or $14 for the week. Otherwise you can hire a
bicycle (the Youth Hostel has some, or else from Mr. Spokes near the Acton
Ferry), or rent a car, or even take an organised sightseeing tour. Cruises on
Lake Burleigh Griffin cost $4.50

POINTS OF INTEREST:

Canberra has 5 signposted Tourist Drives which take in most of the sights.
Each begins at the City Hill Lookout. 3 concentrate on the central area of
Canberra, while the other 2 take in the popular stops on the city outskirts
and beyond. The Tourist Information office will provide you with the
Canberra Sightseeing Guide with Tourist Drives free of charge . Tours 1-4
take approx. three to four hours each with short stops at the points listed,
and Tour 5 will take approx. 7-8hrs. Tour 1 has 16 points of interest – The
Australian National Gallery, the High Court, the Australian War Memorial,
Diplomatic Missions, and the new Parliament House. Tourist Drive No. 2
has 18 ports of call and features the Mint, National Botanic Gardens,
Telecom Tower and Government House. Tour No. 3 has 11 stops including
Mt. Pleasant Lookout, Blundell's Farmhouse, the War Memorial and
Duntroon Royal Military College. Route No. 4 takes in North Canberra,
Canberry Fair, National Exhibition Centre, Cockington Green and
Ginninderra Village, Belconnen, Ginninderra Falls and Lake. Tour No. 5 has
13 ports of call including the Prime Minister's Lodge, Mt. Stromlo
observatory, Cotter Dam and Reserve, Tidbinbilla Deep Space Tracing
Station, Tidbinbilla Nature Reserve, Gibraltar Falls, Tharwa, Cuppacum-

balong, Lanyon, Canberra Wildlife Gardens, Manuka and the Civic Centre.

The three most popular tourist attractions in Canberra are the War Memorial, Parliament House and the National Library.

Tours of PARLIAMENT HOUSE are conducted every half hour from 9 am to 4.30pm when Parliament is not sitting. Enquiries 72 1211. When Parliament is in session it is possible to obtain tickets to the gallery of the House of Representatives by writing, well in advance, to the Principal Attendant, or by telephoning 72 1211. Usually tickets are not required for the Senate Gallery. Afterwards, you might like to see the NEW PARLIAMENT HOUSE construction site on Capital Hill. The exhibition centre is open daily from 9am-6pm.

The NATIONAL LIBRARY, Parks Place, is open 9am-4.45pm seven days a week. Guided tours are conducted at 11.15am and 2.15pm Mon-Fri, but its advisable to book, Ph 62 1440. The classical style library contains nearly two million books as well as maps, pictures, prints, photographs, films, microfilms, newspapers, magazines, and manuscripts.

The AUSTRALIAN WAR MEMORIAL, Fairbairn Ave at the end of Anzac Parade, is open from 9am-4.45pm daily, Ph 43 4211 and houses a massive collection of memorabilia from Australia's involvement in major wars. Allow yourself at least a half a day for this one.

The HIGH COURT OF AUSTRALIA Building is 40m tall and the mural on the northern wall of the great hall depicts the history, functions and aspirations of the High Court. Open 10-4 seven days a week.

There are 70 DIPLOMATIC MISSIONS in Canberra. Most of these are in the suburb of Yarralumla and reflect the architecture of the various countries. Two of them have special exhibitions open to visitors.: Papua New Guinea, Forster Cresc, Mon-Fri 10-12.30 & 2.30-4.30pm; Indonesia, Darwin Ave., Mon-Fri 9.30-12.30 & 2-5 and 10-1 and 2-4 on weekends. Some embassies are open for public inspection on certain occasions during the year (contact the Tourist Bureau for further information).

GOVERNMENT HOUSE, YARRALUMLA, the official residence of the Governor General, is not usually open to the public, but a good view can be obtained from a lookout on Lady Denman Drive between Cotter Road and Scrivener Dam.

The AUSTRALIAN NATIONAL GALLERY houses the National Collection of Art and features permanent and and special exhibitions of Australian and International art. Free guided tours daily, bookings 71 2519. Open 10-5 – admission $2. The NATIONAL FILM AND SOUND ARCHIVE in McCoy Circiut holds public screenings – open 10am-4pm.

The AUSTRALIAN ACADEMY OF SCIENCE is housed in a copper-shelled concrete dome 46m in diameter which rests on arches. The much photographed building is not open for inspection. On the other hand the AUSTRALIAN NATIONAL UNIVERSITY welcomes visitors. It is set in beautiful landscaped grounds in Civic at the foot of Black Mountain.

CIVIC SQUARE in the heart of Canberra is bordered by the Canberra Theatre Centre and has a statue of Thos which symbolises the spirit of the community. Nearby, on Petrie Plaza is Canberra's century old merry-go-round.

The ROYAL AUSTRALIAN MINT, Kent Street, Deakin, Ph 81 1766 is open from 9am-4pm Mon-Fri. From the visitors' gallery you have an excellent view of Australia's currency being minted. An exhibition of coins is on display in the foyer and special coins may also be bought by collectors.

At the ROYAL MILLITARY COLLEGE off Marshead Drive, Duntroon, you can join a conducted tour at 2.30pm Mon-Fri from November to March. Tours start from the Parade Ground entrance by the Officers' Mess. Enquiries (062) 66 6922.

The REGATTA POINT PLANNING EXHIBITION – 'The Canberra of Yesterday, Today and Tomorrow' – is an excellent audio visual introduction for anyone touring Canberra. Open 9-5 seven days a week, Ph 46 8797.

The TELECOM TOWER, Black Mountain rises 195m above the summit of the mountain and affords a magnificent view of Canberra and the surrounding countryside. There are three public viewing galleries, snack bar, revolving restaurant, exhibition room and theatrette. Open 9am-10pm daily. Admission charge.

QUESTACON is Australia's first and only interactive science centre, where science comes alive in over 100 simple do-it-yourself experiments, in the old Ainslie Public School, Cnr. Elourea & Donaldson Sts., Braddon, a block from Civic Centre – Adults $2, Schoolchildren $1 – Open Mon-Fri 10.30am-4.30pm, and some Sunday afternoons. For further details Ph 48 7486.

Australia Post's PHILATELIC EXHIBITION is housed in a special gallery above the GPO in Alinga St. Open 9.30am-5pm, Mon-Thurs, and 9.30am-8.30pm on Fridays. It is Australia's largest and most valuable collection of stamps.

BLUNDELL'S FARMHOUSE, off Constitution Avenue on Wendouree Drive was built more than 120 years ago by the pioneer, Robert Campbell. Open 2-4pm seven days a week, and 10-12 on Wed as well except for June, July and August.

The CHURCH OF ST JOHN THE BAPTIST, Constitution Ave, Reid, and an adjacent schoolhouse (open Wed 10am-12 noon and 2-4pm weekends) preserve much of Canberra's history.

ALL SAINTS CHURCH, Cowper St., Ainslie was formerly the Mortuary Station at Rookwood, Sydney, and was re-erected in Canberra in 1958.

ST MARK'S LIBRARY AND CHAPEL, Blackall St., Barton, has fine wall-hangings – open weekdays 10am-4pm.

The SERBIAN CHURCH, National Circuit, Forrest, has vivid murals covering the walls and ceiling the work of the late Karl Matzek who painted them at the age of 87. (Not open Sunday mornings).

Now we come to LAKE BURLEY GRIFFIN. This man made lake is a major ornamental feature of the city and a popular recreation, fishing and wildlife area. In the lake near Regatta Point is the CAPTAIN COOK MEMORIAL. The towering water jet and associated lakeshore terrestrial globe were erected to commemorate the bi-centenary of Captain Cook's

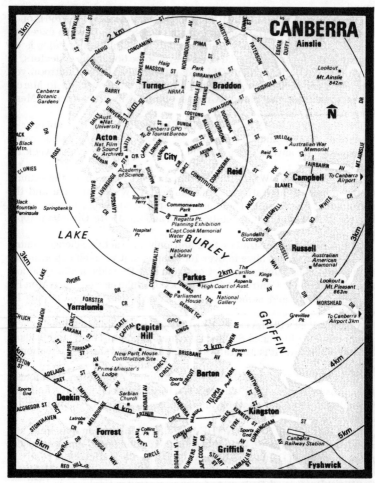

discovery of Australia. The jet sprays water 140m into the air and operates from 10am-12 noon and from 2-4pm daily.

THE CARILLON situated on Aspen Island near Kings Avenue Bridge, was a gift from the UK Government to mark Canberra's 50th jubilee. The 53 bell carillon is one of the world's largest. Free recitals Sundays 2.45-3.30pm, Wednesdays 12.45-1.30pm and holidays as advertised.

The Limestone Pottery Gallery, 60 Limestone Ave., Ainslie, Ph 48 7658, has Australia's largest exhibition of counted thread cross-stitch. The Old Canberra Brickworks Kiln 3, Antique Centre, Denman St., Yarralumla, has unusual bric-a-brac, prints etc. – open Wed-Sun 11am-5pm. The Institute of Sport has daily guided tours through the complex.

FESTIVALS: The Canberra Festival is held each March and usually lasts ten days.

FACILITIES: Ice Skating at the Phillip Centre, Irving St., Phillip; Roller Skating at the Showground; Regular Race Meetings are held at Queanbeyan; There are numerous golf courses and swimming pools but swimming in Lake Burley Griffin is not recommended; Canoes, pedal boats, and sailing boats can be hired at Dobell's at Ferry Wharf, Acton at weekend and holidays; Tennis and squash are also catered for and there's plenty of areas for bushwalking.

OUTLYING ATTRACTIONS:

CANBERRY FAIR, Cnr. Federal Highway and Antil Street, represents a 19th century Australian village. It has restaurants, winery, kid's pub, steam railways, circus, art & crafts – open daily.

CANBERRA WILDLIFE GARDENS, Mugga Lane, Red Hill. Australian and exotic animals and birds – open 9am-5pm daily.

COCKINGTON GREEN, Barton Highway has an outdoor display of miniature buildings and gardens of Britian – open 10am-4pm daily and nearby GINNINDERRA VILLAGE has craft shops and restaurant.

COTTER DAM, 22km west is a good spot for picnics and river swimming.

At GINNIDERRA FALLS, W. Belconnen there are nature trails around the falls and gorge. Lanyon, 30km south, is an historic homestead with beautiful gardens, and close by is the Nolan Gallery – open 10am-4pm Tues-Sun.

Rehwinkel's Animal Park, Macks Reef Road off the Federal Highway, 24km north of Canberra, has koalas, wombats, parrots, camels, deer, etc. – open daily 10am-5pm.

The Tidbinbilla Deep Space Tracing Station is 40km southwest of Canberra – open 9am-5pm daily – and features spacecraft and antenna models, and audio-visual presentations. Nearby is a Nature Reserve with walking trails – guided evening walks in summer.

BRAIDWOOD, about an hour's drive east, is a charming 19th century village with many interesting old buildings and craft shops.

QUEANBEYAN, in NSW, is virtually a suburb of Canberra and offers more in the way of night-time entertainment than Canberra does.

COFFS HARBOUR – Pop. 17,000

LOCATION:
On the coast half way between Sydney and Brisbane.

CLIMATE:
Average Temperature: January max. 26.5 deg. C – min. 19.0 deg. C; July max. 18.5 deg. C. – min. 6.6 deg. C; average annual rainfall 1759mm; wettest six months October to March.

CHARACTERISTICS:

The Great Dividing Range is very close to the coast here and its hills are covered with banana trees. Other fruits such as kiwifruit and avocados also flourish here in its sub-tropical climate.

HOW TO GET THERE:

AIR. Eastern Airlines fly to/from Sydney/Newcastle/Maitland/Taree/Port Macquarie/Lismore/Coolangatta/Brisbane. Air NSW fly to/from Sydney and Casino.

BUS. Ansett Pioneer, Greyhound, VIP, Deluxe, McCafferty's, Gold Coast Intertour and Skenners all stop at Coffs Harbour on their Brisbane/Sydney Pacific Highway route.

RAIL. XPT Service from Sydney.

CAR. On the Pacific Highway, 566km from Sydney, and 429km from Brisbane.

TOURIST INFORMATION:

Coffs Harbour, P.O. Box 757, Ph (066) 52 1522.

ACCOMMODATION:

There is a wide variety of accommodation ranging from mountain resorts to international standard beachfront hotels, to motels and over 35 caravan parks and a large selection of holiday flats. Contact the Tourist Office for full details.

Some names and addresses: The Tahitian Holiday Apartments, opp. main surf beach, Ph 52 2379 – 2 bedroom for 7 days for 2 fr. $189 – for 4 fr. $231; Sunseeker Holiday Units, 150m fr. beach, 7 Prince St., Ph 52 2087; Sapphire Pines Beach Resort 7 days fr. $315 for 2, or $357 for 4; Park Beach Hotel/ Motel, Ocean Pde., Ph 52 3833 – RO $20-25 double; Sapphire Gardens Holiday Resort, Pacific Highway, Ph 53 6282 – sites $8-$10 double – on site vans $16-22 double; Bananacoast Caravan Park, Pacific Highway, North Coffs Harbour, Ph 52 2868 – cabins from $100 per week and on site vans from $60 per week; Coffs Harbour Tourist Parks on site vans fees remain constant throughout the year! Phone 52 1694.

EATING OUT:

The Dragon Licensed Restaurant has a wide range of Cantonese meals. For that special night out, try Oscars International, suite 1, The Centre, Cnr. Castle & High Sts., Ph 51 2266. The Coffs Harbour Golf Club welcomes visitors and has snackbar facilities and a dining room. Coffs has the largest McDonalds in Australia which is open 24 hours. The Coffs Harbour Jetty has cuisine from around the world in a 400m strip: The Pier Hotel serves breakfast, lunch and dinner Australian style; Sala's Place has an island atmosphere; Jade Court serves Chinese meals; Chez Andree – French Cuisine; Avanti's has International Cuisine; Tomargoes serves French Cuisine; the Gaslight is a bistro and Pizza Restaurant; The Tandoori Oven serves Indian Cuisine; The Fishermans Katch specialises in seafood, and the Ploughman's Inn serves good old Aussie tucker; Coffs Harbour Catholic Recreation & Sporting Club, 61A High St., Ph 52 1477 has a family bistro which serves lunch and evening meals.

POINTS OF INTEREST.

The Big Banana, of course. Its the landmark of Coffs Harbour. You can ride the tractor train through a working banana plantation, and take in the panoramic views of the surrounding countryside and ocean. It is located on the Pacific Highway 3km north of town.

The Woolgoolga Adventure Villiage is a wonderful children's park which reflects the fun side of the Banana Republic. They can meet the Bananasaurus, play in the space shuttle, etc. The Kumbaingeri Wildlife Sanctuary is 14km north and is open daily and worth a visit.

Bruener Park Flora Reserve is 9km north west in Kororo and offers fine views of the coast.

Muttonbird Island where the mutton birds return to breed each summer is a delightful walk.

MUSEUMS: Jarrett's Natureland Museum; Military Museum; Historical Museum.

FESTIVALS:

Agricultural Show is held in May.

FACILITIES:

27 hole golf course, bowling greens, fishing (deep sea, estuary and beach) 4 lane boat ramp in safe harbour, horse racing (25 meetings p.a.), tennis, squash, water skiing, sailing, joy flights, Aquajet Water Slide, putt putt, ten pin bowling, roller skating, sailboard and catamaran hire.

OUTLYING ATTRACTIONS:

WOOLGOOLGA has a large Sikh community which has built a lavish temple and a superb curry restaurant.

For adventurers: Nymboida Whitewater Rafting Expeditions on the Nymboida River – Phone (066) 54 1788 for further details.

Mount Seaview Safaris, Ph 52 7433, have been operating for two years and take you places that only 4WD vehicles can go. You will see spectacular rainforests and plateau country where waterfalls abound.

George's Gold Mine is an authentic relic of the gold rush days and is run by a fair dinkum bushie, George Robb. George takes visitors on a 90min guided tour that features a walk into the underground Bayfield Mine to examine a vein of gold bearing quartz, as well as an exhibition of the old stamper battery in operation.

Valley Trails Horse Rides offer 2 hour escorted trail rides through the Pine Creek State Forest – both experienced and inexperienced riders are catered for.

Bushwhacker Canoe Expeditions will take you on a two hour journey down the Bellinger River in safe Canadian canoes, with experienced escorts who allow you to set the pace – Ph 55 8607.

Nambucca Heads, 114km south, is another popular holiday resort. It has a wide range of accommodation from premier hotels to flats and caravan parks. Attractions: Nambucca Historical Museum, Mary Boulton's Pioneer Cottage, The Pub with no Beer (Taylor Arm) – the venue for the Easter Country Music Festival and Fair, the historical Star Hotel, Kew House Toy and Doll Museum, Swiss Toymakers 5km north, Orana Mineral and Art Museum, Valla Pots Pottery, Seaview Shell Museum, Worm Farm and Brown's Cows a dairy farm with tours. A 2 hour river cruise leaves from the RSL car park. Lookouts: Rotary Lookout – spectacular view over the Nambucca River and Warrell Creek estuaries and south to Smokey Cape; Shelly Hill Lookout – view north to Coffs Harbour; Lions Park Lookout on Nambucca Headland; Yarrahapinni Lookout (turn off highway at Rosewood Road near Warrell Creek railway viaduct south of Macksville and follow signs). Facilities: Windsurfer and jetski hire, boat and canoe hire, fishing trips, boat ramps, 3 golf courses, 4 lawn bowls clubs, gymnasium and indoor cricket, squash courts, tennis courts, swimming pool, horse riding, 4 licensed clubs, 6 hotels, 16 motels and 9 caravan parks.

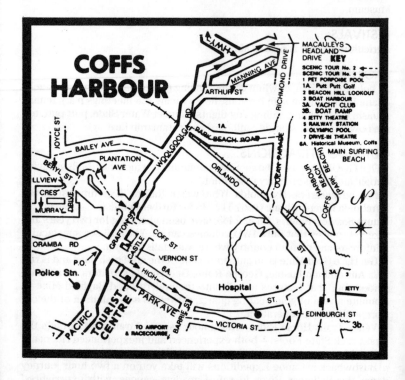

COOMA – Pop. 8,000

LOCATION:
In the Snowy Mountains near the NSW/Victorian border. Distance from Canberra 114km; Sydney 420km; Threadbo 97km; Charlotte Pass 105km; Perisher 98km; Adaminiby 52km; Mt. Selwyn 99km; Tumut 186km.

CLIMATE:
810m above sea level; Average temperatures: January max 25.7 deg.C – min. 11.2 deg. C; July max. 9.8 deg. C – min. -1.3deg. C.; Annual rainfall 450mm.

CHARACTERISTICS:
Gateway to the Snowy Mountains which conjures up visions of fashionable skiers hurtling down ski slopes before sipping their apres-ski drinks, but that is only one facet of the Snowy Mountains. One of Australia's engineering marvels is also to be found here, the Snowy Mountains Hydro Electric Scheme, which captures the water from the melting snow and channels it through the mountains to the interior. The mountains are a carpet of wildflowers in summer and there are numerous trails for bushwalkers. The many lakes and rivers are an aquatic paradise for those wishing to get away from it all. In summer Lake Jindabyne (three times the size of Sydney Harbour) is ablaze with sailboard and catamaran sails and for $5.00 for 30 days or $10.00 p.a., you can fish the lakes and rivers for your share of the trout. When you've had enough water sports, head for the Yarrangobilly Caves between Cooma and Tumut. Four of the caves are open to the public and are among Australia's finest. After your tour of the caves, what better way to recuperate than to have a dip in the thermal pool which is a constant 27 deg C all year round.

TOURIST INFORMATION CENTRE:
119 Sharp Street, Cooma, phone (0648) 21108 or 21177. Hours: 8.30am to 8.30 p.m. daily except Christmas Day. Free one-hour films are screened for visitors daily at 10am, 4 & 7pm. Recorded snow and road reports may be obtained by dialling (0648) 21108, 24 hours a day in winter.

HOW TO GET THERE:
AIR. Air NSW operate daily services to Sydney and a weekend return service from Brisbane in winter. Kendell Airlines operate a daily service to Melbourne and, in winter, services to Brisbane and Adelaide. Limited coach connections between airport and Cooma, otherwise taxis.
COACH SERVICES: Ansett Pioneer operate services from Sydney and Canberra and Snowliner Coaches provide services to Bega and Canberra.
RAIL: From Sydney via Canberra daily with connections to Melbourne from Goulburn.
ROAD: From Sydney via the Hume Highway 420km or via Bega along the

coast 542km. From Melbourne via the coast 730km or via the Alpine Way 664km.

ACCOMMODATION:

19 Motels, 9 Hotels, 3 Caravan Parks all with on-site vans, cabins or flats. Youth Hostel at Thredbo and CYTA Lodge and Salvation Army Hostel at Cooma North. Visitors' Centre has detailed information or see NRMA Accommodation Guides.

Some names and addresses: The Marlborough Motel, Monaro Hwy, Ph 2 1133 – RO $42-50 double; Alkira Motel, 213 Sharp St., Ph 2 1888 – RO $43.50 double; Swiss Motel, 34 Massie St., Ph 2 1950 – B&Lt.B $24-30 double; Pine Hill Lodge Private Hotel, Snowy Mts. Hwy, Cooma West, Ph 3 1267 – RO $25-35 double; Snowtels Caravan Park, Snowy Mts. Hwy, Ph 2 1828 – sites $7.50 double – onsite vans $20-23 double – cabins $22-25 double.

EATING OUT:

Cooma has 19 restaurants, 12 cafes, 7 hotels serving counter lunches/teas, 5 take-away shops and 3 licensed Clubs as well as 4 picnic areas.

POINTS OF INTEREST:

Tourist Drive markers signpost an easy drive through and around Cooma, taking in the town's many points of interest. The first marker is at Centennial Park near the Visitors' Centre, from there it goes past Cooma Creek, Lions Lookout, the Murrumbidgee Water Filtration Plant, Snowy Mountains Authority Information Centre, the Snowy Memorial, Festival Pool, Nannygoat Hill, Cooma Cenotaph, Cooma Prison, Lambie St., Raglan Gallery, Mt. Gladstone, Alpenthaler Park, Southern Cloud Park, Christ Church, the Lookout, Polo Flat and back to the centre.

The Snowy Mountains Authority Information Centre open Mon-Fri 8am-4.30pm and 8a.m.-12 noon Sats and public holidays has displays and models of the Snowy Mountains Scheme, and film show, Mon-Fri at 11am and 3 pm. Ansett Pioneeer run Snowy Mountains Scheme Tours to Adaminaby, Old Adaminaby, Providence Portal, Kiandra, Cabramurra, and visit Tumut 2 underground Power Station, or you can drive around the scheme yourself.

For those who are energetic, there is the Lambie Town Walk. Located within Cooma, the walk passes through residential and natural areas of scenic and historic interest. One part of the walk is through the town area (5km) and the bushland section is also 5kms, and takes approximately two and one-half hours.

FESTIVALS:

Tumut's Festival of the Falling Leaf in April-May.

FACILITIES:

Bowling club, golf course, horse riding, swimming pool (heated) Oct. to March, snooker, squash centre, tennis courts, gliding, ski hire shops, car hire depots and taxis.

OUTLYING ATTRACTIONS:

Snow fields – Mt Kosciusko, Thredbo, Perisher, Guthega, Mt. Selwyn and Charlotte Pass. In winter all the resorts are humming with life and each has its good points.

MT. SELWYN is the lowest at 1614m and is very popular with families and school groups, as it has very gentle beginners' slopes. There is only about 3km of dirt road now, and you can ski down to the lifts from the car park, which has been surfaced and is much cleaner now. The lift tickets have the lowest prices in the NSW skifields. It has 13 lifts with an uphill capacity of 9,500 skiers per hour. The resort usually closes some time in September. Nearest accommodation: Providence Portal, Adaminiby and Talbingo – no accommodation at Mt. Selwyn.

GUTHEGA is also very popular with families and offers some terrific skiing. Its only drawback, the village is at 1630m and the slopes are at 1960m, so you have to take the chairlift to the top to ski. It also has about 8km of steep dirt road. The lift prices are lower than Perisher/Smiggins or Thredbo but its a friendly place and the lift queues aren't long as the management limits the tickets to 1800 per day. It has 9 lifts. Accommodation: It is primarily a club lodge village as it only has one commercial lodge. Most people drive in daily from Wilson's Valley or Jindabyne.

PERISHER/SMIGGINS is the largest of the resorts and it has a sealed road right to the bottom of the lifts. There are 30 lifts with an uphill capacity of 30,000 per hour but, despite this, there are often long queues. It has an elevation of 2054m. Accommodation: There are several commercial lodges but the great majority drive in each day from Jindabyne or Berridale.

THREDBO Village has an elevation of 1340m and the ski slopes are at 2040m. The village has a European atmosphere and is delightful even if the roads in it are narrow, and parking at the lodges is limited. There is a sealed road right to the parking area at the bottom of the chairlift which has room for 1000 cars. There are 14 lifts with a capacity of 11,200 per hour. Accommodation: There are self catering apartments, commercial lodges or the luxury Thredbo Alpine Hotel, or cheaper accommodation at Jindabyne or Berridale.

CHARLOTTE PASS is the most isolated resort with access by oversnow transport only. The Kosciusko Chalet has 40 rooms and the Alitji and Stilwell club lodges sometimes have space available for non-members. The village is at 1760m, and the highest slope is 1980m. There are 5 lifts with an uphill capacity of 3,000 per hour.

Cross country skiing has also become extremely popular in recent years and has opened up new horizons for many. If you do go cross country skiing please observe the basic rules. Always carry waterproof clothing with you, some food, know where there is shelter, carry a map and compass, don't be afraid to turn back if the weather or conditions deteriorate and advise the appropriate authorities of your destination and expected time of return. At Cabramurra there are 30km of marked trails as well as a day shelter for use by all skiers. Cabramurra, 1488m, is Australia's highest permanently inhabited town. It is the headquarters of the Upper

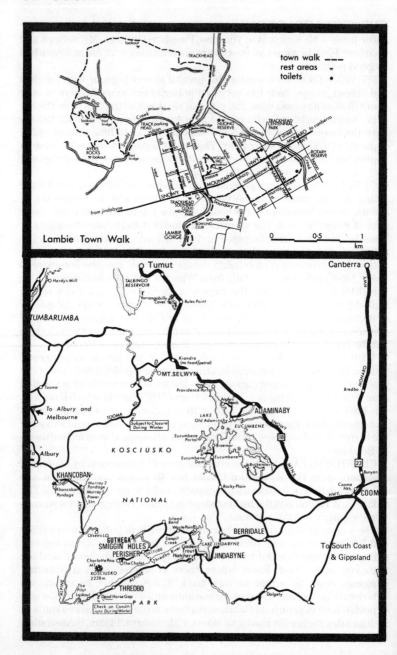

Lambie Town Walk

town walk ---
rest areas *
toilets •

0   0.5   1
km

Tumut Development of the Snowy Mountains Authority. Petrol and food are available and limited accommodation.

Boating & Fishing – Lake Eucumbene, Lake Jindabyne, Lake Blowering, Lake Talbingo and Lake Jounama. Trout are plentiful but an Inland Fishing Licence is necessary.

Bushwalking: Kosciusko National Park – for free maps etc. contact one of the ranger stations – Sawpit Creek, Blowering, Yarrangobilly or Tumut. Maps and other information are also available from National Parks and Wildlife Services, 189 Kent Street, Sydney.

Caves: Yarrangobilly, off the Snowy Mountains Highway between Adaminiby and Tumut. There are usually 4 caves open to the public, but during school holidays the rangers take groups through another cave using miners helmets – a great attraction for the kids. There is picnic area at the caves and a thermal swimming pool with a water temperature of 27 deg.C all year round. There are also several bushwalks.

Trout Farms: Eucumbene Trout Farm, Berridale, open 9am-5pm – off season 12 – 5pm; Snowy Mountains Trout Farm below Blowering Dam, 9am-5pm.

ADAMINABY, 53km from Cooma is the home of 'The World's Largest Trout'. The town was moved to its present site in 1956/7 to allow for the filling of Lake Eucumbene.

KIANDRA is now just a dot on the map, with a few ruins dotting the landscape. During the gold rush of the 1860's it was a town of 15,000. The National Parks & Wildlife Service put out a walking tour map for the Goldseeker's Track which takes you past some of the more interesting sights.

TUMUT is also worth visiting, particularly during autumn when its deciduous trees are at their most spectacular. While you're there you might like to drop in to the millet broom factory open 9am-2.30pm, or to the Tumut Lime & Marble workshop.

The Alpine Way joins Thredbo with Khancoban, winds through some spectacular scenery, and is well worth driving along if you have the time. Snow Chains must be carried in winter and the road is not suitable for caravans.

DUBBO – Pop. 32,000

LOCATION:
Mid-western NSW on the Macquarie River at the junction of the Newell and Mitchell Highways. Distance from: Sydney 416km; Brisbane 862km; Melbourne 818km; and Adelaide 1,207km.

CLIMATE:
Average temperatures: January max. 31.6 deg. C – min. 18.3 deg. C; July 15.0 deg. C – min 2.9 deg. C; average annual rainfall 584mm; height above

sealevel 262.4 m; average number of rainy days – 74.

CHARACTERISTICS:

Dubbo is known as the Hub of the West. It's a prosperous service centre for the fertile farmlands around it.

HOW TO GET THERE:

AIR. Air NSW and Hazelton have daily services to Sydney, and Hazelton has a daily service to Canberra & Orange.

BUS. Ansett Pioneer and Greyhound stop at Dubbo on their Melbourne/Brisbane/Gold Coast runs. The usual restrictions apply e.g. you must have an Australia wide bus pass or have travelled interstate by public transport.

RAIL. An XPT service runs to Dubbo.

CAR. From Adelaide via the Sturt Highway to Mildura, and then the Mid Western or the Barrier and Mitchell Highways; from Brisbane via the Cunningham Highway to Goondiwindi and then the Newell Highway; from Melbourne via the Hume Highway to Seymour, the Goulburn Valley Highway to Tocumwal and then the Newell Highway; from Sydney via the Great Western Highway to Bathurst and then the Mitchell Highway.

TOURIST INFORMATION:

232 Macquarie St., Ph (068) 82 5359 – open 9am-5pm daily.

ACCOMMODATION:

22 motels, 1 hotel/motel, 3 hotels and 5 caravan parks. For detailed information contact the tourist information office.

A few names and addresses: Blue Gum Motor Inn, Cobra St., 82 0900 – RO $47-$53 double; John Oxley Motel, 119 Macquarie St., Ph 82 4622 – RO $35-$40 double; Castlereach Hotel, Cnr. Brisbane & Talbragar Sts., Ph 82 4877 – BB $34-$36 double; Midstate Caravan Park, 21 Bourke St. – site $5 double – overnite van $17 double; Dubbo City Caravan Park, Whylandra St., West Dubbo, Ph 82 4820 – site $7 – overnite vans $16-19 double – cabins $24 double.

EATING OUT:

The Dubbo RSL Club, Wingewarra St., Ph 82 4411 welcomes visitors. The Forest Lodge Motor Inn, Cnr. Wheelers Land & Myall St., Ph 82 6500, has a licensed restaurant and cocktail bar. The Countryman Motor Inn, 47 Cobra St., Dubbo, Ph 82 7422 also has a licensed restaurant. Leightons Restaurant, 34-38 Cobra St, Ph 82 9511 is open 7 days and has a special supper menu on Thurs, Fri & Sat nights. Philippe's French Restaurant, 208 Brisbane Street, Ph 82 5554 is open weekdays for lunches and 7 days for dinner. West Dubbo Bowling Club's Restaurant is open 7days for lunch and dinner. The Old Shire Restaurant & Gallery, Macquarie & Bultje Sts., Ph 81 8318 is fully licensed, but you can also BYO. Edelweiss Restaurant, 215 Macquarie St., Ph 82 7391 serves steak, seafood and fondues. For Chinese try the Kingsway, 195 Macquarie St., Ph 82 7499. The Copper Kettle, Cnr. Darling &

Church Sts,. Ph 82 6506 serves Lebanese & Vegetarian meals. And for the family there is a McDonalds at 22-24 Cobra Street or Big W's Snack Bar in the Orana Mall, Cnr. Wheelers Lane & The Mitchell Highway.

POINTS OF INTEREST:

The city itself is best seen by following the signposted TOURIST DRIVE which starts at the Civic Centre, Darling St.

A HERITAGE WALK commences at the Museum and takes in many historic buildings around the city.

The MUSEUM (234 Macquarie St) is open daily 9am-5pm and exhibits include a village square with 14 shop exhibitions – admission charge.

The OLD DUBBO JAIL in Macquarie Street has many items of interest including the original gallows – open daily 9am-5pm – admission charge.

At the DUBBO MILITARY MUSEUM, Peak Hill Rd., Dubbo, Ph 82 0790 you can see a Neptune bomber, a Vampire Jet a Dukw etc. – open 10am-4.30pm daily – admission charge.

You can milk a cow, ride in a sulkie and see many other farm activities at DUNOON FARM, Cnr. Newell Highway & Camp Road, Ph 82 0790. Adults $5.Children $3. Open 10am-4.30pm.

At the YARRABAR POTTERY you can see a working pottery and the craftsman at his wheel – open daily 9am-5pm – 12km south.

The TROY SALEYARDS, 6km north on the Newell Highway – turn east at the railway crossing and follow the signs – are an unusual tourist attraction. Hundreds of buyers from all over Australia flock to the saleyards as cattle, sheep, horses and pigs go under the auctioneers hammer. The Tourist Information Office has details of sale times.

The WESTERN PLAINS ZOO, Obley Road, Ph 82 5888 is Dubbo's main tourist attraction. Open daily from 9am-4pm. The best way to see this open range zoo is to hire a bicycle or a moke. There are 6km of sealed roads as well as walking paths and plenty of picnic facilities.

FACILITIES:

Golf, lawn bowls, tennis, fishing, sauna, cinema, swimming pool, ice skating rink, Brisbane St, ten pin bowling at Windsor Pde., East Dubbo (daily 9am-11pm), slot car racing at Valley View Raceway with 60m of track, 2/148 Brisbane St, squash courts, Brisbane Street, horse racing, waterslide in Victoria Park, paddle boats and canoes can be hired at Lions Park on the western bank of the Macquarie River and water skiing. Bicycles can be hired from Wheelers Cycles, Cnr. Brisbane and Bultje Sts., Ph 82 9899 and The Bike Shoppe, Cnr. Darling St and Wingewarra Sts., Ph 81 8755 – Mon-Fri 9am-6pm and Sat & Sun 9am-12.30pm.

On the second Sunday of the month Markets are held in the Showground and hundreds of stallholders sell everything from plants and toys to furniture -from 10am-1pm.

FESTIVALS:

Orana Country Music Festival is usually held during the Easter period. The

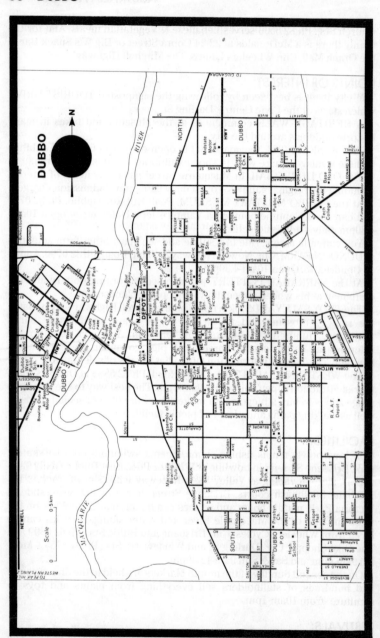

Dubbo Agricultural Show is held in May. The Loo to Loo Canoe Classic is held in October.

OUTLYING ATTRACTIONS:

The RADIO TELESCOPE near Parkes. Turn off the Newell Highway 20km north of Parkes and its 6km along the road. The Visitors' Centre is open daily except for Good Friday, Anzac Day, Christmas Day and Boxing Day. An education liaison officer is on duty at all times. Teachers can obtain information leaflets, worksheets and details of night observing sessons by writing to The Manager, CSIRO Astronomy Education Centre, P.O. Box 2870, Parkes. The Parkes telescope will form part of the Australia Telescope which is due for completion in 1988.

The MUGINCOBLE Wheat Terminal, 8km from Parkes on the Eugowra Rd., is open for inspection Mon-Friday by appointment 62 2225.

The PEAK HILL open cut gold mine, 35km north of Parkes, consists of two holes of enormous depth which can be viewed from the lookouts.

PARKES can best be seen by driving along the Tourist Drive of 33km which takes approximately 90mins.

Ben Hall, the bushranger, is burried in the FORBES Cemetary. The Sandhills Vineyard at Forbes has an antique copper distillery as well as wine tasting and barbecue facilities.

WELLINGTON, on the Mitchell Highway, 50km south-east of Dubbo, has a clock museum and bottle house. The Wellington Caves are 8km south of the town and inspections are held daily on the hour.

At NARROMINE, 40km west of Dubbo, is the Western Plains Gliding and Soaring Centre on the site of the old RAAF Training Aerodrome.

TRANGIE, 36km west of Narromine, is the home of a world recognised agricultural research station and cotton farm. There are several cotton farms between Trangie and Warren.

GILGANDRA, 66km north of Dubbo, has a museum displaying Aboriginal artefacts, bottles, shells and minerals; the Gilgandra Observatory and display centre; and the Endeavour Galleries.

COONABARABRAN, 96km north-east of Gilgandra, is the astronomy capital of Australia, and a visit to the Siding Spring Observatory is a must. It is also the gateway to the rugged Warrumbungle Ranges which are popular with bushwalkers.

GOSFORD – Pop. 39,000

LOCATION:
On the Central Coast just north of Sydney.

CLIMATE:
Average Temperature: January max. 25.0 deg.C – min. 19.0 deg.C.; July max.

17.5 deg. C.- min. 9.2 deg.C; Average Annual Rainfall 1164mm; The heaviest rain falls between October and March, much of it from storms.

CHARACTERISTICS:

Largest town on the Central Coast – once just a popular holiday resort but now a dormitory 'suburb' of Sydney. The Central Coast stretches from the northern bank of the Hawkesbury River to Lake Munmorah in the north, and takes in the resort towns of Terrigal, The Entrance, Toukley, and Budgewoi as well as other smaller places. There is a string of ocean beaches along the coast and behind them a string of lakes which make this area an aquatic playground.

HOW TO GET THERE:

AIR. A commuter sea plance service runs from Rose Bay, Sydney to Gosford (regular departures) – Aquatic Airways.
BUS. V.I.P. call in at Gosford on request on their Brisbane/Sydney Pacific Highway route. Some of the Deluxe services call in at Gosford on their Sydney/Brisbane runs.
RAIL. Good electric train service from/to Sydney, and the State Rail Authority has mini-fares, family fares and combined rail/coach tours.
CAR. Take the Pacific Highway from Sydney and then you have the choice to stay on the highway, or take the F3 Expressway. Distance from: Sydney 83km; Brisbane 930km.

TOURIST INFORMATION:

Gosford City Tourist Association 200 Mann Street, Gosford – (043) 25 2835 – open Mon-Friday 9am-5pm and weekends 9am-3pm. Tuggerah Lakes Tourist Association, Marine Parade, The Entrance (43) 32 9282 – Mon-Fri 9am-5pm & weekends 9am-4pm; Tuggerah Lakes' Visitors Centre, Victoria St & Main Rd., Ph 96 1666 – open daily 10am-3pm.

ACCOMMODATION:

Along the coast there is all sorts of accommodation available, from premier hotels, to camping grounds, from guest houses to holiday flats. Whatever type of accommodation you are seeking you will find something to suit your taste or purse. The Tourist Information Offices will be only too pleased to assist you.

Some names and address in Gosford itself: Gosford Motor Inn, 23 Pacific Highway, Gosford, Ph 23 1333 – RO $44-49 double; The Willows Motor Inn, 512 Pacific Highway, North Gosford, Ph 28 4666 RO $53 double; Rambler Motor Inn, 73 Pacific Highway, West Gosford, Ph 14 6577 – $39-46; Bermuda Motor Inn, 73 Pacific Highway, West Gosford, Ph 24 4366 – $43-$48; Kowara Lodge Motel, Kowara Road, Somersby Plateau, West Gosford, Ph 40 2305 – $35-45 double; Gosford Hotel, Cnr. Mann & Erina Sts., Ph 24 2634 – $25-30 double; Wyoming Caravan Park, 520 Pacific Hwy, Wyoming, 1km north of P.O., Ph 28 4358 – sites $8-9 – on site vans $19.

EATING OUT:

There are Pizza Huts at Gosford, Woy Woy and Long Jetty; Homestead Chicken are at the cnr. Pacific Highway and Hely St., West Gosford, Ph 24 1053; Moutan Restaurant, Woy Woy Leagues Club, Blackwall Rd., Woy Woy, Ph 41 3566 welcomes visitors seven days a week for lunch and dinner. The Skillion Family Restaurant, Skillion Arcade, Terrigal; Cobb & Co Restaurant, 154 Terrigal Drive, Ph 84 1166; Lord Charlie's Waterfront Restaurant, 61 Masons Pde., Gosford, Ph 24 6705; Tails Coffee Shop, 112 Mann St; Fabbs Waterfront Restaurant, 27 The Entrance Road, The Entrance, Ph 32 5545; Tuggerah Lakes Memorial Club, main road between Long Jetty and The Entrance, Ph 32 3399; Everglades Country Club, Dunban Rd., Woy Woy, Ph 41 1866; Mingara Club, Adelaide Road, Tumbi Umbi, Ph 88 3277; Ettalong Beach War Memorial Club, Memorial Ave., Ettalong Beach, 41 1166; The Terrigal Memorial Country Club, Dover Road, Wamberal, Ph 84 2661 – open Wed-Sun 12-2pm & 6pm-8.30pm.

POINTS OF INTEREST.

Old Sydney Town is an authentic and entertaining re-creation of Sydney Cove in its first years. It is perched high on the hills behind Gosford at Somersby , and every day you can see men & women in period costume enacting life in Sydney as it was between 1788-1810 – open daily during school holidays – otherwise Wed-Sun 10am-5pm – bus service from Gosford station or day tours from Sydney.

Australian Reptile Park, Pacific Highway, North Gosford, Ph 28 4311 – open daily from 8am has a giant dinosaur outside the gates. It was established by Eric Worrell on its present site in 1958 and it has a wide variety of reptiles on display. Venom is milked from the snakes and supplied to the Commonwealth Serum Laboratories to produce antivenenes – talks and demonstrations, and swimming pool and picnic area.

The 'Eastern Dragon' Gosford Wharf, Dane Drive, is an authentic Chinese Junk built in Hong Kong. It now cruises Brisbane Waters – contact the Tourist Information Office for details.

Pioneer Park on the waterfront at Point Frederick has been landscaped and many of Gosford's early pioneers are buried in the cemetery.

The Starship Cruises & Ferry Service departs Gosford and the Entrance Public Wharves twice daily – fares – round trip: Brisbane Waters: Adults $5 – Tuggerah Lake: $7.50.

FESTIVALS:

Gosford's Waterfront Festival is held during the last week of September and the first week of October.

FACILITIES:

Fishing, swimming, boating, ten pin bowling, squash, lawn bowls, golf and tennis.

OUTLYING ATTRACTIONS:

The crystal clear waters right along the Central Coast offer some of the best

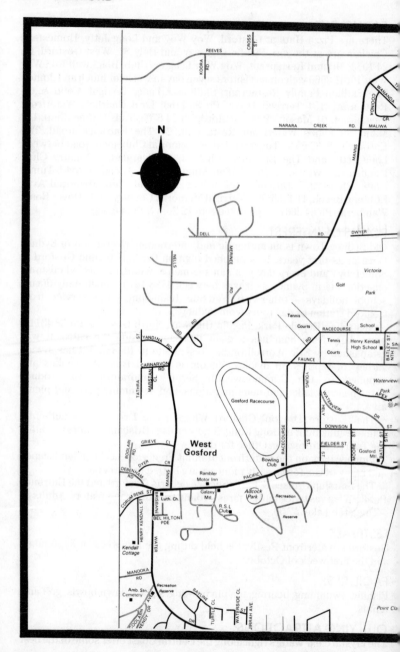

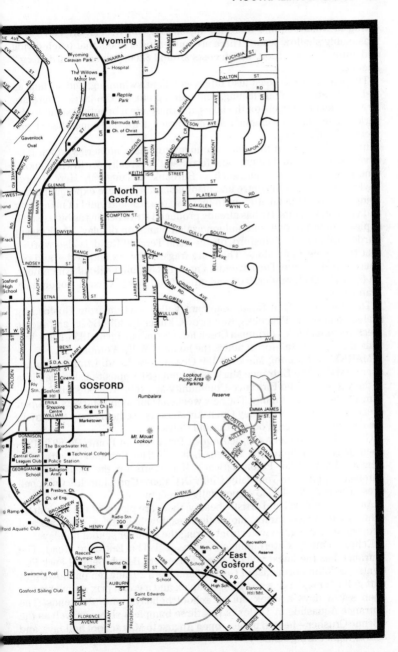

diving in Australia, and there are fascinating old wrecks off Terrigal in reasonably shallow water. There are numerous schools that teach diving and, after 5 days tuition, which costs around $200, you are awarded a 'C' licence.

The whole of the coast also offers excellent swimming, and surfing, as well as boating, sailing, fishing, sailboarding etc. on the lakes. There are large flocks of Pelicans on the lakes and these are a beautiful sight. In the park at The Entrance channel, Marine Parade, a local fish merchant feeds them at 3.30pm daily.

In the hills behind the coast are many top-class nurseries which take advantage of the mild climate and fertile soil. It is really worthwhile taking time to visit some of them, such as Burbank, at Tuggerah. Here George Taylor has a research centre and plant laboratory where experiments are being conducted in an attempt to increase the size and yield of many fruit and vegetable plants. He has already produced strawberries as big as small apples. There are over one million azalea plants on display. The Fragant Garden 13km east of Gosford, off the main Terrigal Road, is also worth a visit for the perfume alone. There are fragant flowers and herbs, and pot pourri etc. is on sale. The Lavender Patch, Lot 3, Cullens Road, Kincumber, Ph 69 1611, has lavender, lace and gifts of Old World Charm – open daily 10am-5pm.

The Ferneries, Oak Road, Matcham Valley – 11km from Gosford by sealed road – has Peacocks, Kangaroos, Emus, Paddle Boats and picnic areas. Askania Park, Ourimbah Creek Rd., Ourimbah, Ph 62 1855, has a 3km walk through the rainforest and is the home of Willy Wombat.

MARKETS: Ettalong Markets, 189 Ocean View Road, Ettalong feature over 60 stalls. The Entrance Markets, Denning St. opposite Lakeside Plaza is the venue for The Entrance Community Markets with 80 stalls – open 8am-12 noon every Sunday. The new weekend Ourimbah Markets are open every weekend. The Toukley Open Air Markets are held every Sunday in the car park between Woolworths and Coles.

GALLERIES: Gallery 460, 460 Avoca Drive, Green Point, Ph 69 2013 – open daily 11am-6pm; The Pottery Loft, 360 The Entrance Road, Erina Heights, Ph 67 6680; Patonga Beach Handcrafts on the Beachfront at Patonga – open 10am-7pm daily; Dinky Di Gallery, Cnr. Church & Campbell Cres., Terrigal, Ph 84 6493 – open daily 9am-5pm.

As well as natural and artistic beauty, there are plenty of entertainment centres with video games, movie theatres, bowling alleys, carnivals and circuses, etc. along the waterfront during the summer school holidays.

Eclipse Family Entertainment Centre, 131 The Entrance Road, The Entrance has the latest video games. Forresters Beach Central Park Fun Centre, is 20km north east of Gosford and has a 20 lane ten pin bowl, putt putt golf course, large waterslide complex and a grand prix racing track – open seven days a week during school holidays, and weekends. The Entrance Aquaslide in Taylor St has three bumpless slides as well as the Cosmic Crusher – heated pools – open August to May school holidays, and also at night during January.

Norah Head Lighthouse is open for inspection Tuesdays and Thursdays during school holidays – check with Tourist Office for times.

Maybareen Farm, George Downes Drive, Kulnura, Ph 76 &1323, has large walk-through avaries, and handheld feeding of farm animals. The cows are milked at 11.30am.

Central Coast Winery Pty. Ltd., 17 Kerta Road, Kincumber, commenced operations in 1976 and its first product was Orange Spumante which is made from naturally fermented oranges from Mangrove Mountain. Other products include Pina Colada, Old Pillory Port, Marsala, Coffee Supreme and table wines – open 9am-4.30pm Mon-Fri and Sat 9am-4pm.

At Railway Crescent, Lisarow, only a few km. from Gosford are the Kitchens of Sara Lee, Ph 28 3333 – guided tours Mon-Fri 10am and 1.30pm – bookings essential.

Vales Point Power Station, Doyalson, Ph 58 8171, has guided tours of 90 mins duration from 8.30am to 1.30pm Sundays to Wednesdays and Public Holidays – bookings essential.

The Smokey Mountain and Grozzly Flats Steam Railroad is 10km north of Wyong on Mountain Raod, Warnervale. Models trains carry visitors on a 4km track – open Sundays and public holidays, and Tues-Thurs during the May and September school holidays. Trains operate every half hour – Ph 92 3559.

Watagan Forest Drive links Wyong to Cessnock by the shortest possible route, a distance of 82km across the forests of the Watagan Mountains, through magnificent mountain scenery with several picnic areas and bushwalks.

BROOKLYN, on the Hawkesbury, doesn't really belong to the Central Coast, but it's the place where the ferries servicing the Hawkesbury River leave from. One unique service is the river postal service which carries mail, food, beer, medicine etc. to the oyster farmers, fishermen and riverfolk who live along the river. It is a popular trip with tourists as it is unique and relaxing at the same time.

The Brisbane Water National Park, between Woy Woy and Kariong, contains the Bulgandry Aboriginal engraving site. This site is easily accessible to tourists and affords a good view with no risk of damage to the engravings.

Munmorah State Recreation Area, 28km north of Wyong, has wildflowers, coastal heathland and rugged cliffs, and makes an excellent day trip from Gosford.

GOULBURN – Pop. 24,000 (district 12,000)

LOCATION:
196km south-west of Sydney and 93km north-east of Canberra.

CLIMATE:
Average summer max 26 deg C, min 12 deg C; average winter max 12 deg C, min 0.5 deg C; average annual rainfall 671mm; 638m above sea level.

CHARACTERISTICS:
Australia's oldest inland city dating back to the earliest days of the colony. Has beautiful cast iron lace work on many buildings. Wheat was grown in the locality as early as the 1820s and to-day, primary industry is still its most important industry, but several large secondary industries are now located there. It is also an administrative centre for several State Government Departments. It was the last town in the British Empire to become a city by virtue of the Royal Letters Patent, becoming a Bishopric in 1863. Home of 'Rambo' the 14m high ram at the Big Merino complex.

HOW TO GET THERE:
CAR. Via the Hume Highway from Sydney or Melbourne or the Federal Highway from Canberra.
BUS. Most of the major coaches lines stop here on the Sydney/Melbourne and Sydney/Canberra/Melbourne runs.
RAIL. On the main Sydney/Melbourne line.

TOURIST INFORMATION CENTRE:
2 Montague St., Goulburn, phone (048) 21 5343. Open: 9-5 Mon-Fri and 9.30-3.30 Sat, Sun & public hols.

ACCOMMODATION:
Excellent and varied – 11 motels, 1 hotel/motel, 7 hotels and 3 caravan parks.

Some names and addresses: Posthouse Motor Lodge, 1 Lagoon St., Ph 21 5666 – RO $50 double; Parkhaven Motel, Lagoon St., Ph 21 4455 – $34-40 double; Lilac City Motor Inn, 126 Lagoon St., Ph 21 5000 – RO $50 double; Big River Motel,2 215 Prince St., Ph 42 4028 – RO $30-40 double; Roche's Hotel, 85 Victoria St., Ph 42& 2866 – RO $20 double; Grafton Hotel, 97 Fitzroy St., Ph 42 2000 – B&B $28-30 double. Governors Hill Carapark, Hume Hwy, Ph 21 7373 – sites $6.50 double – onsite vans $22 double; Goulburn South Caravan Park, Hume Hwy, Ph 21 3233 – sites $5 double – onsite vans $29 for 4 – cabins $26 for 4.

EATING OUT:
Goulburn has sophisticated restaurants, coffee bars, family-style cafes and licensed clubs, so whatever your budget you will find something to suit.

Some names & addresses: Bojangles, 95 Auburn St., Ph 21 6666; Buen Amigos Mexican Restaurant, Posthouse Motor Lodge, Lagoon St., Ph 2165666; Alex's Fish Cafe, 78 Auburn St., Ph 21 2779; BP Pitt Stop, 32 Clinton St., Ph 21 4642; Lotus Chinese Takeaway, 80a Auburn St., Ph 21 4888; McDonalds, Hume Highway, North Goulburn, Ph 21 8055. The Astor Hotel, Cnr. Auburn & Clinton Sts., has counter lunches as does the Empire Hotel, Auburn St.

POINTS OF INTEREST:

20 historic sites can be viewed in two hours on a walking tour – Visitors' Centre has information. The cast iron decoration on many of the buildings has been the subject of much research and photographic record. Some of the historic buildings are open to the public e.g. The Court House, Garroorigang, Gulsons Brickworks and Pottery and Bishopthorpe, by appointment.

The Big Merino complex has a craft centre, educational area, lookout and restaurant.

Visit the Goulburn Yurtworks to see the only makers of Yurts (round-houses based on Mongolian tents).

The Rocky Hill War Memorial dominates the town and is Goulburn's landmark.

The Black Stag Deer Park has fallow red deer, as well as Australian wildlife.

There are also quite a few art galleries and craft shops, and the Applied Arts & Sciences Museum has collections of early gramphones, music boxes and model steam engines, as well as rocks and minerals and local wool samples.

FESTIVALS:

The Lilac Festival is held the October long weekend. Argyle County Fair held at Riversdale in November each year and Carnivale, part of the NSW Government sponsored festival, is held in September each year.

FACILITIES:

Leisure Centre offers ten pin bowling, roller skating, and amusement area. There is a bicycle track at Victoria Park. Regular race meetings are held by the local racing club. Lawn bowls, golf, tennis, carpet bowls, darts, indoor cricket, swimming and fishing are also catered for.

OUTLYING ATTRACTIONS:

The Burgonia State Recreation Area, 35km south-east, is an extensive plateau overlooking deeply dissected gorges in the north and west, and deeply incised valleys of the Shoalhaven River in the east. The views are magnificent. The Jerrara Falls can be seen from Adams Lookdown, and there is a walk down into the gorge there – camping and picnic area.

The Pejar Dam Aquatic Recreation Reserve, 25km north-west on the Crookwell Road, is one of the best trout fishing areas in the south-east region. Fishing Licence is required. Only non-powered boats are permitted, as are windsurfing, swimming etc.

Pelican Sheep Station, 10km south of Goulburn on the Braidwood Road, offers tours for groups. Contact Eric and Hope Sykes, Ph 21 4920. Different breeds of sheep are shown as well as shearing displays. Luncheon tours and accommodation are available.

Braidwood 86km south, has been classified as an historic town by the National Trust. It has a museum-tourist centre and an extensive craft shop, open daily except Tues & Wed. Information about this town is also available from the Goulburn Tourist office. There are some delightful drives around this town including the Araluen Valley.

Bywong Gold Mining Town is 28km north of Canberra, Ph (062) 97 4943. It is open to the public Sat, Sun & public and school hols from 10am-4pm. It is a unique historical restoration project based on authentic documents, maps and pictures. Gold mining and panning, old diggings, miners' makeshift village, blacksmith display and a public water supply built by Chinese well-diggers in 1894.

KATOOMBA/WENTWORTH FALLS
Pop. 14,000

LOCATION:
In the Blue Mountains 105km west of Sydney.

CLIMATE:
Distinct seasons. Cooler than Sydney all year round. Occasional snow falls in winter, usually July. Does not last.

CHARACTERISTICS:
Old World Style. In the Twenties and Thirties, the Blue Mountains was THE Holiday Capital of Australia. Special steam trains like 'The Honeymoon Express' and 'The Caves Express' laboured up the mountain grades filled with honeymoon couples.

To-day many of the old hotels and guest houses have been restored to their former glory and now exude nostaligc art deco magnetism.

The Blue Mountains derive their name from the haze caused by droplets of eucalypt oil dispersing into the atmosphere from the gum trees.

HOW TO GET THERE:
RAIL. Electric trains approx. every 2 hrs. from Sydney. The State Rail Authority have Day-a-Away Rail Tours and Mini Holidays to Katoomba at package prices.
CAR. From Sydney along the Great Western Highway and the F4 Freeway 105km; from Canberra via the Federal Highway, Hume Highway and Great Western Highway 326km.

TOURIST INFORMATION:
Echo Point open 9am-5pm daily, phone (047) 82 1833.

ACCOMMODATION:
Blackheath 4 motels, 2 hotels, 4 guest houses and holiday cabins. Hampton: Hotel/Motel.

Jenolan Caves: Caves House and 8 Bush Cabins.
Katoomba: 13 Motels, 2 hotels, 8 guest houses, 2 caravan parks, and numerous holiday flats & cabins.
Kurrajong: 1 hotel/motel, 1 motel, 1 health farm and 1 camp. Lawson: 1 hotel.
Leura: 3 motels, 1 hotel, 1 guest house, 1 caravan park and several holiday flats.
Youth Hostels: North Springwood, Hawkesbury Road, Hawkesbury Heights, phone (047) 54 1213. Katoomba YHA, Wellington Road, Katoomba, phone (047) 82 1416.

EATING OUT:
The National Trust classified Paragon Cafe.

Katoomba has numerous restaurants and take-aways as well as motel and hotel dining rooms which are open to the public. The RSL and Golf Clubs also welcome visitors. The Paragon Cafe is a reminder of the past and is well worth a visit.

LOCAL TRANSPORT:
Blue Mountains Explorer Bus operates Sat., Sun & Public Hols – 2 routes – Adults $6.00 Child/Pens. $3.00, Family Tickets 2 adults & up to 4 children $16.00, 1 adult & up to 4 children $11.00 full day; Weekend Rover – Adult $9, Child/Pens $4.50. Tickets available on bus, the railway station or the Tourist Information Office. Blue Mountains/Jenolan Caves Special Ticket – Adult $29 with Family and Pensioner concessions available. Contact Golden West Tours (047) 82 1866. Car Hire: Cales Ph 82 2917, or Bryants Ph 82 3651, Taxis: Radio Cabs Ph 82 1311.

POINTS OF INTEREST:
The famous Three Sisters at Echo Point have decorated many postcards and the view down into the valley is magnificent. It is possible to walk down the giant staircase (1000 steps) into the valley below and along to the valley station of the Scenic Railway and catch the train to the top. The 310m track drops 207m into the valley below so it is an exciting ride, up or down. At the top is the Skyway, a cable car which travels out about 450m over the Cook's Crossing and affords magnificents views of Katoomba Falls, Orphan Rock and the Jamieson Valley. There is revolving restaurant in the complex.

From the bottom of the Three Sisters it is also possible to walk along to the Leura Cascades and climb up beside the waterfall.

For the less energetic there is a 20km Cliff Drive along the edge of the escarpment from Katoomba to Wentworth Falls. There are numerous bushwalks and waterfalls, some of which are floodlit at night, along the way.

The Everglades Gardens, Denison St., Leura are one of Australia's great gardens, and have been classified by the National Trust. They are delightful no matter the season. The autumn tones beckon as do the azaleas and rhododendrons in spring – admission charge.

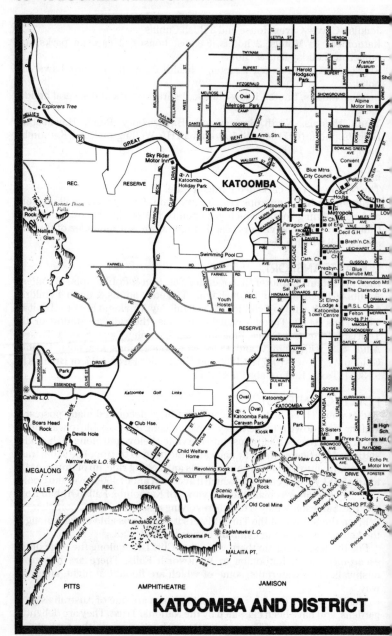

KATOOMBA AND DISTRICT

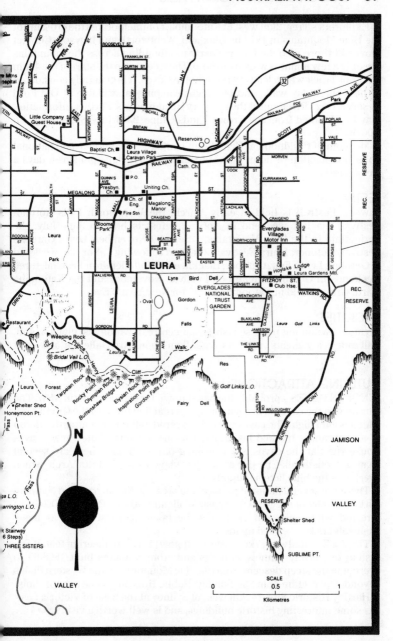

Explorers's Tree, 2km west of Katoomba, commemorates the crossing of the Blue Mountains in 1813 by Blaxland, Wentworth and Lawson. Convict graves of those who died during early roadbuilding across the mountains are only a few minutes walk from here. The tree is also the start of the 42km Six Foot Track which leads to the Jenolan Caves. It is generally considered to be a three day walk, and overnight camping is available at Old Ford Reserve, Coxs River and at the Forestry Headquarters. Further information may be obtained from the Crown Lands Office, 23 Bridge St., Sydney, Ph 2 0579.

Museum of Childhood at Echo Point contains 3000 antique and national dolls, a collection of notes coins etc. and is open 9am-5pm seven days a week, gratis.

FESTIVALS:
Lawson Festival is held in early March; the Wentworth Falls Autumn Festival, the last weekend in April; Yulefest is held in June/July; the Springtime in the Blue Mountains, 1 Sept.-30 November; Leura Gardens Festival, October; Leura Festival, weekend following Labor day weekend in October; Leura Fair, October; Blackheath Rhododendron Festival, three weekends in October; Glenbrook Festival, November and the Katoomba Mardi Gras, is held in Katoomba Street on New Year's Eve.

FACILITIES:
Olympic swimming pool, squash & spa centre, lawn bowls, cinema, golf, trail rides, joy flights, markets Sats. 9am-noon. Art Galleries and craft shops.

OUTLYING ATTRACTIONS:
JENOLAN CAVES – probably the best-known limestone caves in NSW. The entrance to the caves is in a narrow gorge reached through the Grand Arch which is 24m high. The caves were discovered in the 1830's after the victim of a bushranger tracked his attacker to his hideout in the caves. Caves House right at the caves is a charming old hotel, and there are several beautiful bushwalks in the area. The view from Carlotta Arch which overlooks the blue lake, is superb.

There are several national parks in the area e.g. Kanangra Boyd National Park, 68,276ha of rugged wilderness; Wollemi National Park, 450,000 ha of forested wilderness, but care must be taken in these areas as many bushwalkers have ended up lost.

The Zig Zag Railway (7km east of Lithgow) is an engineering feat. It is a system of railway tunnels, cuttings and stone viaducts built 1866-69 to overcome the steep descent from the Blue Mountains to the Western Plains beyond. Open 11am-4pm Sat, Sunday, Public Hols and some schools hols.

Hartley Historic Site, 140km west of Sydney at the base of Victoria Pass, has some interesting historic buildings, and is well worth a visit.

LIGHTNING RIDGE – Pop. 1,112

LOCATION:
770km north-west of Sydney only 60 odd kilometres from the Queensland border.

CLIMATE:
Long hot summers and short cold winters with summer temperatures dropping as much as 20 degrees at night.

CHARACTERISTICS:
An old fashioned, carefree, tomorrow will do if it can't be done today atmosphere, which is treasured and preserved by local residents as a valuable way of life. The only place in the world where wet puddling can be seen (the operation which is used to separate opal 'nobbies' from the clay in which they are found).

TOURIST INFORMATION:
Morilla Street, Tel. 29 0565.

HOW TO GET THERE:
AIR. Airlines of NSW. Fokker Friendship from Sydney to Walgett on Tues, Thurs & Sun. Service vehicle to and from Lightning Ridge. Lightning Ridge Air Service, phone 290 666.
RAIL AND COACH. From Sydney via Dubbo Tues., Thurs. & Sats and returns on the same days. From Sydney via Narrabri Mon, Wed & Fri and returns on the same days.
CAR. From Sydney travel along the Mitchell Highway to Gilgandra, and then north along the Castlereagh Highway. The road is bitumen sealed right into the town itself.

ACCOMMODATION:
Motels: Black Opal Motel, Opal St., Ph 29 0518 – RO $40-42 double; Lightning Ridge Motor Village, Onyx St., Tel. 29 0304 – RO $44; Wallangulla Motel, Morilla St., Tel. 29 0542 – RO $41-43; Caravan & Camping Parks: Crocodile Park, Morilla St., Tel. 29 0437 – sites $6 double – onsite vans $16 double;

Lightning Ridge Park, Harlequin St., Tel. 29 0532 – site $5 double – onsite vans $22 double; Lorne Holiday Station, Tel. 29 0366 – sites $4 double – bunkhouse $8ppn; Tram-o-tel, Morilla St., Tel. 29 0613.

EATING OUT:
Take-aways: Bus Stop Coffee Shop; Harlequin, Maude's Cafe, Morilla St, Roadhouse Cafe, Morilla St.; Digger's Rest Hotel, Opal St., Miner's Mate Restaurant, Opal St.; Nobbies Restaurant, Onyx St; and Lightning Ridge Hotel, Onyx St., and Lightning Ridge Bowling Club, Morilla St.

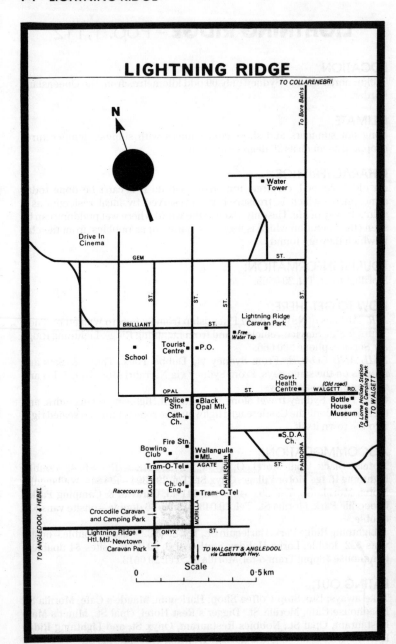

LIGHTNING RIDGE

N

TO COLLARENEBRI

To Bore Baths

Water Tower

Drive In Cinema

GEM ST.

ST.

BRILLIANT ST.

Lightning Ridge Caravan Park

Free Water Tap

School

Tourist Centre ■ P.O.

Govt. Health Centre ■

OPAL ST. WALGETT RD. (Old road)

Police Stn. ■ ■ Black Opal Mtl.

Cath. Ch. ■

Bottle ■ House Museum

To Lorne Holiday Station Caravan & Camping Park
TO WALGETT

Fire Stn. ■

Bowling Club ■

Wallangulla ■ Mtl.

■ S.D.A. Ch.

Tram-O-Tel ■

AGATE ST.

HARLEQUIN

PANDORA

KAOLIN

Ch. of Eng. ■

■ Tram-O-Tel

MORILLA

TO ANGLEDOOL & HEBEL

Racecourse

Crocodile Caravan and Camping Park

Lightning Ridge Htl. Mtl. ■ Newtown Caravan Park

ONYX ST.

TO WALGETT & ANGLEDOOL via Castlereagh Hwy.

Scale

0   0·5 km

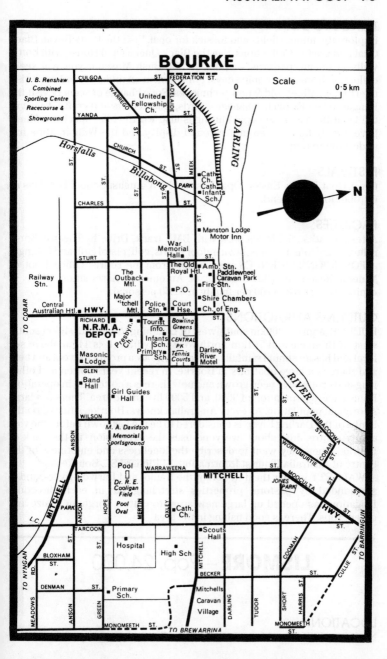

THINGS TO DO:
Explore the mining fields and fossick for opal. Visit the Betty Bevan Black Opal and Cactus Collections. See the Black Queen Opal House with bottle walls in unique patterns – crafts. At the Bush Museum you will see a collection from early mining days. For a look at an underground mine visit the Drive-in Mine – old & new techniques. For a change of scenery visit the Kangaroo Hill Fauna Orphanage – birds, animals arts and crafts. A visit to the Opal Bazaar to see opal cutting is also worthwhile. Spectrum Mines have a daily film and an underground display and the Walk-in Mine has underground tours.

FESTIVALS:
Great Goat Race – Easter; Opal Festival NSW August School Holidays or October long weekend.

FACILITIES:
Artesian baths, children's park with BMX track, Drive In Theatre, horse riding, laundromat, tennis, lawn indoor bowls, golf, pistol club and fishing.

FOSSICKING LICENCES are available from the Tourist Office, Dept. of Mineral Resources (02) 231 0922 or Automobile Association Office in capital cities. Cost: $5.00 per family or $2.50 personal.

OUTLYING ATTRACTIONS:
BOURKE, approx. 300km south-west of Lightning Ridge and 946km south-west of Brisbane and 781km north-west of Sydney. It is 110m above sea level and has an annual rainfall of 325mm. The area produces wool and beef and there is a large abattoirs in Bourke. In recent years cotton and other irrigated crops have been grown and now there is a cotton gin in operation. Bourke has a population of 3600, and 5000 live in the area. There is a large Aboriginal population. As every Australian knows, Bourke, situated on the banks of the Darling River, is considered to be the last town before the vast empty centre. Just about everyone uses the expression 'at the back of Bourke' when they want to describe the loneliness and emptiness of the centre of Australia. Tourist Information, 14 Richard St., Bourke.

WALGETT is near the junction of the Namoi and Barwon rivers, and is surrounded by pastoral properties stretching far in each direction. Irrigation has opened up large new areas to cotton, sorghum, maize and other crops. There is good fishing in the area.

LISMORE – Pop. 24,000

LOCATION:
Northern NSW inland from Ballina on the Bruxner Highway.

CLIMATE:

Average Temperatures: January max. 29.6 deg.C – min. 18.9 deg. C ; July max. 19.9 deg. C. – min. 6.0 deg. C.; average annual rainfall 1349mm; wettest months Dec-May.

CHARACTERISTICS:

The commercial, cultural and sporting capital of the North Coast region. It is the administrative centre for Federal and State Government departments, as well as the commercial and retail hub of the region. The surrounding countryside is extremely fertile and all types of agriculture are found in the region. Tropical fruits such as bananas, avocados, pineapples, bananas and macadamia nuts are widely grown. Dairying is also popular and the hills away from the coast are still timbered. There has been much controversy in recent years over logging.

HOW TO GET THERE:

AIR. Eastern Airlines fly to/from Brisbane/Coolangatta and Newcastle daily. Air NSW have daily flights to/from Casino/Sydney with a connecting bus service to Lismore.

BUS. Ansett Pioneer, Greyhound, Deluxe, VIP, and McCaffertys all stop at Lismore on their Sydney/Brisbane Pacific Highway route.

RAIL. Regular service to Sydney and Murwillumbah.

CAR. Along the Pacific Highway from Sydney and Brisbane – 780km from Sydney and 222km from Brisbane.

TOURIST INFORMATION:

Summerland Coast Tourist Authority, City Hall, Ballina St., Ph (066) 21 1519.

ACCOMMODATION:

Arcadia Motel, Cnr. James Rd & Bruxner Highway, Goonellabah (8km east) $27-38 double; Sylvan Lodge Motor Inn Motel, Cnr. Dawson & Orion St., Ph 21 2524 – RO $38 double; Civic Hotel, Molesworth St., Ph 21 2537 – RO $24-32 double; New Tattersalls Hotel, 108 Keen St., Ph 21 2284 – B&B $26-28 double.

Black Bass Caravan Park, Bruxner Highway, Ph 21 2585 – sites $6-8 double – on site vans $15-22 double; Lismore Tourist Caravan Park, Dawson St., Ph 21 6581 – sites $4.50 double – on site vans $18-20 double; Lismore Palms Caravan Court, 60 Brunswick St., Ph 21 7067 – sites $7 double – on site vans $20 double; There is a Youth Hostel at Granny's Farm, Nimbin, Ph (066) 89 1333 – $6 ppn and one at 78 Bangalow Road, Byron Bay, Ph (066) 85 6445 – $6 ppn.

EATING OUT:

The Gollan Hotel, Cnr. Woodlark & Keen St. serve meals as do most hotels. Try the Golf Club and the local RSL club.

POINTS OF INTEREST.

Lismore was the queen of the river towns last century, as the river was only navigable by trading schooners to here. The logs from 'The Big Scrub' were floated down stream to Lismore.

Cedar Log Memorial – a giant cedar log is displayed in the small park behind the city hall as a permanent memorial to the first cedar loggers of the Richmond Valley.

Claude Riley Memorial Lookout 3km north-east along the New Ballina Cutting offers a fine view of the city.

Robinson's Lookout, also called Girard's Hill lookout, is 2km south of the city centre. It offers views of the city, the river and the surrounding countryside. There is a walking track that joins onto Wilson's walk, which starts at Albert Park and is 6.5km long. It takes you through Wilson's Park, a rainforest remnant with many trees identified by plaques where you can spot local bird life.

Lismore Lake is 2.5km from Lismore on the Casino Road. There are coin-operated gas barbecues and a swimming pool, children's playground and a BMX track. It is a popular with water skiers.

The Richmond River Historical Society Museum contains a fascinating collection of Aboriginal artefacts and pioneer relics as well as geological specimens.

The Regional Art Gallery houses fine collections of paintings, pottery and ceramics.

An Aboriginal Bora Ring adjoins Tucki Tucki Cemetery. The Ring overlooks the Steve King's Plain and the mid-Richmond valley. It is one of several tribal ceremonial grounds in the district, and has been fenced and marked with a description board.

The Media Complex, Ballina Road (Bruxner Highway) 8km east of the city, houses a newspaper, radio station and television studio – phone 24 2433 to arrange inspection.

The Northern Rivers College of Advanced Education is the only higher education institution on the north coast of NSW. It offers quality degree and diploma courses in the arts, education, science, nursing and business.

The Richmond Riverboat moored at Lismore Quay is a fully licensed cruise boat – for bookings phone 21 3710.

FESTIVALS:

September is the month when its all happening: the Cavalcade of Horse; the Lismore Cup, which is the highlight of the racing calendar in Lismore; the Countrycarna and Country Music Jamboree; and the Annual Spring Garden Competition. The North Coast National Show is held in the third week in October each year.

FACILITIES:

Roller Skating at Roskell's Roller World, North Lismore; Lismore Grand Prix, South Lismore, is a racing circuit where you are the driver; You can learn to water ski at the Lismore Lake Ski School; The Lismore Bowl is open daily from 9am-midnight for ten pin bowling. Lawn bowls, tennis, swimming, squash, and also golf are all catered for as well as horse-racing.

OUTLYING ATTRACTIONS:

Inland: ALSTONVILLE is an attractive village 19km east of Lismore on the way to the coast. The Tropical Fruit Research Station has inspections on Mondays and Thursdays at 10am. They have extensive plantations of tropical fruits such as avocados, lychees and custard apples. Summerland House with No Steps is a unique rehabilitation project providing job skills and training for the handicapped. It also has avocados, macadamia nuts, tropical stone fruit, lychees and citrus fruits on sale, as well as a craft cottage and fruit packing house. Devonshire teas are available on weekdays – open from 9am-5pm daily. The Lumley Park Pioneer Transport Museum on the highway has vehicles from days gone by – everything from horse drawn carriages to early petrol powered machines.

At Bexhill, 10km from Lismore, is an open air cathedral. The pews are fashioned from logs whilst behind the stone altar and cross are magnificent views of the Corndale Valley.

At Bungawalby you can visit the Tea Tree Oil Plantation on Thursdays when you can see the complete extractive process from distillation to bottling of this unique Australian oil.

Condong's Madura Tea Estate, Clothiers Creek Road, is open for inspection 11am-5pm Tues-Sun.

CASINO, 30km from Lismore, is the 'Capital of Cattle Country'. The town was surveyed in 1855 and has many early buildings, such as the post office, hospital, court house, and school. The Richmond River runs through the town and there are many scenic drives along the river. The Folk Museum in Walker St. has old photographs, Aboriginal artefacts etc. from colonial times – open 2pm-4.30pm Fridays and Sundays.

Dunoon Village is known as the Macadamia Capital of Australia. It is only 14km from Lismore and may be inspected from May to December. Nuts and nut products can be purchased Mon-Thurs 9am-4pm & 9am-1pm Fri in season.

Fernleigh Grass Ski Park has fully qualified instructors and all equipment is available for hire. There are barbecue facilities, a swimming pool and tennis court – open weekends and school holidays – Ph 87 8268.

Goonellabah's Blue Hills Bonsai, Blue Hills Road, is open daily 9am-5pm for inspection.

NIMBIN is in the centre of an area where alternative lifestyles are very popular. In fact, one could say this was the birthplace of alternative lifestyle in Australia in the 1970's. To-day, the residents have mellowed and have won acceptance by the rest of the community. They have instigated reform on local councils etc. Nimbin has a unique style and character of its own and, unusual local crafts may be purchased at the Nimbin Flower and Gift Shop and at the Nimbin Gallery. Just 4km from Nimbin Village are the Kewarra Rose Gardens open daily 9am-5pm – over 400 rose bushes including a green rose. Nimbin Rocks, or Needles, are an unusual rock

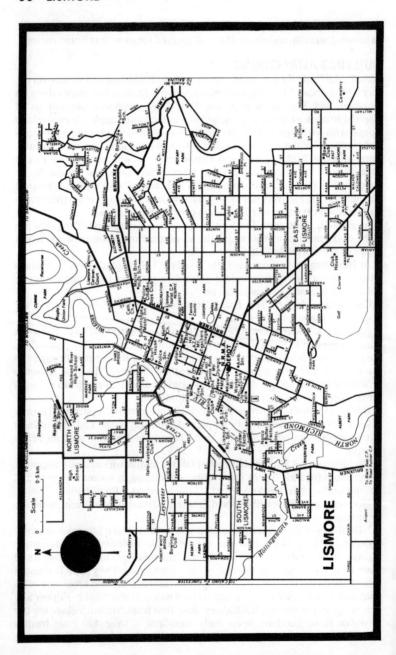

LISMORE

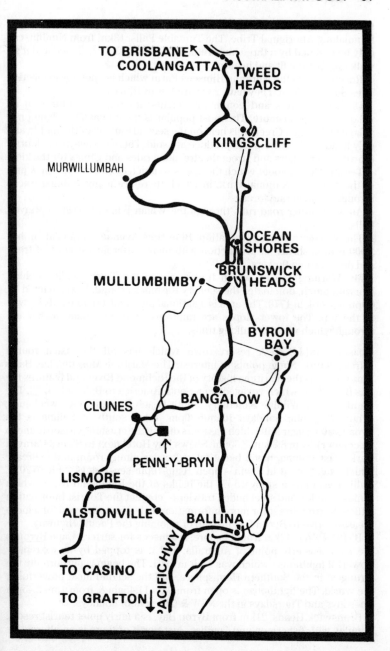

formation 3km on the Lismore side of Nimbin. They are a sacred site of the Bundjalung Aboriginal Tribe. The Tuntable Falls, 13km from Nimbin, can only be reached by a three hour return hike along the creek bed and it's a walk only for the fit and healthy.

Rosebank has the Noranne Hibiscus Farm which is open for inspection Tues-Sun 9am-5pm. They have 230 varieties of Hibiscus.

Dances, markets and community nights are regular features in all villages around Lismore. The most popular is the one at The Channon, a village on Terania Creek. It is held on the second Sunday of the month and only hand-made articles and produce are sold. There is always a colourful crowd with buskers and street theatre, pony rides and games for the kids.

Terania Creek, about which there was so much controversy, is now part of the Nightcap National Park, in which there are many walking tracks through tropical rain forest.

An all weather road runs through the Whian Whian Forest to Minyon Falls.

The Wyymara Protea Plantation, Blue Hills Avenue, Goonellabah, has 2,000 protea shrubs in production with many different varieties of fresh and dried protea flowers.

Mt. Warning 1157m, which towers above the Tweed Valley behind Murwillumbah, dominates the scenery for miles around. It was named by Captain Cook in 1770. The area is a national park and a road winds its way to the top. The lower slopes are rainforest with heathland higher up, through which wander walking trails.

Coastal: BALLINA: A resort town which has all the usual tourist infrastructure. Some points of interest: The Maritime Museum, Las Balsa Plaza records the maritime history of the Richmond River and features the Las Balsa Raft which voyaged from South America to Ballina in 1973. The South Ballina Wildlife Sanctuary, South Beach Road, is open weekends, school & public holidays 10am-5.30pm. 19km south of Ballina is the Broadwater Sugar Mill which has tours during the crushing season (June to December) from 8.30am-3.30pm. Shaws Bay Hotel next to Shaws Caravan Park, East Ballina, has a beautiful red cedar dining room and staircase which was carved in Spain – open 10am-10pm seven days – Ph 86 2034. Ballina also has a shipyard on the banks of the Richmond River, which builds wooden and steel hulled trawlers – contact the Tourist Information Office, Norton Street for more information. Take the coast road for a more pleasant drive to Byron Bay instead of rejoining the Pacific Highway.

BYRON BAY, 42km from Lismore, is a mecca for surfers. Cape Byron is the most easterly point of Australia, and it is topped by an extremely powerful lighthouse which was built in 1901. The beam is purportedly the strongest in the Southern Hemisphere, and the second most powerful in the world. The lighthouse is open from 9am-11.45am & from 1pm-2.45pm Tuesdays and Thursdays in the NSW & Qld. school holidays.

Brunswick Heads, 21km from Byron Bay, is a fairly quiet tourist resort, popular with fishermen and families. Just north of there is an alternative route along the coast to Kingscliff, another popular surfing beach.

MITTAGONG – Area Pop. 28,500

LOCATION:
Southern Highlands of N.S.W. about 90mins drive from Sydney.

DISTANCE FROM:
Sydney 109km; Wollongong 72km; Canberra 175km; Nowra 67km.

CLIMATE:
Average Temperatures: January: max. 25.0deg.C – min. 18.4 deg. C.; July: max. 10.2 deg. C – min 0.2 deg. C.; 640m above sea level. Rainfall varies from 760mm in the north and west to 1140mm at Moss Vale and 1950mm at Robertson.

CHARACTERISTICS:
Called the 'Garden Playground' of Sydney, Wollongong and Canberra. It enjoys distinct seasons: Autumn sees the leaves a blaze of red and yellow; Winter is crisp and invigorating; in Spring native wildflowers and tulips bloom in a mass of colour and in Summer perfect days are followed by pleasant, mild nights.

HOW TO GET THERE:
ROAD: Along the F5 or the old Hume Highway from Sydney; Along the Illawarra Highway via Macquarie Pass from Wollongong; Via Kangaroo Valley and Fitzroy Falls from Nowra or Berry. Daily bus service between Moss Vale and Nowra and Canberra. Interstate coaches depart on a regular basis.
TRAIN: Several services daily from Sydney, and Canberra incl. the XPT. Also a Motor Rail service to Wollongong on Sundays.

TOURIST INFORMATION OFFICE:
Southern Highlands Tourist and Travel Association, Winifred West Park, Hume Highway, P.O. Box 305), Mittagong, 2575, phone (048) 71 28 88. Open 9-5 seven days excl. Christmas Day – open until 8pm Fridays. It is surrounded by tulips in early spring.

ACCOMMODATION:
6 Motels, 2 hotels and a caravan park with on-site vans.
   Some names and addresses: Braemar Lodge, Cnr. Hume Hwy & Braemar Ave., Ph 71 2483 – RO $39-45; Melrose Motel, Hume Hwy, Ph 71 1511 – RO $36-42; Mittagong Motel, Hume Hwy, Ph 71 1277 – RO $38-40; The Poplars Motel, Hume Hwy, Ph 89 4239 – RO $43-50; Mineral Springs Motel, 150

Hume Hwy, Ph 71 1506 – RO $33 double; Mittagong Caravan Park, Hume Hwy, Ph 71 1574 – sites $6 double – onsite vans $13-18.

POINTS OF INTEREST:

Mittagong has many beautiful sandstone buildings and is well known . for its dedication to the arts and crafts .Victoria House, is well worth a visit, as are the Sturt workshops. The area boasts several bushwalks including the one to the historic Box Vale Mine. Lake Alexandra, with its prolific birdlife, is one of the many delightful picnic spots in the town and is the venue for the carnival activities of the annual Dahlia Festival.

FESTIVALS:

Dahlia Festival is held each February. The Bowral Tulip Festival is held each October. The Buxton Village Fair takes place in September. The Bundanoon Festival is held each April and Kangaroo Valley Country Music Festival is held on the Sunday of the October long weekend.

FACILITIES:

R.S.L Club, several restaurants, coffee shops and take-aways, supermarket, 24 hour petrol station, speciality and craft shops and nurseries. 18 hole golf course, bowling club, roller skating rink, swimming pool complex, tennis courts, car rental agencies and taxis.

OUTLYING ATTRACTIONS:

The relatively unspoiled WOMBEYAN CAVES are 65km from Mittagong along a very scenic road, which is rather narrow and unsealed. It takes approx. 90mins for the 65km but its worth it. 5 caves are open to the public and there is a camping area and on-site vans. There is another road to the caves from Goulburn which although largely unsealed, has a much better surface.

THIRLMERE'S Railway Museum is worth a visit. West Parade, Thirlmere, (046) 81 8001 Adults $3.00 Children $1.00. Steam trains run from Picton to Thirlmere on some Sundays and holidays from autumn to spring.

BOWRAL'S Corbett Gardens are the show piece of the Tulip Festival held each October but the whole town looks a picture at this time. The people seem to take a pride in their gardens. Bowral is also worth a visit in autumn when the European deciduous trees are ablaze with colour.

Only 14km from Mittagong is BERRIMA one of the best remaining examples of an 1830's country town. It is a delightful place to wander around as it has many craft and antique shops, as well as trendy restaurants.

BUNDANOON, 32km south of Mittagong, becomes Brigadoon for a day each autumn and celebrates with a street parade, pipe bands and traditional highland games. It has an 'olde worlde' charm and was a popular holiday destination in the twenties and thirties. It overlooks the Morton National Park with its many bush walks. If you stopover in Bundanoon then

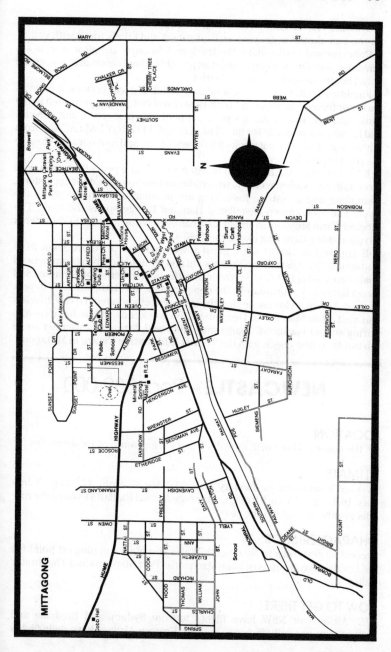

MITTAGONG

you should vist the Glow Worm Glen a 25min walk from the end of William Street. You should begin your walk at sunset and take a torch with you.

Reflectorised marks show the track and, because the glow worms are sensitive, you should keep as quiet as possible. Bundanoon also boasts the only Theatre Restaurant in the district.

Facilities include 3 motels, a holiday hotel, 2 guest houses, a caravan park, conference facilities, a Youth Hostel and camping is permitted in the National Park. It also has a swimming pool, bowling green, and bicycles and horses are available for hire. The 81m high FITZROY FALLS 28km from Mittagong, offer walking tracks for the energetic, and lookout very close to the road for the less energetic.

KANGAROO VALLEY is also worth a visit. It is a peaceful region with mountain and valley scenery, waterfalls and meadows. Canoeing, fishing, swimming and gemstone fossicking are popular along the banks of the river. The well-known castellated Hamden Bridge spans the river. The Pioneer Farm Museum in an old farm has been reconstructed to show what a typical dairy farm was like in the 1880's.

If you would like to see a ghost town, then vist JOADJA 30km from Mittagong. The Australian Kerosene Oil and Mineral Company commenced shale processing in 1878 to provide paraffin oil and kerosene for home and street lighting. Unfortunately, the company failed with the lifting of import duty on American kerosene, and the town was abandoned. To-day, tourists can visit from March 1 to December 1 on weekends, public holidays and during school vacations. Joadja may be closed during wet weather so its advisable to first check with the Tourist Information Centre in Mittagong.

NEWCASTLE – Pop. 389,000

LOCATION:
On the coast 171km north of Sydney and 827km south of Brisbane.

CLIMATE:
Average Temperatures: January max. 27.2 deg. C – min. 17.9 deg. C; July max. 16.9 deg. C – min. 6.0 deg. C.; Average Annual Railfall 1134mm; the rain falls evenly throughout the year.

CHARACTERISTICS:
Second largest town in New South Wales and ideal stopping off point for the holiday playgrounds of Lake Macquarie, Port Stephens and The Hunter Valley.

HOW TO GET THERE:
AIR. Airlines of NSW have flights to/from Sydney and Brisbane and Aeropelican has daily flights to Sydney. Eastern Airlines have daily flights

to/from   Sydney,   Maitland,   Tamworth/Armidale/Brisbane/Lismore/
Coolangatta and Taree, Port Macquarie and Coffs Harbour and Canberra.
BUS. Ansett Pioneer, Greyhound, VIP, Deluxe and Kirkland Onmnibus,
McCaffertys and Skenners Coachline all stop in Newcastle.
RAIL. On the Sydney/Murrwillumbah line with regular services.
CAR. From Sydney via the Pacific Highway through Hornsby and then via
the F3 Expressway; From Brisbane via the Pacific Highway through Tweed
Heads and along the coast or via the New England Highway through Glen
Innes and Armidale.

TOURIST INFORMATION:

Newcastle City Council, King St., Ph (049) 26 2333 ext. 254 – open Mon-Fri
9am-5pm; Hunter Region Tourist Information Centre, Pacific Highway, Ph
64 8005 – open daily 10am-3pm; Tourist Organisation of Port Stephens,
Victoria Pde., Ph 81 1579 – Mon-Fri 9am-5pm – Sat, Sun & public hols 10am-
3pm. For more information on all tourism facilities in the Hunter Region
call the Hot Line on 008 025858 toll free throughout Australia.

ACCOMMODATION:

The more moderately priced motels and hotels are found in the suburbs –
check with the Tourist Information Office for details. Newcastle Parkroyal
Motel, Cnr. King & Steel Sts., Ph 26 3777 – RO $60-80; Newcastle
Travelodge, Shortland Esp, Ph 25576 – $73 double; Novocastrian Motor Inn,
21 Parnell Pl., Ph 26 3688 – RO $65-75 double; City Motel, Cnr. Burwood &
Darby St., Ph 2 5855 – RO $51 double;
    The Casbah Hotel, 471 Hunter St., Ph 2 2904 – RO $35-45 (Fri, Sat & Sun
nights less 25%); The Premier Hotel, 1 Brunker Rd., Broadmeadow (5km
SW) – B&B $28 double; Halls Haven Hotel, Cnr. Newcastle & Bluegum Rds.,
Jesmond (10km west) Ph 55 9206 – RO $18 double;
    Raymond Terrace: Bellhaven Caravan Park, Pacific Highway, Ph 7 2423
– sites only $5 double – onsite vans $15 double.; Redhead Caravan Park, 75
Karlaroo Rd, Nine Mile Beach, Ph 49 8691 – sites $9-10 double – onsite vans
$22-27 double.

EATING OUT:

Western Suburbs Leagues Club, New Lambton, Ph 52 5222 has excellent
dining and bistro facilities – visitors welcome. Tubemakers Recreation
Club, Industrial Drive, Mayfield has an a la carte restaurant, bistro and
snack bar and also welcomes visitors. The Casbah Hotel, 471 Hunter St.,
has steak, schnitzel or chicken dinners including a bottle of Lindeman's
wine for $12 double. McDonalds are at Belmont, Broadmeadow and
Charlestown. Newcastle tends to close up early, and it is better to eat early
and buy your supplies at the bottle shop during normal business hours.

POINTS OF INTEREST.

The Civic Centre features a civic park, Captain Cook Memorial Fountain,
City Hall, City Administration Centre, Newcastle Region Art Gallery, War

Memorial Cultural Centre, Baptist Tabernacle and St. Andrews Presbyterian Church.

The Christ Church Cathedral is worthy of inspection.

Fort Scratchley, off Nobbys Road at the eastern end of the city dates back to the 1840's. This installation came under attack in June 1942 – tours of the underground gun emplacements, casements and magazines on weekends 12noon-4pm.

At Williamtown's RAAF Base you can see the new Hornet FA18 flighters and visit the excellent Aircraft Museum on the base. Conducted tours of the base are available by prior arrangements on Wednesday mornings at 10am sharp – please phone Sgt. Thompson on (049) 28 6480 to arrange a visit.

King Edward Park and Sunken Garden overlooking the ocean is a popular picnic spot. An obelisk erected in 1850 overlooks the park and affords a 360 degree view of the city.

Local History Museum in Brown St., Ph 61 4820 – open Sundays 1pm-5pm.

Newcastle Region Maritime Museum at Fort Scratchley – exhibits include maritime technology, a model collection and photographs – open Tues-Sun 12noon to 4pm.

Newcastle University – a self-guided tour brochure will assist the visitor to explore the University.

Nobby's Lighthouse is just a few minutes from the centre of Newcastle at the northern end of Nobby's Beach – not open to the public.

The Regional Art Gallery has a Dobell collection and other art treasures, plus Australia's largest collection of contemporary Japanese ceramics – open weekdays 10am-5pm, Sat 1.30pm-5pm, Sundays and public holidays 2pm-5pm; the Von Bertouch Galleries, 61 Laman St., Cooks Hill Gallery, 67 Bull St.

The Australian Commercial Glassblowers, Clyde St., Hamilton, Ph 69 6862, welcome visitors at any time to watch glassblowing.

At Merewether Heights, Hickson St., hang-gliders often add colour to the spectacular seascapes to the north and south.

The Science and Technology Centre at 854 Hunter offers visitors the opportunity of a hands-on educational experience.

The great steel-producing plants adjoin the city, and visitors can wander along the docks in the shadow of ships from all over the world.

FESTIVALS:
Mattara Festival is held each September.

FACILITIES:
Aquajet, Parry Street, Newcastle West, Ph 26 3469; Supa Putt Golf, cnr. Griffiths and Turton Rd., Broadmeadow, Ph 52 1344; Roller Skating at the Showground, Broadmeadow, Ph 61 3455; Ten Pin Bowling, Olympic Bowl, Mayfield, Ph 68 3795; Sunnyside Squash Tennis Centre, 11 Broadmeadow Road, Broadmeadow, Ph 61 3951.

OUTLYING ATTRACTIONS:

BARRINGTON TOPS National Park, just inland from Newcastle, is one of the most spectacular alpine regions in Australia. The vegetation in this sanctuary varies from sub-tropical rainforest in the valleys, to alpine on the plateau.

LAKE MACQUARIE, which stretches from the southern suburbs of Newcastle south to near Doyalson, is Australia's largest salwater lake and is a mecca for thousands of sailors and fishermen. At weekends and in school holidays the water is ablaze with sails. Foreshore parklands can be found at Belmont, Croudace Bay, Warners Bay, Toronto, Coal Point, Rathmines, Wangi Wangi and Morisset, to name but a few, and excellent swimming for all ages is found at many of these places.

PORT STEVENS is described as a Blue Water Wonderland only three hours drive from Sydney. It is certainly a popular tourist area. Scuba diving, sailing, surfboarding, fishing, and swimming are all possible here. Nelson Bay is the commercial centre of the area and offers holidaymakers all types of shopping as well as superb restaurants specialising in local seafood. It is also the home port of a fishing fleet which brings in large catches of prawns, fish and local lobsters. There is also a boat harbour and marina. Shoal Bay, just inside the port entrance, has all the usual tourist infrastructure such as motels, holiday flats and entertainment. For something different drop into Bobs Rose Farm, Marsh Road as it is the largest commercial rose and flower farm in the Southern Hemisphere and you can ride the tractor train through the rose bushes.

On the other side of Port Stephens are the twin towns of Tea Gardens and Hawks Nest. They also offer good fishing and prawning and aquatic sports. The beach at Hawks Nest is long and not too crowded, and the surf is usually good. There is a good range of accommodation. It is possible to journey along the Myall River from here to the Myall Lakes, which abound in birdlife, beautiful scenery and peace and quiet. The area around Mungo Brush and Legges Camp, either side of the punt at Bombah Point, is a terrific place to camp and you usually can moor your boat right at your camp site. The lakes are ideal for canoeing and houseboats can be hired. From there the road to Seal Rocks takes you along a narrow strip of land between the ocean and the lakes. It is a great spot even if it does get crowded at holiday times. The major tourist centre of the Great Lakes are the twin towns of Forster-Tuncurry which are renowned for their beaches, fishing, boating, seafoods and temperate climate all year round.

Lastly, we come to the Hunter Valley. The name brings two things to mind, coal and wine. Mining towns are dotted throughout the valley and vineyards are found at Pokolbin near Cessnock.

CESSNOCK is 52km from Newcastle and 185km from Sydney and is the gateway to the wineries. There are approx. 30 wineries in the area and most of them welcome visitors, and have cellar sales. Quite a number have picnic facilities or restaurants attached, and it is a very pleasant spot to spend a day or a weekend, although it can get quite crowded at weekends. The Cessnock Tourist Office or the NSW Government Tourist Bureau will

NEWCASTLE CITY

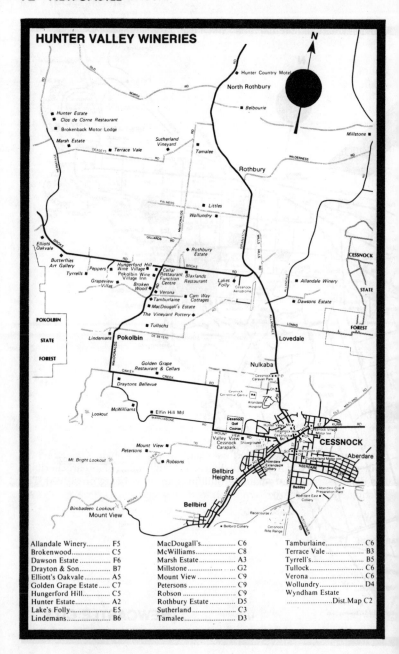

HUNTER VALLEY WINERIES

provide you with opening times and a list of the wineries.

Near KURRI KURRI is the Richmond Main Colliery Museum but opening days are limited so check with Cessnock Tourist Office (Ph (049) 90477) – hours 10am-6pm daily in summer and 10am-4pm in winter. The historic Wollombi Village 31km south-west of Cessnock has a wealth of historic buildings, including St. John's Anglican Church, the Court House and the double-storey sandstone Post Office. There is a Grass Ski Park on the slopes of the Watagan Range at Mulbring, 17km east of Cessnock, 25km west of Toronto. There are ski-tows and slopes of varying degrees of difficulty – open weekends April to October.

PORT MACQUARIE – Pop. 24,400

LOCATION:
On the east coast of NSW, 416km north of Sydney, at the mouth of the Hastings River.

CLIMATE:
Average Temperature: January max. 25 deg. C – min. 18 deg. C.; July max. 18 deg. C. – min. 7 deg. C; Average annual rainfall 1563mm; Hours of Sunshine: Summer 7; Autumn 7; Winter 5; and Spring 7. The CSIRO suggests that Port Macquarie has the most ideal climate in Australia. A warm off-shore current combines with the surrounding barrier of hills to form a pocket, which produces this climate.

CHARACTERISTICS:
A major coastal tourist resort and retirement area. It is the most historically significant town along the coast between Newcastle and the Queensland border. It was founded in 1821 as a settlement for convicts banished for crimes committed in New South Wales. Although much of its early heritage has disappeared, the remaining buildings are now being preserved. The Hastings valley provides some lush mountain scenery.

HOW TO GET THERE:
AIR. Eastern Airlines and Oxley Airlines have daily flights to/from Brisbane/Coolangatta and Newcastle; East-West have daily flights to/from Sydney.
BUS. Ansett Pioneer, Greyhound, McCaffertys, VIP and Skenners all stop at Port Macquarie.
RAIL. Train to Wauchope and then bus to Port Macquarie.
CAR. From Sydney take the Pacific Highway; From Brisbane either the Pacific Highway along the coast or the Cummingham Highway to Warwick, the New England Highway and then the Oxley Highway back to the coast.

TOURIST INFORMATION:

Port Macquarie Tourist Information, P.O. Box 84, Horton St., Port Macquarie, Ph (065) 83 1293.

ACCOMMODATION:

Port Macquarie has over 40 motels, and over 100 holday flats, plus guest houses, hotels and approx. 15 caravan parks. Then there are the nearyby resorts of Lake Cathie, North Haven and Laurieton. So accommodation should not be a problem, except perhaps at Christmas time. The Tourist Information Centre would be able to help you further.

A few names and addresses: Beachfront Regency Motor Inn, 40 William St., Ph 83 2244 – RO $42 double; East Port Motor Inn, Cnr. Lord & Burrawan Sts., Ph 83 3277 – RO $33-36 double; Aquatic Motel, 253 Hastings River Drive, Ph 83 7388 – RO $32-45 double; Port Aloha Motel, 3 School St., Ph 83 2455 – RO $24-44 double; Lighthouse Beach Caravan Park, 50 Hart St., Ph 82 0581 – sites $7-10 double – onsite vans $18-32 double; Melaleuca Caravan Park, 128 Hastings River Drive, Ph 83 4498 – sites only $8-10 double – onsite vans $19 double; Sundowner Aflat, Hastins River Drive, Hibbard, Ph 83 2799 – sites $5.50 double – onsite vans from $32 double

EATING OUT:

You can choose from French, Chinese, Bavarian, Spanish, traditional Aussie, vegetarian, seafood, pancakes or crepes – the choice is endless. The local seafood is a treat that shouldn't be missed.

POINTS OF INTEREST:

The Church of St. Thomas the Apostle was built by convicts, in 1828. It has the original box pews made from local red cedar, and an 1857 barrel organ which plays 33 hymns. It is the only organ of its type in Australia. In the church grounds is the old hospital dispensary, now a simple chapel. The hospital was across the road, where St. Agnes Catholic Church now stands.

The court house dates from 1869 and faces the museum, which was built in the 1830's as a store. The museum has relics from convict and pioneer days – open 9.30am-12.30pm and 2-5pm Mon-Sat & 2-5pm Sundays. The RSL Club stands on the site of the stockade built by the convicts. The cemetery beside Kooloonbung Creek in the heart of Port Macquarie, is where many convicts and officers are buried.

The Town Beach has sheltered swimming for childern at its southern end. Flynns Beach and Lighthouse Beach are noted for good surf. There is a vehicular and passenger ferry which plies from Port Macquarie across the river to less crowded beaches and picnic grounds. The clear waters make it an ideal spot for snorkling.

There is an Observatory near Town Beach which is open on Wednesday and Saturday nights.

Some of the local attractions include: King Neptune's Park, Kingfisher Park, Peppermint Park, Thrumster Village Pottery, Sea Acres Sanctuary, and Fantasy Glades.

There are regular cruises on the Hastings River in the holiday season.

At Old World Timber Art, Hastings River Drive, Hibbard, 3km west, rough forest timber is transformed into useful articles. Wood turning demonstrations are given.

At The Weavers Croft visitors can watch weaving and spinning, and learn about different types of wool – open 9am-5pm Tues-Sun at Calwalla Crescent and Amaroo Parade, off Shelly Beach Road.

Christmas Bells Plain, south of Port Macquarie, is known for the proliferation of the flower from which it takes its name. The bright blossoms appear in January and February.

FESTIVALS:
The Carnival of the Pines is held at Easter, Pioneer Week is held in June/July.

FACILITIES:
Boating, swimming, surfing, fishing, lawn bowls, golf, tennis etc.

OUTLYING ATTRACTIONS:
WAUCHOPE, 18km west, is on the river flats. Timbertown is the main tourist attraction there. It features old steam trains and a sawmill. 1km from town, at Lilybank, canoes can be hired and much of the Hastings River is suitable for canoeing. There are many tranquil stretches suitable for the novice, but experienced canoesists will also find white-water rapids not far away.

KEMPSEY, the commercial centre for the Macleay Valley, is a popular boating, fishing, and watersports resort with a wide range of accommodation. It has several old buildings which are worth seeing. The Victorian court house has an elegant portico, and the post office clock tower is a landmark. All Saints Anglican Church has a beautiful carved wood panel.

SOUTH WEST ROCKS is a pleasing little resort on Trial Bay, near the mouth of the Macleay River. It is also a very popular fishing and boating area.

LAURIETON is one of the three fishing villages which make up the Camden Haven resorts. There are numerous lagoons and waterways within easy reach, and it is a fisherman's delight.

TAREE, 74km south of Port Macquarie, is a very busy market town in rich dairy and timber country. The poet, Henry Kendall, was based here while an inspector of State forests, and a plaque honours his stay.

SYDNEY – Pop. 3,400,000

LOCATION:
The capital of NSW on the shores of beautiful Sydney Harbour.

CLIMATE:

Average Temperatures: January max. 25.7 deg. C – min. 18.8 deg. C; July max. 17.1 deg. C, min. 8.3 deg. C; Average annual rainfall 1216mm; The number of days on which it rains in a month remains fairly constant throughout the year at 11 or 12 but the heaviest rain falls from February to July.

CHARACTERISTICS:

Sydney is a city of of waterways. Australia's oldest and largest city stretches along the coast north to the mouth of the Hawkesbury River, south to Port Hacking and west along the harbour foreshores and the Parramatta and Georges Rivers to the foothills of the Blue Mountains. It takes two hours to drive from the northern to the southern suburbs, a distance of around 70km, as Sydney is lacking a major expressway system and the arterial roads have become terribly congested. The distance along the actual coastline, allowing for all the bays, is 350km. There are so many bays and beaches that even Sydneysiders who have lived here all their lives don't know every beach and bay by name and probably haven't visited more than half of them. The ocean beaches have beautiful white sand and rolling surf. The harbour is always alive with small craft but on fine weekends there are hundreds of craft afloat with brightly coloured sails contrasting with the blue of the water and the sky. The ferries and hydrofoils, which form part of the urban transport system, ply from one side of the harbour to the other no matter the weather. Large white ocean liners sail majestically into the harbour after Pacific cruises, and container ships from all over the world are regular visitors. The Sydney Harbour Bridge and the Opera House 'sailing' in front of it, are Sydney's best known landmarks.

HOW TO GET THERE:

AIR. Sydney is the major gateway to Australia from overseas. All the overseas airlines flying to Australia come to Sydney. You can fly to just about any Australian town of major size from Sydney. There are two major Australian airlines (Australian Airlines and Ansett) and a number of smaller ones e.g. East-West, Air NSW, Eastern Airlines, Hazelton, Sky West, etc. servicing the country towns. A flight from Sydney to Melbourne or Brisbane takes 1hr. 15mins, to Adelaide 1hr. 55mins., to Canberra 40mins, to Hobart 2hrs. 10mins, to Perth 4hrs. 35mins direct. The yellow Airport Express, No. 300, runs between the city and the International and Domestic Air Terminals approx. every 30 mins and costs $2.20.

BUS. Ansett Pioneer, Greyhound, and Deluxe cover most of Australia and VIP, McCaffertys, Across Australia Coachlines, Gold Coast Intertour, Kirklands, Lextours, Olympic East West, and Skenners have smaller networks.

RAIL. The State Rail Authority has been upgrading its tracks and services and now the XPT Supertrains network extends to Albury, Canberra, Dubbo, Armidale, Coffs Harbour and Grafton. The XPT's are fast, smooth and comfortable with air-conditioning, aircraft style seats and big panoramic windows. There are overnight and daylight interstate services to Melbourne, an overnight service to Brisbane, a motorail service to Murwillumbah with bus connection to the Gold Coast and Brisbane. The Alice runs between Sydney and Alice Springs and the Indian Pacific crosses the continent to Perth in 65 hours.

CAR. Sydney/Melbourne is 877km via the Hume Highway, 1048km via the Princes Highway and 959km via the Olympic Way and Hume Highway. Sydney/Brisbane is 1011km via the Pacific Highway and 1033km via the New England and Cunningham Highways. Sydney/Adelaide is 1418km via the Mid Western Highway, 1427km via the Sturt Highway and 1668km via the Barrier Highway. Sydney/Darwin is 4167km via Dubbo, Bourke, Charleville and Mt. Isa. Sydney/Perth is 4000km.

TOURIST INFORMATION:

Your first stop should be the Travel Centre of New South Wales, Cnr. Pitt & Spring Sts., Sydney, phone 231 4444. They have numerous brochures, maps etc. and a large helpful staff. Pick up the latest copy of 'This Week in Sydney', 'Sydney's Top Ten Magazine','Sydney Tourist Guide' and 'Sydney Where Magazine' and you will have plenty of reading, and good tips on what to see and where to go. You could also phone the free Sydney Information Service on 669 5111 which operates 7 days a week from 8 a.m. to 6 p.m. There is also an Information Booth, near the entrance to Martin Place Railway Station which has a free computerised information service, and on the other side of the booth is Halftix – which sells any remaining tickets to Sydney's top shows on the day of the performance from 12 noon until 6pm. If you are a member of an Automobile Association (Australian or overseas) then a trip to the N.R.M.A. office, at 151 Clarence Street would also be a good idea, as they have an excellect Sydney City Book which contains a large amount of relevant information as well as a map of the city. They can also help with maps etc. for other parts of Australia. For all public transport information in and around Sydney phone Metro Trips on 29 2622 from 7a.m. to 10 p.m. 7 days a week.

ACCOMMODATION:

There are all standards of accommodation available in Sydney from hotels like the Hilton and Inter-Continental to budget private hotels offering only the basics. Generally speaking, the cheaper accommodation tends to be around Kings Cross or Central Railway Station but there are exceptions. Bondi Beach is also another area with cheap accommodation. As is usual, accommodation in the suburbs is cheaper than right in the heart of the city. Hostels of course, are the cheapest and there are three official Youth Hostels but as well as those there are several in the Kings Cross area. Some names and addresses:

International Standard: Hilton International Sydney, 259 Pitt St., Ph 266 0610 – RO $145-190 double – suites $250-380; Holiday Inn Menzies Sydney, 14 Carrington St., Ph 2 0232 – RO $135-160 double – suites $250-

650; Hotel Inter-Continental Sydney, 117 Macquarie St., Ph 230 0200 – $160-225 double – suites $325-1500; The Sydney Boulevard, 90 William St., Ph 357 2277 – RO $148 double – suites $250; Regent, 199 George St., Ph 238 0000 – RO $200-280 double – suites $400-1800; Wynyard Travelodge, 7 York St., Ph 2 0254 – RO $123 double.

Good Tourist: The Savoy Apartments, Cnr. King & Kent Sts., Ph 2677 9211 – RO $88 double; The Zebra Hyde Park Motel, 271 Elizabeth St., Ph 264 6001 – RO $75 double – suites $90; Clairmont Inn, 5 Ward Ave., Kings Cross, Ph 358 2044 – RO $65 double; Koala Motor Inn Park Regis, Cnr. Castlereach & Park Sts., Ph 267 6511 – RO $65-85.

Budget: Alice's Tudor Private Hotel, 64 Darlinghurst Rd., PH 358 5977 (opp. Kings Cross Station) $35-45 double; Canberra Oriental Private Hotel, 223 Victoria St., Ph 358 3155 – RO $39-63 double; Criterian Hotel, Cnr. Pitt & Park Sts., Ph 264 3093 – B&LtB $35 double; YWCA, 5 Wentworth Ave., Ph 264 2451 – RO $40-50 double (women or couples) – also has a cheap cafetaria open to the public; CB Private Hotel, 417 Pitt St., Sydney – RO $26 double with $5 refundable key deposit; The Macquarie Hotel, Cnr. Hughes & Tusculum Sts., Potts Point (3mins walk from Kings Cross Station) Ph 358 4122 $30 double; Thelellan Beach Inn, 2 Campbell Pde., Ph 30 5333 – RO $25-27 double.

Hostels: The YHA Hostel, 28 Ross St., Forest Lodge, PH 692 0747 – $8ppn; The YHA at 407 Marrickville Rd., Dulwich Hill, Ph 569 0272 – $8ppn; The YHA Hostel, 262 Glebe Point Road, Glebe, Ph 692 8418 – $12ppn; The King's Cross Backpackers Hostel, 162 Victoria St., Kings Cross, Ph 367 3232 – $8ppn in dorm. or $17-18 double room; Then there's the Travellers Rest Hostel, 156 Victoria St., Ph 358 4606 and the Atoa House at 160 Victoria St., Ph 358 3693 which both charge around the same.

Students might also like to try one of the University Colleges but these only take in travellers in the vacations, and preferably students. Some names and addresses: Warrane College, Ph 662 6199, University of NSW, Kensington (men only) full board $22 day for students staying at least one week; at New College, Ph 662 6066, Kensington RO $18 per day for students and $25 for non-students. The colleges around the University of Sydney, Camperdown tend to be booked out with conferences but you might like to try Wesley College, Ph 51 2024, St. John's Cllege, Ph 51 1240, Sancta Sophia College, Ph 51 2467, International House, Ph 660 5364. They all charge around $18 RO.

Camping Grounds: As is usual in a big city, the camping grounds tend to be in the far outer suburbs. This can be an advantage for people who don't like driving in heavy traffic in unfamiliar cities, provided public transport is nearby. A few conveniently located parks: SOUTH: Heathcote Tourist Park, Princes Hwy, Ph 520 8816 (only a few hundred metres from the railway station – electric train) – sites $9 double – onsite vans $20-30 – NORTH: La Mancha Cara Park, Pacific Hwy, Berowra, Ph 456 1766 – sites $11 – onsite vans $30-$32 – electric train; Sundowner, Cnr. Lane Cove & Fontenoy Rds., North Ryde, Ph 88 1933 – sites $11 – onsite vans $32-$40 – bus; WEST: Nepean River Caravan Park, Mackellar St., Emu Plains, Ph 35 4425 (only a few hundred metres from the railway station – electric train) – sites $11 – onsite vans $22-26.

Serviced Apartments: Contact the Sydney Visitors Apartments, 57-59 York Street, Sydney, Phone (02) 290 1166 – Cost: 1 bedroom $65-70; 2 bedroom $80; studios $50-60.

EATING OUT:

Sydney has a wide variety of excellent restaurants from international standard to BYO (bring your own (wine)). If you are staying some time in Sydney you might like to buy a copy of 'Cheap Eats in Sydney' from one of the bookshops. All the International standard hotels have at least one restaurant and one bistro e.g. Airport Hilton International, 20 Levey St., Arncliffe, Ph 597 0122. Cyranos Restaurant, Cambridge Inn, 218 Riley St., Surry Hills, Ph 212 5500, Intercontinental Hotel 117 Macquarie St., City, Ph 230 0200, Garden Court Restaurant, Phillip St., Ph 230 0700 or the Sydney Hilton, 259 Pitt St., City, Ph 266 0610. Also in this price range are Boronia House, 624 Military Rd., Mosman, Ph 969 2099, Guiseppes, 123 Blues Point Rd., McMahons Point, Ph 922 5601, Balthazar, 71 York St., Ph 29 7292, Primos, 76 Elizabeth Bay Rd., Elizabeth Bay, Ph 358 4516. For more economically priced food: Centre Point Tavern, entrance in Pitt Street – good variety; For good curry and fast service try the Malaya, 787 George St. (opp. Central Railway) phone 211 0946; The Warung Indonesia, 117 York St., phone 290 2232 also has fast service and reasonable prices; The London Tavern, 119 Pitt St also have a good variety of dishes; Tahe Natraj BYO Indian Restaurant, 423 Pitt St.(between Goulburn & Campbell Sts.), Ph 212 6213 serves meat curries for around $8 and vegetarian curries for $5.50. For good Chinese meals head for Dixon Street, the main street of Chinatown. There are numerous restaurants catering for all price ranges; Woolworths, cnr. George & Park Sts and Coles, Cnr. Pitt, George & King Sts. both have upstairs cafeterias serving breakfast and lunches at very reasonable prices. There are plenty of places doing take-away food but you will get a good variety downstairs in the MLC Centre, Martin Place and downstairs at Centre Point, Cnr. Pitt, Market & Castlereagh Sts. Of course there are several McDonalds, all found in George Street, the first near King Street and the others further up towards Central Railway. The Argyle Tavern, 18 Argyle St., The Rocks, Ph 27 7782, is a theatre restuarant featuring the Jolly Swagman show and authentic Australian dishes. If you feel like Seafood, then head for either Doyles On The Beach at Watson's Bay just inside the Heads, Phone 337 2007, or the Manly Pier Seafood Restaurant, West Esplanade (on the pier next to Marineland only 200m from the wharf), phone 949 2677. There are so many restaurants in Sydney that it is impossible to mention them all here. If you want to go further afield then there are terrific restaurants in Paddington, Balmain, Glebe, Redfern, Surrey Hills, Mosman and along the coastal suburbs. Right on the outskirts of town is the Berowra Waters Inn, Berowra Waters, Ph 456 1027. It is right on the water's edge, has exquisite food but you will need to book well ahead – expensive.

LICENSED CLUBS are an institution in New South Wales. Nearly every large country town has one or two and Sydney has scores. They all have poker machines which subsidise their other activities e.g. restaurants, shows and bars. The locals need to be members or to go with a member to be admitted, but interstate or overseas visitors are welcome. You will need your passport or drivers licence to get in. They are so much part of the way of life here, that a visit to one is almost mandatory.

LOCAL TRANSPORT:

All comes under the umbrella of the Urban Transit Authority. Sydney has a fast and efficient electric train service coupled with a bus and ferry service. There are two free buses operating in the city area: the No. 777 shoppers' shuttle service operating Mon-Fri every 10-15 mins between 9.13 am and 3.43 pm from the Domain Parking Station. It travels past the Mitchell Library along Macquarie St past Parliament House, then along Market St., Clarence St and York St to Wynyard Park (behind Wynyard Station) from there along King St to Pitt St and back to the Domain; the other free service is the No. 666 Art Gallery Service which operates daily except Good Friday and Christmas Day. It commences its run at 10.10am from Hunter Street just around the cnr. from George Street and leaves every 30 minutes. The first service reaches the Art Gallery at 10.30 and the last one leaves there at 5 pm. The next cheapest way to travel around Sydney is to buy a weekly Travelpass. These are available from railway stations, Government bus depots, Manly & Circular Quay ferry wharves or the Travel Centre 11-31 York Street, Sydney. The Bus-Ferry Travelpass for the central zone costs $8.30, or the train-bus-ferry Travelpass costs $10.30 and includes the eastern suburbs zone. There is also a Day Rover Ticket for train-bus-ferry which costs $5.50 and is valid after 9 am weekdays and anytime on weekends or public holidays. There are also Family Weekend Tickets for $5 per family for the Sydney Surburban Area and $7 for the outer Metropolitan Area. Family groups must include one adult (maximum two) and at least one child (no limit to number of children).

TAXIS: RSL Cabs Ph 699 0144, Legion Cabs 2 0918, Taxis Combined Services 399 0488. CAR RENTAL AGENCIES: Budget Ph 339 8888, Thrifty Ph 357 5399, Hertz Ph 357 6621, Avis 357 200, Half Price Ph 267 7177, Betta Ph 331 5333. Most of the car rental agencies have offices in Kings Cross. Prices do vary so it pays to shop around.

HELPFUL ADDRESSES:

Consulates: American Consulate General, T & G Building, Cnr. Elizabeth & Park Sts, Ph 264 7044; British High Commission, Gold Fields House, Sydney Cove, Ph 27 9731; Canadian Consulate General, 8th Floor, AMP Centre, 50 Bridge St., Ph 231 6522; New Zealand Consulate General, 60 Park St., Ph 267 3511; Japanese Consulate General, Bent Street, 231 3455; German Consulate General, 13 Trelawney St., Woollahra, Ph 328 7733. Airline Offices: Australian Airlines Ph 693 3333; Ansett Ph 268 1555; East West 233 3700.

SIGHTSEEING:

You can take public transport or walk around the city area, but if you prefer to have some commentary but don't want to take an organised sightseeing tour, then take the red Sydney Explorer Bus, No. 111. This service runs around an 18 km route at roughly 16 minute intervals from 9.30 am to 5 pm daily and the drivers deliver a commentary on the city landmarks. Passengers can get off at any of the stops and pick up a later bus at their leisure and all for $7.50. You purchase your ticket on the bus when you will also be given a 'Sydney Explorer' Guide Book with detailed information on what there is to see and do at each of the 20 stops. Your explorer ticket also permits you to use any regular bus between Central Station and Circular Quay or The Rocks on the day of purchase up until midnight. The route covers most of the places of interest in Sydney and are what you will want to see whether you walk, catch public transport, the explorer bus or an organised tour: 1. Sydney Harbour; 2. Sydney Opera House; 3. Royal Botanic Gardens; 4. Parliament House; 5. Mrs. Macquaries Chair; 6. Art Gallery of N.S.W.; 7. Kings Cross; 8. Macleay Street; 9. Elizabeth Bay House; 10. Potts Point; 11. The Australian Museum; 12. Central Railway; 13. Chinatown; 14. Town Hall; 15. Sydney Tower; 16. Wynyard; 17. The Rocks; 18. Village Green; 19. Pier One; 20. Rocks Visitors' Centre. Another similar service is run by Sydney Double Decker Tours which operates daily every hour from 10am – 4 pm from Circular Quay at cost of $6.50.

If you do decide to take an organised coach tour or the Sydney Explorer Bus, there is one walk which I feel every visitor to Sydney should take. Start at Circular Quay, take a glance to see if there is a cruise liner docked at the Overseas Terminal, there often is and these ships are a magnificent sight. Stroll along the quay towards the Opera House, past the ferries leaving for the north shore of the harbour as well as those leaving for harbour cruises. It is always a busy place but often in the middle of the hustle and bustle you will see someone fishing from the wharf. Its only a short walk to the Opera House which is a magnificent building. Work started on the building in March 1959 and it was officially opened by the Queen in October 1973. Guided tours are conducted daily 9am-4pm and last 45mins, leaving from the Exhibition Hall. It is possible to walk all around the building along the edge of the harbour. On the northern side there is a cafeteria which has outdoor tables and it is a good excuse for a rest. The prices are a little inflated but the view from the terrace tables is unsurpassed even though its often a little breezy. From there you get a superb view of 'The Coathanger' as the locals affectionately call the Harbour Bridge. The majestic 503m long span is an engineering feat. The bridge, which was completed in 1932, took nine years to construct. It was built out from either shore and when the two halves met they were only 7cm out of alignment! After your refreshment stop, walk on to the Botanic Gardens. Just after you walk into the gardens you will see a glimpse of Government House on the hill on your right. It was built in 1845 in Gothic Revival style and is surrounded by beautiful lawns and gardens – not open for inspection. Follow the path along the edge of Farm Cove all the way to Mrs. Macquarie's Chair. This is a good vantage point from which to take photos of the Harbour Bridge, Opera House and the Royal Botanic Gardens with the tower buildings in the background. There are park benches at regular intervals and it is very relaxing just to sit and watch the harbour scene. Follow the road around Mrs. Macquarie's Chair and you will see Garden Island Dockyard where there are usually RAN ships tied up. Just above the swimming pool head back into the gardens (there are several gates along the top road). Have a look at the cacti garden and the Pyramid hot house and exit through one of the gates in Macquarie Street. Walk along Macquarie Street to Martin Place which is a pedestrian mall. It has plenty of seating and an amphitheatre where free lunchtime concerts are held in summer. At the George Street end is the GPO which was built between 1866 and 1886 in Italian Renaissance style and is notable for its carvings and sculptures. In front of the GPO, is the Cenotaph dedicated to the men and women who died serving the country in wartime.

In the city centre there are a few buildings of particular interest and another walking tour will take you past them. Start at:

Centrepoint shopping complex and Sydney Tower on the corner of Pitt, Market and Castlereagh Streets. There are pedestrian overpasses across Pitt and Castlereagh Streets and underpasses beneath Market and Castlereagh Streets making it possible to walk around the city's large department stores in comfort, no matter the weather. On top of Centrepoint is the 325m tower which can be seen from all over Sydney. There are two rotating restaurants and two observation levels, from where the view of the entire city is unsurpassed day or night. On a clear day you can see forever, well, 70km anyhow. The tower is open daily 9.30am-9.30pm except Sun & Public Hols. when it is open from 10.30am-6.30pm.

Walk along Market Street to George Street and you will see the Queen Victoria Building, which occupies a whole city block bounded by George, Market, York and Druitt Sts. It was built in 1893 and contained a vegetable market and shops surrounding a Galleria. Its central dome is 19m in diameter and clad with copper. It was allowed to fall into disrepair, and after extensive refurbishing it was re-opened in late 1986. It is a unique piece of Victoriana and contains some interesting shops. Well worth a visit.

On the opposite corner of George and Druitt Sts. is the Sydney Town Hall which was built between 1868 and 1889 in French Renaissance style. Its concert hall houses a pipe organ which ranks with the biggest and best in the world. The Sydney City Council Administrative offices occupy the modern tower block at the rear of the building. Next to the Town Hall in George Street is St. Andrew's Anglican Cathedral which has twin towers reminiscent of York Minster. Cross over George Street and walk along Park Street to College Street. Park Street disects Hyde Park, the city's most central open space. A war memorial stands at the southern end and there is a sunken garden and the Archibald Fountain at the northern end. The Australian Museum is on the corner of College Street and William Street, as Park Street is called on the other side of College Street. The Museum is well worth a visit.

Continue down College Street past the bowling green to St. Mary's Roman Catholic Cathedral. This is actually the third church to stand on this site as the first two were destroyed by fire. Construction of this building began in 1866 and the original work was completed in 1882. It has recently undergone extensive renovations and new bells were installed in the tower. This beautiful Gothic style cathedral is almost surrounded by parkland. Cross over College Street to Hyde Park and rest while you watch the Archibald Fountain. When you're ready, cross over to Macquarie Street where there are several examples of the convict, Francis Greenway's splendid works: St. James Cathedral on the left and across the street the Mint, Hyde Park Barracks and the Supreme Court. On the same side of the street is Sydney Hospital, built in the 1880's and Parliament House.

Further along Macquarie Street is the Library of New South Wales known to most Sydneysiders as the Mitchell Library. Cross over Macquarie Street and walk along Bent and Spring Streets to Pitt Street and Australia Square. The round tower building has a revolving restaurant on top and was for many years the best vantage point in the city. Walk up Pitt Street across Martin Place and King Street and you come to the Strand Arcade. This arcade runs between Pitt and George Street and was built in 1891. It was partly destroyed by fire in 1976 but has been painstakingly restored and contains many interesting shops. As you stroll through you will see original gas lamps, mosaic floor tiles and cedar shop fronts.

The Rocks is a fascinating area and you will probably want to spend a few hours here at least. The Rocks Information Centre, 104 George St., The Rocks, Ph 27 4972, puts out brochures on walking tours and you can see a film on the area. It is housed in the former City Coroner's Court building.

Some other interesting buildings are: The Argyle Centre, cnr. Argyle and Playfair Sts., which is now an arts and craft centre housed in a huge warehouse complex opening off old cobble stone courtyards. You can see artists, silver smiths, glassblowers, copper workers etc. – open 10am-4pm daily; The Sydney Observatory, Observatory Hill, which was used as a girls' school for many years; the Geological and Mining Museum housed in the enlarged electric light station built in 1902; Cadman's Cottage built in 1816 – Sydney's oldest dwelling; The Old Spaghetti Restaurant, 80 George St. which has an old Bondi Tram as well as other memorabilia.

The Harbour is so much part of Sydney that you will want to take at least one trip across it and every visitor to Sydney should visit the Taronga Zoo as not only is it a good place to see Australian native animals, but if affords a magnificient view of the harbour and city. The best way to get there is to take the ferry from No. 5 wharf across the harbour and then the bus to the top gate and walk down the hill through the exhibits. How long will it take to see the zoo? The sign at the main gate reads '45 minutes if you don't look at anything; 60 minutes if you look a little; all day, if you look at lot.' It is possible to buy combined train/ferry/bus and Zoo entry tickets from railway stations.

Another popular harbour trip is across to Manly. Most people take the hydrofoil one way and the ferry the other. On the way you will pass Fort

Dennison, a rock island first used to confine convicts during which time it acquired the grim name 'Pinchgut'. The fort was built in 1841 to protect Sydney Town against possible invasion. Manly has a harbour beach and a surf beach, boutiques, stores, hotels, restaurants, recreation areas and entertainment facilities. Manly Coaches have sightseeing tours of Manly and North Head which cost $2 – phone 938 4023 for further information.

If you would like to see more of the harbour you might like to take a Captain Cook Harbour Cruise which leaves from Circular Quay, or an all day sailing cruise aboard the 65ft 'Blue Skies', which leaves from the Opera House Wharf. If you would like to hire a boat and do your own thing, Waltons Boatshed, Balmoral Beach, Ph 969 6066 hire out yachts, sailboats, power boats, rowboats and canoes. A word of warning: There are sharks in the harbour and you should only swim in the enclosures.

Another interesting area is KINGS CROSS which was known as Queens Cross until the turn of the century. It has been the centre of bohemian life since the early days. By day it doesn't look much different to many of the older inner city suburbs but at night, it comes alive with crowds seeking the bright lights and entertainment. The El Alemein Fountain down Darlinghurst Road is quite unusual as it is shaped like a dandelion. Kings Cross has a Wax Works at The Village Centre, Springfield Ave., if you like that sort of thing.

ELIZABETH BAY HOUSE, Onslow Avenue Elizabeth Bay is only 5mins walk from Kings Cross Station and bus 311 from Hunter Street stops at the door. It is an elegant colonial mansion dating from 1835.

VAUCLUSE HOUSE, Olola Avenue, Vaucluse, was the home of William Charles Wentworth a noted barrister, explorer and statesman. Bus 325 from Circular Quay stops at the front gate.

If you still have some time for sightseeing in Sydney then you might like to visit some other museums:

The Power House Museum, Cnr. Omnibus Lane & Mary Ann St., Ultimo; Museum of Applied Arts & Sciences, Harris St., Ultimo.

SUBURBAN ATTRACTIONS:
PADDINGTON is a picturesque suburb only a few kilometres from the city centre. You can catch any of the Bondi buses. It has rows of Victorian terrace houses with beautiful iron lace lovingly restored. Newtown and Balmain also have many beautifully restored terrace houses. Victoria Barracks, Oxford Street, is a fine example of Georgian military construction. The 225m main block was designed to take a British regiment of those times, 800 men. A sentry has manned the gate 24 hours a day for more than 130 years. The Guard is ceremonially changed every Tuesday morning. Not far up the road from the barracks is Centennial Park, Sydney's largest park covering 220ha. Its nine lakes attract many species of water birds. It is a popular place with joggers, and bicycles and horses are available for hire.

UNIVERSITY OF SYDNEY is a mellowed gentle sandstone blend of Tudor and Gothic architecture and green lawns. The Great Hall has a Royal

Window which illustrates the monarchy from the Normans to Queen Victoria. The carving on this building took six years. The Fisher Library at the University contains more than 400,000 volumes and the Nicholson Museum contains Egyptian, Etruscian, Greek and Roman art. The University is in Parramatta Rd an extention of Broadway.

BONDI BEACH is probably Australia's best known beach. It is not really much different to any of the other ocean beaches in Sydney. It has become famous because it is the closest one to the city centre, but there are buses to many other beaches which you might like to see e.g. Bronte, Coogee, Palm Beach, or Dee Why.

BOTANY BAY, south of Sydney, is where Captain Cook first set foot on Australian soil. Sydney's main north/south airport runway extends out into the bay. There is a park along the foreshore from just south of the airport to Dolls Point. The bay is popular with boating enthusiasts but is infested with sharks. There is a swimming enclosure at Brighton le Sands and another at Dolls Point. At Kurnell, inside the southern headland, there is an obelisk and museum commemorating Cook's landing. On the northern headland at La Perouse, there is a memorial to the Frenchman who arrived in Botany Bay a few days after the arrival of the First Fleet in 1788. Just offshore at La Perouse is Bare Island, a small island linked to the mainland by a causeway. A fort was built on the island late last century as a deterrent to Russian invasion! It is an historical site and open for inspection from 9am-3.30pm daily. It still has two cannon, and on special occasions they have even been fired.

PARRAMATTA is 24km west of the city centre and a suburb of Sydney, but in 1788 Parramatta was the second settlement in Australia. The Parramatta Tourist Information Centre and Hopkinson's Coach Lines conduct bus tours on the last Thursday and third Sunday of each month at a cost of $3. There is also a signposted tourist drive around the attractions. Look for the Historic Houses Route signs. Call at the Information Centre, Prince Alfred Park, Market St., Ph 630 3703 for a map. Parramatta was the site of Australia's first orchard, vineyard, tannery, legal brewery, woollen mills, observatory, steam mill, market place and fair. Australia's wool industry had its beginning here also. Some of the interesting buildings are: Elizabeth Farm House was built in 1793 by John Macarthur; The Experiment Farm Cottage, 9 Ruse Street, was built for James Ruse in the early 1800's – open Tues-Sun 10am-4.30pm; Tudor Gatehouse, Parramatta Park is open for inspection Sun 1.30-4.30pm – an old steam train runs through the park on the 3rd Sunday of the month from 1-4.30pm; Brislington was built in 1821 by John Hodges and is situated in the Parramatta Hospital grounds, cnr. George & Marsden Sts. – open every 4th Thurs & Sundays from 10am-4pm; St. John's Church of England was opened in 1803 and extensively altered in 1852; Old Government House.

CUMBERLAND STATE FOREST, 95 Castle Hill Rd., Pennant Hills, is an urban forest including an arboretum planted with many Eucalyptus and

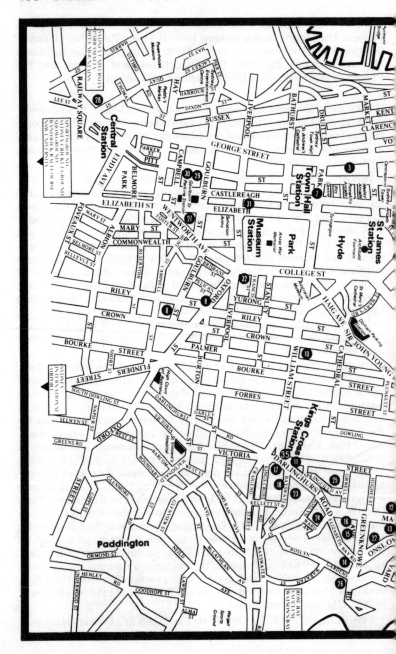

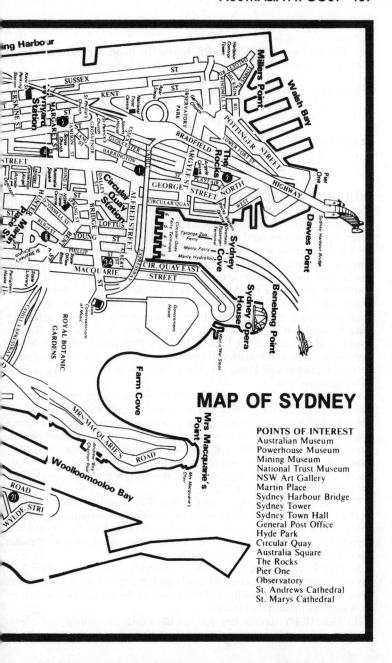

MAP OF SYDNEY

POINTS OF INTEREST
Australian Museum
Powerhouse Museum
Mining Museum
National Trust Museum
NSW Art Gallery
Martin Place
Sydney Harbour Bridge
Sydney Tower
Sydney Town Hall
General Post Office
Hyde Park
Circular Quay
Australia Square
The Rocks
Pier One
Observatory
St. Andrews Cathedral
St. Marys Cathedral

Rainforest trees. There are walking trails including a sensory trail for blind and disabled people.

Not far from there is KOALA PARK, Castle Hill Road, West Pennant Hills. There you can see koalas, kangaroos, wombats, echidnas etc.

FESTIVALS:
Festival of Sydney held from New Year's Eve to the end of January – see the local newspapers for the daily programme.

FACILITIES:
Sydney has all the sporting and recreational facilities you could expect of a city of its size – consult the yellow pages of the phone book for details.

OUTLYING ATTRACTIONS:
The ROYAL NATIONAL PARK is 30km south of the city just past Sutherland, and is the second oldest national park in the world. It is a very popular place on weekends in summer, and the traffic is often banked back for a few kilometres at the park gate as the cars pay their entrance fee. There is a Youth Hostel in the Park at Garie Beach. Audley is a popular picnic spot on the river and you can hire dinghies there. There are numerous bushwalks ranging from 1km to 15km or more. Some of the longer walks start at Heathcote and Waterfall railway stations and from Bundeena which can be reached by ferry from Cronulla. The beaches are splendid and not as crowded as the inner city beaches. The Sydney Tramway Museum is on the Princes Highway near Loftus Railway station at the edge of the national park. It has 30 tramcars and about 600m of track – open Sundays and Public Holidays and Wednesdays during school holidays 10am-5pm.

KU-RING-GAI CHASE NATIONAL PARK is 24km north of the city. The park also has numerous bushwalks and some magnificent Aboriginal rock carvings which are quite easy to find. The higher parts of the park afford magnificent views across Pittwater. On the edge of the national park is Waratah Park, Home of 'Skippy' the bush kangaroo. The park has koalas, kangaroos, dingoes, emus, wombats, eagles, etc. Forest Coach Lines bus No. 56 to Duffy's Forest departs Chatswood Railway Station at 11.05am weekdays – open daily 10am-5pm.

EL CABALLO BLANCO, Camden Valley Way, Narellan, Ph 606 5444 is worth a visit as it has dancing horses, sheep shearing, swimming pool and water slides, train ride, pony rides and trail rides. The El Caballo bus departs Campbelltown Station Wed-Sun at 10am and departs El Caballo Blanco at 4pm.

AUSTRALIA'S WONDERLAND is an Australian type of Disneyland. You pay one entry fee and you can ride and watch the shows all day long. A bus takes visitors to and from Rooty Hill station to the park, which is located on Wallgrove Road, Minchinbury.

HAWKESBURY RIVER lies just to the north of Sydney and winds through a natural forest area. One of the best ways to see it is to join the

Riverboat Mail Run. Catch an electric train to Hawkesbury River Station and join the boat there. The State Rail Authority has a tour on Wednesdays departing Sydney Station at 8.15am returning at 6.38pm – cost $35.

ORGANISED TOURS:

You may prefer to visit the outlying attractions on an oranised tour. There are many companies operating in Sydney. Some names and addresses: Ansett Pioneer Tours, Ph 268 1331; Clipper Tours, Ph 888 3144; Australian Pacific Tours, Ph 693 2222; AAT Kings, Ph 27 2066; The State Rail Authority also has Day-a-Way tours and mini holidays.

TAMWORTH – Pop. 34,500

LOCATION:

It is situated mid-way between Sydney and Brisbane on the New England Highway, at the junction of the Oxley Highway. Distance from: Sydney 453km; Melbourne 1,152; Adelaide 1,446; and Brisbane 589km.

CLIMATE:

Average summer temperatures: max 30.6 deg C and min 16.8 deg C; average winter temperatures: max 16.3 deg C and min 4.0 deg. C. It is 389m above sea level and has an annual rainfall of 650mm. Wettest months: December 71mm and January 85mm. Occasional snow falls in winter in the 'tops' area around Nundle 60km south.

CHARACTERISTICS:

It was the first city in Australia to have street lighting powered by electricity. To-day it is better known as the 'Country Music Capital'.

TOURIST INFORMATION:

Tamworth Visitors' Information Centre, C.W.A. Park, Cnr. New England Highway & Kable Ave, Ph (067) 66 3641 Mon-Fri and 66 3646 Sat. mornings.

HOW TO GET THERE:

AIR. Air NSW have several flights daily between Tamworth and Sydney with connections to other country towns. Eastern Airlines fly to Brisbane, Coolangatta and Lismore. East-West fly to Armidale and Sydney. As it is 'home base' they have the best connections out of Tamworth.
BUS. On the main Brisbane/Sydney, Brisbane/Melbourne and Brisbane/Adelaide route, and Ansett-Pioneer, Border Coaches, Deluxe, Greyhound, Intertour and McCafferty's Coach Companies all serve Tamworth. Most of the services are daily.
RAIL. Tamworth is served by the Northern Tablelands XPT. The State Rail Authority of NSW has introduced a Tamworth Country Caper in their Rail

Stay-a-Way packages. Contact your nearest railway booking office for further information.

CAR. Tamworth is midway between Sydney and Brisbane on the New England Highway at the Junction of the Oxley Highway.

ACCOMMODATION:

22 motels, 1 hotel/motel, 3 hotels and 5 caravan parks. No Youth Hostel. For details contact the Tourist Information Office.

A few names and addresses: Tamworth Flag Inn, New England Highway, Ph 65 7022 -RO $44 double; Golden Grain Motor Inn, New England Highway, ph 65 3599 – RO $30 double; Oasis Hotel/Motel, Armidale Rod, Ph 28 7292 – RO $24 double. Thunderbird Caravan Park, New England Highway, Pk 67 9356 – sites $5 double, overnight vans $18 double.

EATING OUT:

4 licensed clubs which provide lunch and dinner, activities and artists for the pleasure of members and guests. Visitors are more than welcome. There are a number of fully licensed restaurants offering first-class meals and pleasant surroundings, a number of venues for more relaxed and informal dining, and a number of 'quick'n'easy establishments which cater for the diner on the run.

POINTS OF INTEREST:

Tamworth has two Tourists Drives, the first features the city and attractions, and the second features a little bit of country scenery. Just follow the blue arrows.

Tamworth is the Country Music Capital, and, as such, has many related sights e.g. the Hands of Fame Stone, CWA Park, features the handprints of musicians and singers famous in the country music scene. The Roll of Renown at the Radio Centre, Goonoo Goonoo Road dates from 1977, and features bronze plaques, each of which bears the name of the winner of the annual Country Music Award.

The Folk and Historic Museum, cnr. Marius and East Sts., houses the first aeroplane which was built in NSW, some aboriginal artefacts, and collections of guns, coins, swords, stamps and old bottles. Open 8.30-5.30pm Mon-Fri and 8.30am-1pm Sats, gratis.

The V.Guy Kable Memorial Arts Building, Marius St., houses Russian objects of art, Australian silverware, a coin collection, a philatelic display as well as works by renowned artists. Mon-Fri 10am-5pm, Sat 9-11.30am & Sun 2-5pm.

The Kamilaroi Walking Track in Oxley Park offers a scenic bushland walk with panoramic views.

The Regional Music Centre in Marius Street has been classified by the National Trust. It is a former Dominican Convent which is now used for musical studies, and regular Concerts are held there – for further information, phone 66 6911.

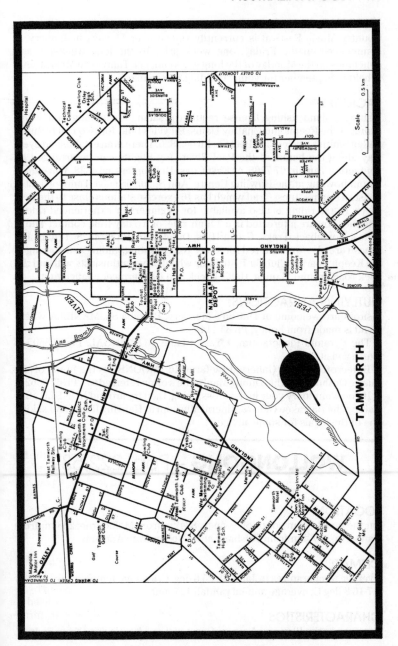

FESTIVALS:

Country Music Festival is currentlly staged over 11 days in January. It commences on the Friday, one week prior to the long weekend, and concludes on the Monday of the long weekend. The Tamworth Music Camp is held in September for young budding musicians.

FACILITIES:

Fishing (inland fishing license required), sailing, swimming and water skiing at the Keepit and Chaffey Dams. Bicycles built for two can be hired at Reg Smith's Cycles, 310 Peel St., Ph 66 2825. There is an established cycle way along the banks of the Peel River. Joy Flights can be arranged by contacting Tamair, 67 7208, or East Coast Helicopters, 66 4328. You can go tenpin bowling at the Bowling Centre, Ann St., ph 65 6653. Tamworth also boasts a Fun'n'Fitness Trail which has 16 exercise stations close to the Peel River. Horse riding is also available for beginners or experienced riders. Whether you are interested in a 1 hour ride, or a 5 day trek, contact Tim & Julie's Horseback Treks, Green Hills, Dungowan, Ph 69 4328. Tennis and squash are also well catered for as are roller skating, gliding and soaring at the Keepit Soaring Club 69 7640. Four wheel drive enthusiasts will find the back road around Manilla, Hall's Creek and Bendermeer challenging.

OUTLYING ATTRACTIONS:

Visitors are welcome at Dutton's Meadery, Barraba St., MANILLA where mead is made from honey, Ph 85 1148.

The Pyramid Planetarium, 4 Yarrol Lane, KOOTINGAL, Ph 67 3505 is worth a visit.

Braecroft Cottage Gallery, Braefarm Rd., MOONBI, is the home of the Aussie Outhouse or the 'Dunny Man' as he's often referred to – Ph 67 3662.

If you want to try your luck at fossicking, then try around NUNDLE after visiting the Barrakee Gem & Mineral Museum at Hanging Rock, and asking one of the locals for some advice.

WOLLONGONG – Pop. 222,539

LOCATION:

On the coast 80km south of Sydney, 824km from Melbourne; 238km from Canberra, 1073km from Brisbane and 1339km from Adelaide.

CLIMATE:

Average temperatures in Jan 17.8-25.6 deg. C; average temperatures in July 8.7-16.8 deg C; average annual rainfall 1275mm.

CHARACTERISTICS:

Gateway to the Illawarra Leisure Coast just one hour's drive from Sydney.

Wollongong's setting is unique. On one side it is bordered by the beautiful Pacific Ocean and on the other by an imposing mountain range. Large stretches of lush rainforest and parkland, coupled with its beautiful beaches and lake, make the region a haven for nature lovers.

HOW TO GET THERE:

BUS. Watts operate a service to/from Sydney airport. Ansett Pioneer, Greyhound and Deluxe stop at Wollongong daily on their Sydney/ Melbourne via the Princes Highway services. The usual intrastate regulations apply i.e. you must have an Australia wide bus pass or be travelling interstate.

RAIL. Regular service from Sydney – approx. 70-90mins.

CAR. Via the Princes Highway to Waterfall and then the F6, or continue along the highway and turn off at the Stanwell Park turnoff for a spectacular drive along the coast. Another interesting route is via National Park to Stanwell Park, turn off just past Sutherland.

TOURIST INFORMATION:

Leisure Coast Tourist Association, 87 Crown Street open 7 days, tel. (042) 28 0300.

ACCOMMODATION:

Illawarra's Leisure Coast boasts a comprehensive range of accommodation from caravan parks which dot many of the beaches and lakesides, to an international style resort hotel, leisure village, quality motels, hotels, holiday units and superb convention facilities.

Some names and addresses: North Beach International, 6 Cliff Road, North Wollongong, Ph 27 1188 – RO $75-105 double ; Centre Plaza Hotel. Cnr. Crown & Station Sts., Ph 29 7444 – RO $40 double; Cabbage Tree Hotel/ Motel, Cnr. Princes Highway & Anama St., Ph 84 4000 – RO $30 double; Imperial Hotel, Lawrence Hargraves Drive, Clifton, Ph 67 1177 – RO $24; North Wollongong Hotel, Flinders St., North Wollongong, Ph 29 4177 – $35 double; Wollongong Surf Leisure Resort, Dalton Park, Towradgi, Ph 28 0300 – 4km north of PO on the beach front – sites $5 double – onsite vans $25 double has kiosk, restaurant, indoor/outdoor tennis courts, bmx track,; mini golf, cricket nets, games room, table tennis, video room and bicycle hire. The park is right next to the northern cycle track.

EATING OUT:

Wollongong's cosmopolitan community offers you a wide choice of superb restaurants, snack bars and coffee lounges. For those who want to boogie the night away, there are many night clubs and discos as well as the licensed clubs.

Some names and addresses: Barnies Family Restaurant, 309 Crown St., Ph 29 7444 – $7-8 range; Heidi's German Restaurant, Cnr. Corrimal & Market Sts., Ph 27 1110 – $8 range; Terrace Restaurant, 34 Young St., Ph 29 2902 – $10-12 range; Charcoal Tavern, 18 Regent St., Ph 29 7298 $10-12 range. During business hours a good place to eat is the Food Court, bottom level of the Gateway on the Mall shoping complex, Cnr. Crown & Kiera Sts. They have tables in the centre and you can choose from Chinese, Italian, Austrian, Mexican, crepes, chicken, pies, kebabs, hamburgers etc. from $1.40 up to around $4.50 for a meal. You can buy take away there, or opposite in Crown Central and eat it at the outdoor tables in the Mall. If you would like to eat at one of the clubs, then try the Fraternity Bowling & Recreation Club, 11 Bourke St., Fairy Meadow, Ph 83 3333 or the Wollongong Ex-Services Club, , 82 Church St., Ph 28 8522.

POINTS OF INTEREST:

Most historic buildings can be visited on a walking tour commencing at Flagstaff Hill (parking available). The sights visited are Wollongong Head Lighthouse, Breakwater Lighthouse, Belmore Basin, Drill Hall, Throsby's stockman's hut monument, Market Square, Illawarra Historical Museum, Congregational Church, Wollongong Courthouse, St. Michael's Provisional Cathedral, Wollongong Uniting Church, Town Hall, Wollongong East Post Office, Tourist Information Office, St. Francis Xavier's Provisional Cathedral and Andrew Lysaght Park.

Mount Kembla Historic Village 7km from Wollongong was the sight of the 1902 mining disaster, but is full of art and crafts centres to-day. A visit to the Botanic Gardens and Rhododendron Park are especially rewarding in springtime. The Wollongong City Art Gallery, cnr. Keira & Burelli Sts, has a fine collection of modern and traditional paintings.

Magnificent views of the coast line can be obtained from Mount Kembla Lookout, Sublime Point and Bulli Lookout, all of which are only about 15-20mins drive from the centre of town. The Golden Fleece Restaurant and the Panorama House Restaurant at Bulli Tops both have magnificent views of the coast.

Kelly's Falls, 2kms off the Princes Highway at Stanwell Tops, has a picnic area and easy walking tracks to the falls. Flannel flowers are abundant in spring and early summer. Nearby is Symbio Koala Gardens where Australian native animals rub shoulders with many exotic species.

While you are in the area drive to Bald Hill lookout where there is a memorial to Lawrence Hargrave and, if the wind is favourable, you will see many brightly coloured hang-gliders as well as a magnificent view.

Call into Stanwell Park in the valley below and browse through Articles Art Gallery, and have a devonshire tea on the outdoor terrace.

South of the city is Lake Illawarra which is renowned for fishing and prawning, and is often ablaze with colourful sailing boats and sail boards.

Bass Point is popular with scuba divers as it is a protected area with no fishing allowed, and large groper and many smaller fish may be seen.

The Illawarra Escarpment State Recreation Area has many fine walking trails through the rainforest – phone 29 4756 for details.

Australia's largest steel mill is located around the foreshores of Port Kembla Harbour through which it exports millions of tons of coal each year from the surrounding mines, as well as steel from the steelworks.

Wollongong also has two bicycle tracks. The one to the north starts at North Beach and goes to Corrimal 14km away, and the southern one starts near the Windang bridge and skirts the shores of Lake Illawarra.

FESTIVALS:
Festival of Wollongong is held each year in November.

FACILITIES:
Cinemas, drive-in theatres, ten pin bowling (Corrimal & Warrawong), bicycle hire (Stuart Park – Lotap Cycles), car rental depots (Budget 83 4244 & Auto Rentals 29 7766), catamaran and sailboard hire (Lake Illawarra & Belmore Basin), tennis, squash, horse riding, golf, joy flights at Albion Park Aerodrome, fishing, leisure centre with heated pools (Beaton Park), horse racing (Kembla Grange), and indoor cricket (Fairy Meadow). Deep sea charter boats leave from Belmore Basin. Ice skating at Dalton Park, Towradgi and Roller Skating at Thirroul.

OUTLYING ATTRACTIONS:
KIAMA famous for its blowhole is 119km south of Sydney but only 30mins drive from Wollongong. The blowhole is floodlit until 9.30 pm. Unfortunately, it only blows' in 'nasty' weather these days. A visit to the restored Railway Terrace Houses is more rewarding as they feature craft shops and restaurants.

MINNAMURRA FALLS, 15km west of Kiama, are situated in a dense subtropical rainforest, and plunge some 50m into a deep gorge. There is a delightful walk from the parking area through the rainforest to the actual falls. The round trip takes about an hour.

At JAMBEROO Recreation Park, about 14km west of Kiama, one can grass ski, enjoy the two lane waterslide and bobsled track, or take a chairlift to the summit of the hill which affords extensive views of the coast.

BARREN GROUNDS NATURE RESERVE, 25km west of Kiama on the Jamberoo Mountain Road affords magnificent views from the lookout, and has an unique hanging swamp and bird observatory.

There are two wineries in the area: The Silos, Princes Highway at Jaspers Brush (south of Berry) and the MacCarthur Estate Winery, Mt. Kiera Road, Wilton. Both of the wineries have restaurants and MacCarthur's have a bush dance on weekends, and operate a bus from Wollongong so patrons don't have to drive. It's a great night out.

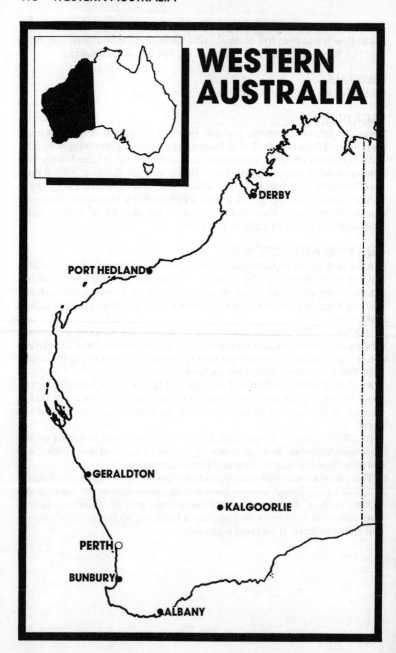

ALBANY – Pop. 15,222

LOCATION:
On King Georges Sound at the start of the Great Australian Bight 406km south-east of Perth.

CLIMATE:
Average temperatures: January max. 25.8 deg. C min. 13.3 deg. C; July max. 15.7 deg. C min. 7.4 deg. C; No. of days per year with temperature over 30 deg.C 15.9; No. of days per year with temperature over 40 deg.C 0.6; average annual rainfall 809mm.

CHARACTERISTICS:
Gem of the Southern Ocean and WA's leading holiday centre. The harbours, rivers and estuaries provide excellent fishing, while the sandy beaches, rugged coastline and nearby mountains provide a variety of things for the visitor to do. Former whaling centre and coaling stop for early steam ships on the U.K./Australian run.

HOW TO GET THERE:
AIR. Skywest have flights to/from Perth Sundays to Fridays.
BUS. The Westrail bus leaves East Perth Terminal 11 times weekly and travels to Albany via Kojonup or York. Greyhound Eaglepass tickets are valid on this service. Deluxe stop here on their Adelaide/Perth via Albany service three times weekly.
CAR. From Perth either via the Coast Road or the Albany Highway 405km.

TOURIST INFORMATION:
Albany Tourist Bureau, 171 York St., Ph (098) 41 1613 – open Mon-Fri 8.30am-5.30pm, Sat 9am-12 and Sundays and public holidays as required.

ACCOMMODATION:
9 motels, 6 hotels, 2 private hotels, 8 guest houses, holiday flats, 12 camping grounds. Contact the Tourist Information Office for full details.
A few names and addresses: Ace Motel, 314 Albany Hwy, Ph 41 2911 – $454 double – family $59; White Star Hotel/Motel, Stirling Tce., Ph 41 1733 – RO $24 double; Parkville Colonial Guest House, 136 Brunswick Rd., Ph 41 3704 – RO $24 double; Mt. Melville Caravan Park, Cnr. Lion & Wellington St., Ph 41 4616 – site $9 double – on site vans $18 double; Tourist Village Caravan Park, Lot 4 Albany Hwy, Ph 41 3752 – site $7 double – on site vans $76 double – cabins $30; The Lilacs, 151 Frenchman Bay Road, Ph 41 2390 – cabins $120-$160 weekly. Youth Hostel, 49 Duke St., Ph (098) 41 3949 – $6ppn.

POINTS OF INTEREST.
The wide main street, York Street, slopes gently down to the sea. It is lined

with a variety of shops, many of them with fine Victorian shop-fronts. The Town Hall was built in 1887 and next door to it are the modern Library and Municipal buildings. Dog Rock is the huge, granite outcrop on the main road to the Town Beach. It looks like the head of a blood hound sniffing the breeze.

On the foreshore is a replica of the 'Amity' one of the first ships to sail into the Sound. A link with the past is also found in the local cottage industries. You can watch craftsmen and women work at weaving, pottery, painting, screen printing and blackboy turning.

For a panoramic view drive to the summit of Mt. Clarence. The road is steep but safe. On its scrubby slopes there is a small colony of noisy scrub birds which were believed to have been extinct until they were re-discovered here in 1961. At Two Peoples Bay there is an interesting display, incorporating a tape recording of the calls of various birds found in this area.

At Whaleworld, Princes Royal Harbour, Frenchman's Bay, 21km from Albany, you can visit the old Whaling Station and Museum – open daily 9am-5pm. The history of all the wool industry in Western Australia is outlined at Albany Aerodrome. A film, shearing and fashion parades are incorporated in the demonstration.

Spectacular views of the town, harbour, farmlands and mountain ranges can be obtained from the John Barnesby Memorial Lookout, Mt. Melville.

Albany Residency Museum tells the story of Major Lockyer's landing in 1826 – open Mon-Sat 10am-5pm and Sun & holidays 2-5pm.

The Old Farm, Strawberry Hill is modelled on the English estates of the 18th century – open 10am-12noon & 2-5pm late August to Easter and daily 2-5pm rest of the year.

Patrick Taylor Cottage at 31 Duke St has over 2,000 display items including period costumes, old clocks, silverware, kitchenware – open daily 2pm-4.30pm.

The Old Gaol built in 1851 is now a museum and is open for inspection daily 1.30pm-4.15pm public holidays, school holidays and Easter 10am-4.15pm.

Some of the beaches: Middleton Beach has a long stretch of sand edging clear, unpolluted water; Emu Point Beach, where you can park your car on the beach itself as the sand is solid. It also has a tidal swimming pool and a launching ramp. The fishing is good at Oyster Harbour.

Follow the well-signposted roads out of Albany to the Torndirrup National Park which has one of the most rugged coastlines in Australia. The park has blowholes and a natural bridge, and from The Gap, where there is a 24m drop, you can see Eclipse Island and West Cape Howe the most southerly point of WA.

FLORA: Jarrah, marri and sheoak are the principal trees. Spectacular shrubs include the scarlet banksia, the bright red swamp bottlebrush, the golden showy dryandra, pink, yellow and cream cone flowers and the white Southern Cross. Orchids abound, while the yellow and red Albany catspaw is seen in sandy woodlands. Hiding in dense swamps is the Albany pitcher plant, while on swamp margins the curious red and white swamp daisy may be seen. July to October are the best months for flowers, but there is always something in flower around Albany.

FAUNA: Lizards, kookaburras, parrots, robins, wrens and finches; also kangaroos, bush wallabies and emus off the beaten track.

FACILITIES:

There is a boat charter service which caters for the keen fisherman. Water sports are very popular on the Princess Royal Harbour. There are several golf courses, and lawn bowls, tennis and squash are all catered for.

OUTLYING ATTRACTIONS:

The STIRLING RANGE National Park has beautiful scenery and excellent bushwalks. For the more energetic there are several mountains which can be climbed e.g. Ellen Peak 1012m – approx. 8 hour return.

DENMARK, 55km west of Albany, has fine beaches, both ocean and bay. It is a favourite family holiday spot due to its safe swimming and fishing. There is a varied choice of accommodation. However, from December to March it is best to book in advance. A visit to Winniston Park which is packed with English antiques is a must, as is a visit to Copenhagen House in Strickland Street which has beautiful local craft items.

The Great Southern Wine Area around Albany/Denmark/Mt. Barker has 14 wineries, 8 of which are open for cellar sales. The main grape varieties are Cabernet Sauvignon, Rhine Riesling and Shiraz. It's best to get a list and a map of the wineries from the Tourist Information office before venturing off, as many of the vineyards are off the main road and are only indicated by small signs. It is also best to pack a picnic lunch as shops are few and far between.

Some of the most striking of all the southern scenery is the green forests and rivers which run down to the inlets and estuaries around WALPOLE and NORNALUP. You can fish on the coast or in the rivers, hire canoes, swim or follow the forest roads to the Valley of the Giants, and through the pretty tinglewood forests.

MANJIMUP is known as the gateway to the tall trees. It's only a short drive to Warren National Park, One Tree Bridge and the four superb karri trees, the Four Aces. PEMBERTON is situated in the superb karri forests. At the Pemberton Sawmill you can see the big timber being sawn. Just 1.6km from the Post Office is the Trout Hatchery. If you aren't afraid of heights then a climb up the 153 rung ladder to the top of the GLOUCESTER TREE (61m) is worth the effort for the superb view.

ESPERANCE has many natural attractions; the climate which is temperate; a brilliant blue bay which sweeps around the coast; beaches which are great; magnificent headlands; and the endless rolling plains burst into colour with wildflowers every spring.

At the nearby Recherche Archipelago islands there are colonies of sea lions , and regular launch trips from Esperance will take you through the islands.

Something you shouldn't miss is the Pink Lake which changes colour depending on weather conditions. Sometimes it is even purple. The colour is caused by an algae called Dunalella Salina.

The Municipal Museum between Dempster Street and the Esplanade has a major Skylab display, as it was near here that a large piece of skylab fell to earth.

You get a good view of the town and surrounding countryside from Rotary Lookout.

Cape Le Grand National Park, 56km east, offers something for everyone, whether it be fishing, walking, studying wildflowers, photography or just lazing on secluded beaches.

Further east is the Cape Arid National Park at the start of the Great Australian Bight.

There is a variety of accommodation available in Esperance including a Youth Hostel.

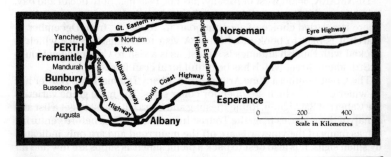

BUNBURY – Pop. 21749

LOCATION:
At the southern end of Koombana Bay 175km south of Perth.

CLIMATE:
Average temperature: January max. 27.5 deg C min. 17.7 deg C; July max. 16.8 deg. C, min. 8.2 deg C; No. of days p.a. with temperature over 30 deg.C 29.7; No. of days p.a. with temperature over 40 deg.C 0; average annual rainfall 882mm; wettest six months May-October.

CHARACTERISTICS:
The major seaport and administrative centre of the South West region. The largest centre in WA outside the metropolitan area. It is an expanding industrial centre with a wealth of natural and manmade resources. It is surrounded by much of WA's best agricultural land, and the area is rich in minerals as well. Ilmenite, rutile and zircon have been discovered in the

sands along the coast. Bauxite is also found nearby. But Bunbury is primarily still a holiday centre, and each year thousands flock here to enjoy all the holiday pleasures and to use the city as a base to visit the many beauty spots of the South West.

HOW TO GET THERE:

BUS. The Westrail bus departs East Perth Terminal 5 times weekly. Deluxe stop at Bunbury on their Perth Adelaide route via Albany.
RAIL. The Australind Express departs Perth Railway Station 6 times weekly.
CAR. Either from Fremantle to Mandurah and along the Coast Road, or from Perth to Armadale, then via the South Western Highway to Bunbury.

TOURIST INFORMATION:

Bunbury Travel Information Centre, Sterling St., (097) 21 4737 – open Mon-Sat 9am-5pm, Sun & public hols 10am-4pm.

ACCOMMODATION:

Bunbury has 6 motels, 5 hotel/motels, 3 hotels, many guest houses and 6 caravan parks. No youth hostel. For further details contact the Tourist Information Office.

Some names and addresses: Admiral Motor Inn, 56 Spencer St., Ph 21 7322 – RO $45-49; Welcome Inn, Ocean Drive, Ph 21 3100 – RO $44-53; Te-Kianga Guest House, 1 Symmons St., Ph 21 5171 – B&B $28 double; Wellington Hotel, Victoria St., Ph 21 2067; Bunbury Village Caravan Park, Cnr. Bussell Highway & Washington Ave., Ph 25 7100 – sites $7 – onsite vans $16-20 double – chalets $25 double – flats $15 double; Riverside Caravan Park, 5 Pratt Rd., Eaton, Ph 25 1234 – sites $5 double – onsite vans $16.

EATING OUT:

Bunbury has no shortage of restaurants in all price brackets. Some of the better ones: The Amalfi and the Lord Forest Hotel Restaurant.

POINTS OF INTEREST:

The Scenic Drive travels along Stirling and Oliver Streets to Koombana Drive where the estuary foreshore is bordered with lawns. This Drive leads to Koombana Park with a golf course, camping and caravan parks, all situated on a peninsula between Koombana Bay and the Leschenault Inlet. The Ocean Drive follows 8km of coastline with sparkling clean beaches facing the broad horizon of the Indian Ocean. You pass Ocean or Back Beach which is a good place for a swim. At Bunbury Harbour you may drive along the breakwater which extends deep into Koombana Bay. From there you can get a good idea of the extent of the modern harbour facilities. The Inner Harbour development programme has involved the diversion of the Preston River into Leschenault Inlet which has meant extensive dredging and reclamation. Bunbury is now one of the best man-made deepwater ports on the west coast of Australia.

Boulter's Heights are a short drive up Haig Crescent. This popular lookout has a picturesque waterfall which adds to the beauty of the surroundings.

The Art Gallery has some excellent examples of Australian paintings.

The Lighthouse is a distinctive landmark as it is painted in black and white checks which makes it stand out boldly. Opposite the BP Roadhouse is the smallest church in Australia, St. Nicholas. It was built in 1842.

The old timber jetty located off Henry Street is 1,830m in length and is no longer used for shipping. It is a popular fishing and crabbing spot. Bunbury is known as the home of the blue manna crab which may be found, in season, in the Leschenault Inlet.

Old steam locomotives run from Bunbury to Collie through the Darling Ranges – contact the Travel Information Centre for details.

The Gemstone and Rock Museum on the Old Coast Road at Australind has an outstanding collection which features rare Bunbury agate, fossilised crabs etc. – open daily 10am-5pm.

On the Perth side of Australind along the Old Coast Road is a signpost on the left to the Scenic Drive. This narrow road skirts the estuary, providing good entry spots for crabbing or picnicking. The Scenic Drive rejoins the Old Coast Road after 5km. Wellesley Road Wildlife Park off the Old Coast Road has many varieties of Australian native animals – open 10am-5.30pm daily. There are regular cruises on the Collie River.

FESTIVALS:
Koombana Festival is held towards the end of February.

FACILITIES:
Football, cricket, hockey, baseball and basketball. Water sports are very popular in Bunbury and Koombana Bay is the venue for sailing, boating and water skiing. There is an olympic pool off Parade Road, Withers. Golf, lawn bowls and tennis are also catered for. Trotting meetings are held at Donaldson Park.

FLORA: The uncleared coastal plain around Bunbury still has jarrah, marri and tuart. Sheoaks, woody pears and peppermint are common. In the swampy areas paperbarks are found. The undergrowth is shrubby and wattles, native buttercups, sarsaparilla, clematis, myrtles and banjines are found. Mangroves, samphires and sedges grow on the shores of the inlet.

FAUNA: Black swans, pelicans, ducks, sandpiper, mudlarks, wagtails and magpies thrive there. Emus, kangaroos and other bush marsupials may be sighted.

OUTLYING ATTRACTIONS:
MANDURAH only an hour's drive south of Perth, is a popular coastal resort. Attractions: The Deer Park 16km north on the Pagononi Road; Cacti Garden and Wildlife Park adjacent to Mandurah Raceway; Halls Cottage; Barvarian Castle and Adventure Playground on the Old Coast Road south;

Cruises on the 'River Queen' on the Murray River and Peel Inlet.

PINJARRA: Attractions: Endenvale homestead; Hotham Valley Tourist Railway based at the Pinjarra Station runs regular excursions in Autumn and Spring. The Timber Trainway runs between Pinjarra and Boddington through a magnificent section of forest, inaccessible by car.; Athlone Angora Stud and Goat Farm 16km east on the Dwellingup Rd is an ideal attraction for the family; At Alcoa Refinery tours are conducted regularly. The HARVEY DISTRICT is a popular bush walking area. The Harvey Weir built in 1916 provided WA with its first controlled irrigation scheme; Myalup and Binningup Beaches along the Old Coast Road are ideal for boating, swimming and fishing.

COLLIE (37km west). Attractions: The Steam Train Museum and Tourist Mine are situated at the entrance to Collie and there is a Historical Museum opposite. All Saints Anglican Church has beautiful murals, stained glass, a 400 year old cross and candle sticks of beaten brass; The Minninup Pool where the Collie River widens out is a good swimming spot and picnic area.

BUSSELTON on the shores of Geographe Bay has a famous old jetty 2kms long. Wonnerup House 10km east off the Bussell Highway is a typical colonial style house built in 1859. The Whistle Craft Shop and Miniature Railway which hauls people around on log jetties over a simulated log hauling railway line is on the Basse Highway (Nannup Road) 11km from Busselton – open school holidays and weekends – includes an adventure playground, animal nursery etc. The Bunyip Craft Centre 7km from the centre of town is where over 100 local craftsmen bring their work to sell. Busselton has several good restaurants as well as plenty of cheaper ones.

Some names and addresses: The Olde Raj, Indian Restaurant, Shop 2, 28 Queen St; Commercial Hotel has counter meals as well as a dining room; Roseys, 70 The Causeway is open nightly from 6.30pm; Sugar & Spice Buffey, 53 Prince St. does lunches and morning and afternoon teas; Golden Inn Chinese Restaurant, 9 Albert St.

There are two routes from Busselton to Augusta both having outstanding scenery. The first and shortest is to travel west to Vasse and then turn south following the Bussel Highway. This route takes you through some of the best farming areas in Western Australia with undulating green pastures and a backdrop of kauri forests.

The first stop along this route is COWARRAMUP which is the beginning of the South-West's prime vineyard region. There are 22 wineries in the district 17 of which have cellar sales. Get the brochure 'The vineyards of the South' from the Tourist Bureau for more information. There are many excellent restaurants in the area.

MARGARET RIVER lies in a rich dairy, cattle and timber region with vineyards emerging as one of the major industries. The renowned Mammoth, Jewel and Lake Caves are nearby and should not be missed – Guided Tours last approximately 1 hour. Tours for the Mammoth leave at 11am & 3pm daily, the Lake at 9.30am & 1.30pm and the Jewel at 9.30am, 11.30am, 1.30pm & 3.30pm – more frequently during holiday periods. The Mammoth Cave is 21km south of Margaret River, the beautiful Lake Cave

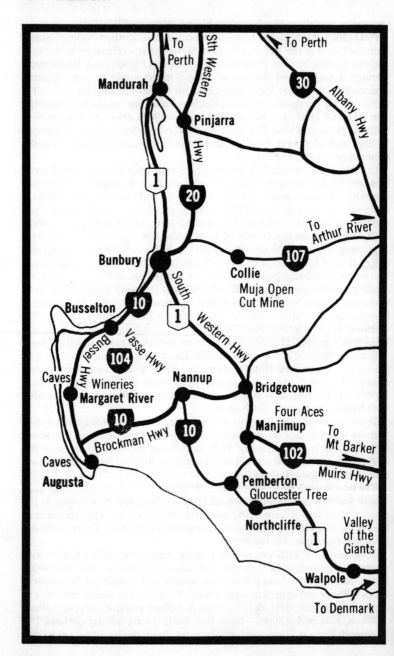

is a further 2km south and a further 14km south or 8km from Augusta, is Jewel Cave. Between Lake and Jewel Caves is the splendid Boranup Scenic Drive and lookout picnic area. The drive takes the visitor through some of the most impressive timber country in the South-West. South of Boranup Drive is Hamelin Bay which is acclaimed as a superb swimming, fishing and boating beach.

The second route to Augusta takes you from Busselton to Dunsborough and then south through Yallingup on Caves Road.

Before you reach YALLINGUP are the Yallingup Caves which are open daily 9.30am-3pm or 9.30am-4.30pm during the holiday period. Yallingup Beach is claimed by many surfers to be unequalled in Australia and many championships are held here.

AUGUSTA, 301km south of Perth, stands high on the slopes of the Hardy Inlet overlooking a splendid vista of trees, tranquil estuary waters and the wild ocean beyond. 9km south is the Cape Leeuwin Lighthouse which stands at the most south-westerly tip of Australia – tours from 9.30am-3.30pm every hour in non-holiday periods and half-hourly during holidays. It is a splendid area for boating.

DERBY – Pop. 3000

LOCATION:
At the southern end of King Sound 723km north of Perth – Gateway to the Kimberley Gorges.

CLIMATE:
Average temperatures: January max. 33.3, min. 26.2 deg C; July max. 28.5 deg. C., min. 13.6 deg C; No. of days p.a. with temperature over 30 deg.C – 279; No. of days p.a. with temperature over 40 deg.C – 44.; average annual rainfall 627mm; wettest six months December-May.

CHARACTERISTICS:
One of the best known towns in the Kimberley region. The narrow channels between the islands off Derby have strong rips and currents, as well as a 11.6m variation between high and low tides.

HOW TO GET THERE:
AIR. The airport is 9km west of the town with daily services by Ansett WA to Perth and Darwin. There are also less frequent services to Geraldton, Gove, Groote Eylandt, Kalgoorlie, Karratha, Kununurra, Learmonth, Newman, Paraburdoo, Port Hedland and Tom Price.

BUS. Ansett Pioneer, Greyhound and Deluxe buses stop at Derby on their Perth/Darwin route.

CAR. On the Great Northern Highway 723km north of Perth and 1731km from Darwin.

TOURIST INFORMATION:
Derby Tourist Bureau, Clarendon Street, Ph (091) 91 1426.

ACCOMMODATION:
Derby Boab Inn, Loch St., 91 1044 – RO $64 double; Spinifex Hotel, Clarendon St, Ph 91 12133 – RO $50-55; Coronway Lodge Private Hotel, Cnr. Sutherland & Stanwell Sts., 91 1327 – RO $25-30; King Sound Hotel/Motel, Delewarr St., Ph 91 1166 – RO $80; Willare Bridge Roadhouse Private Hotel, Great Northern Hwy, Ph 91 4775 – RO $10ppn; Derby Caravan Park, Rowan St., Ph 91 1022 – sites $6.50 – overnite vans & cabins $15-30. The Y.M.C.A. has a hostel in Loch Street – $24 double and the Tourist Bureau has a list of Guest Houses.

POINTS OF INTEREST.
Derby is half surrounded by tidal marsh, and boab trees line the main street. Boab trees are ridiculously shaped trees resembling a bottle. 7km south of the town is an enormous hollow boab tree with a girth of 14m. According to legend, policemen bringing in prisioners used the tree as an overnight cell before the final trek into Derby. Nearby is Myalls Bore with one of the largest cattle troughs in the southern hemisphere. It is 120m long and 1.2m wide.

The Cultural Centre in Derby houses a regional museum, library and art gallery. It is built of Kimberley colourstone from Mt. Jowlaenga, south-west of Derby. Scenic flights over the Buccaneer Archipelago islands are available.

FACILITIES:
Almost all popular Australian sport is played in Derby – cricket, football, golf, tennis, basketball, squash, horse and car racing and shooting clubs have all been organised. Darts, lawn bowls and swimming are also very popular. The swimming pool is open all year round. The outdoor cinema screens films five nights a week.

FISHING:
The Fitzroy River is the best major barramundi water in the Kimberley. Barramundi live in both rivers and salt water. Live bait or a slow spinner is needed to catch them. The town jetty is a popular place for anglers. A fishing licence is required, which can be purchased from the Court House. Watch out for the hazards of the Kimberley coast: big tides, stone fish, sea snakes, sharks and crocodiles. Always use footwear when wading.

OUTLYING ATTRACTIONS:
BROOME, 222km south of Derby, is a colourful old pearling port. Its cosmopolitan population adds to the atmosphere of the town. Many of the old pearl divers were Japanese, Malays, Koepangers and Filipinos and each year their descendants remember their ancestors in the Festival of the Pearl which is held every September. Chinatown is a fascinating part of old

Broome.

And now to the Gorges.

There is a loop road from Derby via Kimberley Downs to WINDJANA Gorge on the Lennard River and TUNNEL CREEK NATIONAL PARK on Tunnel Creek which rejoins the Great Northern Highway south of Fitzroy Crossing. The Windjana Gorge, about 140km east of Derby, is also called Devils Pass. It is about 5kms long and the limestone cliffs vary between 30 and 90m in height. During the wet season the Lennard River becomes a raging torrent through the gorge, but dries out to form a string of picturesque pools in a spectacular setting. On the north-western cliff face near the carpark, is Pigeons Cave which was the hideout of the aboriginal outlaw of the Leopolds who terrorised police and settlers from 1894 to 1897. 30km east of Windjana Gorge is Tunnel Creek which has eroded a tunnel through the limestone 750m long and up to 12 m high, and 10m wide in places. It is possible to walk right along the tunnel but care should be taken and a strong torch should be used. Don't wear your best shoes as some of the floor is under water. Cave paintings can be seen near the north entrance to the tunnel. At the other end the aborigines used the black dolorite and basalt rocks to make stone axes.

19km north of Fitzroy Crossing is GEIKIE Gorge which was formed by the Fitzroy River cutting through the limestone formations of the Geike and Oscar Ranges. These ranges are part of a fossilised coral reef which is thought to be one of the best preserved fossil reefs in the world. There is a 3km walk along the west bank of the river to the west wall of the gorge. Most of the park is suitable for experienced bush-walkers only, as the terrain is rugged and inhospitable. Walkers must contact the Ranger before commencing their walks. Walking is not permitted on the east bank. The distinctive change in colour on the rock face of the gorge marks the high water level during the wet season. Between November and April there are twice daily cruises on the River. An Inland Fishing Licence is required if you intend to do any fishing. You can swim in the rock pools. There are toilets, showers and barbecues in the gorge and hotel accommodation at Fitzroy Crossing.

The Gibb River road to Wyndham passes many of the West Kimberley gorges. Many are accessible without four wheel drive. BARNETT Gorge, GALVAN'S Gorge, ADCOCK Gorge and MANNING Gorge should satisfy most travellers' desire to hike and explore the rugged rocks. At Mt. Barnett Station you can camp or stay in a caravan and visit the nearby Manning Gorge. 10kms upstream are some beautiful waterfalls. Lennard Gorge is only accessible by 4 wheel drive vehicles.

In the centre of the Kimberleys, on the edge of the Great Sandy Desert, is HALLS CREEK. The site of a goldrush back in the 1880's. To-day it is a cattle centre. There is another China Wall 6km north of Halls Creek but the major attraction in the area is 133km further on near Carranya Station, the Wolf Creek Meteorite Crater. It is 835m wide and 50m deep.

Amid the rugged land of the Kimberleys there is a rich green oasis, KUNUNURRA in the centre of the Ord River Irrigation scheme 101km south east of Wyndham. As a result of the scheme a wide variety of crops are now grown e.g. rice, sugar cane, peanuts, sorghum, fodder crops, sunflower and high protein beans, as well as fruit and vegetables. Lake Argyle which was formed as a result of daming the Ord River in the Carr Boyd Ranges, has many tranquil bays, inlets and islands, and the irrigation canals are a fascinating feature of the district. A panoramic view of the Ord Valley can be obtained from Kelly's Knob 2.4km from town. Hidden Valley, 3km away, has some interesting rock formations and birdlife. The CSIRO's Kimberley Research Station invites visitors to look around but has no guided tours. Among unusual rock formations on the way to the station are some aboriginal rock paintings. South of Kununurra is a huge diamond mine with a visitors' centre at the site. Kununurra has all the facilities you would expect and Ansett WA have flights from Perth, Darwin and Alice Springs. It's on the Perth/Darwin Ansett Pioneer, Deluxe and Greyhound route.

WYNDHAM, the port for the Eastern Kimberleys, is suffering from Kununurra's boom in popularity and doesn't have much to offer. Apart from being a dead end road, it is surrounded by mangroves and you can rarely even swim there.

N.B. Many roads in this area become impassible during the wet season (December to March). Even during the dry season it is best to first check with the Tourist Information Office or the Police, about the condition of the roads before venturing off on your own.

Also, keep a watchful eye open for salt water crocodiles in the north of the Kimberley region and don't forget the box jelly fish are prevalent in the ocean north of the Tropic of Capricorn during the summer months.

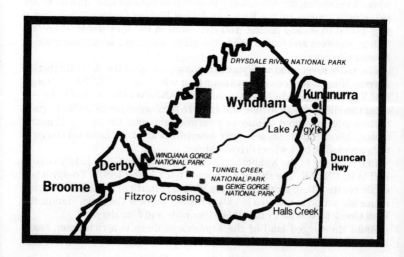

GERALDTON – Pop. 20,895

LOCATION:
On the coast 424km north of Perth. Geraldton is the key port and administration centre for the Mid-West. Ideally situated, a comfortable day's drive from Perth.

CLIMATE:
Average temperatures: January max. 31.6 deg.C, 18.7 deg.C.; July max. 19.4 deg.C, min. 9.2 deg.C; No. of days p.a. with temperature of over 30 deg.C – 75.8; No. of days with temperature over 40 deg.C – 8.3; average annual rainfall 475mm; wettest six months April-September.

CHARACTERISTICS:
It is known as 'Sun City' and is a mecca for sun-lovers because its boasts an average of 8 hours sunshine per day all year round.

FLORA:
Wattles dominate much of the plains and coastal dunes but among them are grevilleas and hakeas, one-sided bottlebrush, smokebush and honeymyrtles. Between July and October over 2,000 different varieties of windflowers are in bloom.

FAUNA:
Mainly rabbits, kangaroos, foxes, some possums, emus, galahs, black and white cockatoos, crows, grey doves and many varieties of small birds.

HOW TO GET THERE:
AIR. Avior Pty. Ltd., Skywest and Ansett WA have daily flights to/from Perth.
BUS. The Westrail bus departs East Perth Terminal six times weekly with alternate routes through Moora and Eneabba. On the Ansett Pioneer, Deluxe, and Greyhound Perth/Broome/Darwin route and Parlorcars route to Perth/Carnarvon/Coral Bay/Exmouth.
CAR. Via the Brand Highway through Eneabba or via the Midland Road through Moora and Mingenew.

TOURIST INFORMATION:
Geraldton Tourist Bureau, Civic Centre, Cathedral Ave., Ph (099) 21 3999 – open Mon-Fri 9am-5pm, Sat 9-12 & Sun & Public Holidays 10am-12.

ACCOMMODATION:
Batavia Motor Inn, Fitzgerald St., Ph 21 3500 – RO $52 double; Greenough Resort Motel, Greenough River Rd., Greenough, Ph 21 5888 – $48.50 double; Hacienda Motel, Curlacher St., Ph 21 2155 – RO $48 double; Geraldton Hotel, 19 Gregory St., Ph 21 3275 – RO $25 double; Palumbos Lodge Guest

House, 311 Marine Tce., Ph 21 4770 – BB \$24 double; Belair Gardens Caravan Park, Point Moore, Ph 21 1997; Youth Hostel, Francis St., Ph 21 2549 – \$5 single.

POINTS OF INTEREST:

From Waverley Heights Lookout (Brede Street) the all-embracing views are truly panoramic.

Fisherman's Wharf at the end of Marine Terrace is where many of the rock lobster boats are moored and where they unload their catches.

Tarcoola Art Gallery, 34 Bayview St., Mt. Tarcoola has a continuous exhibition of Australian landscapes by George Hodgkins – open daily 10am-5pm.

St. Francis Xavier's Cathedral is built in a Spanish colonial variation of baroque and took from 1915 until 1938 to complete. In contrast, the stark, modern architecture of the Cathedral of The Holy Cross is rather austere.

The Point Moore Lightouse is rather difficult to overlook due to its broad red and white stripes. It is 35m high, was built in 1878 and its light is visible for up to 26km.

For a bit of history head for the Geraldton Museum, where the fine displays tell the story of early Dutch wrecks off the Geraldton coast e.g. Batavia, Zeewyk and the Zuytdorp – bronze cannons and cannon balls etc on display – open Mon, Tues, Thurs & Fri 9am-5pm, Sat 9am-12 &2-5pm; Sun & Public Holidays 10am-12 & 2-5pm.

A visit to the Gem and Mineral Museum is a better way to learn about geology than reading a book about it. You will then be able to identify any gemstones which you may chance upon in your travels – open 9am-4pm daily.

Bluff Point Lighthouse Cottage in Chapman Road is the headquarters and library of the Geraldton Historical Society – open Thursdays 10am-4pm.

FISHING:

You can fish for tailer, mulloway and whiting at the Harbour Breakwater, Point Moore, Drummonds Cove and at Coronation Bay (where you might even catch a rock lobster on the reef at night) at Chapman River Mouth, 5kms north of Geraldton, either side of the railway bridge. For tailer, mulloway and herring, try your luck at Shipping Wharf. Abrolhos Islands offer magnificent boat fishing for schnapper, jewfish, mackerel, baldchin groper and trevally as well as reef species. Tourists are not permitted to land on the islands and there is no boat hire service at Geraldton.

FESTIVALS:

The Sunshine Festival is held in September.

FACILITIES:

Swimming, fishing, yachting, lawn bowls, tennis, cricket, squash, pistol-shooting, go-kart racing, horse racing, golf, roller skating and ten pin bowling.

OUTLYING ATTRACTIONS:

GREENOUGH is a quaint little village which has been preserved by the National Trust. Trees grotesquely bending over to the ground are an unusual sight along the flats. Pioneer Museum 19km south is open daily 10am-4pm except Thurs & Fri and has an excellent folk display.

KALABARRI on the coast, 590km north of Perth, has rapidly become a popular holiday resort. It has first-class facilities and is ideal for families. Fishing, swimming or scenic trips to the Murchison Gorges at the Z Bend or the Loop, and the coastal gorges to see further past Red Bluff to the south, all make this an interesting and rewarding holiday centre.

NORTHAMPTON 50km from Geraldton has many fine early buildings e.g. Chiverton House. Horrocks Beach 21km from Northampton on Three Mile Bay is a popular holiday resort with a reef running off the beach, which provides both safe swimming and good fishing. Port Gregory & Lynton are situated 47km from Northampton at the mouth of the Hutt River. The crumbling ruins of the old convict hiring station at Lynton bear mute testimony to the days when it was the convicts who were the miners, road builders and shepherds in the district.

There are aerial tours and boat charters available to view the fascinating Abrolhos Islands – the tours do not land. The beautiful but treacherous reef-surrounded islands have claimed many wrecks over the centuries. They are the main source of supply for the rock lobster fishing industry.

MINGENEW, MORAWA, MULLEWA. Every spring the countryside

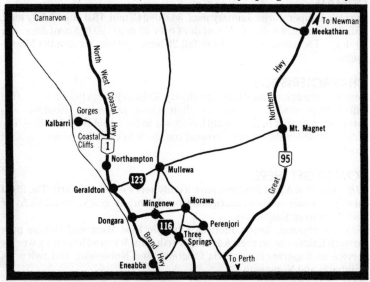

around these towns comes alive with the brilliant colours of wildflowers. Coach tours are arranged from Perth just to see these beautiful floral carpets.

COOMBERDALE Wildflower farm, 200km north of Perth, has a wide variety of cultivated wild flowers which are then dried – open Mon-Fri 9am-5pm.

NEW NORCIA, 132km north of Perth, has a Benedictine Monastery, Colleges, Art Gallery, Museum and Church with beautiful woodcarvings.

THREE SPRINGS, 341km north of Perth, has an open cut talc mine. The talc is transported to Japan and Europe, where it is used to make paper, paint and in the ceramic industry. Not far from the mine are the Pink Lakes.

CUE on the central Murchison Goldfields, 649km north-east of Perth on the Great Northern Highway was once called the 'Queen of the Murchison' when Tom Cue found gold in 1891. As the gold ran out it suffered a steady decline, but with the rise in the price of gold many tourists come here to try their luck.

KALGOORLIE/BOULDER – Pop. 19,848

LOCATION:
In the semi-desert area, 595km east of Perth.

CLIMATE:
Average temperatures: January max. 33.6 deg C, min. 18.3 deg. C; July max. 16.5 deg C, min. 4.8 deg. C; No. of days over 30 deg.C 99.6; No. of days over 40 deg.C 7.8; Average annual rainfall 263mm; wettest six months March-August.

CHARACTERISTICS:
Centre of the State's gold mining industry. Kalgoorlie and Boulder are often called twin towns because of their close proximity. Boulder was established so that miners could live closer to the Great Boulder Mine. The pubs in Boulder stayed open around the clock to cater for miners on shift work.

HOW TO GET THERE:
AIR. Ansett WA and Skywest have a daily service to/from Perth. The flight takes just under one hour and a taxi from the airport costs around $5. Avior also fly to/from Kalgoorlie.
BUS. Greyhound, Ansett Pioneer, Olympic East West and Deluxe pass through Kalgoorlie on their Adelaide/Perth runs. Westrail have a 3 x weekly service to Esperance, once via Calgoolie and Norseman, and twice via Kambarla and Norseman.
RAIL. The Prospector leaves Perth every day except Staturday, and the

Indian Pacific and Trans Australian also stop at Kalgoorlie.
CAR. From Perth via the Great Eastern Highway and Route 94; from Adelaide, Melbourne/Sydney across the Nullabor.

TOURIST INFORMATION:

Cnr. Hannan and Cassidy Sts., Kalgoorlie and Burt Street, Boulder, Ph (090) 21 1413 – Open Mon-Fri & Sat mornings.

ACCOMMODATION:

3 motels, 2 hotels/motels, 10 hotels, 2 private hotels and 4 caravan parks. A few names and addresses: Midas Motel, 409 Hannan St., Ph 21 3088 – RO $65-75 double; The Old Australia Private Hotel, Cnr. Hannan & Martiana Sts., Ph 21 1320 – RO $45 double; York Hotel, 259 Hannan St., Ph 21 2337 – B&B $44 double; Goldminer Caravan Park, Ph 21 3713 – sites $6 – on site vans and chalets $22 double. No youth hostel.

EATING OUT:

There's a wide variety of eating places in Kalgoorlie/Boulder from fully-licensed restaurants, Hotel dining rooms, steak houses to simple cafes, as well as a variety of take aways e.g. Nola's Snack Bar, top end of Hannan St.

POINTS OF INTEREST:

The 'Golden Mile'. You can ride the 'Rattler' (operated by the Kalgoorlie-Boulder Loop Line Preservation Group) around the Golden Mile Mon-Sat 11am and Sundays at 1.30pm & 3pm. The area called the Golden Mile is in fact 2 miles long and a third of a mile wide. There is also a Golden Mile Scenic Drive if you don't want to ride the 'Rattler'.

The Mt. Charlotte Reservoir holds the town's permanent water supply, which is piped in the 563km from a weir at Mundaring in the Darling Range near Perth. The pipeline was first turned on in 1903 and the town went wild. At the official banquet Sir George Reid remarked that 'he had never heard so much talk about water, and seen so little of it consumed'.

As a memorial to the first discoverer of gold in Kalgoorlie, Paddy Hannan, a statue/drinking fountain was erected in Hannan Street. A kurrajong tree marks the place where the first gold was discovered.

The Lions Club Lookout close to the Hainault Gold Mine is a fine vantage point, and you get at 360 deg. view of the surrounding countryside from 60m up.

The Kalgoorlie Town Hall was built in 1903 and has a particularly fine stamped metal ceiling and Victorian style cast seats on the balcony. It also houses the Art Museum on the first floor – open Mon-Fri 9am-4pm.

The Boulder Town Hall is a stately stone building built in 1908 with a distinctive clock tower. The Boulder Block. It's hard to imagine that this half hectare block housed a thriving business centre with 6 hotels which served liquor around the clock. The Golden Mile Museum is housed in the British Arms Hotel in Outridge Terrace – open daily – tours 10.30am to 4.30pm.

The Hainault Mine has been described as one of Australia's most unusual tourist attractions as it provides a unique change for women and children to go underground in a real gold mine in safety – open daily – tours at 10.30am, 1.00pm, 2.30pm and 3.45pm.

At the Eastern Goldfields Historical Society Museum (Boulder City Railway Station) you can see the grace and charm of a past era together with reminders of the hardships of early pioneering life – open daily from 10-12.30pm and 1.30pm-4pm except Thursday.

Hammond Park is a flora and fauna reserve with a lake, rustic bridge and miniature castle. Kangarooos and emus roam free within the park.

If you want to try your luck at fossicking, then first obtain a Miner's Right from the Mines Department, Brookham Street.

FESTIVALS:
The Community Fair is held each March in the Cruickshank Sports Arena, and the social event of the year is the Kalgoorlie Racing Round held each September.

FACILITIES:
Swimming in the Lord Forrest Pool; motor racing at the motorsport complex near the airport; lawn bowls at the Bowling Club, Maritana & Forrest Sts.; gliding, golf, tennis and water polo are also catered for. Car Hire – Herty, Budget, Avis and Letz. Johnston Bikes hire out bicycles for $8 per day. There is a regular bus service Kalgoorlie and Boulder.

FLORA:
There are 60 species of eucalyptus growing in the region including many flowering varieties. Look out for the pale grey-green leaves of the famous sandalwood tree as its not common. The showiest of the wildflowers is the dramatic red and black Stuart desert pea. You will also see hakeas, callistermons, the brilliant red bottle brush, the hop bush and native hibiscus. In spring the fluffy, yellow blossoms of the wattle add gay touches to the landscape.

FAUNA:
There are rabbits, foxes and dingoes as well as kangaroos and emus. If you're lucky you might catch a glimpse of a large racehorse goanna, looking like a fairytale dragon! Several varieties of the eagle family frequent the region and a multitude of parrots and cockatoos. There are also crested pigeons, crows, mallee fowl and the Australian bustard. If you hear a particularly melodious bird song it is probably the pied butcher bird.

OUTLYING ATTRACTIONS:
KAMBALDA 56km south on Lake Lefroy. A few years ago nickel was discovered in Kambalda and the town gained a new lease of life. The old Red Hill Westralia Gold Mine remains standing as a monument to the past. A panoramic view of the whole area including the salt lake, can be obtained

from Red Hill Lookout. Hostess-conducted tours in your own car can be arranged through the Tourist Bureau, Salmon Gums Rd., Kambalda West, Ph 27 2446, at a cost of $10. These tours take in 'hard hat' areas which are normally off limits to tourists. For some thing different, try land yachting on Lake Lefroy.

NORSEMAN, which is referred to as the Eastern Gate to the Western State, is the start or finish of the Eyre Highway. Norseman has been producing gold since 1892 and many of the buildings in the main street are built from timber brought from Esperance by camel train in the early days. Dominating the town is what appears at first glance, to be one of the pyramids – it is in fact, an immense tailings dump. If you are feeling like stretching your legs after a long trip in the car, then the climb to the summit of Peak Charles may be just what you need. The easiest route to the top is marked by posts. Be sure to carry drinks as the climbs takes approximatley three hours up and back. There is also a scenic drive around the town.

COOLGARDIE 40km west of Kalgoorlie. There are a series of 150 markers placed around the town giving a well documented account of Coolgardie's history. Each group of markers describe the immediate site as it was when Coolgardie was the capital of the goldfield, and is usually accompanied by photographs from that period.

The Goldfields Exhibition in Bayley St. is the largest and most comprehensive prospecting museum in WA – open 8.30am-4.30pm.

The Railway Station Museum in Woodward St has an interesting museum of transport – open daily from 9am-6pm. The Bottle & Curio Museum is above the Tourist Bureau – open 8.30am-4.30pm.

The Warden Finnerty's Residence is owned by the National Trust – open daily except Thursdays.

The Coolgardie Animal and Bird Park is 3/4km west of town and has camels, kangaroos etc.

There is a wide variety of accommodation available in Coolgardie including a Youth Hostel.

30km south are the Gnarlbine Rocks which played an important part in the opening up of the goldfields, as they were one of the few watering points known to the early prospectors. A further 18km south are the much larger and higher Queen Victoria Rocks well-known for their sculptured shapes.

WAVE ROCK. To visit Wave Rock near Hyden, turn off the Great Eastern Highway at Merredin. The journey south will take you through the Wheatlands. Under the rich soil lies an ancient granite bed which, here and there, breaks through to the surface. Years of wind, rain and sun have weathered the rocks giving them fascinating shapes and colours. There are several unusual shaped rocks in the district as well as aboriginal paintings. The best known of the rocks is Wave Rock which stands like a frozen ocean wave about to break on the ground below.

PERTH – Pop. 1,000,000
(State Total 1,500,000)

LOCATION:
Perth, the State capital, lies on the Swan River near the south-west coast of Western Australia.

CLIMATE:
Perth has a Mediterranean climate with a short mild winter and a long dry summer. It has the reputation of being Australia's sunniest capital. Average temperatures – January – max 29 deg. C min 17 deg. C; July max 17 deg. C. min 9 deg. C. Summer temperatures may exceed 38 deg. C for short periods. Average annual rainfall 893mm. Wettest months May to August.

CHARACTERISTICS:
Perth is one of Australia's most progressive and attractive capital cities. This sunny, breezy, easy-going city is young and full of fun.

HOW TO GET THERE:
AIR. International services by Qantas and other International airlines. Daily domestic flights by Ansett and Australian Airlines to and from other State Capitals, and East-West Airlines to Sydney via Ayers Rock. Regular services between Perth and Darwin on Ansett WA and Australian Airlines. The airport is 11km from the city centre. Regular bus service or taxis. There is also a good service between the domestic and the new international terminal. Skybus Airport Transfers, Tel. 274 6677, meet all incoming international and domestic flights. Transfer time is approx. 25 mins – cost $3.50. Metropolitan Passenger Transport Trust's Route No. 338 operates between the airport and the city centre every 40-50 mins during the day – cost $1 and transfer time is approx. 35mins. Taxis are readily available and transfer time is 20-25min – cost aprox. $10. Taxi drivers do not expect tips – just round of the fare to the nearest 10 cents.
BUS. Ansett, Deluxe, Greyhound and Across Australia and Olympic and VIP operate services to other state capitals and Ansett, Deluxe and Greyhound have services to other towns in WA.
RAIL. The famous Indian-Pacific train operates between Sydney and Perth. The Trans-Australian operates to Adelaide with connections to Melbourne.
CAR. You can drive across the Nullarbor Plain from the eastern States, or have your car transported across on the train.

CAR RENTAL:
All the big agencies (Hertz, Avis, Budget & Thrifty) have depots here, as well as numerous small ones. It pays to shop around as the prices vary considerably. Campervans and 4 wheel drive vehicles are also available.

CHAUFFEUR CARS:

Limousine services are available from the airport to the city – cost $30-$45 depending upon time and destination – Astra, Ph 328 6939; Deluxe, Ph 325 2817; Budget, Ph 339 8811; Barron, Ph 271 030.

TAXIS:

They are fast convenient and readily available. Charges: $1.20 Flagfall and 55c per km; surcharge weeknights. Main companies: Black & White, Ph 328 8288, Green & Gold, Ph 328 3455, Swan, Ph 322 0111.

PUBLIC TRANSPORT:

Free clipper buses circle the city centre running every 10 mins, Mon-Fri 7.30am to 5.30 pm and Sat 9am-11.30 am from marked stops. Red, Blue and Green Clipper buses (also free) operate other city routes. Check with one of the MTT (Metropolitan Passenger Transport Trust) Offices, 125 St. Georges Terrace, Perth, Town Hall Fremantle, or the Central Bus Station, Perth or by phoning 325 8511. Ferries operate daily 6.45am to 7.15pm from Barrack St. Jetty to Mends St., South Perth (Zoo) – 80 cents one way. MTT buses cover the central business district and suburbs, and have designated departure points in the city, but elsewhere can be hailed at signposted stops. Pay the bus driver, tickets are valid for 2 hours and can be used on MTT trains and ferries with reduced fares on weekend and public holidays. Suburban trains operate from Perth to Fremantle, Midland and Armadale from 5.30am-1am weekdays with a reduced timetable on weekends. Tickets may be purchased at major stations or on trains, and can be used for MTT bus and ferry travel within the time limit of the ticket. Suburban and Bunbury trains leave from the City Station, Wellington Street. Interstate trains and country buses depart from Perth Railway Terminal, East Perth. Tourist Clipper Trips operate on Sundays at 10.30am and 2.14pm visiting many of Perth's beauty spots. Fares adults $4 – book at the MTT offices. Multi-Rider tickets provide discounted ten-ride tickets for unlimited travel on bus, train and ferry services. A special $3.00 all day ticket can be purchased individually or for family groups during the Summer School Holidays. Perth has a network of flat cycleways extending around Perth and the Swan River for easy riding and you can hire cycles.

TOURIST INFORMATION:

WA Travel Centre, 772 Hay St., Perth, Ph 322 2999 and Cnr. High & Henry Sts., Fremantle, Ph 430 5555. The Royal Automobile Club of WA, 228 Adelaide Terrace, Perth, offer maps and touring advice to members of affiliated interstate and overseas Motoring Clubs.

TIME ZONE:

Perth is one and half hours behind Adelaide and 2 hours behind Sydney & Melbourne Standard Time. The Eastern states have Summer Time from October to March and then Perth is 3 hours behind.

ACCOMMODATION:

Perth has a range of excellent hotels, motels and other accommodation. The following prices are a guide only: Premier class singles range from $75 to $115 and doubles from $100-145; Moderate motels and apartments from $65 single and doubles from $40-90; while budget style ranges from $20 single and $30 double. The Travel Centres have accommodation listings including budget and self-catering establishments, plus Homestay and Farm accommodation. Homestay of WA, Lot 40, Union St., Carmel, Ph 293 5347 also handles homestays.

A few names and addresses: Premier – Ansett International, 10 Irwin St., Ph 325 0481; Parmelia Hilton, Mill St., Ph 322 3622.

Moderate: Kings Ambassador Perth, 517 Hay Street, Ph 325 6555; Chateau Commodore, Cnr. Victoria Ave & Hay St., Ph 325 0461; Murray Lodge, 718 Murray Street, West Perth, Ph 321 7441; Marracoonda Motel, 373 Great Eastern Hwy, Redcliffe, Ph 277 7777.

Budget: Criterion, Hotel, 560 Hay St., Ph 324 5155; CWA House, 1174 Hay St., Ph 321 6081; YMCA/WYCA, Jewell House, 180 Goderich St., Ph 325 8488. Self Catering: City Waters Lodge, 118 Terrace Rd., Ph 325 5020; Riverview Apts, 42 Mount St., Ph 321 8963. Youth Hostels: 60-62 Newcastle St., Perth, Ph 328 1135; 46-48 Francis St., Perth, Ph 328 7794; 96 Hampton Rd., Fremantle, Ph 335 3467 – Cost $5 ppn.

EATING OUT:

Perth has a remarkable variety of restaurants and cuisines. The choice runs from simple coffee shops and bistros to luxury-class restaurants. Many inexpensive eating places are found at Northbridge, close to the city. Some medium to high priced restaurants: Bretts, 44 Parliament Place, West Perth, Ph 322 2533; There is a chain of 5 Miss Maud Swedish Restaurants which are quite good, one of them is at 97 Murray St., Ph 325 3900; for good Indian food try the Shoba Indian, 434 William St., Ph 328 5449; you can eat Japanese at the Jana, Mill St., Ph 322 7098; George's by the Terrace, 2 Howard St., Perth, Ph 3222 7577; Golden Eagle Chinese, 130 James St., Perth, Ph 328 5420; The Oyster Beds, 26 Riverside Rd., East Fremantle, Ph 339 1611. For vegetarian or health food try one of the Magic Apple restaurants.

POINTS OF INTEREST:

Start your tour of Perth with a visit to a lookout. The panoramic view will put everything into perspective – the city, river, suburban areas, ocean and the Darling Ranges. Some suggestions: Lions Lookout on the top of the PWD Building, Cnr. Kings Park Rd & Havelock St. – open Mon-Fri 9am-4.30pm and Sept-Jan Sun 9am-4pm – cost 50c. Kings Park's Mt. Eliza lookout and the DNA Lookout Tower provide magnificient views of the city – open at all times. Escorted walking tours of the city are available – contact the WA Tourist Centre. The National Trust of WA, 139 St. Georges Tce., Ph 321 6088 have brochures with several self-guided tours of Perth & Fremantle.

The most important sights: The Town Hall, Cnr. Hay & Barrack Sts. was built by convict labour in the style of an English Jacobean market hall. Barracks Archway, St. Georges Terrace in front of Parliament House is all that is left of the headquarters of the soldier settlers of the enrolled Pension Forces in the 1860's. Tours of Parliament House are conducted Monday-Friday 11.15am and 3.15pm when Parliament is not sitting, and Monday and Friday for 10-15min. when Parliament is in session. Government House in St. Georges Terrace opposite Pier St is the official residence of the Govenor of WA. The Old Courthouse, Stirling Gardens, St. Georges Terrace is Perth's oldest surviving public building. It is built in Georgian style and now serves as offices for the Law Society – open for inspection Tues 9.30am-12.30pm. London Court, between Hay Street and St. Georges Terrace is a Tudor style shopping arcade with its wrought ironwork, hanging signs and other decorations. At each end there are statues, one of Sir Walter Raleigh and the other is of Dick Wittington. St. George and the Dragon appear each quarter of an hour above the clock in St. Georges Terrace. Above the clock face at the Hay Street Mall end, 4 knights on horseback joust above the clock face providing a touch of Olde England in the streets of Perth. Old Perth Boys' School, St. Georges Terrace opposite King St. is the headquarters of the WA National Trust – open Mon-Fri 10am-3pm – Tel. 321 6088. The Cloisters opposite Mill St., in St. Georges Terrace is noted for its attractive brickwork. The Old Gaol in Francis Street is now a museum complex – open Mon-Thurs 10.30am-5pm; Fri-Sun 1pm-5pm; public holidays 9.30am-5pm, Ph. 328 4411. The Old Mill at Narrows Bridge, South Perth, is a restored flour mill built in 1835 – open 1-5pm Sun, Mon, Wed & Thurs and Sats 1-4pm. The Treasury Building, Cnr. Barrack St and St. Georges Terrace is a fine example of Colonial architecture. The Palace Hotel, Cnr. St. Georges Tce & William St. represents the grandeur of the gold-boom era. The Perth Concert Hall, St. Georges Terrace is open for inspection Mon-Sat when not in use. The Perth Entertainment Centre, Wellington Street has tours Mon-Fri at 3pm. The State Reference Library, 40 James St. is open Mon and Fri 9am-5.330pm; Tues, Wed & Thurs 9am-9.45pm; Sat & Sun 2-5.30pm. The Western Australian Art Gallery, James St has traditional and modern exhibitions in a new building – open 10am-5pm daily, Ph 328 7233.

The Western Australian Museum in Francis Street has comprehensive displays, collection of Aboriginal artefacts, vintage cars and a 25m Blue Whale skeleton – open Mon-Thurs 10.30-5pm, Fri-Sun 1-5pm, Ph 3284411. The Post and Telecom Museum, Cnr. Murray and Pier Streets has exhibitions of antique telephones, stamps, morse equipment etc. – open Mon-Fri 10am-3pm, Ph 420 7011. The Aboriginal Traditional Art Gallery at 242 St. Georges Terrace, has some very interesting works of art. It is a non-profit organisation. Kings Park off Kings Park Road, West Perth is one of Perth's great assets as it has delightful views of city and river, gardens, walking tracks and a lookout tower. The 12ha of botanic gardens feature famous WA wildflowers in spring. In the Supreme Court Gardens, Cnr. St. Georges Terrace & Barrack St, is the Music Shell the venue for outdoor summer concerts.

Historic Fremantle: The Fremantle Museum and Arts Centre, Fionnerty Street has an excellent display of the State's maritime history – open Mon-Thurs 10.30am-5pm, Fri-Sun 1pm-5pm, public holidays 9.30am-5pm, Ph 335 8211. The Fremantle Markets, Cnr. South Terrace and Henderson St sell a full range of produce and craft items. The Round House in High Street dates back to 1831 and was originally a gaol – open Wed & Thurs 11am-4pm, Fri 10.30am-4.30pm, Sat & Sun 10.30am-12.30pm, 1.30pm-4.30pm, Ph 335 6422. The America's Cup Museum is in the Rolly Tasker Building, 43 Swan Street – open 9.30am-5pm daly – It has a complete set of models of yachts which have competed in the America's Cup from 1851-1983. The Bannnister Street Workshops are an old warehouse which has been converted into studios and shops for local artists and crafstmen – open Tues-Sat 10am-4.30pm and Sun 1-5pm, Ph 335 9165.

Freemantle Town Hall, Cnr. High and Adelaide Streets is a grand late Victorian building opened in 1887. The massive tower is richly ornamented and features the WA emblem, the black swan, in bas-relief. The Zoo in Labouchere Road, South Perth 4km south of the city has exotic birds and animals in lush bushland settings – open daily 10am-5pm .

FESTIVALS:

The Festival of Perth is held in Jan/February or February/March and has an extensive programme of music, theatre, dance, film, visual arts and outdoor activities. The Perth Cup, Perth's premier horse race, is held each New Year's Day. Western Australia Week is held each June to celebrate Foundation Day. The Perth Royal Show is an 8 day agricultural fair, exhibitions, animals, entertainment held in September/October.

FACILITIES:

Ten-pin bowling, lawn bowls, tennis, para-sailing, horse riding and water skiing can be enjoyed near the city as well as swimming and surfing, windsurfing and yachting. There are 6 private and 8 public golf clubs within easy reach of Perth. There are extensive cycling tracks. Diving and deepsea fishing are also possible. Of course, spectator sports such as cricket, Australian Rules Football, soccer, basketball, tennis, motor racing, horse racing, trotting and show jumping are also popular. Day Cruises on the Swan are well catered for.

OUTLYING ATTRACTIONS:

ROTTNEST ISLAND or Rotto, as the locals call it, is a terrific place to go for a relaxing day. It is 18km from the mainland and can be reached by ferry or by air. There are few motor cars and no traffic lights, and the only means of transport, apart from walking, is by bicycle. The island got its name from the small marsuipal animals which inhabit it. They were mistakenly thought to be rats. They are friendly inoffensive animals and some of them will feed from your hand.

HAVERSHAM Wildlife Park and Zoo, Cnr. Arthur and Cranleigh Rds., West Swan 19km NE, has a collection of rare marsupials, exotic birds and animals – open daily 10am-5pm.

PERRY LAKES off Oceanic Drive, Floreat Park have an abundance of water fowl and birdlife – grassed parklands shaded by native trees and an adventure playground. Bikes are available for hire.

Adventure World, Forest Road, BIBRA LAKE is a magical make-believe world for both children and adults alike, with a large range of attractions for everyone. Ascot Water Playground, 97 Mathieson Rd., Redcliffe has a series of water slides and pools where children can play.

Botanic Golf, Burns Beach Rd., WANNEROO is an 18 hole mini golf course meandering through waterfalls, ornamental pools, exotic gardens and fountains – open Tues-Sat 10am until evening day 1.30pm-10pm.

The Aviation Museum, Bull Creek Drive, Bull Creek has an excellent collection of historic aircraft, aero engines etc. – open Tues, Thurs, Sat & Sun 11am-4pm, Ph 332 4444.

The Museum of Childhood, Hamersley Road, Subiaco has a unique collection of the childhood heritage of Australia – dolls, children's embroidery and script work – open Mon-Sat 10am-3pm and Sun 2-5pm, Ph 381 1103.

The Rail Transport Museum, Railway Parade, Bassendean is a great museum for train enthusiasts – open Sun & public holidays 1-5pm, Ph 277 5278

The Wireless Hill Park and Telecom Museum, Almondbury Road, Ardross, is an early wireless station overlooking Melville Water – open Sat & Sun 2-5pm, Ph 364 1558.

Atlantis Marine Park off Sovereign Drive, Yanchep Sun City, has performing seals, sea lions and dolphins – open 10am-4.30pm daily.

The DARLING RANGE is a popular recreation area within easy reach of Perth. It runs north-south, and the foothills are about 20km from the city. It contains several National Parks:

AVON VALLEY is 50km north east of the city. Hiking is popular and camping is possible. Access: From Perth by road via Midland and Bailup takes about one and a half hours.

WALYUNGA in the upper reaches of the Swan River is about 40km north east, and has swimming and boating facilities. Access: From Perth by road via Midland takes about one and half hours.

JOHN FORREST is a popular recreational area about 26km from Perth with good walking tracks, scenic views, open eucalypt forest, spring wild-flowers. Access: Public transport passes the park boundary. The trip by car via Midland takes about 45mins.

SERPENTINE, 52km south-east, has good walking tracks along Serpentine River above the waterfall. Access: Public transport passes park boundary. From Perth by car via South Western Hwy takes about one and half hours.

YANCHEP, 52km north of Perth, is popular with tourists. It has Limestone Caves (guided tours), spring wildflowers, a lake, koala colony, and birdlife.

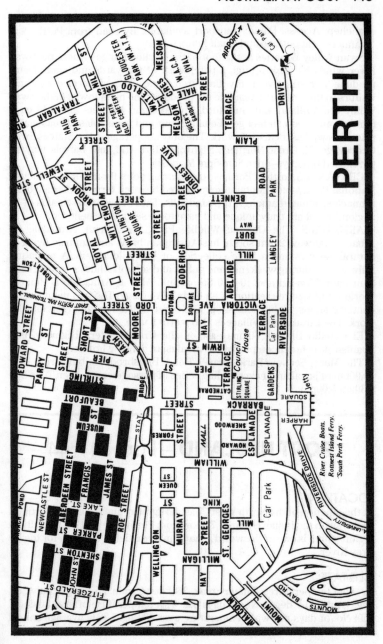

PERTH

Hotel accommodation and limited camping facilities are available at Yanchep. Access: Public transport available. By road from Perth via Wanneroo (about one and a half hours).

Swan Valley Wineries at the foot of the Darling Ranges where the Swan River winds its way through a patchwork of vineyards and small farms produce a distinctive fruity flavoured wine. The vignerons welcome visitors to their cellars to sample the produce. The main towns in the Swan Valley are Midland and Guildford. The Midland Markets are held each Sunday, and you can buy good quality fruit and vegetables at reasonable prices, as well as local craft work. The only cooperage in the State is Swan Cooperage, 52 Great Northern Highway, Hern Hill, and barrels may be purchased directly – open 8am-5pm Mon-Sat.

CERVANTES north of Perth is your starting point for a tour of Nambung National Park, which contains some incredible rock formations, called the Pinnacles, situated amongst the sand hills. These fossilised remains of an ancient forest are truly unique and have to be seen to be believed.

ARMADALE. The Cohunu Wildlife Park, Mills Road, Armadale off Albany Highway, 20km south, has Australian birds and animals living in natural settings and a large collection of WA wildflowers. A miniature railway runs during weekends and public and school holidays – open 10am-5pm daily Mon-Fri and 10-5.30 Sat & Sun. Also at Armadale is Pioneer World a full size re-creation of an early WA village. The two main streets contains shops, blacksmith shop, and other tradesmen and craftsmen at work. The Elizabethan Village is also worth a visit.

El Caballo Blanco, 60kms east on the Great Eastern Highway, is a Spanish style hotel complex with Andalusian dancing horses.

The Maze, Sequoia Park, Neaves Road, Bullsbrook, is built from over 10,000m of jarrah in a never-ending series of passageways – open Tues-Sun 9.30am-5.00pm.

PORT HEDLAND – Pop. 11,144

LOCATION:
At the junction of the North West Coastal Highway and the Great Northern Highway on the Indian Ocean, 1,728km from Perth. The port for the Pilbara region which is one of the world's major mineral fields, and also for the De Grey River.

CLIMATE:
Average temperatures: January max. 36.2 deg.C, min. 25.1 deg.C; July 26.4 deg.C, min. 11.7 deg.C; No. of days p.a. with temperature of over 30 deg.C 259; No. of days p.a. with temperature over 40 deg.C 28.6; average annual rainfall 304mm; wettest six months January-June.

CHARACTERISTICS:
Built on a small island accessible by a 3km causeway. It's Western Australia's fastest growing town. The iron ore mined at Mt. Newman and Mt. Goldsworth is shipped through here, as well as salt which is farmed nearby. The piles of salt awaiting export are an impressive sight.

HOW TO GET THERE:
AIR. Ansett WA & Australian Airlines fly from Perth, and Darwin. Taxis from the airport cost around $15.
BUS. Ansett Pioneer, Deluxe and Greyhound stop at Port Hedland on the Perth/Darwin run. There are also services to Broome and Derby. The trip from Perth takes approx. 24 hours and from Darwin 34 hours.
CAR. Either along the Great Northern Highway or the North West Coastal Highway.

TOURIST INFORMATION:
Port Hedland Tourist Bureau, 13 Wedge St., Ph (091) 73 1650 – open Mon-Fri 9am-5pm, Sat 9am-11am.

ACCOMMODATION:
There's not a lot of choice here. A few names and addresses: The Esplanade Hotel, Anderson St., Ph 73 1798 – RO $34 double; The Hedland Hotel, Cnr Lukis & McGregor Sts., Ph 73 1511 – RO $72-82 double; The Pier Hotel, The Esplanade, Ph 73 1488 – B&B $54 double; Hostels: 3A Kingsmill St. – $6 single; 20 Richardson St., Ph 73 2198 – $5 single. South Hedland Caravan Park, Hamilton Rd., South Hedland, Ph 72 1197 – sites $7 – on site vans $28 double.

EATING OUT:
The Pier and Esplanade Hotels offer counter meals at lunchtime, as does the Hedland Hotel and it also has counter meals on Friday and Saturday nights until 8pm. There are a few shops selling take-away food.

POINTS OF INTEREST:
The Port where the world's largest ore carriers can be seen loading iron ore. These ore carriers are so big that the crew move around the decks on scooters! The engines which bring the ore are also an awesome sight. The fishing is excellent along the Pilbara coast. Mon-Fri there is a daily bus tour of the Mt. Newman Mining Company. The buses leave from the main gate in Wilson Street – details available at the Tourist Office. The Royal Flying Doctor Base in Richardson Street is the headquarters for the Pilbara – open for public inspection.

FESTIVALS:
The Spinifex Spree and the Pilbara Show.

FACILITIES:
Car hire, fishing and swimming, in the pool in McGregor St or the Aquatic

Centre South Hedland preferably, as there are a number of 'nasties' in the sea around here. Race Meetings are held at the Sports Ground Complex which also caters for football, hockey, softball, cricket, soccer and tennis. There is a 9 hole golf course, and a speedway. Horses may be hired at Cooke Point.

OUTLYING ATTRACTIONS:

DAMPIER on the coast 232km south of Port Hedland, is the port for Mt. Tom Price and Paraburdoo. The port handles ships up to 230,000 tons, and there are also ore treatment works. Like at Port Hedland, you will see mountains of salt.

KARRATHA, just north of Dampier, is one of the youngest and fastest growing towns of the Pilbara. It came into being in the 1960's because of the lack of further available land in Dampier. The growth gained further momentum when the Woodside Petroleum North West Shelf Gas Project development commenced.

EXMOUTH is another young town. It was founded in 1967 as a support town for the U.S. Naval Communications Base. Tours of the base can be arranged through the Exmouth Tourist Bureau on week days only. A good view of the base can be obtained from Lighthouse Drive, which climbs steeply to the tip of the Cape Range at Vlaming Head. The range is a national park containing caves with aboriginal paintings, and fossils are often found in the rugged canyons and gorges. Exmouth is known as the game fishing capital of the West. In its waters are found all three types of marlin. There are several excellent charter boat operators. Offshore, on the west coast of the Cape, is Ningaloo Reef, WA's most accessible coral reef. It is a haven for diving, fishing, snorkeling and shell collecting.

CARNARVON is almost as famous for its climate as it is for its bananas. It averages 323 days of sunshine per year. The winters are glorious and although February and March can be very hot, the town is one of the coolest in the North West. It is surrounded by luxuriant plantations of bananas and other tropical fruits, all grown with the aid of water pumped from the sand of the Gascoyne River. 70km north are the Blowholes where water is sometimes forced through the holes to a height of 20m. The Prawning Factory at the mouth of the Gascoyne River on Babbage Island, processes both prawns and scallops, and a tour can be arranged through the Tourist Office. 10km north of the town is Bibbawarra Bore where hot artesian water bubbles at 70 deg. C. O.T.C's Satellite Earth Station on the Brown Range can be visited.

THE PILBARA.

It is an eight hour trip from Port Hedland to NEWMAN which has a population of around 5,000. It is solely a mining town. The Mt. Newman Company has guided tours of its operations, several times daily in winter and at 1pm only in summer. Similar mining activities are also carried out at TOM PRICE and PARABURDOO.

MARBLE BAR (Pop 350) is best known for its reputation as 'Australia's hottest town'. In summer it has consistently high temperatures and the temperature often climbs over 38 deg.C for days on end. The record is 160 consecutive days recorded in 1923-4. The winter months offer the visitors mild daytime temperatures and cool nights. The town gets its name from the unique bar of 'marble' that crosses the Coongan River 5km from the town. Actually it's not marble, it's jasper. Marble Bar is an old mining town, the Old Commet Mine is still operating and the local battery still crushes gold quartz.

Lastly, we come to the main tourist attraction of the Pilbara, WITTENOOM (Pop. 250). It is at the northern end of the Hamersley Range National Park, and the most famous of the Pilbara Gorges, Wittenoom, is 13km south of the town past the old asbestos mines and a number of smaller gorges. The gorges, like others in central Australia, are spectacular. They have sheer rocky walls in which can be seen a variety of colours. Yampire Gorge 24km down the Newman road has blue veins of asbestos. From the Joffre Falls you have a superb view of the 32km long Wittenoom Gorge. There is a 13km walking track circuit which starts from the Asbestos Mine 13km from the town. Contact the Wittenoom Tourist Bureau on Second Avenue for details. There is one motel and one caravan park in Wittenoom and camping is permitted in the National Park.

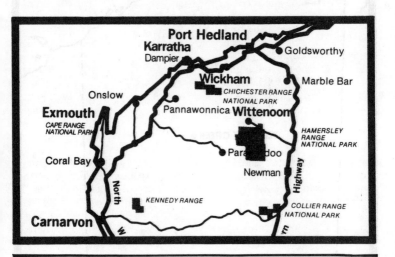

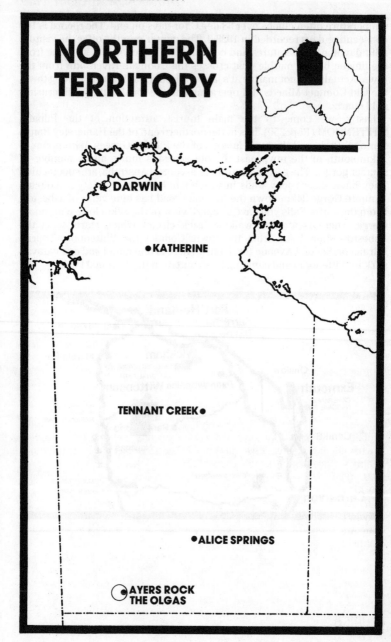

NORTHERN TERRITORY

DARWIN

KATHERINE

TENNANT CREEK

ALICE SPRINGS

AYERS ROCK
THE OLGAS

ALICE SPRINGS – Pop. 20,000

LOCATION:
In the heart of the McDonnell Ranges in the centre of Australia.

CLIMATE:
Average temperatures: January max. 35.9 deg. C, min. 21.1 deg. C; July max. 19.8 deg. C, min. 4.1 deg. C; maximum summer temperatures reach up 42 deg. C but the humidity is always low. 610m above sea level.

CHARACTERISTICS:
The Northern Territory's most famous town, is located in what is almost the geographic centre of this vast continent. The Alice is a place to visit in its own right, but equally, it becomes your base as you explore the wonders of 'The Centre'. It is surrounded by miles and miles of empty plains.

HOW TO GET THERE:
AIR. Ansett and Australian Airlines have direct flights to/from Sydney, Melbourne, Adelaide, Perth, Brisbane, Darwin, Cairns, Mt. Isa and Townsville. Ansett NT fly to/from Tennant Creek, Katherine and Ayres Rock. Ansett also fly to Canberra. Tilair also fly to/from Katherine and Tennant Creek. Ansett WA fly to/from Kunnunura. East West fly to Ayres Rock (Yulara) from Perth and Sydney. Air NSW also fly to/from Yulara to Broken Hill and Sydney. Yulara is 6km from the airport and Alice Springs airport is 15km south of the town and costs about $14 by taxi. There is also an airport shuttle bus which meets flights and takes passengers around to all city accommodation for $4 or $5 return, Ph 52 3843.
BUS. Ansett Pioneer and Greyhound have daily services from Darwin, Adelaide and Mt. Isa/Townsville. Deluxe has services to Darwin, Townsville and Brisbane five days per week. Briscoes have a three times weekly service from Adelaide to Alice Springs.
RAIL. The Ghan runs between Adelaide and Alice Springs (24 hours) and The Alice runs between Sydney and The Alice via Adelaide (48 hours).
CAR. Alice Springs is a long way from everywhere. It's 1525km from Darwin and 1180km from Mt. Isa over sealed roads. The Stuart Highway from Adelaide is sealed to after Coober Pedy but there are still about 270km of dirt between there and the border, and these sections can be cut during rain. It is best to check with the police or the Automobile Association at the town before you come to these sections. The total distance Adelaide/Alice Springs is 1983km. The 'Ghan' offers a motor-rail service to passengers who wish to take their car with them to 'The Centre'.

TOURIST INFORMATION:
51 Todd Street, Alice Springs, Ph (089) 52 1299.

ACCOMMODATION:

A wide variety of accommodation is available from luxury hotels to youth hostels. Contact the Tourist Bureau for a full list.

Some names and addresses: The Sheraton Alice Springs, Barrett Drive, Ph 52 5066 – RO $98 double; The Oasis Motel Gap Road, Ph, 52 1444 – RO $48-62 double; The Todd Tavern Lisenced Hotel, Todd Street, Ph 52 1255 – RO $40-45 – lodge section $30-40 – Dormitory Accommodation $8 per night; Wintersun Gardens Caravan Park, Stuart Hwy, 2km N of PO, Ph 52 4080 – sites $9 double – onsite vans $25 double; Carmichael Tourist Park, Larapinta Drive, Ph 52 1200 – sites $8 double – onsite vans $22 – cabins $20-32 double; Youth Hostel, Todd St. & Stott Tce., Ph 52 5016 – $6 ppn; YWCA, Stuart Lodge, Stuart Tce., Ph 52 1894 – share $14, single $19, double $28.

EATING OUT:

Todd Street is a good place to look for take-aways and coffee shops, and Kentucky Fried Chicken has found its way to The Alice. For a good counter meal head for the Stuart Arms. There are also some classier restaurants like the Il Sorrentino, the Hacienda Overlander Mexican Steakhouse, the Bojangles, and the restaurant in the Old Riverside Hotel.

LOCAL TRANSPORT:

None except for taxis. You either walk, or hire a car or bicycle.

POINTS OF INTEREST:

Your first stop should be Anzac Hill which offers a good view of the town and surrounding ranges. Sunset and sunrise offer best opportunities for photographers, as the hills glow with colour. The National Trust has a useful walking-tour guide to the town's historic buildings, all of which are near the centre of town.

Pitchi Richi Sanctuary is just across the southern Todd River causeway and features the sculpture of William Ricketts.

The Magic Spark Radio Museum located at the Camel Farm Tourist complex, Emily Gap Road, provides a nostalgic look at the communication equipment of yesteryear – open daily.

The School of the Air in Head Street is where teachers communicate with pupils as far as 1,000km away – visiting hours 1.30pm-3.30pm Mon-Fri during term time.

Panorama Guth is a 6m high 360 deg painted landscape of the surrounding countryside. It has a circumference of 60m. Also there is an art gallery featuring many of the Hermannsburg School watercolourists, and a museum of Aboriginal artefacts. – open 9am-5pm Mon-Fri, Sat 9am-12 and 2-5pm, Sun 2-5pm, 65 Hartley Street.

Araluen Arts Centre is the performing and visual Arts Centre for Alice Springs. International and Australian artists provide a high standard of entertainment. It also contains two art galleries and a craft centre.

The Casino, Brent Drive is a hotel resort with gaming room, restaurant, bar and cabaret. The gaming rooms are open from 6pm-2am nightly.

The John Flynn Memorial Church in Todd Mall is a memorial to 'Flynn of the Inland' founder of the Royal Flying Doctor Service.

The Old Telegraph Station was the original communications post – open daily 8am-9pm daily.

The Royal Flying Doctor Base is open to the public 9am-11.30am and 2-3.30pm Mon-Fri and 9am-11am Sat.

Lasseter's Grave is found just inside the gate at the old cemetery. He persihed in the desert in 1931 searching for the now fabled Lasseter's Reef of gold. Albert Namatjira is also buried in the cemetery.

Stuart Auto Museum, just south of Heavitree Gap houses a truly fascinating collection of old vehicles, telephones etc. – open 9am-5pm daily.

The Camel Farm, Emily Gap Road is a good place to learn about these hardy beasts – open daily 8am-5.30pm.

The Residency was built in 1926 and is now used by the Northern Territory Museums and Art Galleries Board for the display of exhibitions, which are constantly being provided from both interstate and overseas.

The Old Timers Museum, south of town on the Sturt Highway, graphically illustrates the early pioneering era of the district – open daily 2pm- 4pm.

The Aviation Museum, Memorial Drive, is housed in the Connellan Hangar on Alice Spring's original airport. It has displays concerning early aviation in the centre – open Mon-Fri 8.30-4pm Sat & Sun 9.30am-4pm. The Kookaburra Memorial is adjacent to the museum.

Chateau Hornsby, 15km from town, produces fine wines – open daily 11am-4pm and for dinner Thurs, Fri & Sat from 7.30pm.

The Mecca Date Garden (Australia's only one) is found on the Old South Road just beyond Heavitree Gap – open daily 9.30am-4.30pm, and there are tours on the hour.

FESTIVALS:
The Bangtail Muster is held each May Day; The Camel Cup camel race is held in May also; The Alice Springs Rodeo is held in August; The Henley-on-Todd regatta is held on the dry Todd River each year in August/September and the Food & Wine Festival is held following the Regatta in September.

FACILITIES:
There are a number of bike tracks and you can hire bikes at Thrifty Bike Hire, Todd Street, Tip Top Jeans Shop, Gregory Terrace. Mopeds are also available for hire at Thrifty or Action Moped at the BP Garage in Todd Street. Other facilities include lawn bowls, golf, hang-gliding, squash, swimming, tennis and horse racing.

OUTLYING ATTRACTIONS:
SIMPSON'S GAP National Park is 23km west of Alice Springs in the colourful MacDonnell Ranges. It is a picturesque cutting through the range. There are some excellent walking trails from the car park.

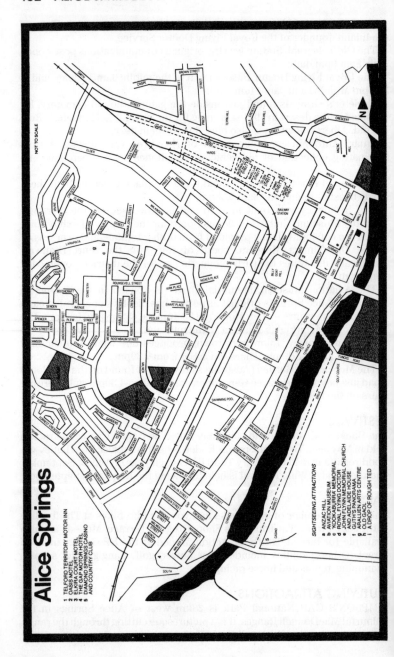

Alice Springs

1 TELFORD TERRITORY MOTOR INN
2 OASIS MOTEL
3 ELKIRA COURT MOTEL
4 THE GAP MOTOR HOTEL
5 DIAMOND SPRINGS CASINO
  AND COUNTRY CLUB

NOT TO SCALE

SIGHTSEEING ATTRACTIONS

a ANZAC HILL
b AVIATION MUSEUM
c 'KOOKABURRA' MEMORIAL
d ROYAL FLYING DOCTOR
e JOHN FLYNN MEMORIAL CHURCH
  AND ADELAIDE HOUSE
f GUTH'S PANORAMA
g ARALUEN ARTS CENTRE
h GAOL
i A DROP OF ROUGH TED

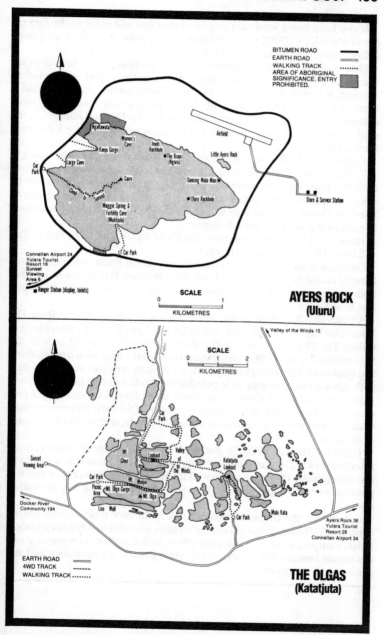

BITUMEN ROAD
EARTH ROAD
WALKING TRACK
AREA OF ABORIGINAL
SIGNIFICANCE. ENTRY
PROHIBITED.

Ngaltawala

Women's Cave

Kapu Gorge

Imati Rockhole

Airfield

Large Cave

The Brain
(Ngoru)

Little Ayers Rock

Car Park

Climb To

Summit

Cairn

Dancing Mala Man

Maggie Spring & Fertility Cave (Mutitjula)

Uluru Rockhole

Store & Service Station

Car Park

Connellan Airport 24
Yulara Tourist
Resort 18
Sunset
Viewing
Area 6

Ranger Station (display, toilets)

SCALE

0   1

KILOMETRES

AYERS ROCK
(Uluru)

Valley of the Winds 15

SCALE

0   1   2

KILOMETRES

Car Park

Sunset
Viewing
Area

Mt. Ghee

Lookout

Valley
of
The Winds

Katatjuta
Lookout

Car Park

Mt. Wulpa

Picnic
Area

Mt. Olga Gorge

Mt. Olga

Docker River
Community 194

Liru Wall

Malu Kata

Car Park

Ayers Rock 36
Yulara Tourist
Resort 28
Connellan Airport 34

EARTH ROAD
4WD TRACK
WALKING TRACK

THE OLGAS
(Katatjuta)

If you keep going west on Larapinta Drive you will come to the turn off for STANDLEY CHASM which is 50km west of town. It is a photographer's delight when the sun is overhead illuminating the red walls.

6km past the Stanley Chasm turn off, Namitjira Drive branches off Larapinta Drive, and if you follow Manitjira Drive you will come to Serpentine Gorge, 100km from The Alice. Further along the same road is Ormiston Gorge, 132km west of Alice Springs, and one of the most colourful and spectacular scenic spots in the MacDonnell Ranges. In the same general area is the Glen Helen Gorge where the Finke River cuts through the range.

HERMANNSBURG on Larapinta Drive, 119km west, was established in 1877 by the Lutheran Church and is home to some 400 Aborigines. At one time the population was double, but recent years have seen a trend by Aborigines to move out to re-establish a more traditional, family-orientated lifestyle. The mission has a wealth of history, but you will need permission to visit, as it is an Aboriginal Reserve.

19km south of Hermannsburg is the Finke Valley and Palm Valley. You will need 4WD transpsort to reach there.

On the way to Ayres Rock is the Virginia Camel Farm, Australia's most famous camel farm. It is 90km from Alice Springs. It is operated by Noel Fullerton and you can have a short camel ride, or go on a safari to nearby Rainbow Valley.

AYERS ROCK (Uluru) is the most famous of the 'sights' out from The Alice. The huge rock juts 348m out of the sand and has a circumference of 9.4km. The Rock is sacred to the Aborigines who associate it with the Dreamtime. There is a 9km walking trail around the base which takes about five hours to walk, taking time to look at the many strange caves and gullies with Aboriginal paintings. It is possible to climb it at one point only, and with the assistance of a hand chain it only takes 2 hours up and back. A pair of sturdy crepe-soled shoes should be worn. The park rangers conduct walks around the area explaining about the plants, widlife and mythology of the area.

THE OLGAS only 32km to the west are a collection of smaller, more rounded rocks. They are equally impressive and are known as Katajuta to the Aboriginals. There are many walking tracks around the rocks and it is possible to climb some of them, but care must be taken as they are rather steep.

In between the Olgas and Ayers Rock is the new multi-million tourist complex, YULARA. It has a Visitors' Centre, international hotels, a budget lodge, camping ground, bank, post-office, petrol station, newsagency and numerous restaurants, supermarket, craft gallery, a pub, police and fire stations and an airport.

DARWIN -Pop. 66,000

LOCATION:
On Beagle Gulf at the 'Top End' of Australia.

CLIMATE:
Average Temperatures: January max. 31.7 deg. C, min. 24.7 deg. C; July max. 30.4 deg. C, min 19.2 deg. C.; maximum temperatures during the summer season reach around 34 deg. C with a relatively high humidity. There are two distinct seasons known locally as 'the wet' and the dry'. The wet lasts from October to April.

CHARACTERISTICS:
Darwin is warm and tropical all year round. It sits astride a peninsula that projects into one of the finest harbours on the Australian coast. It is the seat of Government for the Northern Territory.

HOW TO GET THERE:
AIR. Ansett, Ansett N.T. and Australian Airlines all fly to Darwin. Australian Airlines and Ansett fly to Adelaide, Alice Springs, Brisbane, Cairns, Gove, Melbourne, Mt. Isa, Perth, Sydney and Townsville. Australian Airlines and Ansett WA fly to Port Hedland. Ansett NT fly to Gove, Groote Eylandt, Cairns, Katherine, Tennant Creek and Mt. Isa. Ansett WA fly to/ from Broome, Derby, Kunnunurra and Perth. Tilair fly Darwin to Katherine and Tennant Creek. Darwin is also an international arrival and departure port. Air North also run schedules services throughout the NT, Ph 81 7477. Taxi fare from the airport to the city centre is around $8. There is a special airport bus which costs $2.50 and can be booked by phoning 81 1102 or the No. 5 or No. 8 bus will take you to the city for 30cents.
BUS. Ansett Pioneer, Deluxe and Greyhound all have services to Darwin from Adelaide via Alice Springs, Brisbane via Mt. Isa and Perth via the Kimberleys.
RAIL. No direct service. The nearest stations are Alice Springs or Mt. Isa.
CAR. There are two main highways into the NT: the Stuart from Adelaide which still has about 270km of dirt between Coober Pedy and the Northern Territory border; and the fully sealed Barkly which connects with Brisbane through Mt. Isa. It is also possible to send your car from Adelaide to Alice Springs on the Ghan.

TOURIST INFORMATION:
The Northern Territory Government Tourist Bureau, 31 Smith Street, Darwin, Ph (089) 81 9702.

ACCOMMODATION:
There are approx. 14 motels, 6 hotels, 2 guest houses, 8 caravan parks and a Youth Hostel. Visit the Tourist Bureau for a complete list.

A few names and addresses: Diamond Beach Hotel Casino, Gilruth Ave.,

Mindil Beach, Ph 81 7755 – RO $120 double; Darwin Travelodge, 122 Esplanade, Ph 81 7755 – RO $110 double; Poinciana Motel, Cnr. McLachlan & Mitchell Sts., Ph 81 8111 – RO $62 double; The Palms, 100 McMinn St., Ph 81 4188 – B & LB $55 double; Larrakeyah Lodge, Guest House, 50 Mitchell St., Ph 81 7550 – RO $32-38 double; Overlander Caravan Park, McMillans Rd., Berrimah, Ph 84 3025 – site only $4 double – onsite vans $10-20 double; Pandanus Holiday Centre, Lee Point Rd., Casuarina, Ph 27 2897 – site only $6 double – cabins $14 daily. There are quite a few hostels in Darwin: The big Lameroo Lodge, Ph 81 9833; the Ross Smith Hostel, Ph 81 2162; The Salvation Army Hostel, Ph 81 8188; the Larrakeyah Lodge, Ph 81 2933; and the YWCA, Mitchell Street, Ph 81 8644 & YMCA, Doctors Gulley, Ph 81 8377; The Youth Hostel, Beaton Rd., off Hidden Valley Rd., Berrimah, Ph 84 3107 – $5 ppn.

EATING OUT:

There is a good selection of fast-food shops and take-aways in Darwin Plaza off Smith Street Mall. If you are looking for an evening out then try the Splendor Chinese Restaurant, Jape Plaza, Davenagh St., Ph 81 9292 as they have live entertainment every Fri & Sat night, or Bogarts 25's, 52 Gregory St., Parap, Ph 81 3561, fully licensed and has an a la carte menu. The Beagle Restaurant at the N.T. Museum of Art & Sciences, Ph 81 7791 is Darwin's only seashore restaurant. The Pink Panther Coffee Lounge in the mall – opp. Vic Hotel. Simply Foods, Shop 10, The Track, The Mall has vegetarian and health food – open 10am-2.30pm Mon-Fri, Ph 81 4765. Red Rooster Chicken, Trower Road, Casuarine, Ph 27 8421. Kentucky Fried Chicken, 11 Knuckey St., Darwin, Ph 81 2680 and Bagot Road, Nightcliff, Ph 85 4194. Le Cafe, 444 East Poin Td., Fannie Bay, Ph 81 2221. Indonesian Food at All Food Hall at Harry Chan Arcade, Smith St., Ph 81 5079. The Darwinian thirst is well known and the Darwin stubby holds 2 litres!

LOCAL TRANSPORT.

Car Rental. All the big agencies have offices in Darwin as well as local agencies, so it pays to shop around. Just bear in mind though that Darwin is rather remote and there are a lot of kilometres between Darwin and other towns. Darwin has a fairly good bus service Monday to Friday, but there are no buses on Sundays, and only a limited service on Saturdays. There is a good network of bike tracks and you can hire bikes at the Greyhound Terminal or the Youth Hostel.

POINTS OF INTEREST:

Darwin is easy to tour, just a stroll through the shady Smith Street Mall shows you the new and the old Darwin in one. Focal point of the new mall is the old Vic hotel. Much of Darwin had to be rebuilt after Cyclone Tracy had passed through, but there are stil a few pre-cyclone buildings, and Government House is one of them. This seven-gabled house overlooks Darwin Harbour and was built in 1869. There is an unusual memorial to the cyclone at Casuarina, a steel power pole twisted like a pretzel by the fury of the wind.

Some of the main attractions are:

Darwin Harbour where ferries leave for Mandorah. It takes a half-hour for the 10km trip which shows the beauty of the harbour. Cruises on the harbour are also available as well as more extensive trips to other coastal regions. Boats are also available for hire.

The Artillery Museum: Blockhouses, command posts and observation towers are a reminder of the bombing of Darwin during World War II. Darwin was bombed 64 times in 1942 and 243 people died in the raids.

The Christchurch Cathedral was originally constructed in 1902 as the Lady Chapel for a future cathedral. It was destroyed in 'the cyclone' and has been rebuilt.

The Chinese Temple serves the large number of Chinese people in the Darwin area. There are Buddist, Taoist and Confucian areas and it is open to the public.

The Stuart Memorial honours John McDouall Stuart who left Adelaide on 22 October, 1861 and reached a point east of Darwin in July 1862. The route of this epic south-north crossing became the route for the Overland Telegraph Line and the Stuart Highway.

The Diamond Beach Hotel Casino has blackjack, keno, two-up, mini dice and baccarat for those who want to try their luck, and cabarets, discos and restaurants as well.

The Northern Territory Museum of Arts and Natural Sciences is excellent and includes an art gallery.

The Indo Pacific Marine exhibition is unique in Australia and is believed to be one of only four in the world which have a living coral reef in a series of tanks which are totally self-supporting eco-systems – open 10am-5pm daily from May to October – at other times check with the tourist office. Location: Lambell Terrace at the Roundabout.

At Doctor's Gully thousands of fish come in from the sea to be fed each day at high tide. The sea becomes a frenzied fish fight for bread thrown into the water by visitors.

The Fanny Bay Gaol Museum was in use for nearly 100 years before the last prisioners were transferred to the new Berrimah complex in late 1979. Very few alterations have been made since then and the site now represents a time capsule.

The World's Largest Buffalo some 11km east of the city on the Stuart Highway, is a giant model of a Territory buffalo and the souvenir shop features items related to buffalo.

FESTIVALS:

The Boungainvillea Festival leads up to the annual Beer Can Regatta in June and then there's the Mud Crab Tying Competition in August. In November 1986 the first Mango Harvest Festival was held.

FACILITIES:

Boating, lawn bowls, fishing, golf, horse racing, squash, swimming, tennis and wind surfing. N.B. It's best to do your swimming in the swimming pools from October to May as the sea-wasps invade the beaches during this time.

FISHING:

The NT waters offer some of the most exciting sport angling in Australia. Fishing with hand lines, rods or spears is generally permitted in rivers and billabongs throughout the year without a licence. Amateurs are not permitted to sell any fish they catch, and they are limited to 5 barramundi per day or 10 for any trip lasting more than one day. Anyone with more than 10 Barramundi in their possession is subject to prosecution. There is no bag limit on other fish.

OUTLYING ATTRACTIONS:

YARRAWONGA Wildlife Park, 22km south, has a large collection of animals and birds common to the 'top end' in a simulated natural environment – crocodiles, wallabies, reptiles and birds. If you can't go bush, this is a must.

Crocodile Farm on the Stuart Highway, 35km south just after the Arnhem Highway turn off, has freshwater and saltwater crocs. It is open daily 9am-5pm and feeding times are Wed & Sat at 3pm and Fridays at 11am.

HOWARD SPRINGS, some 30km from the city, is a popular swimming hole.

FOGG DAM, 60km east of Darwin, is a major bird sanctuary and the former site of the ill-fated Humpty-Doo Rice project. 13km closer to Darwin is Graeme Gow's Reptile Park which displays many species of snakes and reptiles – open 8.30am-6pm daily.

WANGI FALLS, 145kms south-east of Darwin (4WD only) is where crystal clear waters from mineral springs tumble hundreds of feet into a serene pool. The cliff face is covered with many varieties of ferns and creepers, and the pool is surrounded by a rainforest of towering trees and palms.

BATHURST & MELVILLE ISLANDS are fascinating places which you can visit on a tour. There are half-day tours to Bathurst Island and full-day tours to Melville Island. These islands are the home of the Tiwi tribe, many of whom make a living from handcrafts, such as carving, silk screen printing and pottery. You may buy wares on the island.

KAKADU NATIONAL PARK, part of which has recently been included on the UN World Heritage List, is one of the most spectacular parks in Australia. It is 150km east of Darwin and lies between the Wild Man and East Alligator Rivers. It has two distinct regions – the floodplains, billabongs and lagoons drained by the Alligator River, and the soaring, rocky Arnhem Land escarpment cut by fantastic gorges, waterfalls and streams. The Kakadu landscape is a production of continual weathering, erosion and sedimentation over some two million years. The Aboriginal rock art here represents a close personal and spiritual relationship between man and his environment. The rock art in Kakadu is among the finest in the world. At Ubirr (Obiri Rock) and Nourlangie Rock, you can see paintings that depict the animal life of the area, an ancient life style and figures of mythical and spiritual significance. These sites are very old and they are still important and significant to the Aboriginal people today. PLEASE KEEP TO THE MARKED PATHWAYS, AND DO NOT TOUCH ANY PAINTED SURFACE. The spectacular waterfalls of Jim Jim and Twin Falls are worth visiting as the surrounding area contains all wildlife common to Northern Australia. Numerous creeks, rivers and billabongs provide excellent fishing opportunities. The most popular way to explore the South Alligator River is aboard the 'Kakadu Princess' which takes tourists on five hour cruises. During the cruise you will probably see magpie geese taking off in large contingents, whistler ducks and elegant white egrets, graceful jabiru, black shags, heron, ibis, crested plovers, black cockatoos, sea eagles, darters and many other species. Accommodation is

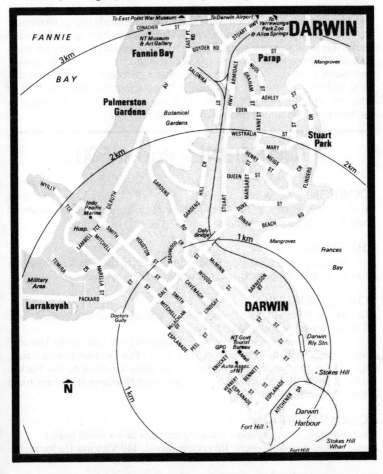

available at South Alligator Motor Inn, Arnheim Highway – RO $90 double; and the South Alligator Caravan Park, Arnhem Highway – sites $6 double – cabins $30-48 double; or you can camp at several locations in the park itself. Kakadu Holiday Village in the heart of Kakadu has air conditioned motel rooms, budget dormitory style accommodation and a caravan park.

ARNHEIM LAND & GOVE: The entire north-eastern half of the top end is the Arnheim Land Aboriginal Reserve which, apart from Gove, cannot be visited without special permission. Gove is the peninsula at the north-east corner of the reserve and at Nhulunbuy there is a bauxite mining centre with a major, deep water export port. Also on the peninsula is Yirrkala, an Aboriginal mission station, which has been a centre for the Aboriginal land rights movement.

N.B. Just a word of warning about CROCODILES. Now that crocodiles are a protected species, their numbers are increasing in the rivers and billabongs in the Top End. Please enquire from the locals before swimming anywhere as, although the Conservation Commission has signposted many dangerous locations, the signs are sometimes souvenired as they are quite unusual. There are two types of crocodiles in the NT, the small Johnstone freshwater crocodile and the larger saltwater crocodile which is found in the tidal region of the rivers. Also don't forget about the Box Jelly Fish or 'stingers' which invade the ocean in the summer months. Only swim in enclosures or swimming pools during this time.

KATHERINE – Pop. 4,500

LOCATION:
On the Stuart Highway 1200km north of Alice Springs, 315km south of Darwin and 1294km from Mt. Isa.

CHARACTERISTICS:
It is a bustling town where the road branches off to the Kimberleys, and is situated on the first permanent river north of Alice Springs.

HOW TO GET THERE:
AIR. Ansett NT and Tillair fly to/from Darwin and Tennant Creek. Ansett NT fly to Ayres Rock and Alice Springs.
BUS. Ansett Pioneer, Greyhound and Deluxe stop off here on the Darwin/Alice Springs route and Darwin/Mt. Isa run and Darwin/Port Hedland run.
CAR. Along the Stuart Highway from Adelaide or Darwin, the Barkly Highway from Mt. Isa, or the Victoria and Great Northern Highways from Western Australia.

ACCOMMODATION:
2 hotel/motels, 6 motels and 4 camping grounds and a youth hostel.
Some names and addresses: Riverview Motel, 440 Victoria Highway, Ph

72 0111 – RO $40 double; Katherine Hotel/Motel, Cnr. Katherine Tce. & Giles St., Ph 72 1622 – RO $52; Springvale Homestead Tourist Park, Shadforth Rd., Ph 72 1159 – RO $40 for motel units – camping sites $8.25; Gardean Holliday Village, Cnr. Giles & Cameron Sts., sites $12 – Cabins $40 double. Youth Hostel, Victoria Highway 2km from the main street, Ph 72 2942 – $4.50 ppn.

POINTS OF INTEREST.

You can visit the School of the Air which plays a vital role in the education of children living on isolated stations in the outback. The school also has its own TV studio, recording facilities etc. – open Mon, Wed & Fri from 9.30am during term time.

You can visit the Sportsmen's Arms which was mentioned in 'We of the Never Never'and the hot springs adjacent to the Katherine River are a popular swimming spot.

FACILITIES:

Boating, lawn bowls, golf course, horse riding, and tennis.

OUTLYING ATTRACTIONS:

KATHERINE GORGE is 32km north-east of the town and there is a daily bus run to the Gorge for $4. There are in fact 13 gorges and each contains fascinating things to see. An increasing number of visitors are exploring the first and second gorges by boat to view the glowing colours, and the towering cliffs which line the waterways. The Johnstone or freshwater croc can usually be spotted lolling along the banks of the river. Many Aboriginal paintings may be seen on the rock faces. There are over one hundred kilometres of marked walking trails in the park.

WATERFALL CREEK NATURE PARK contains the spectacular 100m waterfall known locally as the UDP Falls. There is a rewarding escarpment climb with views to the South Alligator River. Facilities include camping and picnic sites and swimming in the natural pool.

LARRIMAH – 180km south of Katherine. This township was once a main terminus of the now suspended rail service from Darwin. Enjoy a quiet drink at the historic pub. Visitors usually enjoy seeing the crocodiles at the Green Park Caravan Park.

CUTTA CUTTA CAVES NATURE PARK, 27km south is worth a visit. There are twice daily ranger-guided tours of the limestone caves at 10.30am and 1.30pm.

MATARANKA, 105km from Katherine, is a whole new experience with a feeling of 'getting away from it all'. It is said that the thermal pool has therapeutic powers – after a swim in the pool you may not look much younger, but you will feel it. It's a super spot with caravan and camping facilities. There is also a range of excellent accommodation available.

A little south of the Mataranka turnoff at WARLOCK PONDS is the Elsey National Reserve where there is a cairn marking the site of the old Elsey Station, made famous by Mrs. Aeneas Gunn's outback clasic 'We of the

PARKS AND RESERVES OF THE TOP END

All distances marked are from Darwin. Local distances are in brackets. Not drawn to scale.

Cobourg Peninsula Aboriginal Land and Sanctuary

Bathurst Island

Melville Island

Beagle Gulf

Van Diemen Gulf

Yarrawonga Zoo

DARWIN

Howard Springs Nature Park 31 km

Fogg Dam 68 km

(35 km)

STUART

(192 km)

Jabiru 252 km

Berry Springs Nature Park 57 km

Batchelor O

Kakadu National Park

Road often closed in wet season

(134 km)

Adelaide River 113 km

(111 km)

Waterfall Creek Nature Park

(63 km)

(72 km) (38 km)

Daly River Nature Park

(38 km)

Douglas Hot Springs Nature Park

(17 km)

Pine Creek 227 km

Butterfly Gorge Nature Park

(22 km) (44 km)

Umbrawarra Gorge Nature Park

Edith Falls

(46 km)

Katherine Gorge National Park

Katherine Low Level Nature Park

(5km) **KATHERINE** 317 km

(27km)

Cutta Cutta Cave Nature Park

(27km)

Mataranka Pool Park

Mataranka 444km

(3km) (5km)

HWY

N

Keep River National Park 784 km
Kununurra 825 km

Tenant Creek 981 km
Alice Springs 1486 km

Never Never'. The graves of Muluka, head of the property and 'Fizzer', the mailman, two of the characters in the book, can be seen.

PINE CREEK, 50km north of Katherine and 251km from Darwin, is the southern gateway to Arnhem Land. It was the site of the 1872 gold rush and has some historic buildings and a museum.

The turn off to the thermal pools on the Douglas river is approx. 100km north of Katherine, and there are basic camping facilities there. It's about 35km off the Stuart Highway.

ADELAIDE RIVER, 200km north of Katherine and 116km from Darwin, has a War Memorial Cemetery for those killed during the bombing of Darwin in 1942. There are some experimental farms nearby at Tortilla Flats. The beautiful Robin Falls are 12km south of the town and only a short walk off the road.

TENNANT CREEK – Pop. 3,500

LOCATION:
On the Stuart Highway near the junction of the Barkly Highway 2115km from Adelaide, 507km from Alice Springs, 1035km from Darwin, 679km from Katherine and 27km from the Three Ways Junction.

CHARACTERISTICS:
It is in the transitional zone between the Top End and The Centre and therfore offers interesting flora and fauna.

HOW TO GET THERE:
AIR. Ansett NT and Tilair fly to/from Darwin, Alice Springs and Katherine.
BUS. Ansett Pioneer, Greyhound and Deluxe stop here on the Darwin/ Alice Springs route.
CAR. Along the Stuart Highway from Adelaide or Darwin or the Barkly Highway from Mt. Isa.

TOURIST INFORMATION:
Office is located in the Civic Centre, Peko Road, Tennant Creek, Ph. (089) 622 401.

ACCOMMODATION:
2 hotel/motels, 3 motels and 2 camping grounds and a youth hostel. Goldfields Hotel Motel, Paterson St., Ph 62 2030 – B&Lb $52 double; Bluestone Motor Inn, Paterson St., Ph 62 2617 – RO $54 double; Eldorado Motor Lodge, Paterson St., Ph 62 2402 – RO $60; Safari Lodge, Davidson St., Ph 62 2207 – RO $48; Tennant Creek Hotel/Motel, Paterson St., Ph 62 2006 – B&B $40 double; Outback Caravan Park, Peko Road, Ph 62 2459 – site $7 double – onsite vans $15-25; Tennant Creek Caravan Park, Paterson St., Ph

62 2325 -site $7 double, onsite vans $24 double; Youth Hostel, Leichhardt St., Ph 62 2719 – $5ppn.

EATING OUT:

The Dolly Pot Inn, Davidson Street (turn west at Diano Motors) Ph. 622 824 is open daily 7am-midnight. The T.C. Chicken Shop, Paterson Street is centrally located and open Mon-Sat 9am-8pm & 4pm-8pm Sun, Ph 622 283. The Eldorado Restaurant in Paterson Street has an a la carte menu and extensive wine list, ph. 622 158. The Shell 3 Ways Roadhouse 'up the track' has a licensed dining room and bar facilities and is open 24 hours a day.

POINTS OF INTEREST.

Tennant Creek is chiefly a centre for gold and copper mining, and has an export meat-works where approx. 500 head of cattle are slaughtered daily during the season. The town is surrounded by many historic mines dating back to the rush days of the 1900's. It is a modern town with a beautiful, wide tree-lined main street and modern Civic Centre.

From the One Tank Hill Lookout, 2km east of the Tourist Information Office on Peko road, you get a good view of the town and the surrounding landscape.

Mary Ann Dam, 6km north-east of Tennant Creek, is a welcome oasis for visitors. Swimming, picnicking and sailing are popular. Power boats, however, are not permitted. Facilities include BBQ area, tables, boat ramp, pontoon and toilets.

Government Stamp Battery is open for inspection weekdays 9am-Noon and 1-3pm – guided tours 10am and 2pm weekdays. The battery is still used by local prospectors today to treat easily freed gold ores.

Noble's Nob Mine, can be viewed from a vantage point adjacent to the public car park which overlooks the open cut operation. When the mine closed in January 1985, it had produced the most gold of any mine in Australia. Location: Follow the Peko Road for 16km to the turn off, and then follow the directions.

The Devil's Pebbles are 17km north-west, and are a rocky outcrop which has weathered into unusual formations. It is a photographer's delight, particularly at sunset.

FACILITIES:

Olympic swimming pool, golf course, lawn bowls, squash, horse riding, tennis, pistol shooting and fossicking. Car Hire: Budget, Paterson St., Ph (089) 622 646. Tours: Mulga Track Tours & Frew River Safaris, Ph. 622 479.

FESTIVALS:

The Lions annual Goldrush Festival is held in May.

OUTLYING ATTRACTIONS:

THE DEVIL'S MARBLES is a spectacular granite outcrop 108km south of Tennant Creek on the Stuart Highway. It is well known in Aboriginal

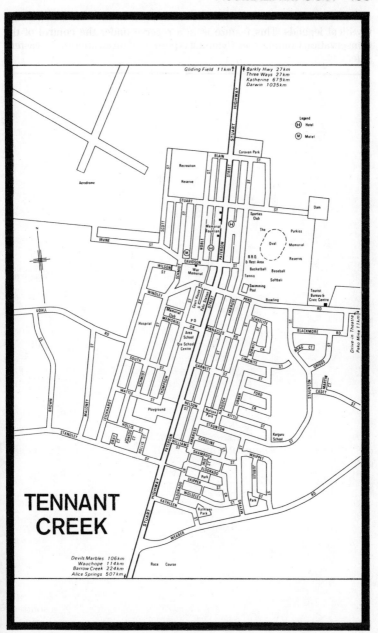

TENNANT CREEK

Gliding Field 11 km↑

Barkly Hwy 27km
Three Ways 27km
Katherine 679km
Darwin 1035km

Legend
Ⓗ Hotel
Ⓜ Motel

Aerodrome

Dam

Caravan Park

Recreation Reserve

Sporties Club

Memorial Fountain

The Oval

Purkiss Memorial Reserve

War Memorial

B.B.Q. & Rest Area
Basketball   Baseball
Tennis   Softball
Swimming Pool
Bowling

Tourist Bureau & Civic Centre

Hospital

Memorial Club

Court House & Rec Station

P O

Area School

Pre-School Centre

Drive-in Theatre
Peko Mine 11am

Blackmore RD

Playground

Nelson Park

Kargura School

Karguru School

Shamrock

Eldorado Park

Skipper Park

Kathleen Park

Jubilee Park

Race Course

Devils Marbles 106km
Wauchope 114km
Barrow Creek 224km
Alice Springs 507km

mythical legends. This feature is in a reserve under the control of the Conservation Commission. Camping is permitted on an area on the eastern side.

BRISBANE – Pop. 1,138,400

LOCATION:
On the banks of the Brisbane River 32km upstream from Moreton Bay.

CLIMATE:
Average Temperatures: January max. 29 deg. C. (84 deg. F) – min. 20 deg.
C (68 deg. F); July max. 20 deg. C. (68 deg. F) – min. 9 deg. C (48 deg.F);
Average annual rainfall: 1148mm – 45.2in.

CHARACTERISTICS:
A mixture of the old and ultra-modern. One of Australia's few capital cities
with an expressway connecting the city centre directly with the main
highways. Whilst Brisbane may not have a magnificent harbour like
Sydney, the winding Brisbane River does make a pleasant backdrop for the
city , and it affords the visitor a relaxing way to see some of Brisbane's
suburbs. The river is ever changing – banks are quite steep around the Story
Bridge ,and flatten out up and down stream. Many of the old wharves have
been moved closer to the mouth of the river, and the public is being given
more access to the riverbanks, and more open-air or side-walk cafes are
appearing, making the most of Brisbane's climate. The Brisbane City
Council has declared 1987 to be 'The Year of the River'. Many people still
think of Brisbane as a backward country town with nothing much to offer,
but it has changed, and is still changing at a rapid rate. As part of the
Bicentennial celebrations in 1988, Brisbane will host the world trade fair,
Expo 88.

HOW TO GET THERE:

AIR. Ansett and Australian Airlines have direct flights to Adelaide, Alice
Springs, Cairns, Darwin, Gold Coast, Hobart, Launceston, Longreach,
Mackay, Melbourne, Mt. Isa, Perth, Proserpine, Rockhampton, Sydney, and
Townsville. Australian Airlines fly to Barcaldine, Birdsville, Blackall,
Charleville, Longreach, Quilpie, Roma and Windorah. Ansett have a direct
flight to Canberra on Mondays. Ansett have a direct flight to Hamilton
Island, and also a direct flight to Port Vila. Air Queensland have direct
flights to Biloela, Blackwater, Bundaberg, Emerald, Gladstone, Maroochy-
dore, Maryborough and Noosa. Henebery Aviation fly to Caloundra. Air
NSW fly Brisbane/Cooma direct on Saturdays in winter, and daily Brisbane/
Gold Coast/Newcastle (Williamtown)/Sydney and 2-3 times weekly
Brisbane/Norfolk Island. Norfolk Airlines fly Brisbane/Toowoomba daily.
Eastern Airlines fly to Armidale daily, Coffs Harbour, Gold Coast, Lismore,
Maitland, Newcastle (Williamtown), Port Macquarie, Tamworth, and
Taree. Sunstate fly to Bundaberg, Maroochydore, Maryborough, Noosa.
East West fly to Burnie and Devonport. Sabair Airlines fly to Kingaroy.

BUS. Ansett Pioneer, Greyhound, VIP, McCafferty's and Deluxe all have the following services: Brisbane/Sydney, Brisbane/Cairns with connections to Darwin and Alice Springs, and Brisbane/ Melbourne Services. Border Coaches have daylight services to Tamworth via Toowoomba, Tenterfield, Glen Innes, and Armidale or Glen Innes, Inverell, Warialda and Moree. They also operate a service from Brisbane to Monto via Esk/Kilcoy, Kingaroy, Murgon, and Gayndah. Skennars have services to the Gold Coast, Sunshine Coast, New England Tablelands, Port Macquarie, Roma area, Mt. Isa and Sydney. Greyhound also have a Brisbane/Alice Springs or Darwin service via Longreach and Mt. Isa. Greyhound have a Brisbane/Toowoomba/ Dalby/Roma service. All the coaches leave from the Transit Centre at Roma Street.

RAIL. The Brisbane Limited connects Brisbane and Sydney, leaving in the evening and arriving early the following morning. The Gold Coast Motorail runs between Sydney and Murwillumbah with a bus connection to the Gold Coast and Beenleigh (outer Brisbane suburb) with a suburban rail connection to the city. The Sunlander and the Queenslander connect Brisbane and Cairns, both leaving Brisbane in the early morning for the two day trip. The Capricornian leaves Brisbane in the early evening six days a week and arrives in Rockhampton in time for breakfast the next day, stopping at various towns along the way. The Westlander runs inland to Roma, Charleville and Cunnamulla twice weekly.

CAR. From Sydney via the Pacific Highway along the coast 1001km, or inland via the New England and Cunningham Highways 1033km.

TOURIST INFORMATION:

Bribane Transit Centre, Roma Street, has laser video discs, computers and touch-screen television monitors, backed up by two-way camera/phones, as well as a traditional information bureau; The Information Kiosk, Queen Street Mall is open six days a week; The Queensland Government Travel Centre, 196 Adelaide St., Ph (07) 31 2211 is open during business hours; and every Friday 'The Courier Mail' publishes a section on 'The Great Outdoors' which details drives, picnic and camping spots.

ACCOMMODATION:

Brisbane has several international hotels, older style hotels, motels, guest houses, private hotels and a youth hostel.

Some names and addresses: Hilton International, Elizabeth St – RO $130 double; Gazebo Ramada, 345 Wickham Tce., Ph 381 6177 – RO $84 double; Gateway Hotel, 85-87 North Quay – RO $80 double; Park Royal, Cnr. Alice & Albert Sts., – RO $105 double; Ridge All-Suites Inn, Cnr. Leichhardt & Henry Sts., Ph831 5000 – RO $70; The Brisbane City Travelodge, at the Brisbane Transit Centre, Roma St., Ph 238 2222; Queensland Motel, 777 Main St., Kangaroo Point – RO $35 double; Tourist Private Hotel/Motel, 555 Gregory Tce., B&B $28; Yale Budget Inn, 413 Upper Edward St., B&B $28 double; Queensland Country Women's Assn, 89-95 Gregory Tc., DBB $53; There are no camping grounds close to the city centre, but then the same can be said of Sydney, or any other big city. If you want to camp then you will have to go to the outer suburbs like Aspley – Aspley Acres Caravan Park, 1420 Gympie Rd., Ph 263 2668 – sites $10 double – onsite vans $25 double – or Victoria Point – Victoria Point Caravan Park, Cnr. Colburn Ave. & Redland Bay Rd., Ph 207 7433 – sites $7 double – onsite vans $25 double. If you are prepared to hire an onsite van then you won't get any closer than the Brisbane Caravan Park, Scott Road, Hawthorne, Ph 399 4878 (5km east). It is rather small, and there are a lot of permanents, but they do have about 15 onsite vans for casual hire, which cost $19 double or $52 weekly. The park is only a few hundred metres from the Hawthorne Ferry, from where there are services straight across the river, with a bus connection on the other side or the Golden Mile Ferry right to the city. The Youth Hostel is at 15 Mitchell Street, Kedron, Ph 57 1245 – $5.50 ppn – 8km from the city. Some of the University of Queensland Colleges do have accommodation available during the vacations if you want to try your luck: International House, Ph 370 9593, Union College, Ph 371 1300 – see phone book for others.

EATING OUT:

Brisbane has many restaurants catering for all tastes and budgets. Most of them offer delicious fresh seafood, and tropical fruit usually features in the menu. Most international standard hotels have at least one good restaurant as well as a bistro, or the like. There are quite a few good restaurants in Fortitude Valley (The Valley).

Some names and addresses: Top of the G, Gazebo Ramada Hotel, 345 Wickham Tce., Ph 831 6177; Gillies Restaurant, The Gateway Hotel, 85 North Quay, Ph 221 0211; Denisons Restaurant, Sheraton Hotel, 249 Turbot St., Ph 835 3535; Ridge Rooftop Restaurant, 189 Leichhardt St, Ph 831 5000; Sweet Patootie, 480 St. Paul's Tce., Valley, Ph 52 9606; Josephine's Restaurant, 247 St. Paul's Tce., Ph 52 3797; Rags Garden The Breakfast Creek Wharf Restaurant, Breakfast Creek Rd., Newstead, Ph 52 2451 serves trawler fresh seafood. At the Breakfast Creek Hotel, Kingsford Smith Drive, Breakfast Creek, Ph 262 5988, you can enjoy your meal outdoors, and even choose your meat if you want a bbq steak. Right on the Queen Street Mall is the New Orleans Restaurant which serves international dishes. It is open 7 days. Squirrels, Cnr. Melbourne & Edmonston Sts., South Brisbane, Ph 44 4603 (near the Performing Arts Complex) is a vegetarian restaurant – a la carte from $9 – buffet from $7. For Chinese food try the Lotus Room, Cnr. Elizabeth & Edward Sts., Ph 221 8546 – open 6 days. Rumpoles on the Quay, cnr. North Quay & Turbot St., Ph 229 5922 offers a $15 pre-theatre dinner and later night suppers.

LOCAL TRANSPORT:

The people of Brisbane still mourn the loss of their trams, but they now have a very efficent electric train system (underground in the city centre), and buses to most suburbs leave from the city centre – day rover tickets as well as fare saver cards are available. For further information on routes, prices etc., contact City Council Bus Information, City Plaza Building, 69 Ann St., Ph 225 4444. Buses to the Redcliffe Peninsula operate seven days a week from outside the Transit Centre – Ph 284 2622 for timetable. Ferries provide across river transport at Newstead/Bulimba, New Farm Wharf/ Hawthorne, New Farm Park/Norman Park, New Farm (Oxlade Drive)/ Mowbray Park, Customs House/Kangaroo Point, Edward Street (Botanic Gardens)/ Kangaroo Point. For suburban train timetables Phone 225 0211, or go to the Information Office, concourse level, Central Station, Ann Street. Skennars operate an airport commuter service – Ph 832 1148 for timetable.

The City Lookabout bus takes you on a fully guided 3 hr tour of the city. It leaves Ann St. (near George St.) at 9.30am Mon-Friday – adults $7.50, child $2.50 and Family $16 – no booking necessary – Phone 225 4444 for further information.

Taxis: Ascot Cabs, Ph 831 3000, Black and White, Ph 229 1000, Blue and White Cabs, Ph 229 1000 and Yellow Cabs, Ph 391 1091.

Car Hire: Avis, 272 Wickham Street, Fortitude Valley, Ph 52 7111, Budget, St. Pauls Terrace, Fortitude Valley, Ph 52 0151. With the opening of the Gateway arterial road, which is 42km long and connects the South-East Freeway at Eight Mile Plains to the Bruce Highway at Bald Hills, the drive through Brisbane has been cut by approx. 30mins.

HELPFUL ADDRESSES:

Airline Offices: Airlines of NSW, Cnr. George & Queen Sts., Ph 226 1111; Air Queensland, MIM Building, 160 Ann Street, Ph 229 1311; Ansett Airlines, 40 Creek Street, Ph 226 1111; Australian Airlines, 247 Adelaide Street, Ph 223 3333; East West Airlines reservations (008) 22 1211; Sunstate Airlines, TAA Terminal Brisbane Airport, Ph 268 666. Consulates: British Consulate-General, 193 North Quay, Ph 221 4933; German Honorary Consul, 307 Queen St., Ph 221 7819. Telephone Interpreter Service phone 225 2233.

OPENING TIMES:

Banks are open from 9.30am to 4pm Mon-Thurs and 9.30am to 5pm Fridays. Shops are usually open from 8.15pm to 5.15pm Mon-Fri and from 8.15am-12 noon Saturdays. The larger stores in the city and 'the valley' are open until 9pm Friday nights, and some of the larger suburban shopping centres are open until 9pm on Thursdays.

POINTS OF INTEREST.

The city centre is best seen on a walking tour, and the new Brisbane Transit Centre is a good place to start. It was only opened in mid-1986 and is an integrated coach and railway terminal at Roma Street. With the building of a rail bridge across the Brisbane River, the Sydney trains now come right to the city centre at Roma Street Station, from where all the long distance country trains leave. The suburban electric trains also leave from here, as well as interstate, intrastate and local buses. There are also long and short term car parks, taxi ranks, a hotel, commercial offices, shops and a tourist information office. Queensland has electrified its railway line from

Brisbane through Gladstone, Rockhampton and inland to its central Queensland Coal Fields. It is a leisurely stroll from the Transit Centre to King George Square and the City Hall. This imposing building is a combined cultural and community centre. An excellent view can be obtained of the city from the clock tower, but try to avoid being up there at 12 noon as its rather noisy. Also facing the square is the Albert St. Uniting Church which is rather dwarfed by the high rise office blocks around it. It is built in Gothic revival style in red brick and white sandstone, and was opened in 1889.

Just around the corner in Ann Street is the Ann St. Presbyterian Church which was opened in 1872. If you continue along Ann Street you will come to Anzac Park and the Flame of Remembrance opposite Central Station. Walk down the stairs and through the park, across Adelaide Street, through the Post Office Square shopping complex, and you will come to the G.P.O. in Queen Street. There is a Postal Museum on the first floor which is open Tues, Wed & Thurs 10am-3pm. Turn right and walk along the Queen Street Mall, through the main shopping centre, and you will come to the Treasury building near Victoria Bridge. It is built around a central courtyard in Italian Renaissance style. Turn left into William Street and you will see the State Library of Queensland which was completed in 1879, and although additions have been made over the years, the original stone facade has been retained. Keep walking along William Street until you come to Margaret Street, then turn left, and then right when you come to George Street and you will see the French Renaissance style Parliament House, which overlooks the Botanic Gardens, which are on the river bank. After all that walking I am sure the gardens will provide pleasant surroundings in which to rest and recuperate. The gardens also afford a view of the Captain Cook and the Story Bridges.

The Old Observatory in Wickham Terrace was built as a windmill in 1829 by convict labour. Due to defects it was never operational and was used as a treadmill, a signal post and meteorological station. (It is rather out of the way, uphill from the city and I find it hardly worth the effort of getting there – others will disagree, of course).

The 1982 Commonwealth Games provided Brisbane with the opportunity to upgrade and improve its public transport and sporting facilities, and now the 1988 World Fair will be held on the south bank of the Brisbane River next to the Cultural Centre, which is due for completion in 1988. The Queensland Cultural Centre, houses the Performing Arts Centre, Queensland Art Gallery and the Museum. The Art Gallery houses an extensive collection of Australian art from colonial times to the present – open daily 10am-5pm – free guided tours Mon-Fri 11am, 1pm, 2pm & Sat & Sun 2pm & 3pm. The Performing Arts Complex is open daily 10am-5pm & Wed until 8pm – guided tours daily on the hour until 4pm.

Close to the city the river is spanned by four bridges, all of which have a unique architectual style, and are worth seeing – the Story Bridge, the Captain Cook Bridge, the Victoria Bridge and the William Jolly Bridge. Brisbane's newest river crossing, the soaring Gateway Bridge, was only opened in 1986, and won the 1986 Special Award of the Instution of

Structual Engineers in London, for outstanding structural engineering.

If you have only limited time in Queensland and can't spare the time for a bush walk, then head for the Wilderness Walk in Koala House, Cnr. Creek & Adelaide Sts. It is a lifelike re-creation of the Queensland bush depicting rain forest, eucalyptus forest, wetlands and a comprehensive collection of Australian animals and birds in their natural habitat. Live koalas are also on display.

The Kookaburra Queen is one of Brisbane's newest attractions, and a luncheon or dinner cruise on this paddlewheeler is a delightful experience. She leaves from the Kookaburra Queen Marina, Howard St., Petrie Bight Mon-Fri at 10am, 12.45 & 7.30pm, Saturdays at 7.30pm and Sun 10am, 12.45pm, 3pm & 6.30pm – Ph 52 3797.

Koala Kruises sometimes run adventure cruises which explore the upper reaches of the Brisbane and Bremer Rivers right to Ipswich. Phone 229 7055 for information and bookings.

SUBURBAN ATTRACTIONS:

The Southern Cross, Sir Charles Kingsford Smith's plane, is preserved in a glass-walled building at Brisbane Airport, Ph 268 9511.

New Farm Park has almost 12,000 rose bushes and a jacaranda and poinciana avenue. Like the Botanic Gardens, it too is situated on the riverbank and although it can be reached by bus, a trip on the Golden Mile Ferry which leaves the Customs House Wharf every hour calls in there.

The Mt. Coot-tha Botanic Gardens and Planetarium Ph 377 8898 is only 10mins drive from the city, and has a large collection of Australian native plants, tropical plants, an ar-d-zone area and tropical plant display dome – open from 7am-5pm daily. The Sir Thomas Brisbane Planetarium in the gardens is the largest in Australia – sessions Wednesdays to Fridays 3.30pm and 7.30pm and Saturdays there is an extra session at 1.30pm and Sundays 1.30 and 3.30pm only. The picnic area at the top of Mt. Cootha is a popular stop for a panoramic view of the city day or night.

Lone Pine Koala Sanctuary, Jesmond Road, Fig Tree Pocket Ph 378 1366, shouldn't be missed. It is situated on the banks of the river and is best reached by boat – The Lone Pine Cruises depart from Hayles Wharf, North Quay daily at 1.15pm – Ph 229 7055. It is Australia's oldest Koala sanctuary and also has a variety of native animals, reptiles and birds – open daily 9.30am-5pm.

Earlystreet Historic Village, 75 McIlwraith Ave., Norman Park, has a collection of old Queensland buildings – open daily 10.30am-4.30pm – Ph 398 6866.

Joss House, Higgs Street, Breakfast Creek, is an historic Chinese Temple built in 1885 with pillars set crookedly as a reminder that nothing in life is perfect.

Miegunyah, 31 Jordan Tce., Bowen Hills was built in 1884 and is a good example of colonial architecture – open Tues,. Wed, Sat & Sun 10.30am-4pm Ph 52 2979.

Newstead House in Newstead Park, Breakfast Creek Road,. is Brisbane's oldest surviving residence. It is on the banks of the river near its junction with Breakfast Creek – open Sunday 2-5pm and Mon-Thurs 11am-3pm.

Spring Hill Galleries, 49 Leichhardt St. (cnr. Berley St), Spring Hill, Ph 832 3814 is within walking distance of the city, and is housed in an historic Queensland home. It is open daily from 10am-6pm.

The Queensland University at St. Lucia is almost completely surrounded by the river and has spacious parklands, and sandstone buildings which are joined by sheltered walkways, called The Cloisters. The Cloisters are decorated with carvings of other universities' coats of arms, sculptures and grotesque faces and animals. It is definitely worth a visit. There are approx. 20,000 students enrolled making it the second largest university in Australia.

The Golden Circle Cannery, Earnshaw Road, Northgate, Ph 266 6122 is open for inspection but booking is essential. They process pineapples and other tropical fruits.

The Mirage Amusement Centre, 2098 Ipswich Rd., Oxley has a water slide, go-kart track and other amusements.

The Brisbane Tramway Museum, 2 McGinn Road, Ferny Grove, Ph 351 1776 has a comprehensive collection of trams.

The Clydesdale Amusement Farm, Dixon St., Strathpine has a variety of amusements and refreshments are available.

Alma Park Zoo and Botanical Gardens, Alma Road, Kallangur feature Australian and exotic fauna, tropical gardens, picnic and bbq facilites – open daily.

The Australian Woolshed, 148 Samford Road, Ferny Hills, Ph 351 5366 has show at 10.45am Mon-Fri and 2pm Sundays – a great Aussie experience for people without the time for the great Aussie outback. There you can see seven different breeds of sheep, see a sheep shorn and see freshly shorn fleece spun into yarn. Every Saturday night there is a Woolshed dance including dinner.

FESTIVALS:

The Warana Spring Festival is held over two weeks in September/October every year. It celebrated its 25th anniversary in 1986. The Redland Strawberry Festival is held the first Saturday in September at the Cleveland Showgrounds.

FACILITIES:

Brisbane has all the facilities one would expect of a State Capital.

OUTLYING ATTRACTIONS:

MORETON BAY AND ISLANDS:

The bayside suburbs of Wynnum, Lota, Manly and Cleveland are great places for boating but only at high tide. At low tide these suburbs all have stretches of mud flats and aren't suitable for swimming except in the enclosures (Wellington Point is the exception as it has sand) but North Stradbroke and Moreton Islands are really worthwhile visiting. They afford

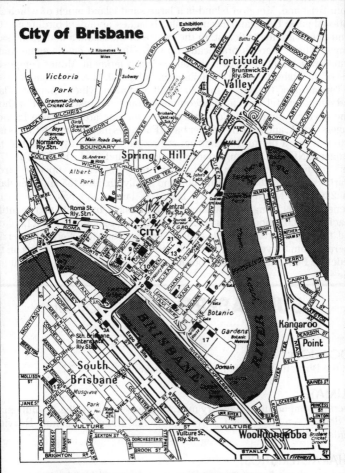

City of Brisbane

1. **Ridge Hotel**
2. **T. A. A.**
3. **Queensland Art Gallery and Cultural Centre.**
3A. **Performing Arts Complex**
4. **Suncorp Theatre**
5. **Sheraton-Brisbane Hotel**
6. **Parkroyal Motor Inn**
7. **Bellevue Hotel Brisbane**
8. **The Gazebo Terrace Hotel**
9. **Mayfair Crest Hotel**
10. **Lennons Plaza Hotel**
11. **Brisbane City Travelodge and Brisbane Transit Centre**
12. **The Melbourne Hotel**
13. **Hilton Hotel**
14. **City Plaza**
15. **The Capital Hotel**
16. **Ansett**
17. **Queensland Conservatorium of Music**
18. **The Gateway Inn**
19. **Queens Wharf Road**
20. **Budget Rent A Car**
21. **Queen St Mall**

the traveller an opportunity to have an island holiday without travelling far from Brisbane. Moreton Island is a large sand island much of which is a national park. The island has unspoiled beaches, abundant birdlife and the sand dunes are magnificient. In the centre of the island amongst the sand dunes, where there is practically no vegitation, one can imagine that a camel train might come over the dunes at any moment. Mount Tempest is one of the highest coastal sand dunes in the world. There is a tourist resort at Tangalooma, the site of the old whaling station, which offers standard and deluxe motel and cabin accommodation and a restaurant. For those who prefer a simpler holiday, there are camping areas at Blue Lagoon, Eagers Creek, and near the ranger base. Facilities include water, toilets and showers but a permit to camp must first be obtained by writing to the Ranger, QNPWS, C/o Tangalooma, Moreton Island 4004 – Ph (075) 48 2710 for further information. Vehicular ferry services operate from Scarborough, Ph 203 6817, Bulimba and Manly Ph 399 6155 and Cleveland Ph 286 2666. North Stradbroke Island is larger and has more varied scenery. It has mangrove swamps, beautiful lakes, bushland and beautiful beaches. Accommodation is available at Amity Point and at Point Lookout and they also have campsites there, and at Dunwich. Vehicular ferries operate from Cleveland Ph 286 2666 and Redland Bay. The beaches on the Redcliffe Peninsula are sandy but its a long walk out to deep water at low tide.

BUNDABERG – Pop. 55,000

LOCATION:
On the Burnett River 398km north of Brisbane.

CLIMATE:
Average temperatures: January max. 30 deg. C – min 21 deg. C – July max. 22 deg. C. – min 10 deg. C.; Average Annual Rainfall 1159mm; Heaviest rainfall – Nov-April.

CHARACTERISTICS:
The Bundaberg district grows approximately one-fifth of Australia's sugar crop but in recent years has become a virtual salad bowl, growing large supplies of tomatoes, avocadoes, pineapples, beans etc. Other rural industries include cattle raising, dairying, pig and poultry raising and tobacco growing and of course, who hasn't heard of the famous Bundaberg rum!

HOW TO GET THERE:
AIR. Air Queensland and Sunstate operate several flights daily to/from Brisbane, Maryborough and Gladstone. Air Queensland also fly to/from Cairns, Mackay, Maroochydore, Rockhampton and Townsville.

BUS. Ansett Pioneer, and Greyhound stop at Bundaburg on their Brisbane/Cairns route.

RAIL. On the main Brisbane/Cairns line. The Sunlander and the Capricornian (both air-conditioned) and the Bundaberg Mail all stop at Bundaberg.

CAR. From Brisbane via the Bruce Highway to the turn off 7km north of Childers. If travelling further north you can rejoin the Bruce Highway at Gin Gin and the trip into Bundaberg only adds 50km to the journey.

TOURIST INFORMATION:

Bundaberg Tourist Information Centre, the Hinkler Glider Museum and the Bundaberg District Development Board are all found on the cnr. Mulgrave and Bourbong Sts, next to the Base Hospital, Ph (071) 72 2406 – open Mon-Fri 8.30-am-5pm & Sat 9.30am-2.30pm.

ACCOMMODATION:

There are over 20 motels in Bundaberg as well as hotels and camping grounds.

Some names and addresses: Bougainvillea Motel Lodge, 73 Takalvan St., Ph 71 2365 – RO $44 double; Bundaberg City Motor Inn, 246 Bourbong St., Ph 72 5011 $43 double; Lyelta Lodge & Motel, 8 Maryborough St., Ph 71 3344 – B & Lt.B Motel, $28 double Guest House $22 double; – evening meal $7 for 3 courses; Gunnadoo Motel, 83 Water St., Bundaberg, Ph 71 4346 – RO $24 double; Park Lane Motel, 247 Bourbong Street, Ph 71 2341 – RO $32 double: Oscar Motel, 252 Bourbong St., Ph 72 3666 – RO $33 double; Royal Hotel, Cnr. Bourbong & Barolin Sts., Ph 71 2201 – RO $26 double; Finemore Trouist Caravan Park, Quay St., (on riverbank), sites $8 double – onsite vans $17-$25 double; Riverdale Caravan Park, 6 Perry St., Ph 72 4731; Oakwood Caravan Park, sites $5 double – onsite vans $16 double. No Youth Hostel.Motels and camping grounds also located on the coast at Bargara and Burnett Heads.

EATING OUT:

Bundaburg has 14 licensed restaurants, 5 BYO Restaurants, 2 licensed clubs, 8 licensed hotels and over 30 coffee lounges, takeaways and snack bars.

Some names and addresses: The Royal Hotel, opposite the post office Ph 71 2201, serves counter lunches Mon-Sat 11.30am-2pm and also has an elegant restaurant which is open 11.30am-2pm & 6pm-8pm. Sugarland Tavern, Johnson Street, Ph 72 7311 has live rock bands and a video disco, as well as counter lunches and dinners. Alexandras Seafood Restaurant, 66 Quay St., Ph 72 7255 – open nightly – licensed. China World, 32 Tago Street, Ph 72 8833 – open Mon-Fri. Granny's Gourmet, Drive In or Take Away sells pancakes, home-made cheese cakes plus hot food. McDonalds, Takalvan St., Ph 72 3969 – open daily. Mexican Border, 27 Elliott Heads Road, Ph 72 1675. The Pumpkin Seed (health foods), 83 Bourbong St., Ph 72 1926 – open 8.15am-5.15pm weekdays & 8.15am-12 noon Sats.

LOCAL TRANSPORT:

There is a weekday bus service to Bargara (Beach), Burnett Heads, Elliott Heads, Moore Park and Gin Gin – contact the Tourist Office for details.

POINTS OF INTEREST.

Bundaberg has several memorials to its most famous son, Herbert John Louis Hinkler (Bert Hinkler) – locally, he was known as Hustling Hinkler. He was the first aviator to fly solo from England to Australia in 1928. Bert Hinkler House, cnr. Mt. Perry Road and Young Street, was shipped to Bundaburg from Southampton, England in 1893. Hinkler designed the house and lived in it from 1926 to 1933. It is now an aviation museum – open daily from 10am-4pm – during school holidays from 9.30am-4.30pm. There are memorials in Buss Park beside the Civic Centre, at the southern end of the traffic bridge and on the Hummock, 10km east of the city on the only hill in the district. The Hinkler Glider Museum contains Hinkler's first successful aircraft in which he flew 35m from the sand dunes of Mon Repos Beach in 1912.

Alexandra Park Zoo is on the banks of the river west of the main railway line.

The Historical Museum, top floor of the School of Arts building in the city, contains a collection of domestic items and farm equipment – open weekdays 10am-3pm.

Bundaberg Rum Distillery has tours Monday-Friday at 1pm. Adequate footwear must be worn (no thongs). Massey Ferguson also has tours on Wednesdays at 1pm – bookings essential 72 1711 – again no thongs or high heels.

The House of Dolls has a wonderful display of dolls dressed in national and period costumes – turn south into Barolin Street and after 8km turn left into Douglas Road, and its about 1km further on your left on the way to Avocado Grove.

The Midtown Marina is a facility of international standard on the banks of the City reach of the Burnett River. The facilities are excellent – power and water are supplied and a ships chandlery is available 24 hours a day to fishing fleets, charter vessels, game vessels and private yachts. Bundaberg ranks with Cairns and Coffs Harbour as one of the 3 principal clearing ports for overseas yachts on the East Coast.

Boyd's Antiquatorium, Bourbong Street West, has motorcycles, vintage cars, coin collection etc – open 7 days from 2-4pm.

The Dreamtime Reptile Reserve has guided viewing with comments on each species of reptile – just past the airport south of the city – Ph 71 5730.

Schmeider's Cooperage, 5 Alexandra Street, East Bundaberg, sells small handcrafted American Oak Casks in its 100 year old workshop – video display showing the full process of a cask being made.

Avocado Grove, 10km south of the Post Office, along Barolin St and follow the signs, has acres of avocados, macadamias, sour sop, lychees and other tropical fruits. A video filmed on location provides information on how they are grown – open 9-5 daily.

Bauer's Gerbera Nursery, Ashfield Road, on the Tourist Route to the Hummock Lookout, has unique varieties of Gerberas – open Mon-Fri all day – prime time August and September.

Bargara Beach, 13km east, offers safe surfing at Nielson Park.

Kelly's Beach has a natural still-water tidal swimming pool and a patrolled beach. It is also the start of the Woongarra Scenic Drive.

Mon Repos Beach with magnificent sand dunes, is the largest and most accessible mainland turtle rookery in Australia. It is an Environmental Park and contains a magnificent Kanaka stone wall and was the site of Bert Hinkler's first flights. Turn left at Bargara State School and follow the signs.

Burnett Heads and The Oaks Beach is 15km from Bundaberg at the mouth of the Burnett River, and is a more developed holiday resort with ample shops, hotel, and caravan parks. The Lighthouse is now located next to the hall. It was taken out of service in 1972 and is now a 107 years old.

Moore Park, 21km north of Bundaberg, is an excellent seaside beach with 16km of firm sandy beach.

Banjo's Horse Riding Centre is only 5 mins from town on the banks of the Burnett River – Ph 72 3357 for bookings – open every weekend and all school holidays, and weekday bookings can be arranged. All rides supervised.

For an unusual treat try some tropical wine which is made from pineapple, passionfruit or other tropical fruit in season – 78 Mt. Perry Road, Ph 71 5993.

FESTIVALS:
The Bundaberg Harvest Festival is held each year in September/October.

FACILITIES:
Boating, fishing, swimming, scuba diving, ten pin bowling, golf club at Bargara, bingo, movies, bowls, croquet, horse riding, tennis, water skiing etc.

OUTLYING ATTRACTIONS:
CHILDERS, 50km south of Bundaberg, has rich red soil and is famous for its avenue of leopard trees, colonial buildings, the Olde Butcher Shoppe and the Hall of Memories. Less than half an hours drive away is Woodgate Beach and Woodgate National Park which has many walking circuits and a special bird-watching shed on the Melaleuca Circuit, the highlight of the park, while an extensive boardwalk allows walkers access to the swampy areas with beautiful flowering water lillies. The beach is popular for catamaran enthusiasts and competitions are held regularly.

BIGGENDEN, 100km south-west of Bundaberg, has the historic Chowey Bridge, the old Mt. Shamrock Gold Mine, the operational open-cut magnetite mine, the Coalsttoun Lakes, Mt. Walsh National Park and the Mt. Woowoonga Forest Reserve.

EIDSVOLD, 250km west via Gayndah, has a truly unique museum housing the George Shaffer Collection – bottle, rock and gemstone collection.

GAYNDAH, 166km south-west of Bundaberg, is famous for its citrus fruit. If one wasn't aware of it before, one could hardly miss the Big Orange complex.

MUDUBBERA is also surrounded by citrus orchards and has the Enormous Ellendale (Big Mandarin). The Golden Mile Orchard has an extensive packing facility. 35km west is the Auburn Falls National Park with its beautiful rock pools and formations.

MONTO, 203km west, is the largest centre of the North Burnett and is the service centre for the surrounding dairy industry. 24km north-east is Cania Gorge with its spectacular sandstone formations, and crystal pools. Walkways and boardwalks extend well into the gorge. 8km further on is the massive Cania Dam with its attractive picnic areas. Gold was discovered at Cania in 1891 and some flecks of gold can be panned from the streams even to-day.

Approximately half way between Gin Gin and Bundaberg, at South Kolan, are 27 mystery craters at least 25 million years old. They are a major tourist attraction with garden setting, observation tower, taped commentary, kiosk, rocks, etc – open daily.

At TIRROAN, near Gin Gin, 65km from Bundaberg at the Daylily Display Centre, Ph 77 6232, there is a collection of thousands of daylilies from China, Japan and America – open Tues, Wed, Fri, Sat & Sun 9am-5pm (prime time October-January).

A day trip to the reef aboard the M.V. 'Lady Musgrave' takes only two and a half hours. Lady Musgrave Island, 49km from the coast, is a truly unspoiled, uninhabited coral atoll where you can stroll through the pisonia and casuarina trees and view the nesting seabirds. The launch trip includes morning and afternoon teas, buffet lunch, snorkelling gear, glass bottomed boat, and bar facilities. Optional extras include introductory dive course and joy flights. Flying boats also leave Bundaberg airport for the 40min flight to Lady Musgrave Island lagoon.

MARYBOROUGH, 113km south, situated on the Mary River has a population of 23,000 and its tree-lined street and Queens Park make it a pleasant city.

HERVEY BAY, 120km south, is a mecca for southern tourists and Point Vernon, Pialba, Scarness, Torquay and Urangan all offer resort accommodation, safe swimming and are a gateway to Fraser Island. Vehicular and passenger ferry services depart from Hervey Bay for the island.

FRASER ISLAND, the world's largest sand island, has an area of 150,499ha. It is a place for the adventurous holidaymaker. There are over 40 freshwater lakes on the island. One of the most spectacular sights on the island are the 40km of coloured sand cliffs between the Maheno and Indian Heads. These have been sculptured by the wind and contain many varying shades. N.B. 4WD vehicles are the only practical means of transport on the island. These can be transported to the island by barge or hired on the island. Orchid Beach Air Services and Sunstate Airlines and Parker's Air Taxis all fly to Frazer Island. If you wish to camp on the island, or bring a vehicle to the island, a permit must be obtained prior to arrival from the Qld. National Parks and Wildlife Service or Forestry Department Offices.

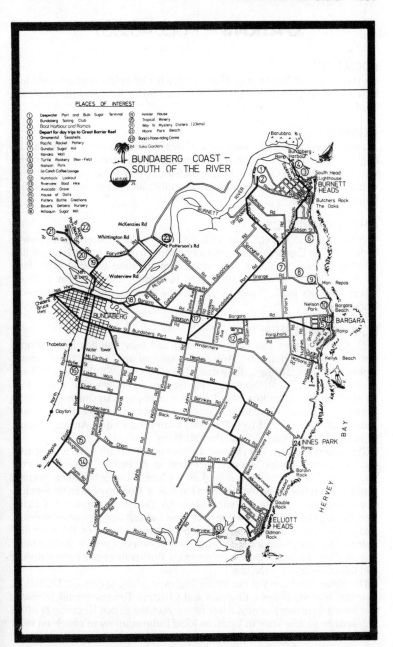

PLACES OF INTEREST

1. Deepwater Port and Bulk Sugar Terminal
2. Bundaberg Sailing Club
3. Boat Harbour and Ramps
4. **Depart for day trips to Great Barrier Reef**
5. Ornamental Seashells
6. Pacific Rocket Pottery
7. Qunaba Sugar Mill
8. Kanaka Well
9. Turtle Rookery (Nov - Feb)
10. Nielson Park
11. La Conch Coffee Lounge
12. Hummock Lookout
13. Riverview Boat Hire
14. Avocado Grove
15. House of Dolls
16. Potters Bottle Creations
17. Bauer's Gerbera Nursery
18. Millaquin Sugar Mill

19. Hinkler House
20. Tropical Winery
21. Way to Mystery Craters (23kms)
22. Moore Park Beach
23. Banjo's Horse-riding Centre
24. Iluka Gardens

BUNDABERG COAST –
SOUTH OF THE RIVER

CAIRNS – Pop. 48,557

LOCATION:
On the shores of Trinity Bay. Most northerly city in Queensland and ideal base for touring Cape York, the northern Barrier Reef and the Atherton Tablelands.

CLIMATE:
Average Temperature: January max. 32 deg. C – min. 24 deg. C; July max. 25 deg. C – min. 17 deg. C.; Extremely high humidity in summer – best time to visit is from May to October, but if you want to chase the marlin, then you will have to come from September-December and put up with the higher humidity.

CHARACTERISTICS:
Cairns has broad streets lined with travellers palms and colourful flower beds, and The Esplanade provides a charming frontage to the bay and has excellent picnic facilities. The rugged mountains, covered with lush rainforest, give Cairns a magnificient backdrop, and the boat harbour where the game fishing boats tie up adds the finishing touch to this tropical 'paradise'.

HOW TO GET THERE:
AIR. Cairns airport has been extended and now handles international traffic as well as domestic. Australian Airlines and Ansett have regular flights to Alice Springs, Brisbane, Darwin, Gove/Nhulunbuy, Hobart, Launceston, Mt. Isa, Melbourne, Perth, Sydney and Townsville. Ansett also flies to Canberra, Hamilton Island, and Rockhampton. Air Queensland fly to Aurukun, Bamaga, Cooktown, Groote Eylandt, Karumba, Kowanyama, Lizard Island, Lockhart River, Thursday Island and Weiper. Ansett N.T. also fly to Darwin. Air Niugini fly to Port Moresby

BUS. Ansett Pioneer, Greyhound, Deluxe and V.I.P. all have a Brisbane/Cairns service. Ansett Pioner, Greyhound & Deluxe have a Cairns/Townsville/Darwin service as well as a Cairns/Townsville/Alice Springs service. Cooktown-Cairns Bus Service has a Cooktown/Cairns service. Coral Coaches operate a Cairns/Atherton Tableland service, a Cairns/Mossman, a Cairns/Cooktown service, and Cairns/Cape Tribution service.

RAIL. The Queenslander and Sunlander trains run between Brisbane and Cairns. The Queenslander is a premier weekly service with first class only. The Sunlander has first and economy class. Both trains leave early morning and take two days for the trip.

CAR. From Brisbane via the Bruce Highway, along the coast, 1720km, a four day trip; via Biloela, Emerald and Charters Towers, inland, 2095km, and also a four day journey. After heavy rain the Bruce Highway is often impassable so it is wise to listen to local radio stations to check on road conditions during wet weather.

TOURIST INFORMATION:

Two Visitors Information Centres: Cnr. Sheridan and Aplin St., – open Monday to Friday from 9am-5pm and Saturday 9am-4pm and 393 Sheridan Street – open 9am to 6.30pm.

ACCOMMODATION:

The Cairns area has over 40 motels, as well as hotels, guest houses, holiday apartments and 20 odd caravan parks. Prices vary considerably depending on the standard of accommodation and the season.

Some names and addresses: Premier Cairns Quality Inn, 209 The Esplanade, Ph 51 8999 – RO $82 double – suites $97-$155; Ramada Reef Resort, Palm Cove, 24km north, Ph 55 3999 – RO $90-114 double; Pacific International Hotel, 43 The Esplanade, Ph 51 7888 (opposite the Marlin jetty) – RO $112-150; Moderate Northern Heritage, 243 Sheridan St., Ph 51 5188 – RO $69 double; Hospitality Inn,137 Lake St., Ph 51 4933 – RO $60 double; Cairns Gateway Lodge, 35 Bruce Highway, Ph 55 4394 – RO $30 double; Newmarket Hotel Motel, Pease St., Edge Hill, Ph 53 4811 – RO $32 double; Budget City Caravan Park, Cnr. Little & James St., Ph 51 1567 – sites $7 double – onsite vans $16-25; Cairns Golden Key Caravan Park, 532 Mulgrave Rd., Ph 54 1211 – sites $7.90 double – onsite vans $22 double; Coles Caravan Park, 28 Pearce St., 53 1163 – sites $6.80 double – onsite vans $22.50 double- cabins $31 double; The Cairns City Youth Hostel, 67 The Esplanade, Cairns, Ph 51 2225 – courtesy pickup bus operates between airport, railway, bus depots and hostel- phone for details. Travel bureau on premises with offers of good discounts on reef trips to YHA members – $6 ppn; Cairns Airport Youth Hostel, The Jungle Club, 28 Collins Ave., Edge Hill – $6 ppn. Hostel is in virgin rainforest within walking distance from airport, near Kuranda railway line and 200m from Bruce Highway. There are also some privately run hostels along The Esplanade which charge around $7 ppn e.g. The Caravalla, 77-81 and 149 The Esplanade.

EATING OUT:

Cairns has some of the best eateries in Queensland. Most of the international standard hotels and motels have at least one restaurant as well as a bistro, or the like. There are plenty of take-aways and many of the hotels in the centre of town serve counter meals. There is a good selection of restaurants.

POINTS OF INTEREST.

There are no sandy beaches in Cairns itself only mudflats, but prolific birdlife gathers there. Palms line many streets, and parks and gardens are a riot of colour from bougainvillea, hibiscus, poinciana and other tropical blooms. The old part of town is to be found around Wharf Street, and The Esplanade. The National Trust has put out a walking tour brochure about this part of town. The Esplanade is 5km long and runs along the side of the bay. This parklike area is a very pleasant place to relax in the cooler parts of the day. Also on The Esplanade is Reef World, which has displays of

Great Barrier Reef marine life – open 9am-5.30pm daily – feedtime time 2pm daily.

The Bulk Sugar Terminal at Smiths Creek handles the sugar from four district mills at Babinda, Gordonvale, Edmonton and Mossman. There are half-hour guided tours on Tuesdays and Thursdays at 3.10pm during the crushing season (mid July to early November).

The Flecker Park Botanic Gardens, Collins Avenue, Edge Hill, are open daily and feature graded walking tracks through natural rain forest to Mount Whitfield, from where excellent views of the city and coastline can be obtained. The Centenary Lakes, Grenslopes Street, Cairns North, are an extension of Flecker Botanic Gardens and were created to mark the city's centenary in 1976. There are two lakes, one fresh water, the other salt. Bird life abounds and barbecue facilities have been provided. Mt. Mooroobool (610M) in the background is the city's highest peak.

The House on the Hill, Kingsford St., Mooroobool (now a restaurant) was built in 1896 for Richard Kingsford, the first mayor of Cairns.

The Laroc Coral Jewellery Factory, Cnr. Armuller and Comport St., Portsmith is generally open seven days a week, and most nights (phone 51 6929 for times).

The paddlewheeler, S.S. Louisa, departs from the Marlin jetty, Trinity Inlet daily at 10am and 3pm for a still-water cruise. The imposing Civic Centre, Cnr. Florence and Sheridan Streets, is the city's cultural centre. A time capsule located in the Civic Centre grounds is to be opened when the city celebrates its second century.

Limberlost Nursery, 113 Old Smithfiled Road, Freshwater is well known for its orchids.

The Royal Flying Doctor Base, 1 Junction St., Edge Hill provides a radio link with isolated stations – visitors welcome Mon-Fri 10am-12noon & 2-4pm. Audio-visual displays outline the various procedures of the School of the Air and the Medical Service.

The Cairns Waterworks, Grafton Street, features a spa pool, waterslide, and four Japanese-style personal spas.

Cairns is a staging place for tours to the Great Barrier Reef, the Islands, the Atherton Tablelands, the Barron Gorge, Cooktown and Cape Tribulation.

FESTIVALS:

The week long Fun in the Sun Festival is held in October.

FACILITIES:

All type of water sports are catered for, as well as the usual sporting activities.

OUTLYING ATTRACTIONS:

GREEN ISLAND:

The island is a true coral cay situated about 29km north-east of Cairns. It grew out of debris washed from its surrounding platform of coral, and is gradually being pushed north-west by prevailing currents. It is only about 1m above high tide and thickly wooded. You can stay on the island in one of the 22 units which cost about $54 DBB per person in the off season and about $74 during the tourist season. The waters still abound with sea life and the beach is beautiful. It only takes about 20 mins to walk about the island. There is an underwater observatory, Marineland Melanesia, which features a large crocodile pool, a fish tank arcade and a display of New Guinea artefacts, and the Barrier Reef Theatre with a film on the reef. There are several ways of getting to Green Island and, of course, they cost varying amounts. You could take the budget launch trip which takes 90 mins and costs $12 for the return trip or you could include a glass bottom boat trip and lunch and the fare rises to $24. Then there is the faster catamaran which makes the trip in 40 mins and costs $22 or, if you include glass bottom boat and lunch, then its $35.

Hayles also run an outer Barrier Reef Cruise which includes 2 hours on Green Island, 3 hours at the Outer Barrier Reef, a ride in a semi-sub. coral viewer, smorgasbord lunch, glass bottom boat, free snorkel gear for $65 (scuba diving available – extra cost); and a Michaelmas Cay Cruise with 2 hours on Green Island, approx. 3 hours on Michaelmas Cay, smorgasbord lunch, glass bottom boat, free snorkel gear and semi-sub. coral viewing for $54.

LIZZARD ISLAND is the most northerly of the resorts and caters to the tastes of the wealthy. During the season, sports fishermen from all over the world come here for the marlin fishing. It is also close to some of the best scuba diving spots on the reef.

THE TABLELANDS:

One of the most popular trips from Cairns is the train trip to KURANDA. The railway line climbs slowly up the Barron Gorge revealing new panoramas around every bend. The train stops at the Barron and Stoney Creek Falls so that passengers can view the falls. The Kuranda Railway Station is a cool, green tropic delight of native shrubs, ferns and flowers. The air here is cooler and crisper than on the coast. There is a popular Youth Hostel in Kuranda, 6 Arara St., Ph (070) 93 7355 – $7 ppn.

On the ATHERTON TABLELANDS some of the places of interest are Mareeba, Tolga Rainforest, Atherton, the Curtain Figtree near Yungaburra, and the crater lakes of Eacham and Barrine (a cruise on peaceful Lake Barrine is a delight). The Chillagoe Caves National Park, has 8 caves open for inspection: The Donna Cave, Pompeii Cave, Bauhinia,, Royal Arch Cave, and the Fairy Caves.

The EVELYN TABLELANDS attractions are the Nerada Tea Plantation, Drawford's Lookout, Millaa Millaa Falls, Mt. Hugh Nelson Lookout, the Crater National Park and Malanda Falls.

NORTH OF CAIRNS:

Just another reminder about the Box Jelly Fish or Stingers which infest the beaches during the summer months!

The turnoffs to the beaches branch off the Cook Highway for approx. the next 20km after leaving the suburbs, the first one being to Machans Beach, then there is Holloway Beach, Yorkey's Knob, Trinity Beach, Clifton Beach, and Palm Cove with the Wild World Bird and Crocodile Park. After that the highway virtually follows the coast until just before the Port Douglas turnoff. Ellis Beach has white sand and coconut palms. Continuing further north you will come to Pebbly Beach with its blanket of multicoloured smooth stones.

Wild World Animal and Reptile Reserve, 22km north of Cairns, is worth a visit. They have an educational commentary and you can see crocodiles being feed – open 9am-5pm daily.

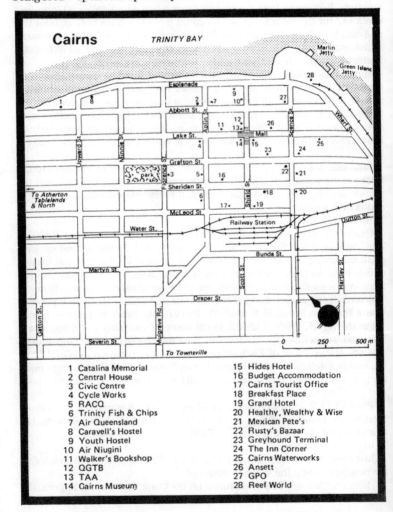

1 Catalina Memorial	15 Hides Hotel
2 Central House	16 Budget Accommodation
3 Civic Centre	17 Cairns Tourist Office
4 Cycle Works	18 Breakfast Place
5 RACQ	19 Grand Hotel
6 Trinity Fish & Chips	20 Healthy, Wealthy & Wise
7 Air Queensland	21 Mexican Pete's
8 Caravell's Hostel	22 Rusty's Bazaar
9 Youth Hostel	23 Greyhound Terminal
10 Air Niugini	24 The Inn Corner
11 Walker's Bookshop	25 Cairns Waterworks
12 QGTB	26 Ansett
13 TAA	27 GPO
14 Cairns Museum	28 Reef World

PORT DOUGLAS, 60km north of Cairns, flourished when miners rushed in their thousands to the Palmer Gold Fields but when Cairns was awarded the railway link to the gold fields, Port Douglas declined. It has a beautiful beach, great restaurants and interesting shops. Ben Cropp's Shipwreck Museum on the jetty has nautical exhibits of historical significance on display – open daily 9am-5pm. The MV Martin Cash makes a daily trip to Low Island, another coral cay, but without the 'tourist attractions' of Green Island. It is certainly worth the trip.

MOSSMAN, 75km north of Cairns, is the centre of a sugar growing district and the administrative centre of the Douglas shire. Take a tour to the Mossman Sugar Mill on the nostalgic Ballyhooley Steam Express along the old tracks through the canefields. The start of the Daintree National Park is only 5km north of the town, and a visit to the beautiful Mossman Gorge is a must. From Mossman you can either head along the coast to Daintree and Cape Tribulation (a deadend road) or take the road to Cooktown, which makes a broad sweep inland before heading back to the coast at Cooktown.

DAINTREE, on the banks of the Daintree River, lies 31km north of the Newell Beach turnoff. If you want to go on to Cape Tribulation then you will have to cross the river by vehicular ferry, which operates daily 6am to 6pm. The Cape Tribulation National Park north of the Daintree River, contains some of the best undeveloped coastal scenery and rainforest in Qld. The famous 'bouncing stones' are found just north of Thornton's Beach. Except after heavy rain, the road to Cape Tribulation can be navigated by conventional two wheel drive vehicles but the Cape Tributation-Bloomfield Road is only suitable for 4WD vehicles. Several of the Cairns coach companies run tours to Cape Tribulation.

COOKTOWN, is 341km north of Cairns and the last 130km are dirt. It is built near where Captain Cook landed to repair the Endeavour in 1770, after it was holed on a reef. As one would expect, there are many relics and memorials to James Cook. Cooktown had a population of 30,000 during the gold rush days of the Palmer River but the population today is only 900. It has a fascinating museum with many old relics. McGraths Bus Service operates a Cairns/Cooktown service three times a week.

GOLD COAST – Pop. 100,000

LOCATION:
The Gold Coast stretches from Tweed Heads on the NSW/Qld Border 32km north to Southport. It is the most famous tourist resort in Australia.

CLIMATE:
Average Temperature: January max. 29 deg. C. - min. 23 deg. C.; July max. 21 deg. C - min. 14 deg. C. Average annual rainfall 1724mm. Driest months July, Aug & Sept.

apartments, guest houses and camping grounds are more dense here than anywhere else in Australia. As a result of this the prices are surprisingly inexpensive and there is really no need to book outside school holidays. During holidays it is essential that you book. Many airlines, bus companies, tour operators, travel bureaus and even the railways offer package deal holidays which are excellent value. All the same I think you can get a better deal if you shop around when you arrive and you can see exactly what you are getting. The motels and camping grounds usually have their vacancy signs prominently displayed, and its not too hard to find a double for $25-30 a night, but if you want to stay longer then its cheaper to rent an apartment or house, but then you will need to have sheets, towels etc. Any of the many real estate agents will be only too pleased to help you. Of course, if you really want to live it up, there are also plenty of international standard hotels but of course, you pay international prices.

SOUTHPORT: Sundale Motel, 20 Queen St., Ph 32 2111 - RO $40 double; Hotel Cecil, cnr. Nerang & Scarborough Sts., B&B $30 double and is very central.

SURFERS PARADISE: Ramada Hotel, Paradise Centre, Ph 59 3400 - RO $100-115 double, suites $120-145; Holiday Inn Surfers Paradise, 22 View Ave., Ph 59 1000 RO $100-115 double, suites $130-600; Chateau Quality Inn, Cnr. The Esplanade & Elkhorn Ave., Ph 38 1022 - RO $73-106, suites $85-106; Gold Coast International Hotel, Cnr. Gold Coast Highway & Staghorn Ave., Ph 92 1200 - RO $110 double, suites $200-900; Golden Gate Resort Motel, 34322 Gold Coast Highway, Ph 31 8299 - RO suites $69-92; Pink Poodle Motel, 2903 Gold Coast Highway, Ph 39 9211 - RO $36-65 double; Silver Sands Motel, 2985 Gold Coast Highway, cnr. Markwell Ave., Ph 36 6041 - RO $28 double; Tara Holiday Village, 52 Cavill Ave., Ph 88 7877 - DBB $74-84; Riviera Motor Inn, 2871 Gold Coast Highway, Ph 39 0666 - RO $28-65.

BROADBEACH: Conrad International & Jupiters Casion, Broadbeach Island, Ph 92 1133 - RO $95-135, suites $245-700; Happy Holiday Inn, 2 Albert St., Ph 50 131 RO $50-79; Broadbeach International Hotel, Victoria Ave., Ph 38 4111 - RO $50 double, suites $75; Casa Blanca Motel, 2649 Gold Coast Highway, Cnr. Margaret Ave., Ph 50 3511 - RO $25-50 double. BURLEIGH HEADS: Fifth Avenue Motel, 1953 Gold Coast Highway, Ph 35 3588 - RO $38 double; The Gregory Motel, Gold Coast Highway, Ph 35 3282 - RO $25;

COOLANGATTA: Beach House Seaside Resort, Cnr. Marine Pde & McLean St., Ph 36 7466 - RO $78 double; Greenmount Villiage Inn, Hill St., Ph 36 1222 - RO $70; Pacific Village, 88 Marine Pde., Ph 36 2733 - daily incl. 3 meals $36; CURRUMBIN BEACH: Golden Moon Motel, Teemangum St., Ph 34 2470 - RO $25 double; Regent Court Motor Inn, 560 Gold Coast Highway, Ph 34 2811 - RO $25-40. PALM BEACH: The Estuary Motor Inn, 1026 Gold Coast Highway, Ph 34 5566 - RO $25 double; Tropic Sands, 1295 Gold Coast Highway, Ph 35 1044 - RO $32-$70; Tally-Ho Motel, 1500 Gold Coast Highway, Ph 35 2955 - RO $20 double;

CAMPING GROUNDS: BURLEIGH HEADS: Rudd Park, Ph 35 2529 - sites $9 double; Paradise Caravan Park, 7 West St., Ph 35 1142 - sites $9 - onsite

CHARACTERISTICS:

The Gold Coast has rolling surf, golden beaches and non-stop entertainment. All around Australia, I have heard that the Gold Coast has been spoilt with all the high rise development, amusement parks etc., but the visitors continue to flock there in their millions (no exaggeration). So it really must have what holiday-makers seek if they are honest with themselves. Of course, the secret may lie in the plain fact that it really does have something for everyone what ever mood they are in. Some sections like Bilinga, Tugun, Currumbin and Palm Beach are less developed than the Surfers area, and the beaches there are not crowded nor shaded by the high rise buildings, and just a few miles inland there are beautiful rainforests and waterfalls. Of course, we mustn't forget the Meter Maids - young ladies who wear gold bikinis and wander the streets putting money in parking meters so that visitors will not be fined when the meter has expired!

HOW TO GET THERE:

AIR.   Ansett and Australian Airlines fly to/from Adelaide, Brisbane, Hobart, Launceston, Melbourne, and Sydney. Air NSW fly to Williamtown, Newcastle. Eastern Airlines also fly to/from Armidale, Brisbane, Coffs Harbour, Lismore, Maitland, Taree and Tamworth. East West also fly to Sydney and Tasmania. Kenney's operate an airport bus and there is a regular bus service operating from Southport right along the coast to Coolangatta.

BUS.   Greyhound, Ansett Pioneer, Skennars, McCaffertys and VIP all stop at the Gold Coast on their Sydney/Brisbane route, Greyhound and Skennars operate a Brisbane/Gold Coast service and McCaffertys operate a Gold Coast/Toowoomba service.

RAIL.   From Sydney to Murwillumbah and then bus to the Gold Coast or to Brisbane.

CAR.   From Sydney via the Pacific Highway 900km. From Brisbane 79km to Southport and 100km to Coolangatta.

TOURIST INFORMATION:

Queensland Government Travel Centre, 38-40 Cavill Ave., Surfers Paradise, 4217, Ph (075) 92 1033 - open Mon-Fri 9am-5pm; Gold Coast Visitors & Convention Bureau, Cavill Mall, Surfers Paradise, Ph (075) 38 4419 & Beach House, Marine Pde., Coolangatta, Ph 36 7765; Tamborine Mountain Visitor Information Centre, Doughty Park, Nth Tamborine - open daily 10.30am-3.30pm except in very wet weather; Travel Centre of NSW, Pacific Highway. Tweed Heads, Ph (075) 36 2634 - open daily 9am-5pm. An extremely useful map can be obtained from any of the Automobile Association Offices, it is called the RACQ Gold Coast City map. It has small detailed maps of Surfers Paradise, Southport, Coolangatta-Tweed Heads, Burleigh, Tamborine Mtn and Nth Tamborine as well as a street index and detailed maps of the entire Gold Coast and hinterland.

ACCOMMODATION:

Accommodation is no problem on the Gold Coast as the motels,

vans $17.50 double;
    COOLANGATTA: Shambrook Caravan Park, Ph 36 7014 - sites $5 double;
    SOUTHPORT: Ashmores Caravan Park, Hinde St., Ashmore, Ph 39 3754 - sites $7.50 - onsite vans $20 double; Holiday World Caravan Park, Nerang-Southport Rd., Ph 39 1777 - sites $7.50 double - onsite vans $20 double - flats $40.
    YOUTH HOSTELS: Coolangatta Rd., Bilinga, Ph 36 7644 - $6 ppn; 2821 Gold Coast Highway, (El Dorado Motel) Ph 31 5155 - $6 ppn.

EATING OUT:
There are more than 300 restaurants on the Gold Coast and numerous take-aways. You won't have to look far for sustenance or a place to rage the night away.
    Some names and addresses: SURFERS: Captain's Table, Cavill Avenue is famous for its exotic cocktails and seafood; The Bavarian Steak House, cnr. Cavill Ave & Gold Coast Highway has a non-smoking dining area and cocktail bar; The River Inn, Ferny Ave on the banks of the Nerang River serves fresh seafood as well as dancing and entertainment; Cavill's International Restaurant, part of Tiki Village, offers indoor/outdoor dining; La Plume de ma Soeur Restaurant, Gold Coast Highway is a BYO restaurant where you can watch the Can Can; Twains International is open from 7pm-3am and has continuous live entertainment; The Penthouse, Orchard Ave is also open until 3.00am and has three floors of entertainment.
    BROADBEACH: The Conrad International has 3 great restaurants as well as the nightclub.
    COOLANGATTA: Oskars on the foreshore is a great place for lunch and dinner - smorgasbord as well as a la carte.
    MAIN BEACH: Grumpy's Wharf Restaurant, 212 Seaworld Drive has a relaxed atmosphere. Most of the hotels have counter meals which are usually good value.

LOCAL TRANSPORT:
Buses travel up and down the Gold Coast Highway from Southport to Coolangatta. The trip takes about 80mins and the services commence around 7am. All the major car rental agencies have offices on the Gold Coast and there are stacks of other smaller agencies. You can also hire mopeds from Surfers Moped Hire, Cavill Ave for around $8 day and also at Coolangatta. Bicycles can be hired at Surfers and Coolangatta. There are many operators offering coach trips to the various attractions. For more information pick up the yellow pages or one of the tourist newspapers.

POINTS OF INTEREST.
SOUTHPORT: Sea World, The Spit, Main Beach, Ph (075) 32 1055 - Australia's largest marine attraction, featuring dolphin and sea lion shows, ski shows, whale and shark feeding and unlimited use of the 11 rides - open daily from 10am-5pm. Southport Yacht Club, MacArthur Parade, Main Beach. Fisherman's Wharf, Main Beach is a unique entertainment centre

with restaurants, tavern, specialty shops, buskers, bands, swimming pool and playground. Australiana and Bottle Museum 3563 Main Beach Parade is open daily 8.30am-5pm and has a comprehensive display.

COOMERA: The big attraction is Dreamworld, a world of fun for everyone - with entertainment, daring rides, waterslides, and all the fun of the fair. At The Palms, Ph 52 2672 international dancing stallions, and miniature horses entertain you from 10.30am-4.30pm daily. Grass ski-ing at Coomera Grass Ski Park.

OXENFORD: Cades County wet'n'wild, Pacific Hwy, is Australia's largest waterpark.

NERANG: On the Nerang/Broadbeach Rd., you can ride in a Tiger Moth open cockpit plane - booking recommended 38 9083.

SURFERS PARADISE: The absolute 'in' place of the Gold Coast. There are always crowds of people wandering the streets no matter the time of the day or night. There are boutiques, side-walk cafes, amusement centres, take-away shops, bars, discos, cabarets, etc. etc. etc. Grundy's is probably worth a special mention as it's one of the landmarks. It is in the Paradise Centre, Cavill Avenue, Ph 38 9011. It occupies almost 3 acres and has rides, games and attractions including a waterslide. Surfers also has a Wax Museum on the Gold Coast Highway.

BROADBEACH: The site of the Gold Coast's only legal gambling casino, Jupiters in the spectacular Conrad International Hotel complex. The casino has over 100 tables of the world's most popular games and the multi-tiered, 1200 seat, international showroom features spectacular production shows. Many airlines, bus companies, travel bureaus, etc. have package deal Jupiter holidays, if you are interested. The Pacific Fair Shopping Centre, Hooker Boulevarde is Australia's most unusual shopping centre. It has open streets with international architecture such as Basin St., Flinders St., the French Quarter, Linden Strasse.

NOBBY BEACH: Magic Mountain, 2209 Gold Coast Highway is another family adventure park with 360 deg. views of the coast and hinterland. There are rides and theatre and fast-food stalls.

MERMAID BEACH'S Traintasia, Gold Coast Highway, Ph 55 2103 is a wonderland of model railways - open Mon-Sat 9.15am-5pm.

BURLEIGH HEADS National Park between Tallebudgera Creek and Burleigh Heads has delightful graded walks through bushland offering fantastic views of the coast. Fleays Fauna Reserve at West Burleigh is worth a visit as they have platypus and other native animals.

CURRUMBIN Bird Sanctuary, Gold Coast Highway, Ph 343 1266 - a National Trust Property where lorikeets feed from handheld dishes at 8.am, 10am and 4pm. Kangaroos, koalas, emus, penguins, waterbirds, and dingoes roam the reserve and every half hour a different group of animals or birds are fed. Seashell Marine Species Museum, 31 Millers Drive, Ph 34 1360 - open daily 10am-4pm.

TUGAN'S Land of Legend, Gold Coast Highway, 1km from Coolangatta Airport is a delightful place for kids of all ages - see the animated hilarious animals, the Pub with No Beer etc.

COOLANGATTA: Twinair operate joy flights over the coast and hinterland from the airport.

TWEED HEADS is in NSW and the RSL Club is very popular because of the poker machines. Tweed Heads also has a 25m heated indoor swimming pool, water slide, ten pin bowling alley and large shopping centre. The Captain Cook Memorial and Lighthouse stands astride the State border on Point Danger. Superb views can be obtained from Razorback hill behind the town. Palm Island Cruises have trips up the Tweed River to see its luxuriant sub-tropical forest, stopping at Murwillumbah for lunch. The Minjungbal Aboriginal Museum, Kirkwood Rd., Sth Tweed Heads, Ph 54 2275, open Tues-Fri 10am-3pm, has videos and displays, and there is a nature walk adjacent to the Bora Ring.

FESTIVALS:
Surfers has a drag racing Speed Festival at Easter.

FACILITIES:
The Gold Coast has all the facilities you could think of and then some more. You can play tennis, squash, golf, ten pin bowling, lawn bowls, and croquet. You can fish, swim, waterski, sailboard, sail etc. There are numerous cabarets, fun fairs, movie theatres, roller skating rinks and so on.

OUTLYING ATTRACTIONS:
There are several beautiful places in the range behind the coast e.g. Natural Bridge or Natural Arch as it is sometimes called. This large cavelike formation has beautiful clear water pouring through it and is surrounded by rain forest. At Springbrook there are several waterfalls and walking tracks and further inland is the Lamington Plateau National Park with many walking tracks. The main pl aces to stay are the guest houses at Binna Burra and O'Reilly's. Tambourine Mountains, 45km north west of the Gold Coast also have spectacular waterfalls and walking tracks. There is also a butterfly farm and thundereggs are found there.

MACKAY – Pop 35,361

LOCATION:
On the coast 1047km north of Brisbane.

CLIMATE:
Average Temperatures: January max. 31 deg. C - min. 22 deg. C; July max. 23 deg. C. - min. 10 deg. C.; Average annual rainfall 1672mm with over 1000mm falling in Jan, Feb & March -driest months June-November.

CHARACTERISTICS:
Mackay is surrounded by miles and miles of sugarcane fields through

which meander tram tracks, upon which run miniature engines transporting the cane to one of the seven sugar mills in the district. Between June and December the night skies turn red with the reflections from the fires in the cane fields, when the cane is burnt just before harvesting. The Mackay district produces about one-third of Australia's total sugar crop, which is exported through the Port of Mackay. North-east of Mackay just off the coast from Shute Harbour, is the Whitsunday Group of Islands containing some of the most popular of the resort islands of the Great Barrier Reef. Although these islands are not coral cays, the scenery is not much different to what one usually thinks of when dreaming of lazing on tropical islands on palm fringed beaches under tropic skies. The beautiful Eungella National Park 84km inland from Mackay has graded tracks leading through rainforest to waterfalls and cool pools.

HOW TO GET THERE:
AIR. Ansett and Australian Airlines fly to/from Brisbane, Melbourne, Rockhampton, and Sydney. Ansett flies to/from Cairns, Hamilton Island and Proserpine. Air Queensland fly to/from Brampton Island, Bundaberg, Cairns, Collinsville, Gladstone, Hamilton Island, Maroochydore, Maryborough, Proserpine, Rockhampton, and Townsville.
BUS. Ansett Pioneer, Greyhound, VIP, and Deluxe all stop at Mackay on their Brisbane/Cairns route. Greyhound and Ansett go through to Shute Harbour, but cannot transport passengers just between Mackay and Shute Harbour due to licence restrictions. McCaffertys also operate a Brisbane/ Mackay service which takes the inland route from Rockhampton.
RAIL. The Sundlander stops at Mackay on the Brisbane/Cairns route.
CAR. Mackay is 1047km north of Brisbane along the Bruce Highway, and to get to Shute Harbour turn off the highway at Prosperpine 124km north, and then its only 33km to the Shute Harbour, from where the launches leave for the Whitsunday Islands. Mackay is 1079km south of Cairns.

TOURIST INFORMATION:
Mackay has an unusual Tourist Information Office, a converted Chinese Junk! It is located on the Bruce Highway just south of town and is open 9am-5pm seven days. The Queensland Government Travel Centre, River St., Ph (079) 57 2292.

ACCOMMODATION:
Mackay has over 28 motels as well as a few hotels and apartments and about 15 caravan parks. You can expect to pay from $40-50 for a double in the majority of the motels and the older hotels usually cost around $21 double. Camping sites usually cost around $6-8 for two, and overnight vans around $18 double.

Some names and addresses: Four Dice Motel, 166 Nebo Rd., Ph 51 1555 - RO $48 double; Tourist Village Motel, 34 Nebo Road, Ph 51 2188 - RO $44-48; Metropolitan Motel/Hotel, Cnr. Gordon & Carlyle Sts., Ph 57 2802 - RO $36 double; Motel Northview, Cnr. Bruce Hwy & Phillips St., Ph 42 1077 -

RO $30 double; The Ambassador Hotel, Ph 57 2368, 2 Sydney St., Ph 57 2368 - B&B $20 double; Austral Hotel, Cnr. Victoria & Peel Sts., Ph 57 2639 - B&B $21. The Backpackers Hostel, 32 Peel St., Ph 51 3728 is not far from the Highway and costs $6ppn.

EATING OUT:
Most of the hotels serve counter meals which cost around $5-7. There aren't too many take-away shops, but then there's quite a few Chinese and other Restaurants, and several of the motels have restaurants which are open to the public.

POINTS OF INTEREST.
Mackay's wide streets are lined with royal palms. The old Customs House and old warehouses on the river bank date back to 1839, when Mackay's port was the river, but because of the enormous tides (around 6.5m), a new artificial port has been built on the coast. As well as having the world's biggest sugar terminal, which may be inspected at 9am Mon-Fri, Mackay has the world's largest coal loader at Hay Point. There is a small boat harbour within the large outer harbour from where Roylen Cruises leave each Monday at 12 noon for 5 day cruises of the Whitsunday Island and outer Barrier Reef. The Spirit of Roylen departs Wed-Mon at 9am and at 10am on Tuesdays for Brampton Island - for further information Ph 55 3066.

Right next to the port is the pine lined Harbour Beach where the surfies hopefully wait for the small waves at high tide. At low tide the water recedes sometimes 2km leaving only shallow swimming holes suitable for children.

Queen's Park in Goldsmith St., East Mackay is a showpiece of tropical palms, shrubs and orchids. The orchid house is open Mon-Fri 10.30am-11am & from 2-2.30pm, and Sundays from 2-5pm.

Extensive views of the town and countryside may be obtained from Radar Hill (along Mt. Bassett Drive) and Rotary Lookout, Mt. Oscar, North Mackay.

Tours of the Racecourse Sugar Mill are conducted Mon-Fri at 2pm during the crushing season from June to November - for further information phone 52 2038.

North of the town are several popular beach resorts e.g. Blacks Beach where scrub covered dunes stretch towards Slades Point. The area is crowded with holiday units, caravan parks, camping grounds etc. and is a popular catamaran and sailboarding area. It also has a netted enclosure which permits swimming in the summer months when the deadly box jelly fish infests the waters north from Mackay.

FESTIVALS:
A Mardi Gras is held each year in April.

FACILITIES:
Lawn bowls, croquet, fishing, swimming, sailing, car racing, golf, squash,

tennis, and trotting.

OUTLYING ATTRACTIONS:
HINTERLAND:

The Eungella National Park is 84km inland from Mackay and the road there follows the Pioneer River and its tributaries up the valley past Finch Hatton, and through Eungella township at the top of the range. Four sugar mills are passed on the way. The road after Finch Hatton has sharp curves and is extremely steep and not suitable for caravans. The view from the top of the range is really spectacular. The Broken River Road leads to a picnic and camping ground within the national park. A permit is required to camp in the park and this should be applied for 6-12 weeks before anticipated arrival.

PROSERPINE, 124km north of Mackay, is the gateway to the Whitsunday Island group and is only 20km from CANNONVALE and AIRLIE BEACH on the shores of Pioneer Bay. These two towns have grown together with the recent tourist development, and there is no shortage of accommodation for those wishing to avoid paying the exorbitant prices charged on the resort islands. It is possible to stay on the mainland and take a day cruise to the various islands. At least it is a good way to see which island you would prefer to holiday on at a later time. If you want to swim at Airlie Beach then it will have to be in a swimming pool as there is no beach to speak of there, you have to head north to Earlando or Dingo Beaches or south to Conway Beach. There is plenty to see on the mainland e.g. The Mandalay Coral Gardens, 3.5km off the Shute Harbour Road are definitely worth a visits as special films show the variety of coral which is found on the reef, and how coral grows, as well as guided tours through the gardens. A diving centre is also located there as well as bbq and picnic facilities - open daily 9am-5pm. Whitsunday Aquariums, Jubilee Pocket Rd., Airlie Beach are open 9am-5pm daily and feature a wide range of coastal fish - feeding time 11am. The Conway Range National Park has walking tracks at its northern end but is largely undeveloped. The Heirloom Doll Museum, 5km from Airlie Beach has dolls from around the world.

SHUTE HARBOUR, 36km from Proserpine, is an important transhipment point for the Whitsunday Islands. Launches depart from here for all the local resort islands as well as sailing boats and launches which may be chartered for day or week trips. Several boats have daily cruises to uninhabited islands and to the outer reef some 60km away. For further information phone 46 6224. Most of these boats will also drop off campers on uninhabited islands. All that you need is camping gear, a permit from the National Parks & Wildlife Office, Conway Range National Park, 1km from Shute Harbour, Ph 46 9430, food and water and the 'Aerogard'. There is plenty of open air and undercover parking available for those visiting the islands. For further information contact The Whitsunday Tourism Association at Airlie Beach on (079) 46 6673. There are also several operators offering flights to the Barrier Reef and Islands e.g Air Whitsunday, Ph 46 9133; Coconut Airways, Ph 45 1277; Hamilton Island

Aviation, Ph 46 9144.

WHITSUNDAY RESORT ISLANDS listed below can all be reached by launch from Shute Harbour:

HAYMAN ISLAND is the most northerly of the group and the resort has only recently been renovated. There are a number of bushwalks on the island and you can also walk out to Arkhurst Island at low tide. There is a broad fringing reef in front of the resort.

LONG ISLAND has three resorts, Happy Bay, Palm Bay and the newer Whitsunday 100. Happy Bay resort is not as commercialised and organised as some of the other resorts, and is enjoyed by many families. Its prices are less than most of the other resorts. Palm Bay is the cheapest island resort on the Whitsundays with 9 units which cost from $54-66 per day and can accommodate 4. They are extremely popular so it is essential to book well ahead phone (079) 46 9233. Whitsunday 100 is geared towards the youth market and it offers all sorts of activities and entertainment - cost accommodation & full board $75-135 ppn.

DAYDREAM ISLAND is the closest island resort to Shute Harbour and it is extremely small, less than 2 km sq, so if you are a keen walker this is not for you. The whole of the resort is built around an enormous swimming pool - accommodation, 3 meals and free use of equipment $89 ppn.

TELFORD SOUTH MOLLE is much larger and has quite a few bush walks. It has a 9 hole golf course, squash court, day and night tennis, quoits, softball, indoor bowls, games room and entertainment. It has 202 units and is one of the larger resorts - cost $82.50-$117 full board ppn.

LINDERMAN ISLAND has a heated pool, golf course, day and night tennis, bush walks, organised games, bush bbq and Adventure Valley a sleep-out, live-out, camp fire experience for 8-14 olds and play groups for younger children. There is also music and dancing, first-run movies, bingo, and pool and beach discos. Cost $86-94 full board ppn.

BRAMPTON ISLAND has many secluded beaches with unspoled bush and tropical foliage, and you can swim out and see underwater coral gardens and myriads of tropical fish just of the beach. There is a 5 hole golf course, archery, tennis, and entertainment. Cost $65-103 full board ppn.

HAMILTON ISLAND is one of the newest resorts and has a large fresh water swimming pool, a 400 boat marina and offers expensive entertainment such as helicopter joy rides, game fishing, parasailing, scuba diving etc. It also boasts shopping facilities, restaurants, squash courts, sauna and an air strip capable of taking small jets. Cost $150-$260 full board ppn.

HOOK ISLAND has no resort development, but it does have a camping area, and if you don't fancy camping on an uninhabited island or a resort island, then this just might be for you. This is one of the most popular day trip destinations for day trippers in the Whitsundays, but the crowds don't stay that long. The Underwater Coral Observatory is 10m under the water and affords visitors the opportunity to see plenty of fish. It is best visited from August to November when the water is clearest and least disturbed.

BOWEN is known throughout Australia for its tomatoes but it also has

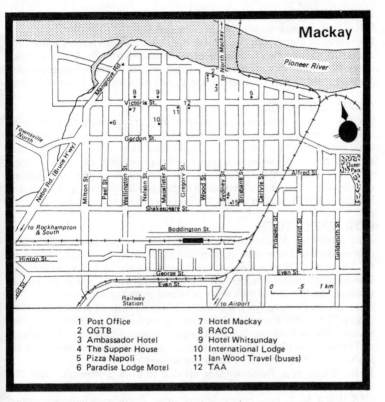

1 Post Office
2 QGTB
3 Ambassador Hotel
4 The Supper House
5 Pizza Napoli
6 Paradise Lodge Motel
7 Hotel Mackay
8 RACQ
9 Hotel Whitsunday
10 International Lodge
11 Ian Wood Travel (buses)
12 TAA

some rather good beaches. It has Golden Arrow signs numbered in sequence to guide tourists around its attractions. They start at the Salt Works. Some points of interest: The Historical Museum, 22 Gordon St. has displays of shells, minerals and Aboriginal artefacts; Abbot Point where coal is shipped overseas.

MT. ISA – Pop. 23,679

LOCATION:

On the Leichhardt River in the Selwyn Range which is the only relief in the north-western flatness. It is a hot, long drive across the sloping plains to the east coast. Mt. Isa is only 201km from the Northern Territory border whilst it is 1,821km from Brisbane and just over 900km from Townsville.

CLIMATE:

It has two distinct seasons – The Wet and The Dry. The Wet lasts from December to March, but the rainfall is not as heavy as further north only averaging 250mm for the four months compared with Burketown, which receives around 700mm during the same period. Average Temperatures: January max. 37 deg. C – min. 24 deg. C; July max. 24 deg. C – min. 10 deg.

CHARACTERISTICS:

The Isa, as the locals call it, is a modern mining town with over 100 clubs and 70 sporting associations. Because of its isolation, the people of Mt. Isa have endeavoured to make life as pleasant as possible and like other outback towns, it exudes a 'tougher' atmosphere than the coastal cities, which is probably the result of the harshness of the surrounding countryside. The mine is Australia's largest producer of copper, lead, zinc and silver. The best time to visit Mt. Isa is in the winter months.

HOW TO GET THERE:

AIR. Australian Airlines and Ansett fly to/from Alice Springs, Brisbane, Cairns, Darwin, Melbourne, Sydney and Townsville. Australian Airlines fly to Cloncurry, Hughenden, Julia Creek, Perth and Richmond. Air Queensland have DC3 flights to/from Cairns with 4 or 5 stops along the way if you would like to see a bit more of inland north Queensland.

BUS. Ansett Pioneer, Greyhound and Deluxe all stop off at Mt. Isa on their Cairns/Townsville/Darwin or Alice Springs routes, and Greyhound operate a service from Brisbane via Toowoomba, Roma, Charleville, Longreach, and Boulia. Campbell Coaches (an associate of Greyhound) operate a Mt. Isa/Karumba (on the Gulf of Carpentaria) service.

RAIL. There is a twice weekly service to/from Townsville and The Inlander takes 21 hours for the 900km journey!

CAR. Its a long, hot, rather boring drive from anywhere and when travelling in wet weather, tune in to local radio stations for the latest road reports. Extreme care should be taken when you meet road trains as these rigs are extremely long. From Townsville via the Flinders and Barkly Highways 900km; From Brisbane via the Warrego, and Landsborough Highways to Cloncurry and then on to Mt. Isa 1821km; 650km from the Three Ways junction on the Alice Springs/Darwin road; and 561km from Karumba on the Gulf of Carpentaria.

TOURIST INFORMATION:

Mt. Isa Tourist Information Centre, Ph (077) 43 7966 is open Mon-Fri 9am-5pm. The North West Qld Tourism and Development Board, Marian St., Ph (077) 43 7966 can help with information to out of the way places.

ACCOMMODATION:

Mount Isa has over 10 motels, 3 caravan parks and the usual assortment of hotels.

Some names and addresses: Burke & Wills Isa Resort Motel, Cnr. Grace

& Camooweal Sts., Ph 43 8000 – RO $55-58; Verona Motel, Cnr. Camooweal & Marian Sts., Ph 32 2014 – RO $56-65; Copper City Motel, 105 Butler St., Ph 43 2033 – RO $35 double; Welcome Inn Guest House, 118 Camooweal St., Ph 43 2241 – RO $24; The Riverside Caravan Park, 195 West St., Ph 43 3904 has sites for $8 double and onsite vans from $20 double; Sunset Caravan Park, 14 Sunset Drive, Ph 43 7668 has sites for $8 double and onsite vans for $19 double; Mt. Isa Caravan Park, 112 Marian St., Ph 43 3252 charges $6.50 for 2 and onsite vans cost $16 double; The CWA Hostel, 5 Isa St., Ph 43 2216 offers accommodation for women and children and costs around $10 ppn; The Youth Hostel, Wellington Park Rd. (opposite the Velodrome) Ph (077) 43 5557 – $6ppn.

EATING OUT:
The Clubs welcome visitors and most of the pubs serve counter meals. Several of the motels have licensed restaurants and there are several restaurants and take-away shops in the centre of town.

POINTS OF INTEREST.
The focal point of the town is the mine and its chimneys. The new lead smelter stack is 265m high and can be seen for miles around. MIM employs one in five of the city's population and most of the others are dependent on the mine. Mount Isa Mines Limited is Queensland's largest single industrial enterprise and its richest. The city dates back only to 1923 when the prospector John Campbell Miles found an ore outcrop, which is now marked by an obelisk. His ashes lie buried beneath a memorial clock near the post office. Mt. Isa was Australia's first company town and an example of early company housing, a tent house, is on display. A far cry from the company house of to-day. Surface mine tours are conducted Mon-Fri at 9am & 1pm and Sat & Sun at 9am in the tourist season. They leave from the Tourist Information Centre and last 2 hours and include a film. There is a charge of $4 for adults and $2 for children – children under 9 not admitted and sturdy footware is a prerequisite. For further information phone 43 7966. The Civic Centre which cost $3m to build and contains a 1000 seat auditorium and a library, is Mt. Isa's pride and joy.

At the city lookout there is a signpost which displays distances to cities all over the world.

Rotary International's Frank Aston Museum and underground mine display is cut into a hill close to the town centre – open 10am-3pm daily.

Lake Moondarra, 20km north of the town, is an artifical lake which is the city's acquatic playground.

Royal Flying Doctor Service Base is also the headquarters for the Qld. C.W.A., School of the Air, and the Cubs and Brownies of the Air. The Base on the Barkly Highway, Cnr. Grace's Bridge is open for inspection from 9.30am-11.30am Mon-Fri.

Fossicking is a popular pastime.

FESTIVALS:
The Rodeo is held in August and the Mt. Isa Show is held in June, the

Festival of Arts in September and the Oktoberfest and Eisteddfod are both held in October.

FACILITIES:

Mt. Isa has very good sporting facilities and the river and lake provide opportunities for aquatic sports.

OUTLYING ATTRACTIONS:

CAMOOWEAL 190km west of Mt. Isa is only a few kilometres from the NT border. It is a supply town for large cattle stations in the vast outback border area. In the 1880's it was an important stop on the great cattle droves. To-day the road trains, transporting cattle to the coast, still stop there.

MARY KATHLEEN is 65km east of Mt. Isa and was established in the 1950's to mine the then largest known deposit of uranium in Australia. The mine was closed in 1963, and was reopened in 1976 after modernisation, only to close again in 1982. The once bustling town is deserted.

CLONCURRY (The Curry) is 177km east of Mt. Isa and the surrounding hills hide many old ghost towns and ruins of early copper mines. The area was a big copper producer until Mt. Isa was developed. Maps of the ghost towns are available from the Court House for those who wish to visit or go gem fossicking. Most of these areas are only accessible by 4WD vehicle. Gold is also found in small amounts around the area. It was here in 1928 that the Flying Doctor Service had its beginnings and a Cloister of Plaques has been erected to commemorate its pioneers, on the site where the first pedal wireless call for help was received. The Mary Kathleen Memorial Park is situated at the eastern end of the town. The park contains a museum which houses one of the best rock collections in Australia, as well as memorabilia of Mary Kathleen and Robert O'Hara Burke's water bottle. The park is open 8am-5pm daily. There is a cairn commemorating the ill-fated Burke and Wills expedition beside the highway where it crosses the Corella River 43km west of Cloncurry. At the nearby Lake Corella there are picnic and bbq facilities. This lake was formed to supply the former mining town of Mary Kathleen. The highest official shade temperature, 53.1 deg. C (127.8F), was recorded in Cloncurry in 1889. Cloncurry's Merry Muster is a weekend event preceding Mount Isa's Rodeo, and is usually held in August. There are mineral springs at Mount Frosty which can be easily reached in dry weather. This popular swimming hole is about 9m deep with practically no shallows. There is also an old limestone mine there and the surrounding countryside is ideal for gem fossicking. From Cloncurry the Burke Developmental Road runs north to Normanton.

NORMANTON 375km north of Cloncurry, is the main town of the Gulf Country with a population of 110. It is 80km from the coast on the Norman River and was once an important port. The wharf has long since rotted, and the cattle trains now transport cattle to the eastern seaboard. The only rail line not linked to the main system in Queensland runs once weekly between Normanton and Croydon, a distance of 151km. Karumba on the mouth of the river is 69km by road from Normanton and is the main centre of the $10m prawning industry in the southern part of the Gulf. The trawlers bring the prawns to Karumba where they are snap frozen and air freighted to the southern states and overseas.

JULIA CREEK is 134km east of Cloncurry, and has massive oil shale deposits quite near the surface.

WINTON 342km south-west of Cloncurry, was the birthplace of Qantas. The Queensland and Northern Teritory Air Service had its first registered office in Winton in 1920 but migrated to Longreach 173km south-west. Winton is synonymous with sheep, and there is a cairn on Winton's town common commemorating the Great Shearers' Strike of 1891-4. In nearby Elderslie Street is Herb Young's waggon the last horse drawn waggon to bring wool to Winton's railhead. Road trains bring cattle from the Channel Country and the Northern Territory to the railway at Winton. Banjo Paterson wrote Waltzing Matilda at Dagworth Station in the Winton area in 1895, and a statue of a swagman has been erected in commemoration near the swimming pool. Australia's hottest artesian bore, 78.95 deg. C, is to be found at Castle Hill west of Winton. At Lark Quarry 5km off the Winton Jundah Road 105km south of Winton dinosaur footprints can be viewed from a suspended walkway.

NOOSA AND THE SUNSHINE COAST –
Pop. 80,000 (Area)

LOCATION:
The Sunshine Coast stretches from Caloundra, 90km north of Brisbane, to Double Island Point in the north, and boasts 55km of white sandy beaches and rocky headlands.

CLIMATE:
Average Temperatures: January max. 29 deg. C. – min. 20 deg. C; July max. 21 deg. C – min. 7 deg. C; Average annual rainfall: 1776mm; Driest months Jun-Sept. A lot of the summer rain falls as evening storms after hot sunny days.

CHARACTERISTICS:
Rather like the Gold Coast was in the 1950's or 1960's, except for Noosa, it has a friendlier not so impersonal air with less razzamatazz. The beaches and surf compare favourably with the Gold Coast, but there are not so many high rise buildings to cast shadows on the beaches in the afternoons. The high rocky headlands and areas of natural bushland divide the resorts, and afford the holiday maker the opportunity to walk along shady paths in the heat of the afternoon, or drop a fishing line into the shallow waters of the rivers and savour the peace and quiet. There are still small secluded

beaches which can only be reached by narrow sandy paths meandering through sand dunes, and the mouths of the rivers are ideal places to fish, canoe, row or sail. The Noosa River, which is navigable to near its headwaters at Tin Can Bay, is home to thousands of birds. The river flows through several lakes on its way to the sea and many houseboats are to be found along its reaches. The pace is slower here than on the Gold Coast, but that doesn't mean there is a lack of entertainment and decent restaurants. Unfortunately, the developers are now concentrating on selling the Sunshine Coast and it is obviously only a matter of time before there are dramatic changes.

HOW TO GET THERE:

AIR. There are three airports serving the region – Caloundra, Noosa and Maroochydore: MAROOCHY (as the locals call it) is equipped to take jets and visitors are transported from there by bus all along the Sunshine Coast - Ansett fly from here direct to/from Adelaide, and Melbourne; Air NSW fly to/from Sydney and Melbourne; Air Queensland fly to/from Townsville, Rockhampton, Maryborough, Mackay, Gladstone, Bundaberg and Brisbane, and Sunstate fly to/from Brisbane. CALOUNDRA: Henebery Aviation fly direct to/from Brisbane. NOOSA: Sunstate fly direct to/from Brisbane.

BUS. Skennars and Deluxe have a Sydney/Noosa service. Skennars also have three services a day to/from Brisbane – Ph 43 1011. VIP stop at the Caloundra turn-off on the Bruce Highway and at Nambour, and from there you can take a local bus to the coast. Greyhound, Ansett Pioneer and Deluxe also stop at Nambour on their Brisbane/Cairns route.

RAIL. from Brisbane to Nambour and then bus to the coast.

CAR. From Brisbane take the Bruce Highway north. The four lane section puts Caloundra within an hour's drive of Brisbane and Noosa is only 61km further on (another hour's drive along the Nicklin and the David Low Ways).

TOURIST INFORMATION:

Noosa Junction Tourist Information Centre, 15 Sunshine Beach Rd., Noosa Heads, Ph (071) 47 3798 – open 9am-5pm seven days; The Noosa Information Cemtre. Weyba Drive, has an audio visual theatre and maps with numbering systems that highlight the Sunshine Coast attractions; Queensland Government Tourist Bureau, Alexandra Parade, Alexandra Headland, Ph (071) 43 2411; The Sunshine Coast Tourist Information Centre, Kawana Waters is open daily 8.30am-5.00pm or call at the office at Noel Burns House, Nicklin Way, Buiddina, Ph (071) 44 5655; The Landsborough Shire Tourist Information Centre, Caloundra Road is open weekdays 8.30am-4.45pm, Sat 9am-4pm & Sun 10am-2pm. There are several tourist newspapers available which provide additional information e.g. 'Sunshine Coaster' or 'Sunshine Holiday'.

ACCOMMODATION:

Accommodation ranges from modestly priced budget units, houses and caravan parks to super deluxe international standard hotels and apartments. Holiday Noosa, Hastings St., Noosa Heads, Ph 47 4011 can arrange accommodation in houses or apartments from Noosa Heads to Sunshine Beach. The Tourist Information Centre can also arrange accommodation as can the Qld. Government Tourist Bureau.

Some names and addresses: NOOSA: Noosa International Motel, Edgar Bennett Ave., Ph 47 4822 – RO $100-200 double; Netanya Noosa Motel, 75 Hastings St., Ph 47 4722; Castaways Holiday Motel, Noosa Coastal Hwy, Ph 47 3488 – RO $50 double; Jolly Jumbuck Homestead Motel, 44 Noosa Drive, Ph 47 3355 – RO $39-45 double; Pine Trees Resort Motel, Hastings St., Ph 47 3200 – RO $35-70 double; Holiday Village, David Low Hwy, Ph 47 3294 – sites $9 double – cabins £20-30 double; All-A-Wah Caravan Park, Mary St., Noosaville, Ph 49 7247 – sites $8 double – onsite vans $18 double; Content Caravan Park, Weyba Rd., Noosaville Ph 49 7746 – sites $7.50 – onsite vans $21 double – cabins $27 double. Youth Hostel Douglas Street, Noosa – cost $6 ppn. MAROOCHYDORE: Blue Waters Motel, 64 Sixth Ave., Ph 43 6700 – RO $36 double; Coachmans Court Motor Inn Motel, 94 Sixth Ave., Ph 43 4099; Wum Palm Motel, Cnr. Duporth Ave & Phillip St., Ph 43 4677 – RO $34 double; Maroochy River Motel, 361 Bradman Ave., Ph 43 3142 – RO $28-31; Youth Hostel, Schirmann Drive, Ph 43 3151 – $6 ppn. CALOUNDRA: Palm Breeze Motel, 105 Bullock St., Ph 91 5566 – RO $33 double; Caloundra Safari Motel, Cnr. Orsova Tce. & Minchinton St., Ph 91 3301 – RO $30-36 double; Palm Breeze Motel, 105 Bulcock St., Ph 91 5566 – RO $33; Shearwater Motel, 79 Edmund St., Kings Beach 91 1744 – Ro $30; Golden Beach Caravan Park, 75 The Esplanade, Golden Beach, Ph 92 1296 – sites $7 double – onsite vans $20 double – cabins $22 double; Ocean Beach Caravan Park, Beerburrum St., Dickey Beach, Ph 91 3342 – sites $6 double.

EATING OUT:

The Sunshine Coast is a gourmet's delight. Dozens of restaurants feature fresh local seafood complemented by delicious sun-ripened tropical fruit such as avocados, pineapples and pawpaws. Beach and river fronts are dotted with picnic tables where visitors can enjoy take-away or picnic food. Some names and addresses of restaurants: NOOSA: Angels Sidewalk Restaurant and Piano Bar open 7.30am for Breakfast and until late – live entertainment most nights, Hastings St.; The Jolly Jumbuck, Family Restaurant, Noosa Drive, Ph 47 3355. For first class dining try Michelles, Hastings St., Noosa Heads, 47 4722 – open 7 days or Jammys on the ocean front, David Low Way, Sunrise Beach, Ph 47 3944. MOOLOOLABA: Goodtime Charlie's Restaurant and Cabaret, The Esplanade, Ph 44 1745 – licensed until 3am. Captain Feather's Charcoal Chicken, Sunshine Beach Road, Ph 47 3425. MAROOCHYDORE: La Terrasse Restaurant, 57 The Esplanade, Ph 32 2914, has exquisite French and seafood cuisine. For a friendly country pub, try the Victory Hotel, Maple St., Cooroy, Ph 47 6355 – counter lunches and dining room or the Kenilworth Hotel, Elizabeth St., Ph 46 0206.

LOCAL TRANSPORT:

Buses: Caboolture Bus Lines, Phj 95 2286; Didillibah Bus Service, Ph 44 2553; Kangaroo Bus Lines, Ph 95 1466; Nambour Bus Service Ph 45 9724l Sunshine Coast Buses, Ph 43 4555; North Arm Bus Service, Ph 46 7377; Tewantin Bus Service Ph 49 7422; Thornely's Bus Service Ph 48 7340; Doonan Ph 47 8649 – phone for up-to-date timetables. Car Rental: Hertz, 10 Aerodrome Rd., Maroochydore, Ph 43 5422 – Noosa Junction Ph 47 3433; Budget Noosa, Ph 47 4510; Maroochydore, Nambour, Caloundra 43 6555 (toll free interstate) (008) 331331; Noosa Car Rental, Noosa Drive, Noosa Heads, Ph 47 3777.

POINTS OF INTEREST:

The Sunshine Coast boasts 60km of good surfing beaches and all the larger beaches are patrolled. Water sports are the most popular attraction and you can try your hand at everything from scuba diving through to water-skiing and sailboarding. Sailing and fishing are also popular and overseas yachts are often tied up at Mooloolaba Harbour. The hinterland has magnificent rainforests and outstanding views can be obtained from the Blackall Ranges.

CALOUNDRA: The Endeavour, Landsborough Parade, Golden Beach, Ph 92 1278 is a scaled replica of Captain Cook's barque – open daily 9am-4.45pm. A good way to see some of the waterways is to either take a cruise on the 'Love Boat' along Pumicestone Passage to Bribie Island, which is the northern most island of Moreton Bay, or a cruise on 'Showboat II' which leaves from the rear of the Endeavour replica daily at 1pm for a two hour cruise. The Seashell Gallery, Nicklin Way has a comprehensive collection of shells, coral and tropical butterflies. The World of Matchcraft, Nicklin Way, is another attraction which is popular with little people as it has miniatures of the worlds greatest attractions made from matchsticks e.g. The Great all of China, Eiffel Tower, Taj Mahal etc. – open daily 9am-5pm.

MOOLOOLABA beach is protected by Point Cartwright and the harbour wall, making it an extremely protected beach which is popular with families and windsurfers. Windsurfers and catamarans can be hired at the Spit. Mooloolaba is home to a large fishing fleet and fresh fish can be purchased from the Mooloolaba Fish Co-op.

ALEXANDRA HEADLAND has great surf and the Boolarong Motel opposite the surf, is renowned for its fine seafood.

MAROOCHYDORE at the mouth of the Maroochy River, is a thriving tourist centre as it has both a fine surfing beach, and the still waters of the river for water skiing, sailing and fishing. It also has good restaurants and other tourist facilities such as Bern Kemp's Gallery of Sand Paintings, 209 Bradman Avenue, which has a collection of natural coloured sand paintings – open Tues-Sat 9am-4pm and Suncity Bowl, Ph 43 2580 for tenpin bowling.

The road north swings away from the coast at Maroochydore and follows the banks of the river to the bridge near BLI BLI where there are many canefields. Also at Bli Bli is Fairytale Castle, a replica 11th century Norman Castle with moat, porticullis and drawbridge. Inside fairytales are depicted in elaborate dioramas – open daily 9am-5pm. Another attraction there is the Suncoast Pioneer Village, David Low Highway, Ph 48 7155 – open daily.

The road then swings back towards the coast past Maroochy Airport and Mt. Coolum to COOLUM BEACH where the surf is great. The road north follows the coast past Peregian Beach, Marcus Beach, and Sunshine Beach to NOOSA. Noosa is the most northerly of the resorts, and has a north facing beach which is extremely unusual, sheltered from the prevailing south-easterly winds by the headland. It has a lively surf and in the 60's and 70's surfers made the resort their mecca, but then it was discovered by the entrepreneurs who bought up large tracts of land and the face of Noosa changed. It has become more cosmopolitan and popular with the upper and middle classes. The natural beauty of the area remains, but the atmosphere is different. The headland is a national park and there are several walks meandering through it to the various attractions e.g. Boiling Pot, Hell's Gates, Paradise Cave. The boutiques and restaurants in Hastings Street are first class with prices to match, and there is no shortage of entertainment. You could be in Double Bay or South Yarra except the weather is probably warmer. Noosa is the place to go if you want to see and be seen. But despite that, it is really a beautiful area. Noosa, Noosaville and Tewantin are practically one town now. The coloured sands at Teewah can be reached by 4WD vehicle along the beach at low tide. Tours are available from Noosaville or Tewantin. Upstream from Tewantin the Noosa river meanders through lakes which are surrounded by wetlands with prolific bird life.

TEWANTIN is a small town in Noosa's Lake District. In the 1870's huge log rafts were guided down the river to Tewantin, where they were sorted before continuing on their way to Brisbane. Five lakes are linked in a waterway network stretching for almost 80km. Lake Cootharabna has a special area for learner water skiers. Many visitors spend holidays on houseboats wandering through the area.

FESTIVALS:
Mooloolaba's Harvest of the Sea Festival is held in May each year. Bribie Island's Festival Week normally starts the first week in October.

FACILITIES:
The Sunshine Coast caters for all watersports and windsurfers, catamarans, cruisers and houseboats can be hired. All sorts of sporting facilities exist e.g. tennis, squash, tenpin bowling, cinemas etc.

OUTLYING ATTRACTIONS:
NAMBOUR is the most southern of Queensland's sugar towns although less and less sugar is being planted due to a combination of low sugar prices, and the booming residential development of the area. Pineapple and other tropical fruit plantations are also found around the district. The Moreton Central Sugar Mill has tours by arrangment from July to

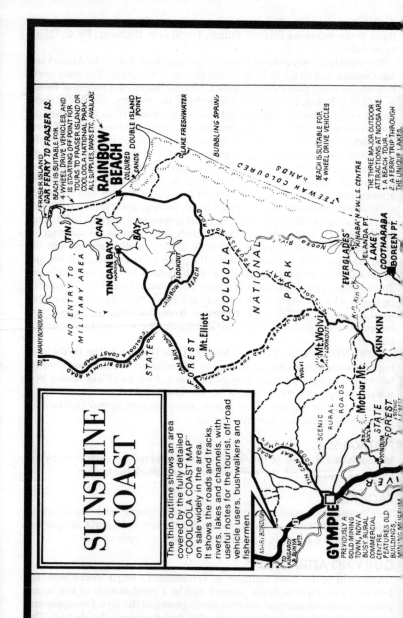

SUNSHINE COAST

The thin outline shows an area covered by the fully detailed "COOLOOLA COAST MAP" on sale widely in the area. It shows the roads and tracks, rivers, lakes and channels, with useful notes for the tourist, off-road vehicle users, bushwalkers and fishermen.

RAINBOW BEACH

FRASER ISLAND CAR FERRY TO FRASER IS. BEACH IS SUITABLE FOR 4 WHEEL DRIVE VEHICLES, AND IS STARTING OFF POINT FOR TOURS TO FRASER ISLAND OR COOLOOLA NATIONAL PARK. ALL SUPPLIES, MARS ETC. AVAILABLE

DOUBLE ISLAND POINT

COLOURED SANDS

LAKE FRESHWATER

BUBBLING SPRING

TEEWAH COLOURED SANDS

BEACH IS SUITABLE FOR 4 WHEEL DRIVE VEHICLES

THE THREE MAJOR OUTDOOR ATTRACTIONS AT NOOSA ARE
1. A BEACH TOUR.
2. A FERRY TRIP THROUGH THE UNIQUE LAKES.

TO MARYBOROUGH

NO ENTRY TO MILITARY AREA

TIN CAN BAY

TIN CAN BAY MARINA

COOLOOLA

Mt.Elliott

STATE

FOREST

COOLOOLA COAST ROAD HIGH SPEED BITUMEN ROAD

RAINBOW BEACH ROAD

TIN CAN BAY ROAD

RAINBOW BEACH

Noosa River

NATIONAL

PARK

"EVERGLADES"

WABA N.P.W.L.S. CENTRE

ELANDA PT.

LAKE COOTHARABA

BOREEN PT.

KIN KIN

COOLOOLA COAST ROAD. HIGH SPEED BITUMEN ROAD FOR FAST TRAFFIC

Mt.Wolvi LOOKOUT

WOLVI

RURAL ROADS

Mothar Mt.

STATE FOREST SCENIC DRIVE

SCENIC RURAL

GOOD BAY BITUMEN ROAD

TIN CAN BAY ROAD

PIE PK PK

WONDUNNA

GYMPIE

PREVIOUSLY A GOLD MINING TOWN, NOW A BUSY RURAL COMMERCIAL CENTRE FEATURES OLD BUILDINGS, MINING MUSEUM

M.R. BOROUGH

TO KGAROY & BUNYA

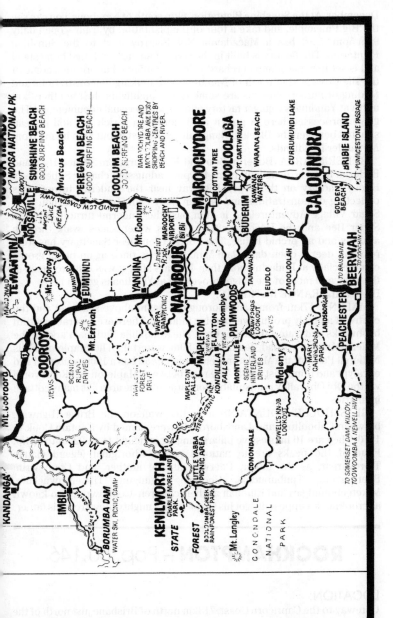

December. At the Sunshine Plantation, 6km south of Nambour, you can see the Big Pineapple, and take a tour of the plantation by train – open daily 9am-5pm. CSR has a Macadamia Nut Factroy next to the Sunshine Plantation. The factory is built in the style of an early colonial homestead and is set in a macadamia orchard – open 9am-5pm. Farmorama, home of the Big Cow, is 6km north of Nambour, and milking demonstrations and feeding of nursery animals are some of the highlights. Just another 3km north at Yandina is a ginger factory with an audio visual documentary. The ginger processed here is grown at Buderim on a rich red soil plateau situated between the Blackall Range and the coast about 8km inland from Alexander Headlands.

BUDERIM AREA: Buderim Zoo and Koala Park, Cnr. Bruce Hwy and Buderim Road is open daily 10am-4.30pm – admission charge; Super Bee's Honey Factory on the Bruce Highway near the Buderim turnoff, has collecting demonstrations and is open daily 9am-5pm – admission free. Sugar Village Adventureland is 1km past the Buderim turnoff between Super Bee and the Deer Sanctuary. It has water slides, walk through avairies and an orchid house. The Forest Glen Deer Sanctuary has free-roaming deer – open daily 9am-5pm. Coffee is once again being grown commercially at Buderim more than 40 years after it was last produced in the area, and most of the ginger processed at Yandina is grown here.

BLACKALL RANGE RETREATS:

MALENY, 17km from Landsborough, is 442m above sea level and the centre of a highly productive dairying industry. There are several beautiful bushwalks and waterfalls in this area. The Kondalilla National Park, off the Maleny-Mapleton Road, features an 80m waterfall. The Mapleton Falls National Park off the Mapleton-Kenilworth Road has a 120m waterfall and eucalypt and rainforest walks. The road between Mapleton and Kenilworth via the Obi Obi valley is unsuitable for caravans. The area has many cottage industries.

GLASSHOUSE MOUNTAINS near Beerwah on the Bruce Highway, between Caboolture and Landsborough, were named by Captain Cook in 1770. They are 10 impressive pillars ranging in height from 229m to 554m. Four of the peaks are in national parks. Aboriginal legend claims Tibrogargan as the father, Beerwah as the mother, and Coonowrin, Beerburrum, Tunbubudala, Coochin, Hgungun, Tibberoowuccum, Miketeebumulgari and Elimbah as their children. Coonowrin, also known as crookneck, supposedly got his shape from a mighty blow from his father.

ROCKHAMPTON – Pop. 50,146

LOCATION:
Gateway to the Capricorn Coast, 713km north of Brisbane just north of the Tropic of Capricorn.

CLIMATE:

Average Temperatures: January max. 31.4 deg. C – min. 21.7 deg. C; July max. 22.7 deg. C – min. 8.6 deg. C; The most rain falls between December and March – approx. 500mm.

CHARACTERISTICS:

'Rocky' is the heart of the beef cattle country. The main breeds are English Shorthorns, Herefords, Braford, Brahman, Africander and Zebu. Rockhampton also has two flour mills and they process wheat from the Central Highlands around Emerald. Ever since Queensland became a separate state, there have been people fighting for the establishment of a separate North Queensland State. A vigorous Capricornia New State Movement is still going strong in the 1980's.

HOW TO GET THERE:

AIR. Australian Airlines and Ansett fly to/from Brisbane, Mackay, Melbourne, and Sydney. Air Queensland fly to/from Bundaberg, Gladstone, Mackay, Maryborough, Townsville and Cairns. Air NSW fly to/from the Gold Coast, and Newcastle. Sabair Airlines fly to/from Gayndah and Monto. Eastern Airlines also fly to the Gold Coast. Sunstate fly to/from Great Keppel Island. Sunstate fly to/from Toowoomba.

BUS. Ansett Pioneer, Greyhound, Deluxe, VIP and McCaffertys all stop at Rockhampton on their Brisbane/North Queensland route. Greyhound also have a Rockhampton/Longreach service 3 times weekly.

RAIL. The Capricornian leaves Brisbane in the early evening 6 days a week and arrives in Rocky for breakfast the next day. The Sunlander and the Queenslander both stop at Rockhampton and leave Brisbane in the early morning. The Midlander runs between Rockhampton, Longreach and Winton twice weekly.

CAR. From Brisbane you can travel to Rockhampton via the Bruce Hwy 713km, or take the inland route via Esk and Biloela 758km. Rockhampton is 1413km south of Cairns.

TOURIST INFORMATION:

The Qld. Government Tourist Bureau, 119 East St., Ph (079) 27 8611 is open 9am-4.45pm and the Capricorn Information Centre at the junction of the Bruce, Burnett and Capricorn Highways.

ACCOMMODATION:

Rockhampton has no shortage of motels and there are plenty of older style hotels near the city centre, and there is a good supply of camping grounds.

Some names and addresses: Riverside International Motel, 86 Victoria Pde., Ph 27 9933 – RO $60 double – suites $55-$120; Duthies Leichhardt Hotel, Cnr. Bolsover & Denham Sts., Ph 27 6733 – RO $35-59 – suites $65-75; Simpsons Motel, 156 George St., Ph 27 7800 – RO $33 double; A1 Motel, 134 Gladstone Rd., Ph 27 4944 – RO $37 double; Municipal Riverside Caravan Park, Reaney St., North Rockhampton, Ph 22 3779 – sites $5.40 double;

Tropical Wanderer Caravan Villiage 394 Yamba Road, Nth Rockhampton, Ph 28 2621 – onsite vans $19-22 double. Youth Hostel, 60 Macfarlane St., Ph 27 5288 – cost $6 ppn. Its about 20 mins walk from the centre of town.

EATING OUT:

Most of the hotels serve counter meals and the steaks in Rocky are particularly big being in the heart of the cattle country. Several of the motels have licensed restaurants and there are the usual take-away places and Chinese restaurants.

POINTS OF INTEREST.

Rocky is the commerical and administrative centre of central Queensland on the banks of the Fitzroy River. Its wide streets are lined with trees and solid buildings, indicating a prosperity dating back to the early days. More than 50 buildings have been classified by the National Trust. Half of them are in Quay Street which runs along the banks of the river. The Australian Estate Co. Ltd. offices were built in 1861. The Customs House was built in 1901 and has a handsome copper dome and a striking semicircular portico. Queens Wharf is all that remains of the quays of this once busy port before the river silted up. St. Pauls Cathedral and St. Joseph's Catholic Cathedral are both built in Gothic style from local sandstone. The Royal Arcade was built in 1889 as a theatre with a special feature, the roof could be opened on hot nights.

The Botanic Gardens in Spencer Street on the Athelstone Range, have an excellent fernery and water fowl feature in the 18ha gardens. They also have an excellent butterfly collection.

The Rockhampton Art Gallery, Victoria Parade, exhibits works which reflect the sparseness of the outback as well as the lushness of the tropical areas – open 10am-4pm Mon-Fri & 7pm-8.30 Wed & 2-4pm Sun.

The Gem and Mineral Centre, 18 Denham St., Ph 27 3910, is open during normal trading hours and you can watch gem cutting and polishing.

The Capricornia Potters Group exhibits its work in Room 4 of Reid's Cultural Centre, Cnr. East & Derby Sts.

Outside the city is a bougainvillea-shrouded home built by the Archer brothers soon after they became the first settlers in 1853, The slab homestead is built by a lagoon which is Queensland's oldest fauna reserve. Another 1850's homestead is Glenmore which has been in the Birkbeck family since 1861 – open for inspection.

St. Aubins' Herb Farm, Canoona Road, opposite the airport, is a National Trust classified home built in the 1870's. It has a thriving herb garden with over 80 varieties of herbs in a natural setting.

FESTIVALS:

The Capricana Festival is held in September as is Yepoon's Pineapple Festival and the Calliope Spring Fair.

FACILITIES:

Rockhampton has all the usual facilities you would expect of a town of over 50,000 people. To get to the beach though you have to drive around 40km to the Capricorn Coast.

OUTLYING ATTRACTIONS:
CAPRICORN COAST:
Just a reminder that the box jellyfish can be present in the sea anywhere north of the Tropic of Capricorn in the summer months.

YEPPOON, is the largest and best known of the resorts which are strung out for 25km along the coast. Others are Keppel Sands and Emu Park. Yeppoon nestles beside hills on the shores of Keppel Bay. Pineapple farms straggle up the hills on one side and the sea is on the other. A Pineapple Festival is held each November. Palms and pines line the main street and shady trees line the road to Rockhampton. There is a 4m difference between high and low tide and at low time trawlers, yachts and dinghies are left high and dry. Just north of Yeppoon a large international tourist resort is being developed by Japan's Iwasaki Sangyo Co. It has been the cause of much controversy and even a bombing. There is an unusual memorial to Captain Cook at Emu Park, a singing ship. The mast, sail and rigging contain hollow pipes, and the ship 'sings' when the wind blows. Double Head shelters the boat harbour at Rosslyn Bay from where the boats leave for Great Kepple Island. If this is your real purpose for visiting Rockhampton, then you may find it more convenient and certainly cheaper to stay at Yeppoon.

GREAT KEPPEL ISLAND Resort has beautiful beaches and the coral may be viewed from glass bottomed boats. There are no motor vehicles on the island and visitors can walk its bush tracks for hours or simply relax on the beach. There is a small camping reserve, Wapparaburra Haven, behind the sand dunes at Fishermans Beach just north of the main resort buildings. You can camp for $10 for 2 per night or they have cabins which cost $45 double per night. There is also a kiosk there which is open from 8am-9pm daily and sells fruit, vegies, some meat, and a few basics, but of course its dearer than on the mainland. The daily tariff at the resort is $152-$190 a double all meals included or $97.50 -$119 single. There is also a Youth Hostel which costs $6 ppn but it's very popular and often booked out so if you plan to stay there, book a few weeks ahead at least. Middle Island, close to Great Keppel Island has an underwater observatory.
INLAND:
The Cammoo Caves, 23km north of Rockhampton and 2km off the Bruce Highway rival the Jenolan Caves in every way. Tours are conducted daily from 8.30am-4pm, Ph (079) 34 2774. Olsen's Capricorn Caverns are about 2km east of Cammoo Caves turnoff and tours operate Sunday-Friday at 8.30am, 10am, 11.30am, 1pm, 2.30pm and 4pm – Phone 34 2883.

MT HAY, 41km west of Rocky on the Capricorn Highway, has a Gemstone Tourist Park where visitors can fossick for thundereggs – admission charge.

MOUNT MORGAN, 38km south-west of Rocky, has a huge opencut mine 2.5km long, 2km wide and 360m deep. The mine has produced gold, copper, zinc, lead and silver. To-day a specialised carbon-in-pulp plant extracts gold from tailings. Inspections of the plant are conducted daily at 9.30am & 1.30pm – admission charge. GLADSTONE, 107km south of Rockhampton, has a long history as a port, firstly exporting sorghum and then as a coal exporter. Now the Queensland Alumina Refinery, the Gladstone Power Station and Boyne Island Aluminium Smelter are all contributing to Gladstone's progress. Only school groups can tour the Qld. Alumina Refinery, but the visitors' lookout is open to the public day and night. The Power Station can be inspected during working hours but booking is essential, and the Aluminium Smelter has conducted tours on Wed & Fri at 9am – bookings essential Ph (079) 73 0211 ext. 223. Launches leave Gladstone for Quoin Island Resort (inside the harbour) and also for Heron Island (2.5hr trip). Heron Island can also be reached by helicopter.

HERON ISLAND is part of the Capricornia Section of the Great Barrier Reef Marine Park. It is a national park and mutton birds come to nest between October and May. It is a true coral cay and the reef is excellent. You can walk out at low tide. It's a great place for snorkling and scuba diving and boats take divers to the most interesting places. There is plenty of bird life, and green and loggerhead turtles nest on the island from October to January and the hatchlings can be seen from late December to early May. Daily tarrif including all meals $80-$325 pp.

TOOWOOMBA – Pop. 63,401

LOCATION:
At the top of the Great Dividing Range 130km inland from Brisbane and having an altitude of 2,000ft (606m). The commercial centre of the rich pastoral area of the Darling Downs.

CLIMATE:
Toowoomba has a temperate climate and therefore is less humid than on the coast, with frosts in winter and rare light snow falls on the highest points of 'the Range'. Average temperatures: January max. 26.9 deg. C – min. 16.5 deg. C; July max. 16.2 deg. C; July max. 16.2 deg. C – min. 4.2 deg. C.

CHARACTERISTICS:
A true 'Garden City' which was first settled in 1849. Originally, the area was thought to be too swampy for a town and the first settlement in the area was at Drayton, now a suburb of Toowoomba. But water was scarce at Drayton and the town of Toowoomba was born. Many German immigrants settled around Toowoomba in the 1860's successfully farming the fertile land. The soil on the Darling Downs is rich, deep, and black. It is extremely fertile but a quagmire after heavy rain, and forms deep cracks in dry weather. Toowoomba is often called 'The Queen City of the Downs'.

HOW TO GET THERE:

AIR. Sunstate fly to/from Brisbane with connections to Bundaberg, Gladstone, Maroochydore, and Maryborough. Norfolk Airlines fly to/ from Brisbane.

BUS. McCaffertys have Brisbane/Sydney service via Toowoomba and also a Brisbane/Roma service which stops at Toowoomba. Ansett Pioneer and Grehound stop at Toowoomba on their Brisbane/ Charleville service and Greyhound also stop there on their Brisbane Longreach Service.

RAIL. There is a daily service from Brisbane. Quite a few people get off the train at Helidon and take the McCaffertys bus to Toowoomba because it is faster than travelling the whole way by rail. A combined rail/bus ticket is available. The Westlander stops at Toowoomba on its twice weekly run to Roma and Charleville.

CAR. From Brisbane travel through Ipswich on the Warrego Highway 130km; From Sydney travel on the New England Highway through Warwick.

TOURIST INFORMATION:

The Toowoomba Tourism and Development Board, Ground Floor, Town Hall Chambers, 541 Ruthven Street, Phone (076) 32 1988 can provide tourists with a map of the Blue Arrow Scenic Drives. The Queensland Government Tourist Bureau, 241 Margaret Street, Toowoomba, Ph (076) 32 2755.

ACCOMMODATION:

There are over 20 motels in Toowoomba as well as 6 caravan parks and several hotels.

Some names and addresses: The Sunray Motor Inn, Cnr. Bridge & McDougall Sts., Ph 34 2200 – RO $43 double; Park Homestead Motor Inn, 88 Margaret St., Ph 32 1011 – RO $52 double; James Street Motor Inn, James & Kitchener Sts., Ph 38 3066 – RO $42 double; Colonial Caraville, 730 Ruthven St., Ph 353 3233 – RO $42 double; The Southern Hotel, Ruthven St., Ph 35 3311 – RO $29 double; Toowoomba Motor Village, 821 Ruthven St., Ph 35 8186 has sites for $6 double and onsite vans for $18-20 double; Garden City Caravan Park, 34 Eiser St., Ph 35 1747 – sites $8 double – onsite vans $17 double. The nearest Youth Hostel is at Jondaryan, at the Jondaryan Woolshed Historical Pioneer complex 3km from Jondaryan – $3.50 ppn.

EATING OUT:

The hotels in the city centre serve good counter lunches and have dining rooms. There is no shortage of take-away places, several of the motels have licensed restaurants and there are several excellent restaurants.

POINTS OF INTEREST.

Toowoomba has beautiful treelined streets with many parks and beautiful private gardens. The city has an active cultural and artistic life. It looks its best in September for the Carnival of Flowers. People come from all over the State to look at the gardens entered in the competitions. There are several categories e.g. new private garden, good neighbours, factory garden etc. The whole of the town seems to take pride in their gardens and they really are a sight to behold. Toowoomba's chosen the violet as its floral emblem as this small, fragrant, flower flourises here. The view from Picnic Point Lookout is truly panoramic. On one side you have the city and on the other side, the whole of the Lockyer Valley with Table Top and Sugar Loaf Mountains in the foreground. The range stretches off into the distance to the south. West of the city is the distinctive Gowrie Mountain and the Kingsthorpe Hills.

The scenic Prince Henry Drive starts and finishes at the eastern end of Bridge Street and follows the clifftop around a small spur of the Great Dividing Range. It is a one-way traffic thoroughfare from which breathtaking views are obtained. It goes through the suburb of Prince Henry Heights and past Redwood Park Fauna Sanctuary.

For a view of the city lights at night drive along Ruthven Street which becomes Crows Nest Road, to the top of Mount Kynoch, the site of the city reservoir. There is a 360 deg. view of the town and the districts of Crow's Nest, Ravensbourne, Lockyer and Gowrie Mountain.

Queen's Park and the Botanic Gardens cover more than 70 acres and provide an attractive display all year round. Laurel Bank Park has a scented garden for blind visitors.

Toowoomba has some fine old buildings including the post office, court house, the White Horse Hotel, and Gabbinar and Clifford House both built in the 1860's as well as the more humble Tawa built soon after allotments were first handed out in 1849.

The old centre of Drayton, now a suburb of Toowoomba, has not been completely lost to development. The Royal Bull's Head Inn, the earliest hotel on the Downs has been restored by the National Trust. The 1850's building incorporates part of the original hostelry. St. Matthew's Church was built in 1887, and contains records dating back to 1850 from an earlier building. It has a splendid hammer beam roof, and the knocker on the vestry door originally graced the Bulls Head where the settlement's first services were held. Smithfield, a stately homestead built at the end of the last century, is now a restaurant. There is also a memorial to author Arthur Hoey Davis (Steel Rudd) who made Dad and Dave famous. Davis was raised at Emu Creek, 20km from Drayton, where he was born in 1868.

Toowoomba has several art galleries which are worth visiting: The Gould's and Toowoomba Art Gallery in the City Hall has an interesting collection of paintings and antiques – open 11am-3pm Mon, Wed & Fri; The Linton Gallery, 421 Ruthven St has paintings, pottery and sculpture – open Mon-Fri 9am-5pm & Sat 9am-noon; The Lionel Lindsay Art Gllery, 27-37 Jellicoe St., has a collection of works by great Australian artists, authors and poets – open 2.15-5pm Mon-Fri; Tia Art Galleries, Old Western Highway (Taylor St) about 7km from the city, display sculptures in wood and have exhibitions of paintings by well known Australian artists – open daily 9am-sunset.

The Cobb & Co. Museum beneath Cobb & Co.'s James St. Depot, has an unique display of horsedrawn vehicles.

The Toowoomba Doll and Model Train Museum has a comprehensive display of dolls and an intriguing garden railway – open Tues-Sun 10am-4pm.

The Teddy Bear Museum, Bell Street Arcade, 29 Bell St is open 10am-4pm Mon, Wed, Thurs & Fri and 2-4pm Sun.

Blue Arrow Drive, a 48km scenic drive well worth following – maps available at the Tourist Information Office.

Toowoomba also has an adventure park, like any other large city these days, Willow Springs Adventure Park.

FESTIVALS:

The Carnival of Flowers is held each year in September and The Green Week is held each April.

FACILITIES:

Toowoomba has all the facilities you would expect of a town with such a large population – golf, tennis, squash, horse racing, lawn and indoor bowls, croquet, swimming pool, cinemas, theatres etc.

OUTLYING ATTRACTIONS:

The Darling Downs are Queensland's main wheat growing area. Neat homesteads speckle the land and a pattern of fields stretches over the horizon. There are not only wheat fields but other grains are grown, as well as sunflowers and other oil seeds, and cotton. Dairy and beef cattle graize on the hills, and sheep further west. No visit to Toowoomba would be complete without a drive through the surrounding countryside.

Cooby Creek Dam is the source of Toowoomba's water supply and a popular picnic spot. Travel along the Crow's Nest Road and turn left 17km from the P.O. and its another 17km further on.

Just past OAKEY, 30km west, is Brookvale Park. It consists of 6 acres of Australian native plants collected from every state in Australia. It has possibly the largest collection of acacias (wattle) trees in the world.

DALBY, 83km west, has two memorials, one to the early settlers and one to the cactoblastis moth, and the scientists who introduced it to control the prickly pear which threatened to overrun the Darling Downs early this century. The destruction that it caused was so horrific that hundreds of farmers were driven off their land. The moth was introduced in 1925 and in 15 months the prickly-pear was under control. Dalby is the centre of the wheat growing area and and there are huge silos in the town.

The BUNYA MOUNTAINS, part of the Great Dividing Range, took their name from a stand of Bunya Pine trees on the slopes and crest. The area was proclaimed a national park in 1908 and has an area of 12,000 ha. Its highest points are Mount Mowbullan, 3,610ft, in the south and Mount Kiangarow, 3,725ft, to the north. This is the largest remaining stand of bunya pines, a species greatly depleted by early rainforest timber getters

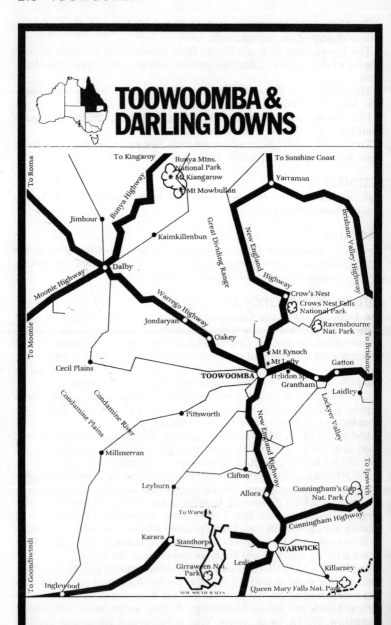

TOOWOOMBA &
DARLING DOWNS

Capt. Cook Bridge, Brisbane

Shute Harbour, Queensland

but the pines aren't the only vegetation in this area. Tree ferns are plentiful in the gullies and there are coral trees, bottle trees, grass trees and orchids are prolific on the cliff faces. There are some beautiful walking tracks through the park, including easy walks to McGrory's Falls, Festoon Falls and the Great Falls on Barker's Creek.

STANTHORPE, 811m, is the main centre of the Granite Belt, which produces much of the State's apple and table grape crop. Stanthorpe is well known in Queensland as it usually has the lowest temperature in the State. There are also quite a few wineries in the area.

CUNNINGHAM'S GAP, which lies between Mt. Cordeaux (1117m) and Mt. Mitchell (1128m) is where Alan Cunningham crossed the Great Dividing Range in 1828 while looking for a way through the range. A cairn has been erected in his memory in the picnic ground at the top of the gap. There are several walking tracks in the area and panoramic views can be obtained from the lookouts.

At the foot of the range is HELIDON SPA pool which has been formed to contain the natural spa waters. The waters are claimed to be beneficial and are bottled and sold around Australia. It is surrounded by delightful picnic grounds and the lake is large enough to water-ski on. The road to Brisbane travels through the Lockyer valley, a rich market garden and fruit growing area.

TOWNSVILLE – Pop. 86,112

LOCATION:
On the coast 1443km north of Brisbane.

CLIMATE:
Average Temperature: January max. 31 deg. C – min. 24 deg. C and high humidity; July max. 25 deg. C, min. 15 deg. C; Average Annual rainfall 1194mm – wettest months Jan-March with an average of 873mm.

CHARACTERISTICS:
The third largest city in Queensland and main commercial centre of northern Queensland. It sprawls along the shores of Cleveland Bay and around the foot of Castle Hill, a 300m high, bare, red granite outcrop, the most prominent feature of the town. The Port of Townsville has regular shipping services to Japan and the United States, handling containers, minerals from Mt. Isa, beef and wool.

HOW TO GET THERE:
AIR. Ansett and Australian Airlines have flights to/from Brisbane, Alice Springs, Cairns, Canberra, Darwin, Hobart, Launceston, Melbourne, Perth and Sydney. Australian Airlines have flights to/from Blackall, Charters

Towers, Cloncurry, Hughenden, Julia Creek, Mt. Isa, Richmond and Winton. Air Whitsunday fly to/from Airlie Beach and Orpheus Island. Air Queensland fly to Bundaberg, Collinsville, Gladstone, Hamilton Island, Mackay, Maroochydore, Maryborough, Proserpine, Rockhampton and Dunk Island. East West have a Townsville/ Devonport service.

BUS. Ansett Pioneer, Greyhound, Deluxe, VIP and McCaffertys all stop at Townsville on their Brisbane/Cairns services. Ansett, Greyhound and Deluxe all have a Townsville/Mt. Isa/ Darwin or Alice Springs service.

RAIL. The Sunlander and Queenslander stop at Townsville on their way to/from Cairns and Brisbane six times weekly. The trip takes approx. 30 hours. The Inlander travels to Mt. Isa twice weekly and takes approx. 21 hours.

CAR. From Brisbane along the Bruce Highway 1443km; from Brisbane along the inland route 1505km. It is important to listen to a local radio station for reports on road conditions during wet weather, as roads in northern Queensland are often cut during heavy rain.

TOURIST INFORMATION:
Townsville Tourist Organisation, Cnr. Sturt & Stokes Sts., Ph (077) 71 2724 is open Mon-Fri 9am-5pm; The Queensland Government Tourist Bureau, 303 Flinder's Mall, Ph (077) 71 3077.

ACCOMMODATION:
Townsville has over 30 motels, hotels, guest houses, hostels and half a dozen camping grounds. Some names and addresses: Sheraton Breakwater Casino Hotel, Sir Leslie Thiess Drive, Ph 72 4066 – RO $87-$205 – suites $200-350; Townsville International Hotel, Crn. Flinders & Stokes Sts., Flinders Mall, Ph 72 2477 – RO $79 double – suites $135;Travelodge, 75 The Strand, Ph 72 4255 – RO $60-95 – suites $150; Hospitality Inn Robert Towns, 261 Stanley St., Ph 72 6908 – RO $56 double – suites $75. Coachman's Inn, Cnr. Flinders & King Sts., Ph 72 3140 – RO $40 double; Civic Guest House, 262 Walker St., Ph 71 5512 – RO $22 double – communial cooking facilities; Coral House Private Hotel, 32 Hale St., Ph 71 5512 – RO $16-25. Sun City Caravan Park, 119 Bowen Rd., Ph 79 2302 – sites $7 – onsite vans $22 double; Walkabout Caravan Park, Cnr. University Rd. & Bruce Hwy, Ph 78 2480 – sites $6 – onsite vans $19 double; The Wills Street Hostel, 23 Wills Street, Ph 72 2820 – $7; Backpackers Budget Accommodation, 205 Flinders Street.

EATING OUT:
Townsville has plenty of hotels serving counter lunches, take-aways, and good restaurants. The international hotels have at least one restaurant and usually a bistro, and if you ask the staff where you are staying, they will usually be able to recommend restaurants in the price range you are looking for.

POINTS OF INTEREST:
Castle Hill (approximately 300m high) offers a panoramic view of

Townsville. It is topped by an octagonal restaurant which commands a 270 deg. view of the town and the bay.

Mount Stuart, 2km south of Stuart, is also an excellent vantage point.

Flinders Mall is virtually the heart of the city. It is a landscaped pedestrian mall with a relaxed atmosphere. The Strand, Townsville's sea promenade, has many parks including the Sister Kenny Park and the Anzac Memorial Park with its Centenary Fountains, waterfall and bougainvillaea gardens. Also along the Strand is the Torbruk Memorial Baths, an olympic sized swimming pool and nearby is a netted enclosure in the sea for the summer months, when the box jelly fish make swimming in the open sea dangerous. Queen's Gardens next to Queen's Park, Kissing Point (a small Army Base with a Military Museum) has a small rock swimming pool. There are another two salt water mesh swimming enclosures one at Rowes Bay and one at Pallarenda, which provide sea bathing safe from sharks, sea-stingers and other marine hazards.

The Town Common Environmental Park is a flora and fauna sanctuary and some rare water fowl, including the primitive magpie geese, may be seen there. In the winter months, at the height of the dry season, as many as 3000 brolgas, along with up to 180 other species of bird, flock to the common's salt-marsh lagoons and waterholes. The brolga is famous for its courting ritual and the park provides visitors with an excellent opportunity to see this dance at close quarters.

Townsville has north Queensland's first licensed casino. If you are feeling lucky you might like to call in, even if its is only for a look and a meal, at one of its two licensed restaurants. The casino is built on the waterfront and has magnificent views of Cleveland Bay and Magnetic Island.

The Tropicforest Garden Estate, 56 Bowen Road, has constructed rainforest walks to a freshwater aquarium containing exotic fish. An underwater observatory reveals what lies below the surface – open daily 8.30am to 5.30pm – devonshire teas.

Copper Refineries Pty. Ltd., Hunter St., Stuart, one of the largest copper refineries in the southern hemisphere, have conducted tours weekdays at 10.30am & 1.30pm – Blister copper produced at Mt. Isa (874km away) is refined and cast into ingots.

Ross River Dam, 21km from the city, supplies 90% of Townsville water needs. There are picnic facilities but no swimming or water sports permitted.

Pangola Park, 7km inland is a good place for a bush picnic. On weekends mini bikes and horses can be hired and there are good bush walks and swimming.

7km offshore is Magnetic Island, a popular holiday resort. Hayles operate a regular passenger service from the Magnetic Island Wharf, 168 Flinders St., phone 71 6927 for times. The trip takes approx. 40 mins. The vehicular ferry operates to Arcadia, in Geoffrey Bay, from Ross St., South Townsville at 8am, 11 & 2pm weekdays and 8am & 2pm on weekends, but it is essential to make early reservations. The trips takes 60 mins. The passenger service is met by an island bus, which also provides visitors with tours of the island. Mini mokes, taxis and bicycles are also available for hire on the island which has 24km of sealed roads. Popular swimming beaches are Picnic, Alma, Radical and Horseshoe Bays. There is a wooden swimming enclosure at Picnic Bay for swimming in the summer months. The resort areas are Picnic Bay, Nelly Bay, Geoffrey Bay (Arcadia), Alma Bay, Radical Bay and Horseshoe Bay. There are 24km of bushwalking tracks on the island and a wide range of accommodation is available – hostels, motels, holiday flats and houses. Dinghies may be hired at Picnic and Nelly Bays. Other attractions include: Shark World Sea-life Aquarium, Nelly Bay open daily 8.30am-5.30pm; Koala Park Oasis; Mountain View Fernery and Orchid Display, Rheuben Tce., Arcadia – open daily 9am-12noon & 2-4pm. Magnetic Island is larger than the other resort islands but the beaches, water, bush and climate are the same and the prices tend to be a lot lower than most.

FESTIVALS:
Pacific Festival is held each June and last 10 days.

FACILITIES:
Townsville has all the usual sporting facilities one would expect in a town of its size – lawn bowls, tennis, squash, etc. Water sports are also well catered for.

OUTLYING ATTRACTIONS:
At CAPE FERGUSON, 47km east of Townsville, the Australian Institute of Marine Science has a laboratory with harbour facilities. Guided tours are conducted on Fridays only by appointment – Ph (077) 78 9211.
NORTH:
   THURINGOWA, Queensland's newest city, stretches from Townsville north along the coast for 112km, and includes some magnificent beaches e.g. Balgal and Saunders Beach.
   CRYSTAL CREEK, Mt. Spec National Park, 67km north, is an enjoyable day's outing. The picturesque bridge across Little Crystal Creek was built during the 1932 depression by the Main Roads Commission. At The Loop, 14km further on, a 1km walking track connects a series of lookouts.
   INGHAM, is 113km north of Townsville and approx. 20km from the coast. Its main industry is the sugar industry, and Victoria Mill is one of the largest raw sugar refineries. Lucinda, 27km away, is a bulk sugar export port with a 5.7km cyclone proof jetty, which dips 2m over its length to follow the curvature of the earth. Dungeness Boat Harbour is the departure point for Orpheus Island launches. Orpheus Island is a quiet tourist resort and National Park in the Palm Group of islands, about 80km north of Townsville.
   TULLY, at the foot of Mt. Tyson 674m, receives the highest annual rainfall of any town in Australia, with an average of 4267mm p.a. The roads to Kareeya Gorge and power station, and south to Murray Falls, take the

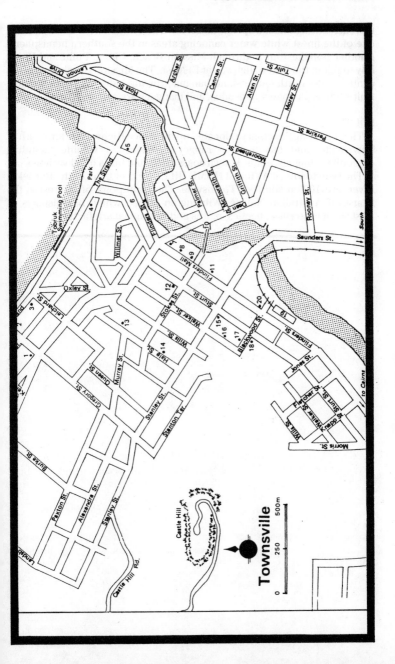

traveller through lush tropical rainforest. The Tully River is claimed to be one of the finest white water canoeing areas in the southern hemisphere. Another popular tour is through Mission Beach, Clump Point and Bingil Bay to rejoin the Bruce Highway at El Arish. The Mission Beach Area is the centre of the north Queensland banana growing industry. Other tropical fruit such as pawpaws, avocados, and mangoes are also cultivated.

SOUTH:

The Billabong Sanctuary is located on the Bruce Highway, 17km south of Townsville, and has a large range of Australian wildlife including crocodiles, dingoes, emus, kangaroos, snakes and birds of all varieties.

The twin towns of AYR and HOME HILL on either bank of the Burdekin River, are 100km south of Townsville. The main point of interest is the House of Australian Nature, Wilmington Street, which has displays of Australian butterflies, beetles, moths and Aboriginal artefacts.

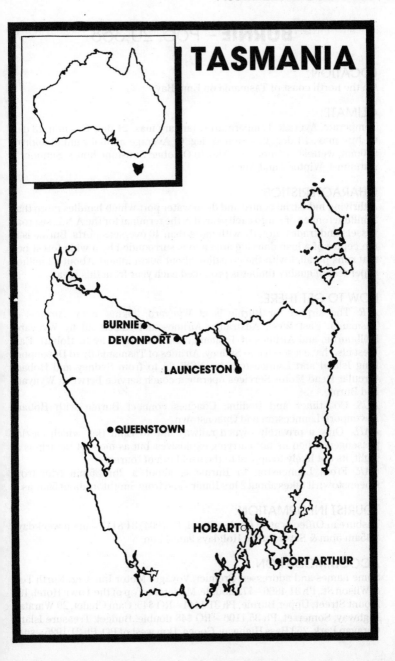

TASMANIA

BURNIE
DEVONPORT

LAUNCESTON

QUEENSTOWN

HOBART

PORT ARTHUR

BURNIE – Pop. 20,368

LOCATION:
On the north coast of Tasmania on Emu Bay.

CLIMATE:
Temperate. Average Temperatures: January max. 21 deg. C. – min. 13 deg. C; July max. 13 deg. C. – min. 5 deg. C; Average annual rainfall approx. 900mm; wettest six months – May to October; Sunshine hours: Summer 7, Autumn 4, Winter 3 and April 6.

CHARACTERISTICS:
A thriving industrial centre and deep water port which handles more than 2 million tonnes of cargo each year. It is the terminal for the A.N.L. sea road vessels and trades directly with more than 40 overseas ports. Burnie is in the centre of a lush dairying area and is surrounded by a wide forest belt that runs parallel with the coastline about 50km inland. About 22 million super feet of quality timber is produced each year from this area.

HOW TO GET THERE:
AIR. The airport for Burnie is at Wynyard, 20kms away. Airlines of Tasmania, East West, Australian Airlines and Ansett all fly Wynyard/ Melbourne, and Airlines of Tasmania and East West fly to Hobart. East West also have a service to Sydney. Airlines of Tasmania fly to Devonport, King Island and Launceston. Air NSW fly to from Sydney and Hobart. Circular Head Motor Services operate a coach service between Wynyard and Burnie.
BUS. Coastliner and Redline Coaches connect Burnie with Hobart, Devonport, Launceston and Queenstown.
RAIL. Only a privately owned railway line to Emu Bay which carries passengers when its not carrying explosives, but as most of the trip is at night, its not likely to appeal to the usual run of tourist.
CAR. From Launceston to Burnie is about a 2hr 35min trip; from Queenstown it takes about 2 hrs 15mins and from Smithton about 50mins.

TOURIST INFORMATION:
Tasbureau Office is at 48 Cauley Street, Ph (004) 31 8111 – open weekdays 8.45am-5pm & Sat & Public Holidays 9am-11am.

ACCOMMODATION:
Some names and addresses: Premier: Voyager Motor Inn, Cnr. North Tce. & Wilson St., Ph 31 4866 – $72 double. Moderate: Top of the Town Hotel, 195 Mount Street, Upper Burnie, Ph 31 4444 – RO $45; Cam Chalet, 20 Waratah Highway, Somerset, Ph 35 1106 – RO $48 double. Budget: Treasure Island Caravan Park, 253 Bass Highway, Cooee, 1km west of PO, Ph 31 1925 – sites

$5 double – on site vans $24 double; Somerset Caravan Park, 5km west, 40 Bass Highwaym, Ph 351185 – site $5 double – on site vans $22 double – cabins $25 double; Youth Hostel, 36 Dodgin St., Wynyard, Ph 42 2013 – $5 ppn (18km from Burnie).

EATING OUT:
Licensed Restaurants: Raindrops, 9 North Tce., Ph 31 4866 a la carte; Mandarin Palace, 63 Wilson St., Ph 31 7878; Alpine Inn, 20 Warratah Highway, Ph 35 1106. BYO: The Electric Jug, 25 Ladbrooke St., Ph 31 5023 for Australian Meals; Li Yin Chinese Restaurant, 28 Ladbrooke St., Ph 31 5413; Rialto Gallery Restaurant, 46 Wilmot St., Ph 31 7718 Venetian and The Steakhouse, 104 Wilson St., Ph 31 5542.

POINTS OF INTEREST.
The Pioneer Village Museum in High Street is Burnie's premier attraction. It is close to the centre of the city, and the entire village is under one roof and has more than 30,000 individual items on display. There's an inn, newspaper office, general store, blacksmith shop, and many authentic replicas of a commercial centre of the 1890-1910 period – open 10am-5pm Mon-Fri and 1.30pm-5pm weekends.

Burnie Park is only a few minutes walk away. It has shady trees, a rose garden and the old Burnie Inn which was first licensed in 1847, and which is open daily for inspection during the summer. There is also an animal sanctuary.

The Civic Centre and Art Gallery in Wilmot Street are also worth a visit.

The Associated Pulp and Paper Mill, Marine Tce., Ph 31 1222, Ext 483, has guided tours at 2.15pm Tues-Fri. During the tour you will see what happens to wood as it is processed into paper. Children under 12 not admitted and women are asked to wear slacks and low heeled shoes. Booking is essential.

Lactose Cheese Factory organises tours to see cheese being made but again, booking is essential.

Round Hill Lookout and Fern Glade are only 3km from town and are well worth a visit.

FESTIVALS:
Australia's largest one-day sports carnival is held in Burnie every New Year's Day. The Agricultural Show is held annually in October.

FACILITIES:
Lawn bowls, boating, fishing, sailing, swimming (pool or sea), golf, bike and horse riding.

OUTLYING ATTRACTIONS:
HELLYER GORGE, is 52km from Bernie on the Waratah Highway which links the north-west with the west coast. The gorge itself is older than time and is a scenic reserve. Nearby are glorious white sandy beaches, tidal

inlets, freshwater streams and pools where campers can pitch their tents in near solitude, and enjoy nature in an undisturbed and timeless area.

WYNYARD, 16km from Burnie, is a pretty town and almost more English than England. It is a major gateway to the north-west coast and a signposted scenic drive leads to Table Cape which offers superb panoramic views, while Fossil Bluff (just beyond the Wynyard Golf Course) is a unique area rich in rare and ancient fossils. Among the importants finds made here is that of a whale bone some 2 million years old. The waters round the town are popular with divers and underwater photographers because of their clarity. Equipment for the scuba diving enthusiast can be hired in town. 7km south of the town is the Oldina Forest Reserve which contains a virtual museum of superb trees. At the Reserve are spacious lawns and picnic facilities. 30km east from Wynyard is Rocky Cape National Park. Some of its geological formations are 700 million years old and some aboriginal remains found there indicate that the area was occupied at least 9,000 years ago, before Bass Strait was formed. There are some very interesting caves . There are several bushwalks in the park, and the one from Sisters Beach to Rocky Cape is noted for its spring displays of wildflowers. The Table Cape Cheese Factory and United Milk Whey Plant are open for inspections Sept-Feb from 10am-noon. The Leisure Ville Holiday Centre has modern self-contained villa units, flats and on site vans and is right opposite a sandy beach (East Wynyard on the Scenic Drive, Ph42 2291).

STANLEY is a classified historic town, and was the site of the first settlement in north-western Tasmania. It has changed very little since its early days. Its most distinctive feature is The Nut, a 150m high rock that dominates the coastal scenery. If you wish to climb it, there is an easy walking track which begins opposite the post office and ends at the summit cairn. Stanley Discovery Centre, Church St., is open daily 10am-4.30pm – admission $1. There is good fishing all around Stanley.

SMITHTON is the administrative centre of the Circular Head municipality of the far north-west. It has one of the largest and most modern butter factories in Tasmania as well as a bacon factory, a large piggery and several sawmills. The district has an ideal climate for growing peas, and a modern factory in the town freezes huge quantities. Air services connect Smithtown with King Island and aerial tours of the many off shore islands may be booked at the airport.

MARRAWAH is at the western end of the Bass Highway, 48km from Smithtown. It is well worth visiting as the wildflowers and native fauna are plentiful and there are several important Aboriginal rock carvings at Mount Cameron. The carvings of circles and bird tracks are similar to ones found in the deserts of the Australian mainland.

KING ISLAND. It's worth flying to as it is virtually a region on its own. It is 64km long and 27km wide at its widest point and has 145km of coastline. It has two main towns Currie on the west coast and Grassy in the south-east. Currie, with a population of approx. 700 is the administrative centre, and Grassy (pop. 600) is a deepwater port, and the site of the scheelite mine. It would appeal to travellers and those who enjoy skin diving, and surfing or shooting. The pheasant shooting season is in June; the duck shooting season in March and April; and mutton-birding takes place in the autumn.

DEVONPORT – Pop. 21,424

LOCATION:
On the north coast where the Mersey River enters Bass Strait.

CLIMATE:
Average temperatures: January max. 21 deg. C – min. 13 deg. C.; July max. 13 deg. C – min. 5 deg. C; Average annual rainfall approx. 800mm; wettest six months May to October; Sunshine hours; Summer 7, Autumn 4, Winter 3 and Spring 6.

CHARACTERISTICS:
Gateway for the car and passenger ferries from the mainland. Devonport was originally two towns which voted to amalgamate in 1893 – Formby, on the west bank of the river, and Torquay on the east bank. Devonport had its beginnings as the centre of a rich agricultural and orchard area. Even to-day, the Mersey Valley remains one of Tasmania's main orcharding districts but nowadays it is also famous for its mushrooms.

HOW TO GET THERE:
AIR. East West, Ansett and Air NSW fly to Melbourne and Sydney. East West, and Airlines of Tasmania fly to Hobart. Airlines of Tasmania fly to Burnie/Wynyard, Queenstown and King Island. Air Queensland fly to/from Dunk Island.
BUS. Tasmanian Redline Coaches and Coastliner Express connect Devonport to Launceston, Burnie and Hobart with a connection to Queenstown from Burnie.
CAR. From Hobart either along the Midland Highway via Launceston, or the Lakes Highway through the midlands and central highlands with 60km of unsealed road which may be snow covered in winter.

TOURIST INFORMATION:
Tasbureau, 18 Rooke Street, Ph (004) 24 1526 – open 8.45am-5pm Mon-Fri & 9am-11am Sat & public holidays.

ACCOMMODATION:
Premier: Gateway Motor Inn, 16 Fenton St., Ph 24 4922 – RO $67 double.
Moderate: Limani Tourist Lodge, 57 Percy St., Ph 24 4928 – RO $30 double; River View Guest House, 18 Victoria Pde., Ph 24 7357 – B&B $30 double;

Edgewater Hotel/Motel, 2 Thomas St., East Devonport, Ph 27 8441 – RO $35 double. Budget: Trade Winds Private Hotel, 44 McFie St., Ph 24 1719 – B&B $20 double; Devonport Caravan Park, Caroline St., East Devonport, Ph 27 8886 – site $6 double – on site vans $20 double; Youth Hostel, 26 Victoria Parade, Ph 24 7197 – $6ppn.

EATING OUT:

Licensed Restaurants: Argosy, Tarleton St., Ph 27 8872; The Green Door Restaurant and Wine Bar, 10 Oldaker St., Ph 24 6000; Gold Panda, 12 Thomas St., Ph 27 8324. BYO: Devonport Chinese, 3 Rooke St., Ph 24 4148; jade Palace, 4 Kempling St., Ph 24 7306 – A la carte; Sir Loins Steak House, 142 William St., Ph 24 7157; The Jolly Frog, 59 Wright St., Ph 27 9238 – a la carte; Sunrise, 140 Fenton St., Ph 24 16331 – a la carte; Taco Bill, Kempling St., Ph 24 6762 – Mexican.

POINTS OF INTEREST.

Mersey Bluff, a headland which provides panoramic views of the coastline, sheltered beaches and various short walks.

Tiagara Tasmanian Aboriginal Culture and Art Centre, Mersey Bluff has displays of carved figures, and tribal signs carved into rocks. The Tasmanian Aboriginals were physically different from their mainland counterparts. Some scientists believe they were originally an African or Polynesian people who drifted to Tasmania on primitive rafts, but a more plausible explanation is that their ancestors crossed over from the mainland when Tasmania was still joined to it. Unfortunately, when the first settlers reached the Derwent in 1803 they began wiping out the aboriginals and by 1876 the entire race of full-blooded Tasmanian Aborigines had been wiped out.

The Wheel House, Victoria Parade has a fascinating collection of pedal powered transport, and is open Tues-Sun 10am-4.30pm.

Bramiches Early Motoring and Folk Museum, 3 Don Road takes you back to the early days of motoring – open by appointment only.

The Maritime Museum, Gloucester Avenue, has a collection of models of early sailing ships that visited Tasmania – open Tues-Sun 2pm-4pm in Winter and from 10am-4.30pm in Summer.

The Devonport Gallery & Arts Centre, 43 Stewart St. is open Tues-Fri 10am-4.30 & Sun 2.30pm-4.30pm.

FESTIVALS:

The Tasmanian Thousands carnival at Devonport, on the first weekend in February, features rich Wheel and Gift races. The Dahlia Festival is also held in February, and an Orchid Show in October. An Apple Festival is held in the Mersey Valley in March.

FACILITIES:

Boating, fishing, swimming, lawn bowls, golf, sailing, greyhound racing, trotting and horse racing, and squash.

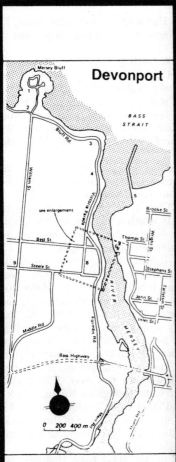

1 Tiagarra
2 Bluff Caravan Park
3 Maritime Museum & Wheel House
4 Youth Hostel
5 Terminal Caravan Park
6 Ferry
7 Bass Strait Ferry Terminal
8 City Centre
9 To Don River Tramway

1 Tasmanian Redline Coaches
2 Ansett
3 TAA
4 Post Office
5 Ferry to East Devonport
6 Tourist Bureau
7 RAC

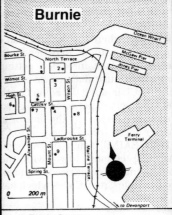

1 Tourist Bureau
2 Webster Travel
3 Ansett
4 TAA (East West agents)
5 Tourist Bureau
6 Pioneer Village Museum
7 Circular Head Motor Services
8 Post Office
9 Tasmanian Redline Coaches

OUTLYING ATTRACTIONS:

The Don River Railway on the Bass Highway towards Ulverstone, has vintage steam locos which haul carriages on a half hour trip along the banks of the Don River.

ULVERSTONE, 18km west, is the 'Woodchopping Centre'of Australia. Woodchopping had its beginnings in Ulverstone back in 1870 when two bushmen got into an argument in a local pub about who was the best man with an axe. With a wager of $50 at stake, they adjourned to a nearby paddock to settle the matter and the sport was born. In 1974 the world champsionship was held in Ulverstone. There is a large unusual War Memorial in the main street. It consists of the 17m pillars joined by bronze chains.

At PENGUIN, 12km west of Ulverstone, you can still see some fairy penguins. It also has some good beaches and you get a magnificient view of the area from the Dial Range which dominates Penguin.

LEVEN CANYON, 36km south of Ulverstone via Sprent, Castra and Nietta, is a spectacular gorge which is worth a visit, as are the Gunn's Plains' Caves. These limestone caves also have glow worms, and conducted tours are held every hour between 10am and 4pm.

CRADLE MOUNTAIN NATIONAL PARK: The northern end of this 1280km park can be reached from Devonport by the road through Gowrie Park, which climbs to the central plateau. It ends on the shore of Lake Dove where the skyline is dominated by the peak of Cradle Mountain (1,545m. Several smaller lakes are scattered across the valley. This area of the park is wild, open moor country broken by deep gorges and forested valleys. However, visitors should not forget this beautiful area is a mountain wilderness where the weather can change abruptly and without warning. For people without experience and the right equipment, it can be a dangerous place in which getting lost is all too easy. Hiking clubs throughout Australia arrange parties to walk through the National Park to Lake St. Clair along the 85km Overland Track from Waldheim, and unless you are a very experienced hiker you should go with one of these parties. For those who haven't the time or inclination to hike, Astral Airways have charter flights from Devonport to Cradle Mountain.

DELORAINE, south of Devonport on the Bass Lake Highway, is a charming country town with the wall of the Great Western Tiers dominating the countryside. Approx. 20km west of the town up in the hills are the Mole Creek Caves which have some spectacular formations.

HOBART – Pop. 180,000

LOCATION:

On the Derwent River Estuary at Storm Bay about 19km from the mouth.

CLIMATE:
Average temperatures: January max. 22 deg. C – min. 12 deg C; July max. 11 deg. C- min. 4 deg. C; Average Annual Rainfall 635mm; Driest months January-March.

CHARACTERISTICS:
The suburbs spread along both banks of the river, up and down the inland valleys, and into the foothills of Mount Wellington which towers 1,354m above Hobart to the west.

HOW TO GET THERE:
AIR. Ansett, Australian Airlines, Air NSW, East West and Airlines of Tasmania all fly to/from Melbourne, Sydney and Brisbane. East/West fly to the Gold Coast and Devonport. Australian Airlines also fly to/from Christchurch (N.Z.). Australian Airlines and Ansett also fly to Launceston. The airport is 16km from the city centre and Tasmanian Redline Coaches have a regular service 34 4577.
BUS. Tasmanian Redline Coaches have services from/to Launceston/Devonport/Burnie/Wynyard/Smithton and to Queenstown. Glamorgan have a Hobart/Swansea/Bicheno service. Peninsula Coach Service operates a Hobart/Port Arthur service. Bushwalkers Transport Ph (002) 34 2226 provide charter transport on a 24 hour basis – phone for further details.
CAR. It is virtually possible to travel to Hobart in less than a day from anywhere in Tasmania. Hobart/Devonport it is just under 300km so that will give you some idea of the distances in Tasmania.

TOURIST INFORMATION:
Tasbureau, 80 Elizabeth Street., Ph (002) 30 0211 – open Mon-Fri 8.45am-5.30pm, Sat, Sun & public holidays 8.45am-11am.

ACCOMMODATION:
Premier: Wrest Point Hotel Casino, 410 Sandy Bay Rd., Sandy Bay, Ph 25 0112 – RO $90 double. Moderate: Argyle Motor Lodge, 2 Lewis Street, North Hobart, Ph 34 2488 – RO $52 double; Mayfair Motel, 17 Cavell St., West Hobart, Ph 34 1670 – RO $47 double; Hobart Tower Motel, 300 Park St., New Town, Ph 28 0166 – RO $42 double; Astor Private Hotel, 157 Macquarie Street, Ph 34 6384 – B&B $39 double. Budget: Sandy Bay Caravan Park, (2km E of P.O.) 1 Peel St., Sandy Bay, Ph 25 1264 – site $6 double – on site vans $24 double; Treasure Island Caravan Park, 10km north) Berriedale Reserve, Main Rd., Berriedale, Ph 49 2379 – site $5 double – on site vans $24 double; Youth Hostels: 52 King St., Bellerive, Ph 44 2552 – $5.50 ppn; 'Woodlands', 7 Woodlands Ave., New Town, Ph 28 6720 – $5 ppn; The Scout Association's 'The Lea', off southern Expressway, Kingston, 8km from GPO, has self contained dormitory Accommodation for large groups – contact the Scout Association, 107 Murray St., Hobart, Ph 34 3885; During Vacations, the University Colleges offer casual accommodation:

Christ College, Ph 23 51990 – RO $11 students & $18.50 for others; St. John Fisher College, Ph 34&8955 is $25.50 ppn and Jane Franklin Hall, Ph 23 2000 $12 ppn.

EATING OUT:

Licensed Restaurants: The Crepe Escape, Centreway, Collins St., Ph 34 2890; Club 50, 50 Victoria St., Ph 34 2566; Nalinas Indian Restaurant, 37 Montpellier Retreat, Battery Point, Ph 23 6653. BYO: Royal Tasmanian Botanical Gardens Restaurant, Domain Rd., Ph 34 4849; Etna Pizza Parlour, 171 Sandy Bay Rd., Ph 23 5314; Capers, 44 Cat and Fiddle Arcade, Ph 34 6367; King Wah Cafe, 159A New Town Rd., Ph 28 3431; Malaysian Tea House, 466 Macquarie St., Ph 34 2175; The Pantry, 143 Liverpool St., Ph 34 9232; Sweeneys, 353 Elizabeth St., Ph 34 9307 – vegetarian.

PUBLIC TRANSPORT:

The Metropolitan Transport Trust buses depart from the central business district for the outer suburbs. Unlimited travel tickets cost $2 and may be used between 9am-4.45pm and after 6.30pm on weekdays, and all day on weekends. Day Rover Tickets also available.

BICYCLE HIRE:

Graham McVilly Cycles, Ph (002) 12 7284 – daily $12.50 – weekly $35 – hourly $2.50.

POINTS OF INTEREST.

Hobart has more than 90 buildings which have been classified by the National Trust, 32 of them are in Macquarie Street and 31 in Davey Street but apart from those, there are numerous other well-maintained buildings still in use to-day. They are one of the city's most attractive and charming features. The National Trust has regular walking tours of the city on Saturday mornings. They start at 9.30-am and last 2-3hrs but if you won't be in Hobart on a Saturday, some of the most interesting buildings are:

Parliament House, part of which was originally the Customs House built between 1835 and 1840. The stone for it came from what is now a lake in the grounds of Government House. The cellars, once the bonded store, still display broad arrows on the brickwork. The Legislative Council chamber has housed that body since 1856. The House of Assembly chamber is housed in a wing built in 1939.

Government House is built in Tudor-Gothic style. It has 70 rooms and 50 chimneys and took from 1840 to 1858 to complete.

The Theatre Royal in Campbell Street – Australia's oldest legitimate theatre is built in regency style and is a reminder of a gracious era.

The Customs House Hotel, Cnr. Morrison & Murray Sts first licensed in 1846. This was the prototype for the hotels of the old Hobart waterfront of the 19th century.

Buildings at Battery Point. The whole area looks much the same as it did a century ago. Houses and cottages are packed into a jumble of narrow

Tasmanian countryside

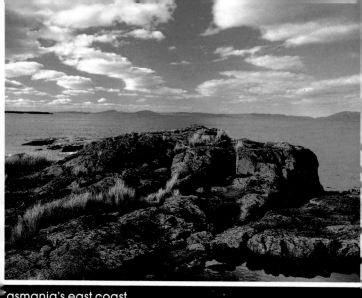

asmania's east coast

streets and lanes which gives the area a maritime atmosphere. The oldest building is the 1818 signal station which was used to relay messages from another station on Mt. Nelson. There is a fine terrace of Georgian sandstone warehouses on one side of Salmanca Place. The other side is where the New Wharf used to be. Nowadays openair markets are held there every Saturday in summer. In winter the markets move into one of the old warehouses. The nearby St. George's Church has Australia's oldest Classical Revival spire.

Other interesting early churches include St. David's Anglican Cathedral, Cnr. Macquarie & Murray Sts., St. Mary's Cathedral, The Scots Church, the Congregational Church, New Town, and the Holy Trinity Church, North Hobart. All of these churches were built in the finest architectual tradition of the great cathedrals of Britain and Europe. St. David's is an excellent example of Gothic Revival style. It's solid silver altar vessels were presented by King George III in 1803. The imposing St. Mary's was built on the site of St. Virgilius, the first Catholic church to be built in Tasmania. Much of St. Marys standstone work had to be rebuilt as the original foundations were faulty. Scots Church was first known as St. Andrew's and the 1830 building is notable for its heavy battlementing. The New Town Congregational Church was built in 1842 in Romanesque Roman style.

Runnymede in Bay Road, New Town. It was built in 1844, is now owned by the National Trust, and is open for inspection daily except Mondays. It is a totally authentic home which was built about 140 years ago and was occupied until the late 1970's.

Hobart's most popular shopping area is around the Cat & Fiddle Arcade which has an animated clock which is activated every hour on the hour. Naturally, you'll see the cat, fiddle, dog, dish, cow and spoon!

One of the main landmarks of the city is the Tasman Bridge which spans the Derwent Estuary just north of the city centre. In 1975 it was struck by a ship causing part of the roadway to collapse, killing 12 people. The nearby Royal Botanical Gardens and Queen's Domain are pleasant places in which to relax after a hectic morning's or afternoon's sightseeing.

Hobart's other landmark is of course, Wrest Point Casino. It was Australia's first legal casino, and is as well known for its lavish stage shows as it is for its gaming tables.

Anglesea Barracks is the nation's oldest military establishment still used by the forces. Some of the buildings date back to the early 1800's and the guns outside the gate are naval cannon cast before 1774. It is open daily and there are guided tours on Tuesday mornings.

Hobart's city centre is extremely close to the harbour. From certain vantage points, it often appears that boats are moored in the streets. Most of the waterfront is recreational area which is frequented by locals and tourists alike. The annual blue water classic the Sydney to Hobart Yacht Race terminates at Constitution Dock right in the heart of the city.

There are quite a few interesting museums in Hobart amongst them the Tasmanian Museum & Art Gallery; the Allport Museum & Library of Fine Arts in the State Library in Murray St. – open Mon-Fri 9am-5pm; the John

Elliott Classics Museum at the University of Tasmania at Sandy Bay; Beatties Historic Photo Museum in the Cat & Fiddle Arcade; the Post Office Museum, Castray Esp – open 9am – 5pm weekdays and 9am-11am Saturdays and the Lady Franklin Museum in Lenah Valley which is built like a Greek temple – open Sundays.

If you are travelling by car then you might like to follow the Golden Arrow tours which start at the Town Hall – see the Tourist Bureau for details of the places around the tour.

On the opposite side of the Derwent, near Risdon Cove, are the Bowen pyramids in Bowen Park. These house historic exhibits including Tasmanian Aboriginal artefacts.

The Bellerive Battery also across the Derwent, was built in the 1880's when a Russian invasion was feared. The Fort affords excellent views of the Derwent Estuary and Mt. Wellington.

If you are a chocolate lover, then you will probably be interested in a tour of the Cadbury factory at Claremont – the Tourist Bureau will give you details of times etc.

The old Cascade Brewery is a striking relic of colonial times and is set picturesquely beside a stream in the shadow of Mt. Wellington. Their bottle collection is open Mon-Fri.

Mt. Wellington, 1270m, has many walking tracks and of course offers a terrific view of Hobart, but it can get cold there even in summer. In winter, it is often dusted with snow.

FESTIVALS:
The Tasmania Festival begins just before New Year with the arrival of the Sydney-Hobart race boats and continues for about a week. The Hobart Arts Festival is held in June and the Royal Hobart Show in October.

FACILITIES:
Hobart has all the facilities you would expect of a capital city – horse racing, car racing, lawn bowls, golf courses, squash and tennis courts, swimming pools, etc.

OUTLYING ATTRACTIONS:
THE DERWENT VALLEY: Head north along the Brooker Highway, past Claremont and Cadbury's factory and then take the Lyell Highway at Granton. At Granton you can see the long Bridgewater Causeway which was built by convict labour. At Boyer, 32km from Hobart, are big newsprint mills which supply about half of Australia's newsprint. Much of it is transported by barge along the river to Hobart. New Norfolk, 35km from Hobart, could almost be a village in England. It is classified by the National Trust as an Historic Town and has many quaint old buildings. Hops are grown in the surrounding countryside. It is also possible to get to New Norfolk by launch from Hobart. 11km from New Norfolk are the Salmon Ponds at Plenty where brown and rainbow trout are raised. 73km from Hobart is the Mt. Field National Park which is on a plateau with mountains

and lakes. There are many bushwalks and also ski-ing in winter.

South along the Coast you come to Kingston-Blackmans Bay one of Hobart's fastest growing outer suburban areas. It has lovely beaches and picnic areas. Blackmans Bay has a small blowhole and lookouts at Doughty Point and Piersons Point offer superb views of Bruny Island and Storm Bay. There is a Motor Museum and an unusual market at Margate, 19km from Hobart. The market has its headquarters in Tasmania's last passenger train. The converted carriages house toy-makers, glass blowers, woodworkers, artists, etc. A few kilometres south is Snug, an apty named village, and 34km from Hobart is Kettering the terminal for the Bruny Island vehicular ferry.

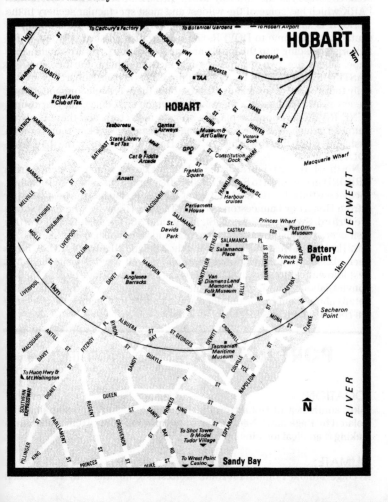

BRUNY ISLAND is a popular holiday destination for campers. The main township is Adventure Bay on the east coast of South Bruny. The island is like two islands as it is quite narrow in the centre.

Further south is HUONVILLE which is the commercial centre for the district. It is a pretty area which provides pleasant rural and seascape scenery. The Huon Valley was a huge apple exporter before Britain joined the Common Market. A cruise on the 'Huon Pride' is a good way to see the countryside. 31km south of Huonville is GREEVSTON which is the administrative centre of the Esperance Municipality which includes Macquarie Island, 1000km south. Timber is an important industry in this area. Greevston is the gateway to the HARTZ MOUNTAINS NATIONAL PARK which has some of the wildest and most spectacular scenery in the world. It is said to resemble the Canadian Rockies. If you take the road south you will come to DOVER, 65km away. It is the last petrol stop for motorists heading into the lonely and rugged country towards South-East Cape. There are two fish processing factories there. Further south is HASTINGS and the FAIRY CAVES (approx. 100km from Hobart). There are daily tours of the caves and a restaurant but there is no accommodation at the caves. At Hastings is a thermal pool which is 27 deg. C all year round. LUNE RIVER is a popular place with gem collectors, and there is also a tramway which still operates taking tourists for a 6km tour through bushland from the township to The Deep Hole across the bay from SOUTHPORT.

North of Hobart is Tasmania's holiday coast which stretches from ORFORD in the south to ST. HELENS in the north. It has sheltered beaches, rocky coastline, terrific surf and great fishing. It also has the best weather – from Hobart or Launceston take the Tasman Highway. The main towns are Orford, Swansea, Bicheno, St. Marys and St. Helens. It is well worth a visit even if its just to sample some of the local crayfish, oysters or fish.

121km north-west of Hobart along the Midland Highway is ROSS. It has been classified by the National Trust and is well worth a visit. One of its best known features is the elaborately carved Ross Bridge built in 1836 by convict labour. There are many interesting buildings in the village and details about them can be obtained at the Tourist Information Centre in the tea rooms, which was originally St. John's Church.

PORT ARTHUR – Pop. Nominal

LOCATION:
95km south-east of Hobart on the Tasman Peninsula. The settlement is isolated by Eaglehawk Neck, a narrow strip of land only 410m across, thus making it an ideal location for a penal colony.

CLIMATE:
Average annual rainfall 1031mm; wettest six months May to October;

Sunshine hours: Summer 8; autumn 5, winter 4 and spring 7.

CHARACTERISTICS:
This old penal settlement was home to 12,500 convicts who lived under the threat of the lash, and an experimental isolation system that often drove them to madness. Escape was rare and many remained to be buried in mass graves on the Isle of the Dead. To-day Port Arthur rests in peace amidst English oaks and expansive green lawns that roll down to the water's edge.

HOW TO GET THERE:
BUS. You can take one of the organised tours from Hobart, or you can catch the Peninsula Coach Service which leaves Hobart Mon-Fri at 7.45am & 3.45pm and leaves Port Arthur at 7.45am & 11am for the return journey. The cost is $8 single or $14 return for the 114km journey.
CAR. From Hobart take the Tasman Highway to Sorell and then the Arthur Highway.

TOURIST INFORMATION:
Port Arthur Information Bureau (002) 50 2107.

ACCOMMODATION:
Four Seasons Motor Hotel, Ph (002) 50 2102 – RO $62; Fox and Hounds, Arthur Hwy., Ph 50 2217 – RO $80 double; Seascape Guest House, Arthur Highway, Ph 50 2367 – B&B $40 double; Tanglewood Host Farm Guest House, Nubeena Rd., Ph 50 2210, B&B $36 double; New Plymouth Holiday Village, Stewarts Bay, Ph 50 2262 – $50 double; Youth Hostel, Ph 50 2311 – $5 ppn.

EATING OUT:
Licensed Restaurants: Four Seasons Motor Inn, Tasman Hwy, Ph 50 2101 and Fox and Hounds, Arthur Hwy, Ph 50 2217.

POINTS OF INTEREST.
The whole of the Tasman Peninsula is promoted as 'Convict Country'. Port Arthur was Tasmania's most infamous convict establishment and now it is Tasmania's premier tourist attraction. Every year thousands of tourists visit Port Arthur. It is difficult to say whether it is because of morbid curiosity, or because they have a genuine interest in treading the paths and halls of one of Australia's really historic ruins. Tasmania was first populated almost entirely by convicts and their soldier guards from Port Jackson in NSW. Subsequently, convicts were shipped directly from England. The settlement operated from 1830 to 1877 when it was abandoned. It was burnt out by bushfire in 1878, but there are quite a few buildings still standing. The most notable being the Penitentiary, the church, the Model Prison, the hospital and guard house. There are still two buildings in use to-day, the lunatic asylum, which has been restored to house a reception centre, an audio visual theatre, a scale model of Port

Arthur of the 1870's and a small museum, and the Commandant's residence, which is now a private home. The whole township area is maintained by the National Parks and Wildlife Service.

The solitary confinement cells can still be seen to-day and anyone who has experienced, even for a few minutes, the claustrophobic darkness of the cells, can well understand why one of the larger buildings in the prison complex was the Lunatic Asylum.

The Museum of Records has actual records of the transportees sent to Tasmania (a long list of prisioners names, their crimes and punishment). The minimum term of transportation was seven years and this was imposed for such offences as stealing a lamb, a sheep, a pig. One prisoner, Joseph Parker, was transported for life for stealing a silk handkerchief. On another list, several men and women were sentenced to transportation for life for the theft of articles of little value. In one case sentence of death for stealing 25/- which was commuted to transportation for life. Even children received long gaol sentences. They were kept separate at Point Puer across the bay. The ruins of the Bakers' ovens and the old school are all that remain to-day.

The Isle of the Dead, the cemetery for Port Arthur, is just off the point and can be reached by the regular ferry.

FACILITIES:
Swimming in the beautiful bays, fishing, canoeing and boating, and excellent bushwalks from 1 hour to 2 to 3 days duration.

OUTLYING ATTRACTIONS:
There were several subsidiary establishments on the peninsula, the Coal Mines settlement at Saltwater River, the Saltwater Creek agricultural centre and the timber mills at Premaydena and Koonya.

SALTWATER RIVER was the site of two outstations, the Coal Mines and the Experimental Farm. The Mine served a dual purpose, it provided fuel for use in the colony and it also was a punishment centre. Cells were even built into mine galleries. The mine was abandoned in 1877 when coal caught alight and smouldered for many years.

EAGLEHAWK NECK is the narrow strip of land joining the Tasman and Forestier peninsulas. During convict times several dogs were chained in close proximity on short chains making escape virtually impossible. Nearby are several remarkable coastal formations – the Remarkable Cave which is accessible when the tide is out, the Devil's Kitchen, Tasman's Arch and the Blowhole as well as the Tessellated Pavement which looks like well laid large pavers.The whole of the area is now a holiday resort with all the usual tourist infrastructure e.g. souvenir and craft shops, horse back trail riding.

Nearby is DOOTOWN, a picturesque group of holiday homes near Tasman Arch. Almost all the houses have names incorporating Doo e.g. Much-A-Doo, Didgeri-Doo, Doo Little.

At KOONYA there is an old-time store that takes you back to the days when lollies were 2 a penny and soap was three pence a cake.

NUBEEN, on the shores of Parsons Bay, is the largest town on the Tasman Peninsula. It is a popular resort. In convict days timber cut from the hinterland was shipped to England from nearby Wedge Bay.

The scenery at Cape RAOUL is quite spectacular as years of weathering has caused the rock to split vertically creating an organ pipe effect.

SORRELL is at one end of a 3300m causeway which was completed in 1872 after 8 years work. It shortened the trip to Hobart quite considerably obviating the need to travel through Richmond.

RICHMOND is as elegant to-day as it was in the 1820's when it was an important military post and convict station linking Hobart with Port Arthur. It has a village green shaded by leafy green trees, and its sandstone buildings house galleries, tea shops, craft boutiques and museums.

QUEENSTOWN – Pop. 4,300

LOCATION:
On the rugged west coast of Tasmania in the midst of a wilderness area.

CHARACTERISTICS:
Firstly and lastly a mining town. After seeing so many trees, your first glimpse of Queenstown may come as a shock because the hills around the town are denuded of trees. This reveals the unforgettable colours of the hills.

CLIMATE:
Averages only 1750 hours of sunshine in a year, while it rains on an average of 320 days per year – annual rainfall over 3000mm.

HOW TO GET THERE:
AIR. Airlines of Tasmania fly to and from Hobart week days and from Melbourne, Smithton and Launceston.
BUS. Tasmanian Redline Coaches connect Queenstown to Hobart, Burnie, Derwent Bridge and Strahan.
CAR. Queenstown is 254km north-west of Hobart along the Lyell Highway, and 175km south-west of Burnie along the Waratah and Zeehan Highways.

TOURIST INFORMATION:
Tasmanian Government Tourist Bureau is at 39-41 Orr Street, Ph 71 1099.

ACCOMMODATION:
The Tourist Bureau has a full list, but here are some names and addresses: Commercial Hotel, Driffield St., Ph 71 1511 – B&B $34 double; Empire Hotel, 2 Orr St., Ph 71 1699 – RO $28 double; Silver Hills Motor Inn,

Penghana Rd., Ph 71 1755 – RO $59 double; Penny Royal, Batchelor St., Ph 71 1804 – RO $58; Pine Lodge Guest House, 1 Gaffney St., Ph 71 1852 – B&B $34 double; Mountain View Holiday Lodge, Penganah Rd., Ph 71 1163 – Bunkhouse $13 double; Mountain View Caravan Park, 9 Grafton St., Ph 71 1332 – onsite vans – cabins $24 double – Bunkhouse $10 double – sites $4 double; No Youth Hostel.

EATING OUT:
Most of the hotels have counter meals.

POINTS OF INTEREST:

The Mt. Lyell Open Cut Copper Mine Tours leave at 9.15am and 4.30pm on weekdays and at 9.15am and 4pm on weekends. There is also a Mining Museum with an interesting collection of photographs.

In the Driffield Street Park is a restored ABT locomotive and a display detailing the history of the Queenstown/Straham railway which was a remarkable feat of engineering.

The Gallery Museum, Cnr. Sticht and Driffield Sts., has mining and household exhibits.

The Western Arts & Craft Centre, Orr Street, sells wood crafts, paintings etc. – open daily.

FACILITIES:
Swimming pool, golf course, gem fossicking and gold panning.

OUTLYING ATTRACTIONS:
ZEEHAN, 38km north of Queenstown, boomed when rich silver-lead deposits were discovered in 1882. By the turn of the Century it was a town of 5,000 and an entertainment 'capital'. Melba and Caruso performed here, but ore ran out and the town declined before the 1st World War. A number of buildings have survived from its boomtime including the Gaiety Theatre, St. Luke's Church and the Post Office. The Museum in the old School of Mines building has many interesting exhibits and models as well as fauna displays and Aboriginal artefacts.

STRACHAN, 40km from Queenstown, is situated on Macquarie Harbour, the only harbour on the west coast. It dates back to the convict days when it was a dreaded place. Many of the convicts who were sent to Sarah Island in Macquarie Harbour found life there was hell on earth, and death was seldom from natural causes. The closure of many mines on the west coast and the building of the railway line from Zeehan to Burnie led to its decline. To-day it is a fishing port, holiday village and a base for trips into the wilderness area around the Franklin River. From Strachan you can take a flight on a sea plane over the peaks of Frenchmans Cap National Park, majestic Lake Peddar, the rapids and gorges of the Franklin River and then land on the tranquil Gordon River. From there you can transfer to a 6 passenger jet boat and travel up stream far beyond the Franklin River over the rapids to the spectacular Angel Cliffs of the Upper Gordon River – For further information contact Wilderness Air, Ph (004) 71 7280. Or if you prefer you can take a half-day scenic cruise on a motor launch which will take you from Macquarie Harbour to the Gordon River, Marble Cliffs, Butler Island, Warner's Landing, Sir John Falls Landing, Gordon Gorge turning at Big Eddie Rapids and returning to Strahan via the infamous Sarah Island and Hell's Gates, the notorious entrance to Macquarie Harbour – cost $25-$28.

FRENCHMAN'S CAP is part of the Wild Rivers National Park and the Lyell Highway passes close to the northern edge of the Cap. There are several bushwalks in the area. You can take a short walk to view the white quartz dome of the Cap and look out over the Franklin River. If you have more time, then you could walk right into the rainforest.

The South West National Park is a true wilderness area around Lake Peddar. The most popular and accessible base for bushwalking is STRATHGORDON which has a motel and a camping and caravan park. However, many of the walks are definitely for experienced bushwalkers only.

LAUNCESTON – Pop. 86,000

LOCATION:
At the head of the lovely Tamar River at the junction of the north and south Esk in the central northern region of Tasmania.It is Australia's largest inland port.

CLIMATE
Average temperatures: January max. 21 deg.C – min. 13 deg.C; July max. 13 deg.C – min. 5 deg.C; Average annual rainfall approx. 750mm; wettest six months May to October; Sunshine hours; Summer 7, Autumn 4, Winter 3 and Spring 6.

CHARACTERISTICS
Known as the 'Garden City' because of its abundance of well-established, beautiful public and private gardens. It nestles in the wide river valley amid the lush green countryside that has given rise to the description of Tasmania as 'this other England'. Launceston is Tasmania's second largest city.

HOW TO GET THERE
AIR. Australian Airlines and Ansett fly to/from Melbourne, Sydney and Brisbane and the Gold Coast. Airlines of Tasmania fly from Melbourne's Essendon airport to Launceston daily and Kendall Airlines fly to Launceston from Mildura and ALbury via Melbourne; and Promair flies from the Latrobe Valley in Victoria to Launceston. Redline operate a coach to/from the airport cost $3 – taxi approx. $10.

BUS. Tasmanian Redline Coaches and Coastliner operate a Hobart/Launceston and Launceston/Devonport, Burnie, Wynard and Smithtown service. For Bushwalkers: Staffords Coaches, Lower Barrington (004) 24 3628 operate coaches from Launceston Airport to Lake St. Clair $40 or Cradle Valley $32; Mountain Stage Line, P.O. Box 433, (004) 34 0442 operate on demand from Launceston to Cradle Mountain $20 or Lake St. Clair $25 and the round trip Launceston/Cradle Mt/Lake St. Clair/Launceston for $40. Ski season transport Launceston/Ben Lomond/Launceston $15 return or $10 single.

CAR. From Hobart 199km via the Midlands Highway (approx. 2hr 30min); from Burnie 143km, approx. 2hr 35min; from St. Helens via Scottsdale 2hr 30min or via St. Marys 1hr 45min.

TOURIST INFORMATION
Tasbureau, cnr. St. John and Paterson Sts., open 8.45am-5.30pm weekdays and 9am-11.30am Saturdays, Sunday and Public Holidays.

ACCOMMODATION

International Hotel: Country Club Casino, Country Club Ave., Prospect Vale, Ph 44 8855 – RO $128 double. Moderate: Abel Tasman Motor Inn, 303 Hobart Rd., Kings Meadows, Ph 44 5255 – RO $44 double; Hotel Maldon, 32 Brisbane St., Ph 31 3979 – B&Lt.B $39 double; Crown Hotel, 152 Elizabeth St., Ph 311 4137 – B&B $30. Budget: Launceston House Hostel, 36 Thistle St., Ph 44 9779 – $6 ppn – family rooms available – bicycles for hire as well as wet weather gear, bushwalking boots, stoves etc.; Treasure Island Caravan Park, Glen Dhu St., Ph 44 2600 – sites $6 double – on site vans $24 double.

EATING OUT

Licensed Restaurants: Shrimps, 72 George St., Ph 34 0584; Quigleys, 96 Balfour St., Ph 31 6971. BYO: Akbar Asian, 63 Climitiere St., Ph 34 0024 – Chinese; Calabrisella, 56 Wellington St., Ph 31 1958 – Italian; Satay House, Kings Court Shopping Centre, Ph 44 5955 – Indonesian; Shafi's Afghan Restaurant, 150 George St., Ph 31 2679; The Smiling Toad, 91 George St., Ph 34 0554 – vegetarian.

POINTS OF INTEREST

There are many quaint malls and shopping centres in the city centre e.g. the attractive Quadrant Mall and Yorktown Square.

Stroll through the streets and you will see some old merchant warehouses like Macquarie House which is now part of the Queen Victoria Museum and Art Gallery in Wellington Street which has a unique collection of Tasmanian fauna and Aboriginal relics, a Planetarium and a reconstructed joss-house – open Mon-Sat 10am-5pm and 2-5pm Sun.

The Old Umbrella Shop in George Street is built entirely of Tasmanian Blackwood and is now preserved by the National Trust.

City Park is spacious with well laid out gardens and beautiful old elm and oak trees. It also contains a small zoo and houses the John Hart Conservatory with its noted displays of begonias, cyclamen and many other hot house blooms.

The Design Centre of Tasmania, cnr. Brisbane and Tamar Streets Park, is open 10am-6pm Mon-Fri, 10am-1pm Sat & 2-5pm Sun. It has displays by Tasmania's best designers and craftsmen.

The Penny Royal Gunpowder Mills is the most imaginative manmade development in the State. It has authenticity plus Disneyland family appeal. It depicts early 19th century gunpowder mills, cannon foundry and arsenal in a landscaped setting of streams and waterfalls. There is a unique canal system and lake complete with a fleet of vessels, two of which fire and proof their guns daily. As well there is a scale model railway system with 700m of track between the Gunpowder Mill and the Penny Royal Watermill complex which also has accommodation – open daily 9am-5pm.

In contrast, the ultra-modern Country Club Casino has gaming tables and live entertainment and modern restaurants for the visitor.

Franklin House, 7km south, is an early settler's home refurnished in colonial style – open for inspection daily 9am-12.30pm & 1.30-5pm.

If you would like to see wool being spun and further processed, then head for Waverley Wollen Mills, Waverley Road – open daily 9am-4pm. At the Tarmar Knitting Mills, Hobart Road – open daily 9am-4pm you can see material being knitted.

A cruise on the Tamar River is a good way to see the surrounding area. Launches and an old paddlewheel steamer operate from Launceston and Beauty Point – contact the tourist bureau for further information.

No visit would be complete without a visit to the Cataract Gorge a few minutes by bus from the city. A 1.6km walk along the face of the towering cliffs terminates in the Cataract Cliff Grounds Reserve from where a chairlift crosses the gorge for a breathtaking view.

FACILITIES
As with all cities of a reasonable size all sports such as lawn bowls, golf, squash, water sports, greyhound and horse racing, and cycling are catered for.

FESTIVALS
Agricultural Show in October and the Launceston Cup (Horse Racing) in February.

OUTLYING ATTRACTIONS
HASPEN is 13km south-west, and is often referred to as being very much like England and Entally House is built like an English farm house – open daily 10am-12.10pm & 1-5pm.

EXETER, 24km north-west, is a centre of a fruit growing area and even the local school has its own farm. At the mouth of the Supply River are the remains of Tasmania's first water-driven flour mill.

BATMAN BRIDGE, 30km downstream, spans the Tamar River at Whirlpool Reach. It was one of the world's first cable-stayed bridges. It is dominated by a 100m high steel A-frame tower which is inclined at 20 deg. from the vertical and leans out 30m across the river and carries almost the entire weight of the 206m main span. The bridge was opened in 1968.

SCOTTSDALE, 70 km north-east, is the centre of the market garden area and has a large food processing factory specialising in deep freezing and dehydrating vegetables. In 1973 the first oil poppies were harvested and they have now become an important facet of rural production in the area. In January and February when the poppies bloom the countryside is a blaze of colour. Lavender is grown around Nabowla, 13km west of Scottsdale and its perfume pervades the air in December when it is in bloom.

BRIDPORT on the coast is 26km north of Scottsdale. It has long white sweeping beaches, lovely fresh water inlets and coloured rocks. It is a popular summer holiday resort with all the usual tourist infrastructure. There is plenty of good fishing and local crayfish tails are exported to America.

BELL BAY on the Tamar River is a fine inland port and there are several industrial processing plants there e.g. Comalco's aluminium smelter and

Tempco's manganese steel furnaces.

GEORGE TOWN is the residential and commercial centre for Bell Bay. It has a beautiful Georgian mansion that has been restored and is open for inspection 10am-5.30pm daily.

BEN LOMOND NATIONAL PARK is 48km south-east of Launceston and has spectacular mountain scenery and is Tasmania's leading ski resort. Access is by a very steep mountain road through a precipitous gorge and across the mountain plateau. In winter, it is often covered by heavy snow. Contact the Tourist Bureau for bus timetable.

LIFFEY VALLEY is a popular destination for bushwalkers and fishermen. There is a large fernery which sells a large variety of ferns. In the reserve are the Liffey Falls which drop into a beautiful rainforest.

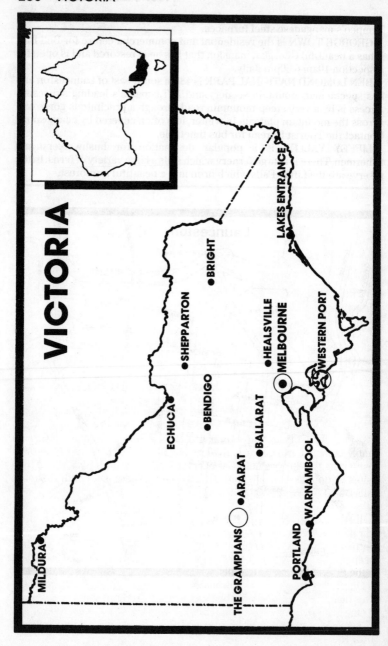

ARARAT – Pop. 8,336

LOCATION:
In the central highlands of Victoria and gateway to the Grampians.

CHARACTERISTICS:
There is a decided Scottish flavour about this area. The Grampians dominate the whole of the landscape. They have craigy slopes on the eastern side and gentler slopes on the western side levelling out into the Wimmera Plains. They are entirely contained within a State forest and are a bushwalker's dream.

HOW TO GET THERE:
BUS. On the Ansett Pioneer, Greyhound and Deluxe Melbourne/Adelaide Western & Dukes Highways route.
RAIL. On the main Adelaide/Melbourne railway line.
CAR. On the Western Highway 545km from Adelaide and 203km from Melbourne.

TOURIST INFORMATION:
Municipal Offices, Ararat Ph (053) 522 23332.

ACCOMMODATION:
Ararat Colonial Lodge, 6 Ingor St., Ph 42 2411 – RO $43-58 double; Statesman Motor Lodge, Cnr. George Rd. & Lambert St., Ph 52 4111 – RO $42-57 double; Ararat Central Motel, 249 Barkly St., Ph 52 2255 – RO $41-50 double; Golden Gate Motel, Western Hwy, Ph 52 2474 – RO $36-41 double; Ararat Hotel, 130 Barkly St., Ph 42 2477 – B&B $26 double; Chalambar Motel, 132 Lambert Street, Ph 52 2430 – RO $33-36 double; Pendock Motel, 367 Barkly St., Ph 52 2430 – RO $34; Commercial Hotel, 191 Barkly St., Ph 52 1014 – B&B $27-33; Turf Hotel, 157 Barkly St., Ph 52 2393 – B&B $26 double; Acacia Caravan Park, Acacia Ave, Ph 52 22994 – sites $7 double – onsite vans $15-20; Pyrenees Caravan Park, 67a Pyrenees Hwy, Ph 42 1309 – sites $7 double – on site vans $16-18 double. There is a Youth Hostel at Halls Gap, Ph (053) 56 4262, $6 ppn..

POINTS OF INTEREST:
Ararat, a former gold mining town, is the commmercial and industrial centre of a prosperous farming and winegrowing region. The average sheep population in the district is around 1,500,000. The town was named by the first settler, Horatio Wills, who, after a rugged trip overland, rested on One Tree Hill overlooking what was later to become Ararat and wrote in his diary 'This is Mt. Ararat for, like the Ark, we rested here'. The lookout on One Tree Hill provides a panoramic view of the city and surroundings.

There are many old public buildings built of bluestone but the imposing Town Hall is an exception.

The Langi Morgala Museum, Queen Street, has the Mooney Collection of aboriginal weapons and effects, steam locomotives and machinery. It is open Wednesday afternoons and weekends.

The Ararat Regional Art Gallery, Town Hall Building, specialises in wool and fibre pieces by leading craftsmen – open Mon-Fri 11am-4pm & Sun 2pm-5pm.

Montara Vineyard, Chalambar Road, Ph 52 3868 is open for tastings and sales to the public Mon-Sat 10am-5pm.

FESTIVALS:
Golden Gateway Festival in October.

FACILITIES:
Lawn bowls, croquet, horse racing, swimming, tennis, trotting, and squash.

OUTLYING ATTRACTIONS:
Midway between Ararat and Stawell is the little township of GREAT WESTERN which gives its name to the fine wines, including the champagne-style Great Western Special Reserve, maturing in the cellars beneath the sloping hills of Seppelts vineyards. Located in the public hall of Great Western is a toll gate, over one hundred years old which was formerly in use on the Great Western Highway.

STAWELL is a former gold mining town and with rising gold prices, the mines may even become profitable once more. There are two 'follow the arrow' tours of the town which take visitors to the Quartz Reefs and Pleasant Creek goldfields areas and include many monuments, historic buildings and sites, open cut mines, a mine adit and the chiming clock on the Town Hall tower with its sculptured group of gold miners which activates on the hour. The North Western Woollen Mills have tours at 10.30am weekdays followed by a bus tour of the town with driver commentary. One of its main attractions is Mini World, a world in miniature. It covers mankind's development and lifestyles in Australia and Asian countries and includes working models, dioramas, automatic commentaries and outdoor features. Stawell is the home of the Stawell Easter Gift, the world's richest track event. Near Stawell, in the Victoria Range and the northern Grampians, are Aboriginal rock paintings. The most striking of them is in Bunjil's cave in the Black Range 11km from Stawell. It depicts Bunjil, a dreamtime ancestor common to most of the tribes of south-east Australia.

HALLS GAP, right in the Grampian Ranges, is a holiday accommodation centre adjacent to Wonderland Forest Park and picturesque Lake Bellfield. It is noted for its large koala population and wildflowers in all seasons. There are many roads and walking tracks in the area which lead to some of the Grampian's most spectacular sights, which include Boroka and Reeds Lookouts, McKenzie Falls and Lake Wartook, Zumsteins Park, Lake Bellfield, Mount William and Roses Gap. Within minutes of leaving Halls Gap, hikers can plunge into dense rainforests with waterfalls, fern glens and wildflowers.

AVOCA, another former mining town, is in the foothills of the Pyrenees Range at the junction of the Sunraysia and Pyrenees Highways. It is picturesquely situated on the banks of the Avoca River and its quiet hills team with black wallabies and grey kangaroos. There is also a growing colony of Koalas.

SKIPTON, south-east of Ararat, has some fine old buildings and a smoked eel factory, which cultivates eels and smokes them for export. To the south at Mt. Widderin, is Victoria's largest volanic caves.

BALLARAT – Pop. 62,600

LOCATION:
Main centre of the Victorian Central Highlands which have a decided Scottish flavour about them. Ballarat was made famous through the Eureka Stockade, the bloody miners' rebellion in 1854. Distance from: Melbourne 113km; Sydney 985km; Adelaide 637km; and Canberra 747km.

CHARACTERISTICS:
Ballarat was a quiet country town until gold was discovered in 1851. Virtually overnight it grew into a city and two years later it had a population of 40,000. The spirt of the early days can be relived at Sovereign Hill a fascinating recreation of a gold-mining township.

HOW TO GET THERE:
BUS. It is on the Melbourne/Adelaide/Perth and Melbourne/Adelaide/ Alice Springs Ansett Pioneer and Greyhound routes and the Melbourne/ Adelaide VIP and Deluxe route. V-Line buses run from Melbourne direct and the trip takes approx. 2 hrs. Greens Buslines, Mair St., operate a weekday service to Bendigo. Railway buses run to a few other towns in the area: Warrnambool, Geelong, Hamilton, Maryborough, and Donald.
RAIL. Regular service from Melbourne takes 2 hrs.
CAR. Just over 110km on the four lane western freeway from Melbourne; from Adelaide about an 8 hour trip.

TOURIST INFORMATION:
The Gold Centre Regional Tourist Office, Lydiard St., Ph (053) 32 2694. Central Highlands Regional Tourist Office, 115 Bridge Street Mall, Bakery Hill, Ph (053) 32 2694.

ACCOMMODATION:
18 motels, 3 hotels/motels, 5 hotels and 4 caravan parks and camping grounds. See the Tourist Information Office for further information.

A few names and addresses: The Eureka Lodge Motel, 119 Stawell St.

South, Ph 31 1900 – B & Lt. B $37 double; Mid City Motel, 19 Doveton St. North, Ph 31 1222 – RO $43-50 double; Old Ballarat Village,613 Main Rd, Ballarat East, Ph 31 3588 – RO $44.50 double – Group Accommodation Lodge $22.50 double B & LB;Brewery Tap Hotel/Motel, Western Hwy, Ph 34 7201 – B&LB $24 double. Shady Acres Tourist & Holiday Park, Western Hwy, Ph 34 7233 – sites $6.50 – overnite vans $18-24 double; Government Camp Visitor Accommodation (Assoc.Youth Hostel), Sovereign Hill, off Magpie St. Ph 31 1944 – $7.50 single for YHA members but $26-32 for others; College of Advanced Education Students' resident on Mt. Helen Campus grounds – $6 single for YHA members (during vacations), Ph 31 1800 extn 388.

EATING OUT:

As usual most of the hotels have counter meals for a reasonable price. Then there's the chain restaurants McDonalds, Pizza Hut and The Pancake Kitchen, 2 Grenville St. If you are wanting to splurge then try Dyer's Steak Table in Little Bridge St. You will find most eating places in Sturt or Bridge Sts.

POINTS OF INTEREST:

For anyone who appreciates early Australian architecture Ballarat's main street includes some of the finest examples of Victorian architecture. The Tourist Office sell a walking tour brochure for 30cents. Montrose Cottage, the first masonry cottage built on the goldfields, is now a museum.

At the western end of the city you can't fail to be impressed by the 22 km avenue of stately trees, the Avenue of Honour, crowned by the Victory Arch. Sovereign Hill Gold-Mining Township/Gold Museum is a living memorial to the gold rush era in Ballarat 1851-1861. It is a fully operational re-created gold mining town. The Gold Museum has a priceless collection of alluvial gold, nuggets, rare coins, etc..

Adam Lindsay Gordon's Cottage which stands in the Botanical Gardens, is filled with personal papers and effects belonging to this Australian poet and his contemporaries. Some original Ballarat vintage trams run on the short track around the Botanical Gardens beside Lake Wendouree. A Paddle Cruiser cruises around the lake daily and offers a commentary describing historic features of the town. The Eureka Stockade Memorial Park near the site of famous civil uprising in 1854 has a stone momument, diorama of the battle with recorded commentary. The Eureka Exhibition which is situated opposite the Eureka memorial guides visitors through a series of computer controlled rooms and scenes depicting the several events relating to the incident. Several other displays of the Gold era are found at the Ballarat Historical Museum in Barkly St. The Ballarat Fine Art Gallrey houses the Norman Lindsay collection and the original Eureka flag is also on display.

The Antique Toy Gallery is open from 10am-4.30pm Tues-Sun. For the young and the young at heart, Golda's World of Dolls, 148 Eureka St – Mon-Thurs 1-5pm and weekends 10am-5pm. The Shell House has several mosaic works on display created by placing shells in concrete.

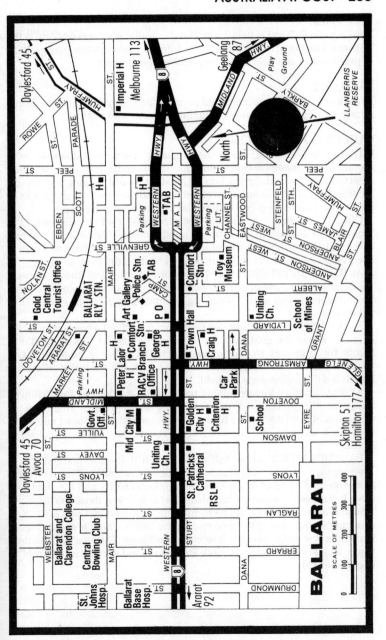

FESTIVALS:

The Begonia Festival is held every March – Ballarat's floral emblem is the Begonia. The Royal South Street Eisteddfod is a seven week smorgasbord of performings arts held during September and October.

FACILITIES:

Lawn bowls, croquet, fishing, gold panning, golf, greyhound racing, horse racing, rowing, sailing, squash, swimming, tennis, and trotting.

OUTLYING ATTRACTIONS:

KRYAL CASTLE, 8km along the Highway towards Melbourne, is a reconstructed medieval castle built into the foothills. It offers real family entertainment with daily displays of jousting, sword fighting and similar medieval pursuits. A licensed tavern in the castle serves food and drinks of old England and a medieval banquet is held each Saturday night.

CLUNES, 40km north, was the first place that gold was discovered in Victoria and as you will see from the solid sandstone home and town hall in the main street, became a wealthy town. Clunes holds a 'Back to' Festival every September. The town is surrounded by 22 extinct volcanos.

At HEPBURN SPRINGS, near Daylesford, are the well-known mineral water baths which are open daily between August and June and of course the mineral drinking spas. Take along a container to get some spa water to 'take-away'.

At DAYLESFORD you can see the remains of five furnaces and a 24m chimney where the gold from the surrounding district was smelted into ingots for transport to Melbourne. Each December a large Highland Gathering is held in Victoria Park during which the Australian Highland Pipe Band Championships are held.

AVOCA, another former mining town in the foothills of the Pyrenees Range at the junction of the Sunraysia and Pyrenees Highways, is picturesquely situated on the banks of the Avoca River. Its quiet hills teem with black wallabies and grey kangaroos. There is also a growing colony of Koalas.

BACCHUS MARSH, about half way between Melbourne and Ballarat, is where brown coal is mined in a massive open cut operation. The town itself is surrounded by market gardens and apple orchards and the road into town is flanked by massive elms planted in memory of those townspeople who served in World War I. The Border Inn was used by Cobb & Co. as a changing station during the gold rush of the 1850's. There is also a chicory kiln and a few architecturally interesting buildings. The nearby Lederderg Gorge and Werribee Gorge are both State Parks and attract visitors from all over the world.

BENDIGO – Pop. 52,741

LOCATION:
Almost in the centre of Victoria. At the junction of the Calder Highway, McIvor Highway, the Northern Highway and the Loddon Valley Highway. Distance from: Melbourne 151km; Adelaide 661km; Sydney 892km; Canberra 653km.

CHARACTERISTICS:
Bendigo was once one of the richest gold mining towns in Australia and is proud of its mining history and has preserved relics of the period as lasting reminders for present and future generations. The most tangible of these is a complete mine, in working condition right in the town, the Central Deborah Mine.

HOW TO GET THERE:
BUS. Bendigo is on the Greyhound and Ansett Melbourne/Mildura route, and on the VIP and Deluxe Melbourne/Adelaide route. There is also a mini-bus service between Ballarat and Bendigo.
RAIL. Regular service and the trip from Melbourne takes about 2 hrs.
CAR. From Melbourne on the Calder or McIvor Highway; from Sydney the Hume Highway and Midland Highway.

ACCOMMODATION:
18 motels, 1 hotel/motel and 3 hotels and 7 caravan parks. See the Tourist Office for details. A few names and addresses: All Seasons Motor Inn, 479 McIvor Hwy, Ph 43 8166 – RO $45-50 double; Oval Motel, 194 Barnard St., Ph 43 7211; City Family Hotel, 33 High St., Ph 43 4674 – RO $26-35; Ascot Lodge Caravan Park, 15 Heinz St., White Hills, Ph 48 4421 – site $7.50 double – overnite van $18.50 double. No youth hostel.

EATING OUT:
There are numerous pubs serving counter lunches and teas e.g. Lake View Hotel in McRae Street. There are numerous coffee shops and hamburger shops and of course the cafeterias in the department stores as well as McDonalds, Ollies etc.

POINTS OF INTEREST.
Tourist brochures tell the visitor to Bendigo that the vintage talking tram travels at 100 years an hour! It runs twice daily except for weekends and school holidays, when it departs hourly. It commences its 8km trip through the city at the Deborah Mine and detours to the Tramways Museum, then out to Emu Point and the Joss House and return, and has a synchronised taped commentary broadcasting information about more than 50 historic points of interest as it passes each of them. Bendigo has no fewer than 26 buildings classified by the National Trust. The Central Deborah Goldmine

only ceased production in 1956 and has been fully restored as a working exhibit (above ground level) – open daily 9am-5pm. The Chinese Joss House at Emu Point has been restored to its original condition by the National Trust. At Sandhurst Town you can ride the express to Gold Wash Gully diggings for an entertaining and educational re-enactment of life on the diggings. This turn of the century town features arts and craft stores. The Bendigo Pottery at Epsom is the oldest pottery works in Australia – guided tours and sales. The Bendigo Woollen Mills are also interesting as are Ettrick Spinning Wheels. The Mohair Farm and Woodstock Pottery on the Maryborough Road are also of interest, as are the Cherry Berry Farm Water Adventure Land and Dawson's Cacti Gardens.

FESTIVALS:

The Easter Fair has been staged for more than a century. The three day

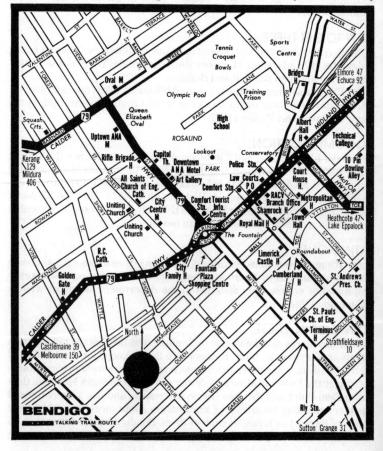

carnival includes a parade on the Saturday, a walking of the dragon' ceremony takes place on the Sunday when a small lion wakes Śun Loong' with fireworks. Sun Loong is a 100m long and is the largest known ceremonial Chinese dragon in the world. It is a colourful feature of the major procession on the Monday afternoon.

FACILITIES:
Lawn bowls, golf, tennis, swimming, croquet, horse racing, and trotting.

OUTLYING ATTRACTIONS:
CASTLEMAINE, 38km south, nestles in a dip of the Great Dividing Range and is built on several low hills. It has many unspoiled buildings erected during the period when vast quantities of gold were being taken from the ground. In the Castlemaine Market there is a wonderful collection of large photographs of Castlemaine mining scenes that are on permanent display. At Leanga-Nook, just out of Harcourt near Castlemaine, is a fine Koala Park Reserve where koalas roam freely.

BRIGHT – Pop. 1,545

LOCATION:
In the foothills of the Victorian Alps 312km from Melbourne.

CHARACTERISTICS:
Gateway to the Victorian Alps and famous for its autumn leaves.

HOW TO GET THERE:
AIR. To Albury/Wodonga and then bus. *BUS.* Ansett Pioneer, Greyhound, VIP, or Deluxe, to Albury/Wodonga and then local bus.
RAIL. To Albury/ Wodonga and then bus.
CAR. From Melbourne: either the Hume Highway to Wangaratta and then the Ovens Highway 310km; The Princes Highway to Bairnsdale and then the Omeo Highway 545km. From Sydney Via the Hume Highway to Albury/ Wodonga and then the Kiewa Valley Highway 650km.

TOURIST INFORMATION:
Adrian Smith, Caltex Service Station, 1 Anderson Street, Bright, Ph (057) 55 1509. Rock Cavern, Beechworth, Ph (057) 28 1374.

ACCOMMODATION:
The Bright Central Booking Agency handles all types of accommodation for Bright and District, Phone 55 1944 or write to 1 Anderson St., Bright 3241. Some names and addresses: High Country Inn, 13 Gavan Way, Ph 55 1244 – RO $46-54; Pinewood Hotel/Motel, 91 Gaven St., Ph 55 1277 – RO

$38-42; Bright Haven Motel, 1 Delany Ave., Ph 55 1033 – RO $35-45; Oriental Lodge Guest House, 2 Ireland St., Ph 55 1074 – DBB $36 ppn; Rosedale Guest House, 117 Gaven Street, Ph 55 1059 – DBB $32 ppn; Golfers Flats, Toorak Ave., Ph 55 1670 – Holiday season $250 per week – October/November $125 per week. Alpine Caravan Park, 1 Mountbatten Ave., Ph 55 1064 – sites $6-7 double – onsite vans $16.50-25 double – cabins $28 double; Bright Municipal Caravan Park, Cherry Ave., Ph 55 1141 – sites $6 double – onsite vans $20 double; Youth Hostel, (formerly Star Hotel) Main Street, Beechworth, Ph 28 1425 – $6.25 ppn.

EATING OUT:

Alps Pizza and Pasta Restaurant, 94 Gavan St., Ph 55 1526; Barnabys, 98 Gavan St., Ph 55 1050; Bright Restaurant, 10 Barnard St., Ph 55 1987; Bogong View Motor Inn, 35 Delaney Ave., Ph 55 1422; Crazy Kangaroo, Gavan St., Ph 55 1838; Glorias Pizza and Pasta Restaurant, 94 Gavan St., Ph 55 1526; Golden Chopsticks, Ovens Highway, Ph 55 1191; Pinewood Bistro, Gavan St., Ph 55 1277; Ragamuffins Restaurant, 74 Gavan St., Ph 55 1770 and Red Carpet Inn, Gavan St., Ph 55 1255.

POINTS OF INTEREST.

Bright indeed deserves its name. This pretty village sparkles against its backdrop of dark green-clad hills. In summer, the lighter green of the deciduous trees contrast with the gums and pines. In autumn, the brilliant yellows, golds and reds truly glow in the sunshine. Photos of Bright's autumn leaves have graced many calendars and postcards. Bright is one of Australia's longest established holiday destinations, having welcomed visitors for more than a century. Bright's first guide book was published in 1887. It included maps of walking tracks and bridle paths, specially marked and graded according to degree of difficulty. These are still popular to-day – maps of the tracks are available at Bright's Tourist Information Centre. Some of the most popular walks are to the Clearspot, Huggins and Mt. Porepunkah lookouts which offer a panoramic view of the village.

Bright's Court House (1861) and the Log Lock-up (1874) are National Trust classified, while the Powder Magazine (1871), A.J. Lock's shop (1860's) and the old weatherboard house (1850's) are recorded. Bright's Historical Museum has been established in the town's disused railway station. There is a 6km walking/bicycle track from Bright to Wandiligong which starts at the Bright carpark.

The Edelstein Gallery, Mountbatten Ave., Ph 55 1715 has a comprehensive gem and rare mineral collection as well as the largest cuckoo clock in Australia – open daily school & public holidays 10am-5.30pm othersiwe Mon-Sat 1pm-5pm and Sun 9am-5.30pm.

The Old Mill Park & Roller Skating Rink, Mill Road, Ph 55 1137 has a skateboard track, minigolf, half court tennis, bocce, pedal car and cycle track, giant slide, shetland pony rides, indoor roller skating rink, and one hour trail rides through the bush and pine forests – open daily.

FESTIVALS:

The Festival of the Autumn Leaves.

FACILITIES:

In summer the weir across the Ovens River provides a clean, fresh swimming pool beside the lovely Memorial Park. There is a sports centre with swimming pool, trampolines, squash court, table tennis and a sauna. An amusement park for children offers a roller skating rink, mini-golf, skateboard and bicycle tracks and a maze. There is also a golf course and, of course, trout fishing in the nearby rivers.

OUTLYING ATTRACTIONS:

THE SNOW COUNTRY: The major ski centres are Falls Creek, Mt. Buffalo and Mt. Hotham. Private bus companies operate day-trip services from Albury-Wodonga to Falls Creek, Mt. Hotham and Mt. Buffalo. The availability of a buses depends on demand. The buses are most readily available to Falls Creek – the most popular destination from Albury-Wodonga. Ski Lifts: Falls Creek has 22, Mt. Hotham 9, Mt.Buffalo 8 Slope gradings: Falls Creek has 20% beginner, 60% intermediate & 20% advanced; Mt. Hotham has 30% beginner, 30% intermediate & 40% advanced; Mt. Buffalo has 80% beginner, 15% intermediate & 5% advanced.

Combined length downhill runs: Falls Creek 34km, Mt. Hotham 14km and Mt. Buffalo 5km.

Combined length marked cross-country trails: Falls Creek 8km, Mt. Hotham 50km, and Mt. Buffalo 10km.

Mt. Beauty lives up to its evocative name, fulfilling the expectations of visitors who travel up the lovely Kiewa Valley towards the mountains. In summer they come to water ski and windsurf on Mt. Beauty Pondage, or to bushwalk – the National Park Rangers at Mt. Beauty take summer torchlight expeditions to view rare possums – inquiries to the National Parks Office (057) 57 2693. There is an all weather airport for gliding and parachuting in summer, and charter planes in winter ferrying interstate skiers. It is the headquarters of the Upper Kiewa Valley Hydro-electric scheme and tours of the Kiewa and other power stations are available – bookings are advisable although not essential. In winter, it is a base for skiers.

Falls Creek is one of Victoria's best known and most popular skiing areas, yet in summer it has even more to offer the holidaymaker. Falls Creek is tucked under the very edge of the Bogong High Plains, overlooking the Kiewa Valley and the Bogong High Plains have to be seen to be believed during December and January. During these months, organised Alpine windflower tours are available for walkers, including family groups. There are nine walking trails which take from 90 mins. to all day. It is essential that walkers sign the intention books at the various departure points and wear suitable footwear, and carry a jumper, gloves cap and waterproof jacket regardless of the weather conditions.

Victoria's highest mountain, Mt. Bogong 1986m, is found here. There are many commercial and self-contained lodges available winter and summer, and the information centre, restaurants, bars and shops are open year round. The road from Wangaratta and Wodonga via Mt. Beauty-Tawonga is sealed right to the village.

Porepunkah, 6km from Bright, is the gateway to the Mt. Buffalo National Park, which is an ideal family ski resort and summer holiday centre. Mt. Buffalo has self-guided walks offering spectacular terrain and scenery. Obviously, it is essential to stay on the tracks. Leaflets are available at the Chalet which is one of the oldest guest houses in Victoria. The mountain possesses incredible rock formations, and in summer boasts alpine wild flowers and birdlife, including the lyrebird.

Mt. Hotham at 1863m is Australia's highest ski resort. It is novel in that the village is at the top of the ski-runs. Mt. Hotham is renowned for its excellent coverings of powder snow, so appreciated by top-ranking skiers. Beginners also appreciate this soft snowcover which gently cushions the inevitable tumble or two. In summer, it is a delightful retreat with walking trails which wind around the mountains and along the ridges.

Myrtleford, 32km from Bright, is the centre of the hops and tobacco growing industries. A drive from Myrtleford to the historic homestead of Merrigang offers a close look at many hop farms and visitors are welcome at Merrigang – enquire at the Tourist Information Office for opening times. The harvesting of tobacco and hops takes place during February and March. There is good trout fishing in the local streams. There is also a large timber mill which accepts 40 semi-trailer loads of logs daily, and nothing is wasted – pinebark chips are used for landscaping, logs for timber planks and off-cuts and waste are converted to pulp, which is used to make 500,000 rolls of toilet paper daily.

ECHUCA – Pop. 7,940

LOCATION:
Close to the junction of the Murray, Campaspe and Goulbourn Rivers. Distance from: Melbourne 200km or 2½hrs drive.

CLIMATE:
Average daily temperatures: January max. 31.9 deg. c – min. 16.7 deg. C ; June max. 15.2 deg. C – min. 3.7 deg. C. Average annual rainfall 451mm.

CHARACTERISTICS:
Echuca has a long and colourful history as a result of once being one of Australia's largest inland ports. It handled cargo from about 100 river boats, as well as goods brought in by rail from Melbourne. The award winning television series 'All the Rivers Run' captured much of the romance and

feel of Echuca as it was in its river boat days.

HOW TO GET THERE:

BUS. From Melbourne, Ansett Pioneer have a special same day return fare to Echuca $22.00 – available Tues, Wed, Thurs & Sat only. Greyhound stop at Echuca on their Sydney/Adelaide run.

RAIL. Regular service from Melbourne.

CAR. At the junction of the Murray Valley Highway and the Northern Highway and the Cobb Highway.

TOURIST INFORMATION:

Murray Tourism Information Centre in the old Customs House, Cnr. Murray Esplanade and Leslie St. Echuca Information Centre, 642 High St.

ACCOMMODATION:

Echuca has 13 motels, 2 hotel/motels, 1 guest house and 4 caravan parks. Some names and addresses; Hopwood Motor Inn, Northern Hwy, Ph 82 2244 – RO $40-46; Caledonian Hotel Section, 110 Hare St., Ph 82 2100 – BB $36 double; Echuca Caravan Park, Crofton St., Ph 82 2157 – site $7 double – overnite van $16-18 double. For something different you could hire a houseboat from Magic Murray Houseboats, Ph (054) 82 2177. Youth Hostel – Rich River Inn, 21 Warren St., Ph (054) 82 4287 – $6.25 single.

EATING OUT:

The Echuca Hotel serves counter meals. The Bridge Hotel Restaurant has an excellent menu and wine list. The Cock'n'Bull is a BYO restaurant. The Coffee Pot Sandwich Bar is good for a quick snack. Vagg's Shamrock Hotel has a restaurant and you also can get something to eat at the Echuca Port Food House. For a cantonese, malaysian or vegetarian meal head for the River Palace BYO Restaurant. The Steam Packet Motel has a BYO Tavern. For that quick cup of coffee try The Tangled Garden, 433 High St. The Licensed Clubs in Moama welcome bona fide visitors for meals or drinks. There is also an Ollies Family Restaurant at 221 Ogilvie Ave.

POINTS OF INTEREST:

The Port of Echuca is open daily 9.15am-5pm. The wharf, river boats, barges and buildings have been restored. Tickets (passports) are available from Port Visitors Centre & Souvenir Shop opp. wharf. Your Passport, valid all day, admits you to the following features: Paddlesteamers Pevensey, better known as 'Philadelphia' from 'All the Rivers Run' and Adelaide, an historic logging boat – both tied up at the wharf; a ten minute film which tells the Port story; the escape tunnel from the former cellar bar at the Star Hotel; the Paddlesteamer Gallery with river scenes of the last century; and the Bridge Hotel upstairs galley.

The Historical Society Museum opp. Hopwood Gardens has old river charts, photographs etc. – open weekends, public and school holidays 1-4pm.

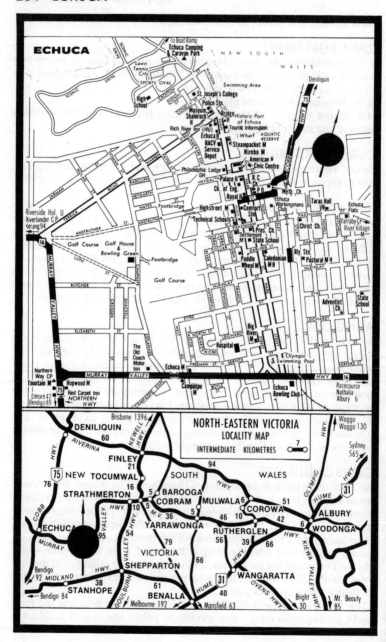

Echuca also has a Wax Museum, Bond Store, Murray Esplanade. The Coach House Carriage Collection features a collection of authentic horsedrawn vehicles – 57 Murray Esplanade – open daily.

The Alambee Folk and Auto Museum, 711 Warren St., has vintage and veteran cars, and a working model railway.

River Cruises: 2 day/night cruises aboard P.S. Emmylou – departs Wed and Fri; One hour trips on the P.S. Canberra or the P.S. Pride of the Murray; or M.V. Tisdall Princess floating restuarant.

If you are interested in vintage and veteran cars then head for the Alambee Folk and Auto Museum in Warren St.- open daily from 9am.

Tisdall Winery, Cornelia Creek Road, Ph 82 1911, is open daily for tastings and cellar sales. Over the road from there is Joalah Fauna Park open from 10am Wed-Sat – morning and afternoon teas available.

The Echuca Aquarium at 601 High St., Ph 82 2459 has a fine display of tropical fish and goldfish. Reptiles are also on display, and venmon is milked from them – open daily.

FESTIVALS:

The Rich River Festival is held over 10 days in October and concludes with the annual wine and food day.

FACILITIES:

Boating, bowls, bush walking, croquet, fishing, golf, horse racing, horse riding, sailing, swimming, trotting, water skiing, bingo, and bicycle and canoe hire.

OUTLYING ATTRACTIONS:

KYABRAM, only 31km from Echuca, is becoming well known as an Arts and Crafts centre in the Goulburn and Murray Valleys. The Stables Pottery and Craft Centre has an unique and unusual display of locally made pottery, woodturning, copperware, glass blown goods, lead lighting, dried flowers and numerous hand crafts – open daily except Mondays. The Kyabram Fauna Park has hundreds of Australian animals and birds which roam freely around the park. It also has a miniature railway, playground kiosk – open daily 10am-6pm seven days a week.

THE BARMAH FOREST is a 20 min. drive from Moama and the tourist bureau has leaflets. At Barmah just off the main Moama Raod, is Alinta Holiday farm with animals, birds, refreshments and onsite vans. Koonbar Tours, Kondrook organise half day billy tea and damper tours of Red Gum forest country, Ph (054) 53 2281. The Moama Markets are held alternate Saturdays at Moama Sporting Complex. Canoe through spectacular and unspoiled river country, Barmah Moira red gun forest on a day or overnight canoe tour – book through Echuca Travel Centre, 203 Hare St., Echuca.

HEALESVILLE - Pop. 4,526

LOCATION:
In the Dandenong Ranges just north-west of Melbourne.

CLIMATE:
The climate can be brisk in winter with snow on the higher peaks.

CHARACTERISTICS:
The Dandenong Ranges are an ever-changing scenic treat within a hour's drive of Melbourne. They contain ash forests, streams meandering through moss-covered gullies, ferns and orchilds. Sherbrook Forest Park is recognised as the best place in Australia for seeing and hearing lyrebirds. Attractive little towns and villages dot the hills, and city people come for the fishing, walking, riding or just to enjoy the view.

HOW TO GET THERE:
BUS. Marysville Coach Co., Lyell St., Marysville, Ph (059) 63 3206, has day and half day tours to scenic attractions in the area.
RAIL. Suburban train to Lilydale with connecting buses to Healesville.
CAR. From Melbourne take the Maroondah Highway to Healesville.

TOURIST INFORMATION:
217 Maroondah Hwy, Healesville, Ph (059) 62 5873.

ACCOMMODATION:
Healesville Motor Inn, 45 Maroondah Hwy, Ph 62 5188 - RO $36-40; Sanctuary House Healesville Motel, Badger Creek Rd., Ph 62 5148 - B&LtB $42-44; Healesville Maroondah View Motel, Maroondah Hwy, Ph 62 4154 - RO $30-36; Terminus Hotel, Harker St., Ph 62 4011 - BLtB $36 double; Park Drive Motel, 316 Maroondah Hwy, Ph 62 5000 - B&LtB $35$38 double; Strathvea Guest House, Myers Creek Rd., Ph 62 4109 - DBB $100 double; Badger Creek Caravan Park, Don Rd., Ph 62 4328 - sites $8-9 - on site vans $20-26 double; Healsville Caravan Park, River St., Ph 62 5888 - $6-8 - onsite vans $20-25; Ashgrove Caravan Park, Don Rd., Ph 62 4398 - sites $6 double - on site vans $20 double.

EATING OUT:
Mount Rael Restaurant, Yarra Glen Road, Ph 62 4107 - BYO Australian Cuisine; Park Drive Motel, 316 Maroondah Hwy, Ph 62 5000 - BYO English Cuisine; Sanctuary House Motel-Guest House, Badger Creek Rd., Ph 62 5148 - International/Australian Cuisine BYO; Strathvea County House, Myers Creek Road, Ph 62 4109 - Australian Cuisine BYO.

POINTS OF INTEREST.
Healesville was one of Melbourne's most popular spring-summer-autumn

holiday resorts at the turn of the century. It is still popular with holiday-makers who enjoy observing nature, horse riding, golf, walking, hiking or exploring the semi-rural and bushland roads of the area.

Above the town is Toolangi State Forest, criss-crossed with logging roads, some of which have good surfaces for general touring. A popular half-day trip is Tealesville-Toolangi along Chum Creek Road returning by Myers Creek Road.

Colin MacKenzie Wildlife Sanctuary is Healesville's premier attraction. Most of the enclosures are natural looking. There are five walk-through aviaries and some birds are not caged and just pop back for a feed. There is a nocturnal house, a platypus house, and reptiles, as well as bbq and picnic facilities.

Yenbena Cultural Centre, Badger Creek Road, Ph 62 3453 promotes and displays the artistic skills of aborigines. Cultural activities are held each weekend.

Badger Creek Ceramics, 217 Maroondah Hwy, Ph 62 5873, displays arts and crafts from the district, and is the Information Centre.

FACILITIES:
Lawn bowls, swimming, tennis, golf, and fishing.

OUTLYING ATTRACTIONS:
A nice trip from Healesville is to St. Filans, Marysville, Camberville, McMahons Creek, Warburton, Yarra Junction and Lilydale.

MARYSVILLE is just 95km from Melbourne, and there is snow on nearby Lake Mountain and Mt. Margaret from June to October. The road to the south through Camberville traverses the Cumerland Valley where the States tallest hardwoods cover the slopes of Mt. Arnold and Mt. Observation. Visit the Cumberland and Cora-Lynn Falls, Robert's Lookout and the Meeting of the Waters. Only an hour's walk, or a short drive away are the Stevenson Falls, which cascade 83m in three mighty jumps and are the tallest falls in Victoria. For those who are more energetic, there is an alternative return route via Keppel's lookout. This walk takes approx. 2.5hrs.

Another day trip from Healesville is to the wineries of the YARRA GLEN district:

Fergussons Winery, Wills Rd., Yarra Glen, Ph 652 237, has tastings and tours and a colonial style restaurant specialising in roasting on the spit.

Kellybrook Winery & Restaurant, Fulford Road, Wanga Park, Ph 722 1304, has tastings 9am-6pm Monday-Saturday & noon-6pm Sundays.

Linville Fruit Wines, Linithgow Monbulk-Seville Roads, Seville, Ph 64 4697, is open from November to April 10am-5pm Mon-Sat.

Prigorje Winery, Maddens Lane, Gruyere, Ph 64 9279, has tastings 9am-6pm Monday-Saturday & noon-6pm on Sundays.

Settlement Vineyards Pty Ltd., Settlement Rd., Yarra Junction, Ph 67 1428, has Australian Cuisine, and Live Music, and is open Fridays, Saturdays, and Sundays for dinner.

St. Huberts Wines, Cnr. St. Huberts Road & Maroondah Hwy, Coldstream, Ph 739 1421, has tastings 10am-6pm Saturdays and noon-6pm Sundays.

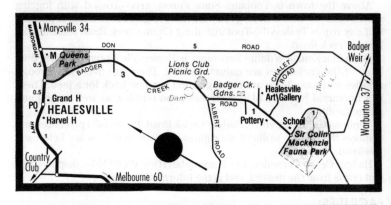

LAKES ENTRANCE – Pop. 3,414

LOCATION:
On the north-eastern coast of Victoria at the entrance to the Gippsland Lakes in an area known as the Victorian Riviera.

CLIMATE:
The Victorian Riviera has a Mediterranean climate and also its own Fohn (wind) which blows from the north-east across the highland, where it loses its moisutre and is warm by the time it reaches the lakelands.

CHARACTERISTICS:
The Holiday Capital of the Victorian Riviera which is one of the largest and most popular resort areas in Victoria. In summer the usual population is multiplied several times over. It also has one of Australia's largest fishing fleets which supplies both fish and scallops to the Melbourne and overseas markets.

HOW TO GET THERE:
BUS. Greyhound have a Melbourne/Bega service which stops at Lakes Entrance in the early afternoon and Ansett, Greyhound and Deluxe stop at Lakes Entrance on their Melbourne/Sydney Princes Highway run. The trip takes just under 12 hours from Sydney, or just over 5 hrs. from Melbourne. Deluxe and Greyhound stop here in the middle of the night/early hours of the morning which might present some problems with accommodation.

CAR. From Sydney travel via the Princes Highway; from Melbourne travel via the Princes Highway, or turn off the Princes Highway at Dandenong and travel the South Gippsland Highway along the coast and up to Sale. where it rejoins the Princes Highway.

ACCOMMODATION:

There is a wide range of accommodation available – approx. 16 motels, 2 guest houses, three hotels, approx. 40 blocks of flats and 22 caravan parks many with on site vans and cabins, and well as holiday flats.

A few names and addresses: Abel Tasman Motor Lodge, 643 The Esplanade, Ph 55 1655 – $35-63 double; The Hotel Central Motel, Princes Hwy, Ph (051) 551 821 – $36-50 double; Lakes Jakaranda Holiday Flats, 59 Church St., Ph 55 1511; Paradise Holiday Flats, Lake Bunga Beach Road, Ph 55 2934; Fountain Court Holiday Apartments, Lake St., Ph 55 1949; Whiter's Caravan Park, 43-79 Roadknight St., Ph 55 1343; Silver Sands, 33 Myer St., Ph 55 2343 – sites $8 double – on site vans $19-35 double; Idleours Caravan Park, Cnr. Princes Hwy & Whiter St., Ph 55 1788 – sites $8-10 – on site vans $18-33; Sunnyside Caravan Park, 60 Myer St., Ph 55 1735 – sites $6.50-10 – on site vans $17-30.

EATING OUT:

Pinocchio Inn, BYO, 569 Esplanade, Ph 55 1680 has fresh fish, Italian style pasta, grills and poultry and children's serves are available; The Scallop Pot Restaurant in the Glenara Motel Complex, is fully licensed and specalises in seafood – Phone 55 1555; The Hotel Central Motel, Princes Hwy, Ph 55 1977 has excellent Bistro meals for lunch and dinner and nightly entertainment in the season; Tres Amigos, another BYO Restaurant has take away and children's meals; There is also a floating restaurant, the Sloop John D, BYO, at the western end of the Boat Harbour – open 7 days – closed Sundays during June, July and August.

POINTS OF INTEREST:

The best way to explore the lakes is by boat. If you haven't a boat you can either hire one or take a trip on the Thunderbird, Victoria's largest catamaran ferry, or on the ML Bluebird – cruises leave at 9.45am and 2pm – special full day, luncheon and night cruises are advertised on the notice boards- Peel's Tourist & Ferry Service, 3 Laura St., Ph 55 2346.

A view of the whole lakeland area can be obtained from Jemmy's Point. This is the northern end of Ninety Mile Beach which stretches from Lake Tyers to Seaspray and is one of Australia's most unspoiled beaches.

Cavecraft, on the Esplanade, has a good display of local crafts including wool mohair, pottery and jewelley – Ph 55 9239 – open 7 days 8am-8pm.

Homestead Colonial Crafts, Falks Lane, Kalimna West, has an extensive variety of hand-made crafts from the East Gippsland region – open Wed – Sun.

The Big Boomerang, Aboriginal Art Museum, Princes Highway, Ph 55 1505, has genuine Aboriginal artefacts on display and for sale as well as an informative audio visual display – open 9am-5pm daily.

Nyerimilang Homestead, overlooking Lake Victoria, has beautiful formal gardens and is surrounded by farmland and natural bushland.

Two Museums worth visiting: The Gone with the Wind Museum and Shell Museum.

The Forests Commission conducts regular forest tours which depart from the Esplanade during the holiday season.

During the holdiay season Lakes Entrance becomes a carnival town, with sideshows, ferris wheels, carousels and dodgem cars.

FESTIVALS:

The Kinkuna Festival is held in May; the Bairnsdale Festival is held in March and the Sale Festival in October.

FACILITIES:

Boat hire, swimming, fishing, sailing, golf, lawn bowls, bush walking, tennis, water ski-ing etc.

OUTLYING ATTRACTIONS:

BAIRNSDALE was the port for its pastoral hinterland in the days before road transport. Now it supports a number of secondary industries. Attractions: Eagle Point has silt jetties which are the second largest in the world after those of the Mississippi; St. Mary's Church which is famous for its unique murals, painted ceilings and other works of art; Macleods Morass Game Reserve which covers 418ha and has been developed as a Water Fowl conservation area. At the Jolly Jumbuck Craft Centre you can see naturally greasy wool being spun. They also have leather work and pottery on display. The Blue Arrow Tour around Bairnsdale takes you past the town's points of interest. Pick up a leaflet from the Tourist Information Centre, 63 Main St. for details.

BUCHAN CAVES, 56km north, have beautiful limestone formations. Two of them are open to the public, the Royal and Fairy Caves. There are guided tours at 10am, 11am, 1.15pm, 2.30pm and 3.45pm daily. Facilities include a reserve for day visitors and overnight campers, and a motel. Whilst in the area you could also take a 2 hour walk to the 'Pyamids' an unusual rock formation, or picnic at the junction of the Buchan and Snowyn Rivers and swim, fish or go canoeing. Just off the Basin Road, is the Old Chimney silver and lead mine.

NOWA NOWA, on the highway 24km from Lakes Entrance, is a saw milling town but you could also try your luck fossicking as there are good deposits of red jasper, shell fossils and other gem stones.

McLENNAN STRAITS between Wellington and Victoria Lakes is one of the districts best fishing spots.

GLENALADALE NATIONAL PARK is west of Bairnsdale through the rich vegetable and dairying area of the Mitchell Valley. The main feature of the park is the Den of Nargun, which is a cavern which has been gouged out by a river. It is reached along a track from the car park and the walk takes approx. 30mins.

PAYNESVILLE is a popular boating, yachting and fishing resort on the lakes. It has an interesting church, the Anglican St. Peters.

MALLACOOTA, 111km along the coast near the NSW border, is surrounded by the Croajingalong National Park. It is situated in one of Victoria's most remote and peaceful lakeland settings. There are many walking tracks through the national park with its prolific birdlife. There is also excellent fishing in the river, surf and from the rocks, and game fishing boats may be chartered. At Gypsy Point, 14km from Mallacoota, you can have a quiet counter lunch and shake hands with Joe, the friendly kangaroo who shakes hands with visitors. The Double Creek Nature Trail starts at the picnic area by Double Creek, and takes about 30 minutes to walk. From Bastion Point, a colourful rocky outcrop overlooking Mallacoota harbour, there is a magnificient view of the coastline.

SALE, 104km on the Melbourne side of Lakes Entrance, is the operations centre for the nearby Bass Strait oil fields. You should try to see the magnificent Oil and Gas display depicting the discovery, development and production of the major offshore oil reserves. There is also a large RAAF flying training base. Cullinen Park, off Foster St., is the site of the historic Port of Sale where, in days of yore, steamers tied up after their long trip from Melbourne. There is a 4km drive around Lake Guthridge which is a sanctuary for native birds. There are also roads leading to the southern end of Ninety Mile Beach.

MELBOURNE – Pop. 3,000,000–

LOCATION:
On the shores of Port Phillip Bay.

CLIMATE:
Melbourne's climate is midway between maritime and continental, and very changeable. Average Temperatures: January max. 26 deg. C – min. 14 deg. C; July max. 13 deg. C. – min. 6 deg. C.; average annual rainfall 656mm.; driest months June to August.

CHARACTERISTICS:
Capital of the State of Victoria which is often called the Garden State.

HOW TO GET THERE:
AIR.   Regular services from all other capital cities and also from overseas.
BUS.   Ansett Pioneer, Greyhound, VIP, Deluxe, Across Australia Coachlines, Gold Coast Intertour, Dyson's Bus Services, Olympic and East West all have regular services to/from Melbourne.
RAIL.   From Sydney and Adelaide with connections to other capital cities.

Also an extensive network to Victorian country towns.

CAR. From Sydney via the Hume Highway 875km – via the Princes Highway 1058km – via the Olympic Way 961km – via Canberra/Cooma/Cann River 1038km. From Adelaide via the Western & Dukes Highways 726km – via Princes Highway West 910km.

TOURIST INFORMATION:

VTC Retail Offices, 230 Collins St., Ph (03) 52 619 9444; Victorian Tourism Commission, Level 7, Building 'D', World Trade Centre, Cnr. Flinders & Spencer Sts., Ph 619 9444; Melbourne Tourism Authority, 20th level, Nauru House, 80 Collins St., Ph 654 2288. Travellers' Aid Society of Victoria, 2nd Fl., 281 Bourke Street and Spencer Street Railway Station, City, Ph 654 2600, 654 2887, 672 2873 – Tourist Centres open 8am-8pm Mon-Sat & 10am-6pm Sun.

ACCOMMODATION:

Deluxe: Hyatt on Collins, 123 Collins St., Ph 657 1234 – RO $150 double; Menzies at Rialto, 495 Collins Street, Ph 62 0111 – RO $135 double; Parkroyal on St Kilda Rd., 562 St Kilda Rd., Ph 529 8888 – RO $135 double. Moderate: The Commodore, 4 Queens Rd., Ph 26 62411 – RO $64 double; The Australia Hotel 266 Collins St., Ph 63 0401 – RO $90; Palm Lake Motor Inn, 51 Queen St., Ph 529 7233 – RO $74 double. Budget: Georgian Court, 21-25 George St., East Melbourne, Ph 419 6353 – RO $34 double; Spencer Private Hotel, 44 Spencer St., Ph 62 6991 – RO $26 double; Youth Hostel, 122 Flinders St., Ph 654 5422 – $7.50 ppn; Appartments: Albert Heights Exec. Appartments, 83 Albert St., Ph 419 0955 – $58 double; George Powlett Lodge, Cnr. George & Powlett Sts., East Melbourne, Ph 419 9488 – $50 double; George Street Apartments, 101 George St., East Melbourne $28-40 nightly. For something different try the Australian Home Accommodation Centre, Suite 4, 209 Toorak Rd., South Yarra, Ph 241 3694 for accommodation in private homes. Accommodation is available in some university colleges during vacations: Chissholm College, La Trobe Uni, Ph 478 3122; St. Hilda's College, University of Melbourne, Ph 347 1158; Queens College, University of Melbourne, Ph 347 4837; Ormond College, University of Melbourne, Ph 347 2014; Monash University, Mannix College, Ph 544 8895. The colleges are not particularly cheap but are good places for meeting other students.

EATING OUT:

Melbourne has over 1600 eating houses from small streetside cafes to full-fledged restaurants covering 60 international cuisines.

A few names and addresses: For an unusual experience try the Colonial Tramcar Restaurant and dine while you travel through Melbourne – dinner Tuesdays to Sundays – bookings Ph 596 6500. Oz Eats, 813 Hampton Street, Brighton, Ph 592 2026 – specializes in traditional 'Aussie Meals'. The Last Laugh Theatre Restaurant, 64 Smith St., Collingwood, Ph 419 6226 is open for dinner & show Mon-Sat – comedy disco. The Melbourne Underground,

22 King St., Ph 61 4701 is open from noon-4pm & 10pm-5am Mon-Fri and 8pm-7am Fri & Sat – fully licensed – dancing. The Spaghetti Theatre, 185 Collins St., Ph 63 5787 – open noon-11.30 Mon-Sat & noon-8.30pm Sun – BYO & live entertainment. Austria House, 419 Spencer St., Ph 329 5877 has Austrian Cusine – BYO – open 7 days for lunch/dinner. Tijuana Taxi Mexican Restaurant, 62 Little Collins St., Ph 63 2752 – Fully Licensed/BYO – open for dinner 7 days. Chinese Noodle Shop Restaurant, 331 Clarendon St., Sth Melbourne, Ph 699 4150 – family restaurant – BYO.

LOCAL TRANSPORT:

All comes under the umbrella of The Met, Melbourne's public transport system covering trains, trams and buses, operated by the Metropolitan Transit Authority, and divided into ten neighbourhoods.

Ticket prices are based on how many neighbourhoods you are travelling in and for how long, with two-hour, daily and weekly travelcards being available. Tickets covering the inner Melbourne area are priced as follows:

Two-hour ticket $1.20

Daily Travelcard $2.30

Weekly Travelcard $11.20

TRAMS: Just about 'the symbol' for Melbourne. These old-fashioned trams still provide transport for thousands of commuters and are a big draw-card for visitors. The every day trams are painted green and yellow but if you are in Melbourne on a Sunday, keep your eyes open for the brightly painted ones!

CITY EXPLORER BUS: Designed as an easy method of transport between Melbourne's major inner-city attractions, the double decker 'City Explorer Bus' operates every day except Mondays between 10am-4pm, and it departs from Flinders Street Station on the hour – cost $7 adult, $3 child, $12 family (2 adults and 2 children).

TAXIS: Taxis can be hired off the street, at taxi ranks, major hotels or by phoning one of the taxi companies. A 30 cent telephone booking fee is charged and flag fall is $1.10. Tariff One operates between 6am and 6pm Mon-Fri, costs approx. 53.2 cents per km. Tariff Two operates between 6pm and 6am Mon-Fri and between and 1pm Sat to 6am Mon and costs approx. 64.1 cents per km. Some telephone Nos:

Arrow Taxi Service Ltd. 417 1111 Astoria Taxis 347 5511

Blacks Cabs & Eastern Group 567 3333 D & D Cyma Taxi 791 2111

Embassy Private Hire Service 329 9444 Silver Top Taxi 345 3455

Frankston Radio Cab Pty.Ltd. 786 3322 Regal Combined 810 0222

North Suburban Taxis Ltd. 480 2222 West Suburban 689 3455

CAR RENTAL: There are plenty of agencies but most will not rent vehicles to drivers under 21 years of age. Current international licences are acceptable in Australia. Some Agencies: Astoria, 630 Swansea St., Carlton, Ph 347 7766; Austourer Rentals, 327 Princes Highway, Werribee, Ph 741 1800; Budget, 13-21 Bedford St., North Melbourne, Ph 320 6222; Hertz, 94 York St., South Melbourne, Ph 699 0180.

FERRY SERVICE: A ferry service for passengers and cars to and from

Tasmania operates on Mondays. Wednesdays and Fridays and takes 14 hours – contact the Tourist Bureau for further information.

BIKE HIRE LOCATIONS: Alexandra Avenue (opp. Botanic Gardens); Jells Park Glen Waverley; Richmond – Yarra Boulevard and Kevin Bartlett Reserve; Westerfolds Park, Templestowe. Bikes can also be delivered to your hotel. Cost: $4 per hour, $9 for 4 hours – $10 dep for 2 bikes and you will need some identification e.g. driver's licence, passport, credit card.

BIKE TRACKS: Carrum-Patterson River 4km; Elwood-Brighton 5km; Glen Iris-Malvern 4km; Nepean Highway 4km; Moonee Ponds Creek 12km; Mordialloc-Edithvale 3km and Yarra Boulevard 11km.

POINTS OF INTEREST.

Carton & United Breweries Tour, 16 Bouverle St., Carton, Ph 342 5511 have free tours lasting approx. one hour – booking essential – free tastings.

Chinatown, Little Bourke Street, abounds with Chinese restaurants and stores – features oriental archways.

Diamond Valley Railway, Lower Eltham Park, Altham, Ph 439 2493 – open Sundays, Public Holidays and Wednesdays in school holidays 1pm-5pm – miniature passenger carrying railway featuring steam, diesel and electric trains.

Fantasy Egg Farm, Wonga Road, South Warrandyte, Ph 876 2311 is open 9am-5pm seven days a week and sells chickens, homemade ice cream and other farm produce. It also has water buffalo, emus, kangaroos and deer.

Jam Factory Shopping Centre, 500 Chapel Street, South Yarra, Ph 240 0537 – open Monday-Thurs 9am-5.30pm, Fri 9am-9pm. and 9am-12.30pm Saturdays. Originally a factory for the manufacture of jams for IXL for over 70 years. The restored building is now a large shopping complex.

Maritime Trust of Australia's, HMAS Castlemaine, has been transformed into a maritime museum with displays of model ships, relics, pictures, etc.

Royal Melbourne Zoological Gardens, Elliot Street, Parkville, Ph 347 1522 – open daily 9am-5pm. It has almost 400 species of Australian and exotic animals displayed in 60 acres of botanic gardens only 10 minutes from the city centre. The Lakeside Restaurant serves 'meals with a view' looking out to Gibbon Island. The Butterfly House exhibits 20 species of Australian butterflies.

The Victorian Arts Centre, 100 St. Kilda Road, Melbourne, Ph 617 8211 – open daily 10am-5pm. Guided tours of the Melbourne Concert Hall and State Theatre complex last approx. 1 hour.

Barque Polly Woodside (Melbourne Maritime Museum), Cnr. Normanby Road and Phayer St., South Melbourne, Ph 699 9760 – open weekdays 10am-4pm and weekends 12 noon-5pm.

Como, Como Avenue, South Yarra, Ph 241 2500 – open daily 10am-4.45pm. Como is an elegant colonial mansion which has been classified by the National Trust, and is set in five acres of gardens. It was built in 1855.

Captain Cook's Cottage, Fitzroy Gardens, Ph 419 8742, is open daily 9am-5pm. It is the original house of the parents of the discoverer of the east coast of Australia which was brought from Great Ayton, Yorkshire,

England in 1934.

La Trobe's Cottage, Birdwood Avenue, South Yarra, Ph 63 5528, is one of the earliest surviving timber portable houses. It was residence of Victoria's first lieutenant general.

Laurel Lodge, 51 Langhorne St., Dandenong, Ph 546 6221 – open Sunday 2pm-5pm – one of Dandenong's original homesteads furnished with period furniture.

Old Melbourne Gaol, Russell Street, Ph 654 3628 – open daily 10am-4.30pm. Built between 1841 and 1864 this gaol remained in use until 1929. It serves as a grim reminder of early convict days, and is probably best known as the place where Ned Kelly was hanged in 1880.

Parliament House, Spring Street, Ph 651 8911 – guided tours when Parliament is not sitting at 10am, 2pm and 3pm Mon-Fri.

Rippon Lea, 192 Hotham St., Eisternwick, Ph 532 9150 – open daily 10am-5pm – closed Christmas Day, Good Friday and mid June to mid August on Mondays and Tuesdays. Built in 1868 by Sir Frederick Sargood, this fifteen room Romanesque style house still retains 5.26 ha of beautiful gardens.

Shrine of Remembrance, between Domain & St. Kilda Roads, Ph 63 8415. The State of Victoria's war memorial built to honour Australia's war dead.

Dandenong Saleyards/Livestock Market located between the Dandenong Railway's Goods Yard and Cheltenham Road – Sale Days: Monday vealers, bullocks and sheep; Tuesdays, fat cows, bulls, pigs, calves and poultry; Fridays, horses and saddlery – third busiest saleyard in Victoria.

Nearby Parks & Gardens:

Albert Park Lake 2.8km south of the city centre. This lake and recreation area is popular with bike-riders, joggers, sailors and picnickers.

Carlton Gardens, bounded by Nicholson and Rathdowne Sts. and Victoria Pde., feature superb trees and the Royal Exhibition Building built in 1880.

Flagstaff Gardens bounded by King, Latrobe and William Streets – surrounded by historic buildings.

Fitzroy and Treasury Gardens bounded by Spring, Wellington, Clarendon, Albert & Lansdown Streets, Fitzroy.

Kings Domain includes Alexandra and Queen Victoria Gardens with floral clock and Pioneer Woman's Memorial Garden.

Royal Botanic Gardens between Alexandra & Domain Rds., South Yarra, Phone 63 9424 – open daily 7am-7.45pm in summer and 8.30am-5.15pm in winter. The gardens cover 41ha and have 12,000 species of native and exotic plans. Also in the gardens is The Craft Cottage – open 10am-3pm daily Mon-Fri. Voluntary guides conduct free guided walks every Tues, Thurs and Sundays at 10am and 11am except public holidays.

Museums:

Alma Doepel, Sailing Ship, berthed at 20 Victoria Dock, Ph 417 5100 is open daily 10am-4pm. It is a 1903 Australian sailing ship being restored as a Maritime Museum and sail training ship.

ANZ Banking Museum, 380 Collins Street, open Mon-Fri 9.30am- 4.30pm.

Museum of Victoria, 322-328 Swanston Street, Ph 669 9884 – open Mon-Sun 10am-5pm. The science section is responsible for collecting, preserving and displaying the state's technological and scientific heritage. A new children's museum has recently been opened within this building. The State Library of Victoria is also housed in this complex.

Railway Museum, Champion Road, North Williamstown, Ph 51 6146, is open weekends and public holidays 1pm-5pm and Wednesdays 1pm-4pm.

Performing Arts Museum, 100 St. Kilda Road, Ph 617 8211 is open Mon-Sat 11am-6pm, and has a lively programme of regularly changing exhibitions, and covers the whole spectrum of the performing arts. Ten unique sight and sound exhibitions throughout the year.

Museum of Chinese Australian History, 22 Cohen Place, Ph 662 2888 is open Mon, Wed, Thurs & Fri 10am-4.30pm, and 12noon-4.30pm weekends. There are historic artefacts and photographs, an exciting multi-screen audio visual display and, the star attraction, Dai Loong, a giant Chinese dragon.

Caulfield Racing Museum, Caulfield Racecourse, Station St., Ph 572 1111 – open Tues and Thurs 10am-4pm – displays great moments of racing history.

The Jewish Museum of Australia, Cnr. Toorak Road & Arnold St., Ph 266 1922, is open 11am-4pm Wed & Thurs and 2-5pm Sunday. It has changing exhibitions displaying Jewish history, culture, religion and lifestyle. Audio-visual presentation and synogogue tours available.

Melbourne Out and About Heritage Walks, 22 Toorak Mews, 382 Toorak Rd., South Yarra, Ph 241 1085 have regular personalised guided walking tours covering interesting aspects of Melbourne e.g. historic buildings, shopping, sightseeing group itineries, and transport arranged to suit special interests.

Melbourne Personally, Suit 611, 6th Floor, 234 Collins Street, Melbourne, Ph 63 1905. Home entertaining for overseas people through dinner parties and luncheons in private homes.

River and Bay Cruises

Maribyrnong River Cruises, 1 Maribyrnong St., Footscray, Ph 689 6431 depart from outside the Anglers Tavern – Regular departures Oct-April Weekends 1.30pm and 3pm.

Melbourne Cruises depart Berth 3, Princes Walk, Ph 63 2054/55 – daily 12 noon to Como Island.

Williamstown Bay and River Cruises departs River frontage, World Trade Centre, Ph 397 2046. Daily scenic cruises of the Port of Melbourne and the historic seaport of Williamstown. Jan-April Sat 1pm and 3pm, Sun 11am, 1pm and 3pm. Weekdays 3pm.

Amusement Parks: Fun Factory, 257 Toorak Road, South Yarra, Ph 340 8274; Luna Park, The Esplanade, St. Kilda, Ph 534 0653.

FACILITIES:

City Baths, Swanston St., Ph 663 5888; Golf Courses: 60 in the metropolitan area – enquiries to Victorian Golf Association, 6 Riddell Pde., Elsternwick,

Ph 528 1555 – most clubs have full hire facilities. Sailing/Sail Boarding are popular on Port Phillip Bay and sailboards may be hired along the bay at Sandringham, Dromana, Frankston, Mount Martha and Sorrento (in summer). Tennis and squash are popular and there are many courts available for hire.

Of course, no visit to Melbourne in the season (March to September) would be complete without seeing an Australian Rules Football match. Reserved seats may be arranged through each club but the majority of tickets are sold at the gate – see the local newspapers for details – price $7 – children & pensioners $1 – under 10's free.

In the summer, many one day Internationals and Sheffield Shield matches are played at the MCG, Yarra Park, Jolimont, Ph 63 3001. Melbourne has two major venues for Greyhound Racing – Olympic Park on Monday nights and Sandown Park on Thursday nights. Harness Racing's main Melbourne venue is Moonee Valley, 16km from city, McPherson St., Moonee Ponds, Ph 370 2633 – every Saturday and some Mondays. Australia's premier event on the Racing Calender is of course, the Melbourne Cup which is held the first Tuesday of November at Flemington Racecourse, Epsom Road, Flemington, Ph 376 0441 (3kms from city centre) – free guided tours of the racecourse take place every race day. There are three other top racecourses in Melbourne – Caulfield, Station St., Ph 572 111 (10km from the centre); Moonee Valley, McPherson St., Moonee Ponds, Ph 370 2633 (6km from the centre); Sandown, Racecourse Drive, Springvale, Ph 546 5288 (25km from the centre).

The major Soccer venue is Olympic Park (1 km from the centre), Swan St., Melbourne. The Australian Tennis Open is held in December at Melbourne's Kooyong Courts (6km from the centre) in Glenferrie Road, Kooyong, Ph 20 3333.

Markets: Queen Victoria Market, Elizabeth Street, – open Tues & Thurs 6am-2pm, Fri 6am-6pm, Sat 6am-12 and Sun 9am-4pm; South Melbourne Market, Cnr. Coventry & Cecil Sts., South Melbourne, Ph 699 4077 – open Wed 6am-2pm, Fri 6am-6pm, Sat 6am-12 and Sun 9am-4pm; St. Kilda Esplanade Art & Craft Market, Upper Esplanade, St. Kilda – open Sunday only 9am-4pm.

Free Entertainment in Parks was introduced by the City Council in 1972, and Melbourne now has the world's leading free entertainment programme, featuring over 37,500 artists and having over 1,700 productions to its credit. From October-April performances are held throughout the week at various outdoor venues, including the Sidney Myer Music Bowl, City Square and Treasury Gardens. During the winter months performances are held every Sunday afternoon at the Town Hall – For information Ph 329 0737. See the newspapers for details of the ABC Orchestral Concerts, Australian Ballet Company performances, the Australian Opera Company performances and the Victoria State Opera performances.

OUTLYING ATTRACTIONS:
MORNINGTON PENINSULA:

Arthur's Seat Chairlift, Arthurs Seat Road, Dromana, Ph (059) 87 2565 – open Sat 1-5pm, Sun 11am-5pm, Public Holidays 11am-6pm, School Holidays 12 noon-5pm & Christmas holidays 10am-6pm, night runs 6pm-11pm.

Cape Schank Lighthouse. Cape Schank Rd., via Rosebud Ph (059) 88 6251 – open Tues & Thurs 10am-12 noon & 2pm-4pm – bookings essential and tour includes visit to the radio beacon room and tower.

Ponderosa Zoo & Wildlife Park, Cnr. Somerton & Oaklands Rd., Oaklands Junction, Ph (03) 333 1524 – open 6 days – closed Tuesdays 10am-5pm.

Phillip Island has many attractions but the most famous is the Penguin Parade which lasts from 1 hour before sunset to one hour after sunset every day of the year, at Summerland Beach, Phillip Island Penguin Reserve, Nobbles Rd., Ventnor, Ph 56 8300. Kingston Gardens Zoo, Tourist Road, Cowes, Ph (059) 52 2038 is open daily 8.30am-6pm. – historic chicory kiln, blacksmith shop also host farm accommodation. Mini Europe, Ventnor Rd., Cowes, Ph (059) 52 2519 has an open air display of miniature buildings. The Australian Dairy Centre, Phillip Island Rd., Newhaven, Ph (059) 56 7583 is open Wed-Sun 10am-5pm and every day during school and public holidays. It has a museum, and a small cheese and candy factory. Tourist Information, RMB 1035, Newhaven, Ph (059) 567 447.

French Island which can be reached by ferry either from Phillip Island or from Stoney Point (Mornington Peninsula) is larger than Phillip, although less developed. The former McLeod Prison Farm is now a tourist resort. Most of the Island is State Park and an ideal place for the keen naturalist and sightseer.

DANDENONG RANGES:

Rhododendron Garden, The Georgian Rd., Olinda, Ph 751 1980 – open 10am-4.30pm winter and until 5.30pm in summer – is a 40ha garden featuring rhododendrons, camelias, azaleas, exotic trees and shrubs, lakes and native fauna.

Tesselaar's Padua Bulb Nurseries, Monbulk Road, Silvan, Ph 737 9305 is where the famous Tulip Festival is held every year. The gardens feature tulips and windmills.

William Ricketts Sanctuary, Mt. Dandenong Tourist Rd., Mt. Dandenong, Ph 751 1300, features a forest scene of sculptural work on the theme of aboriginal mythology and wildlife – open 10am-4.30pm winter and until 5.30pm in summer.

Emerald Lake Model Railway, Emerald Lake Park, Emerald, Ph (059) 68 3455 has the largest HO model railway exhibition in the southern hemisphere – open public and school holidays and weekends 11.30am-3.00pm.

Austraflora Nursery, Belfast Road, Montrose, Ph 728 1222 have a large selection of Australian native plants growing in a natural landscape setting, and in containers.

Puffing Billy, Old Monbulk Road, Belgrave, Ph 754 6800. A 13km steam train journey through the ranges – open Sundays 11am-5pm.

GIPPSLAND:

Coal Creek Historical Park, South Gippsland Highway, Korumburra, Ph (056) 55 1811 – open daily 9am-5pm – Re-creation of an 1890's coal mining railway town with over 40 buildings.

Gumbuya Park, Princes Highway, Tynon, Ph (056) 29 2613 – open Mon-Thurs 10am-5pm – family fun park with toboggan slide, mini cars, mini golf etc.

Wilsons Promontory National Park is shaped like a broad arrow aimed at Tasmania and has some of the State's best beaches. The Prom is best known for its craggy wilderness and rugged grandeur of the coastline. It is a popular holiday area for Melbournians.

WESTERN ENVIRONS:

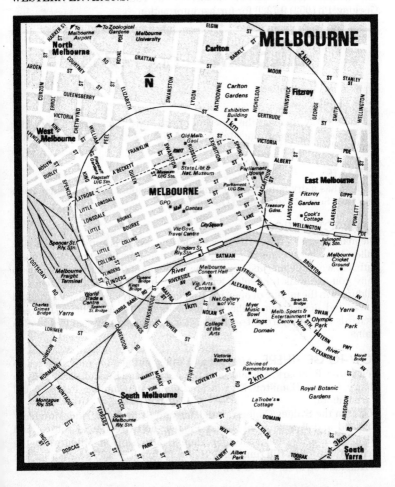

Alpine Toboggan Park, Plenty Rd., Whittlesea, Ph 716 1078 – open Mon-Fri 10am-6pm and public and school holidays.

Barringo Wildlife Reserve, RSD Barringo Rd., Macedon, Ph (054) 26 1680 – open daily 10am-6pm.

Lyndhurst, Lowden's Road, Kilmore, Ph 82 1118 – has guided tours and sheep shearing demonstrations – bookings essential.

Hanging Rock Reserve, Via Woodend, Ph (054) 27 0295 – open daily sunrise to sunset.

Geelong is a bustling port and industrial centre of 130,000, with commercial and cultural amenities befitting Victoria's largest provincial city. It has 160 historic buildings including the Church of St. Peter & Paul, the Customs House, Osborne House. See the Tourist Authority, Ryrie St., Geelong, Ph (052) 9 7220 for further information.

MILDURA – Pop. 17,763

LOCATION:
On the Murray River at the junction of the Sturt, Silver City and Calder Highways. Distance from: Melbourne 557km; Adelaide 401km; Sydney 1036km

CLIMATE:
Mildura has a dry mild winter climate and 400 hours more sunshine each year than Surfers Paradise, in Queensland.

CHARACTERISTICS:
The main centre of the north-west of Victoria, which is known as Sunshine Valley. It is a great place to relax as well as being the threshold to the great outback, which begins just beyond the far banks of the Murray. In Walpeup Shire you can walk for 120km without seeing as much as a vehicle track. Mildura is in the middle of open plain country. Before the area was irrigated it was red desert, but to-day it is surrounded by deep belts of green orchards and vineyards. To the south there are sand dunes and mallee plains.

HOW TO GET THERE: *AIR.* Murray Valley airlines operate services to Melbourne, Renmark, Adelaide and Broken Hill, and Kendell Airlines fly to Albury, Cooma, Hamilton, King Is. Merimbula, Mt. Gambier, Portland and Warnambool.
BUS. On the Sydney/Canberra/Adelaide and Sydney/Adelaide /Horsham/ Portland and Warnambool Ansett Pioneer and Greyhound routes, and VIP's Sydney/Adelaide route. Greyhound also stop at Mildura on the Melbourne/Broken Hill run. Henty Highway Coach Services have a service to Horsham on Mon, Wed & Fri.

RAIL. The Vinelander from Melbourne daily except Saturdays (overnight 10hrs). V/line have a 5 day Mildura Sun Fun tour.

CAR. Along the Sturt Highway from Adelaide; along the Murray Valley Highway from Albury-Wodonga; along the Mid-Western Highway from Sydney; and Calder/Sunraysia Highway from Melbourne.

TOURIST INFORMATION:

Suncity Tourist Office, 41B Langtree Ave., Ph (050) 23 7077. Victorian Government Tourist Bureau in Deakin Avenue.

ACCOMMODATION:

Mildura has 25 motels, 4 hotels, guest houses and serviced apartments and 15 camping grounds/caravan parks.

A few names and addresses: Mildura Motor Inn, 376 Deakin Ave., Ph 23 7377 – RO $48-59 double; Mildura Country Country Club Motel, 12th Street Extention, Ph 23 3966 – B &LB $53 double; Wheatlands Motel, 433 Deakin Ave., – B&B $34 double; Wintersun Hotel, 124 Eighth St., Ph 23 0365 – B&LtB $29-33; Rosemount Holiday House, 154 Madden Ave., Ph 23 1535 – B&B $28 double – weekly B&B $90 pp.; Greensview Holiday Homes, 348 Eleventh St., Ph 23 7207 2 & 3 bedroom units.

Sun City Caravan Park, Cnr. Cureton & Benetook Aves., Ph 23 2325 – sites $7.50 double – overnite vans $19 double; Golden River Caravan Park, Flora Ave, Ph 23 4171 – sites $8 double – overnite vans $20-24 double – cara-cabins $22 double; Apex Caravan Park (on the river bank) Chaffey Bend, Ph 23 2309 – sites $7 double – overnite vans $21 double. No Youth Hostel.

EATING OUT:

At the Grand Hotel, Seventh St you can eat in the Grand Dining Room, the Spanish Grill or the Red Lion Bistro. Restaurant Rendezvous, 34 Langtree Ave., Ph 23 1571 and the Piccola Italia, 27 Deakin Ave., Ph 23 4266 are two of the better restaurants. For take-aways try P.J.'s Deakin Avenue store, 8th Street Food Fair under the T & G clock or Hudak's cakes, 37 Deakin Street for pies pasties and cakes. For a taste of the past, try Foxy's Dinner Den open Wed-Sun for lunch and dinner, 7th St. and Chaffey Ave., Ph 23 1785.

POINTS OF INTEREST:

In 1885 Alfred Deakin, the then Premier of Victoria, persuaded the Canadian brothers George and William Benjamin Chaffey to help plan Mildura. It was laid out in an American grid pattern and most of its streets were given numbers instead of names. The Chaffeys installed pumps to lift water from the Murray. After some initial problems with salt polution, the area became well known for its fruit. Much of Mildura's history is preserved in the Museumn of Local History, which is housed in Rio Vista, the stately home of W.B. Chaffey in Cureton Ave – open 7 days. Also in Cureton Avenue is the Mildura Arts Centre Complex with its displays and art exhibitions.

The Pioneer Cottage, 3 Hunter Street has a pioneering display – open

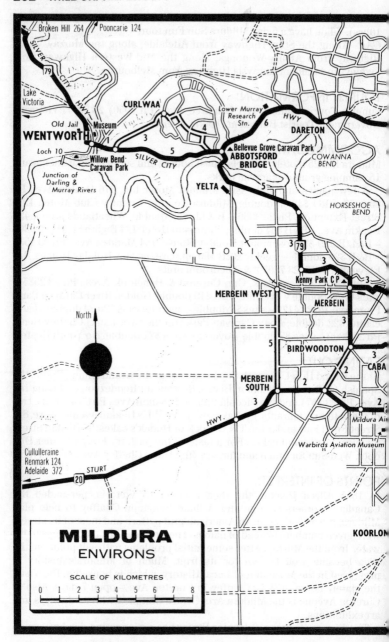

Broken Hill 264 Pooncarie 124

SILVER CITY HWY

79

Lake Victoria

Old Jail

WENTWORTH

Museum

CURLWAA

Lower Murray Research Stn.

HWY

DARETON

Loch 10

Willow Bend Caravan Park

1

3

4

5

6

SILVER CITY

Junction of Darling & Murray Rivers

Bellevue Grove Caravan Park

ABBOTSFORD BRIDGE

COWANNA BEND

YELTA

5

HORSESHOE BEND

VICTORIA

3 79

3

Kenny Park C.P.

3

MERBEIN WEST

MERBEIN

3

North

5

BIRDWOODTON

3

CABA

2

MERBEIN SOUTH

2

2

2

3

HWY.

Mildura Air

Warbirds Aviation Museum

Cullulleraine
Renmark 124
Adelaide 372

STURT

20

KOORLON

MILDURA
ENVIRONS

SCALE OF KILOMETRES

0 1 2 3 4 5 6 7 8

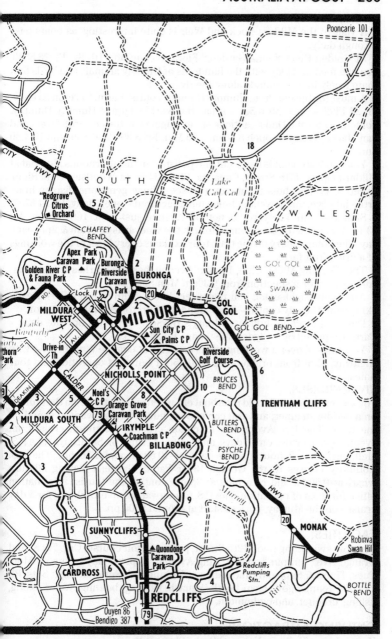

daily, Ph 23 3741.

A visit to the Mildura Lock and Weir is quite interesting, as boats pass through daily.

At Golden River Fauna Gardens, Flora Avenue off 11th St., Ph 23 5540, you can feed and play with the hundreds of friendly animals and birds that roam freely in the grounds along the riverbank.

A must for the children, Humpty Dumpty Tourist Farm, Cureton Avenue, Ph 23 1492 – open Mon-Sat – it has the world's largest Humpty Dumpty. Something for the Dads – antique steam engines on the cnr. 15th Street and San Marco Avenue – open 8.30am-5.30 Mon-Fri 8.30-12.30 Sats and 10-4.30 Sun.

You can watch opals being cut and polished in the afternoons Mon-Sat at Mildura Opals, 17th Street, Cabarita, Ph 23 3469. At Woodsies Gem Shop, Cureton Ave, Nichols Point, you can see a huge gemstone display in an artificial cave, and jewellery being manufactured – open daily, Ph 24 5797.

Suntana Sam Vineyard, Benetook Avenue just past 16th Street, Ph 23 1471, has tractor train tours through the vineyards at 11am & 2pm each day. The commentary on the train tour explains every facet of the workings of a dried fruit farm.

The Working Man's Club, Deakin Avenue, has the world's longest bar, and is open for inspection from 9.30am Mon-Sat.

After your sightseeing you might feel like a swim at Apex Park Beach 3kms from the city centre – drive along the Cureton Avenue extension.

During the school holidays Monty's Horse'n'Cart rides operate daily – Carts are pulled by a Clydesdale team – Ph 24 5816.

You can see over a working citrus property at Orange World, Silver City Highway, 5km from bridge – Ph 23 1045 for hours of operation and tour times.

RIVER CRUISES:

You can experience the old riverboat era when you steam down the Murray on a paddle steamer, and you can choose how long you want to spend on the river. The P.S. Avoca has luncheon cruises, afternoon cruises, an evening disco cruise on Fridays, and a dinner cruise on Saturdays. The P.S. Melbourne has 2 hour cruises daily at 10.50am and 1.50 pm. The P.S. Rothbury cruises to the Golden River Fauna Gardens leaving Mildura wharf at 9.50am and returning at 3pm – contact the tourist information office for days of operation. The P.S. Coonawarra leaves Mildura for 5 day cruises on the Murray – prices start at around $400 pp.

FACILITIES:

Olympic swimming pool, 12th Street; putt putt golf course, Cnr. 7th St and Orange Ave.; ten pin bowling, King Avenue – open 7 days; bingo – Mon, Tues, Thurs & Sats; old time dance at Uniting Hall 8pm-midnight Sats, Ph 23 2208; tennis, golf, lawn bowls, squash, skating, boating, water skiing, fishing, croquet, and badminton.

OUTLYING ATTRACTIONS:

Hattah Lakes/Kulkyne National Park 50km south.

Mungo National Park containing the unique Walls of China – a range of dunes 89km north-west – dry weather road.

WENTWORTH an historic NSW township is 20mins drive from Mildura. The old Wentworth Gaol has been classified by the National Trust. It houses the Morrison collection (old bottles, antiques and Australian artefacts). Also there is the Big Yabbie, an aquarium of native local fish – open daily. The mighty Darling joins the Murray at Wentworthville. At the Darling View Galleries you can see pottery, lead lighting, leather work, crafts etc.

WINERIES:

Stanley Wine Co, Silver City Hwy, Morquong, Ph 23 4341 – open Mon-Sat and Sun afternoons.

Mildara Winery, Merbeln, Ph 25 2302 – open Mon-Fri and Sat morn.

Lindemans Winery, Karadoc (through Red Cliffs), Ph 24 0303 – open Mon-Fri & Sat morn.

Fitzpatrick Estate Wines, Campbell Avenue, Irymple, Ph 24 5843 – open Mon-Sat.

Capogreco Estate Wines, Riverside Avenue between 17 & 18th Sts., Ph 23 6060 – open Mon-Sat.

PORTLAND – Pop. 9,353

LOCATION:
On the coast at Cape Sir William Grant, the only deepwater port between Geelong and Adelaide.

CLIMATE:
Average Temperatures: January max. 22 deg. C – min. 13 deg. C; July max. 14 deg. C – min. 6 deg. C; average annual rainfall 866mm; wettest 6 months May-October; average hours of sunshine: summer 8; autumn 4; winter 3; spring 5.

CHARACTERISTICS:
It is an imposing port with an old, stately air. It is filled with historic buildings from the 1840's era. The Henty Brothers settled here with their flocks of sheep in 1834 before Victoria was proclaimed a separate State. It is the port for the pastoral south-western corner of Victoria and the site of the new Alcoa Aluminium Smelter.

HOW TO GET THERE:
AIR. Kendell Airlines have daily flights to/from Melbourne.
BUS. Greyhound stop there on their Melbourne/Adelaide coastal route. The trip takes approx. 6 hours from Melbourne and 7 hours from Adelaide. There is a weekdays bus service to/from Mt. Gambier which takes approx.

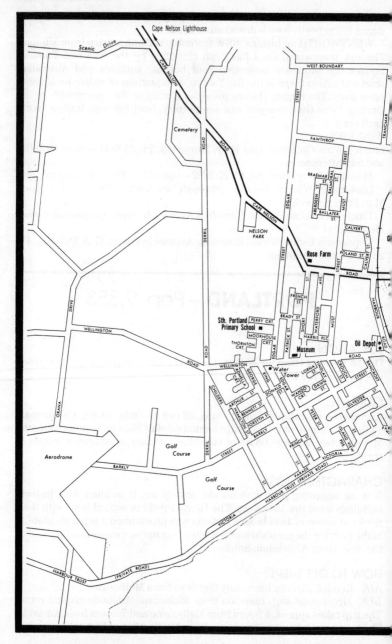

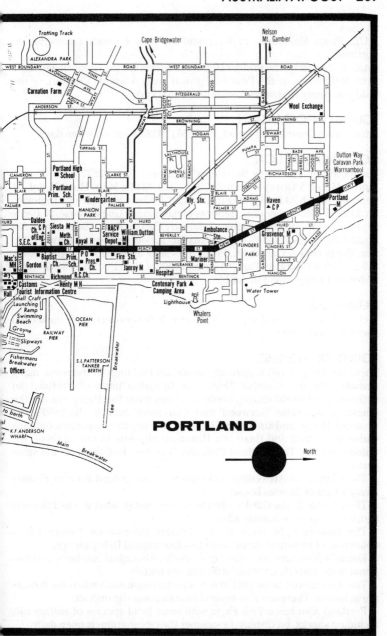

PORTLAND

90 mins.
RAIL. From Melbourne to Warrnambool with a coach connection to Portland.
CAR. Either along the Princes Highway (362km) or the Great Ocean Road from Melbourne, or the Princes Highway from Adelaide (568km), or the Calder & Henty Highways from Mildura (531km).

TOURIST INFORMATION:
Information Centre, Cliff Street, Ph. (055) 23 2671 – open seven days.

ACCOMMODATION:
Marina Motel, 196 Percy St. (Henty Highway), Ph 23 2877 – RO $34-38; Janroy Motel, 5 Otway St., Ph 23 3347 – RO $3438; Macs Hotel/Motel, 41 Bentinck St., Ph 23 2188 – RO $16-19 single; Potland Motel, Henty Highway, Ph 23 2255 – RO $32 double; Selwyns of Sandilands Guest House, 33 Percy St., Ph 23 3319 – RO $20 double; Centenary Carvan Park, 184 Bentnick St., Ph 23 1487 – sites $7 for 4 – on site vans $16-20 double; Haven Caravan Park, Cnr. Henty Hwy & Garden St., Ph 12 768 – sites £4.50-6 for 4 – on site vans $17-22; Daldee Caravan Park, 61 Julia St., 500m from PO, Ph 23 3057 – sites $7 for 4 – on site vans $16 double.

EATING OUT:
Richmond Henty Hotel/Motel, 101 Bentinck St serves counter meals and also has a restaurant.

POINTS OF INTEREST.
There are around 100 historically-important buildings in the town, many classified by the National Trust and all giving parts of Portland an authentic, old-world charm. Some buildings from the Henty era are the bluestone mansions 'Burwood' and 'Claremont' built in the 1850's, the Customs House and the Court House. There are five important old inns dating from 1842 and there is a Historical Museum in one of them, the Caledonian Inn. The Portland Club and Foresters Hall are from the same period.

The Claremont Art Gallery is situated on the ground floor of Franics Henty's former famous house.

The Cottage in the Gardens has been restored to what it was 120 years ago, and is open on Sunday afternoons.

The Historical Museum at the Tourist Information Centre has a collection of historical items, including the original Henty plough.

Kurtze's Museum has a display of shells, Aboriginal artefacts, international dolls, historical items, birds, and old bottles.

The Avonmore Carnation Farm is a picturesque sight when the flowers are in bloom. There are also several rose farms in the district.

Portland also has a Fish Farm with most local species of marine life, including sharks, on display. In summer the Oceanarium is open daily.

In Cape Nelson State Park, 12km south-west of Portland, high-school

Melbourne city

McKenzie Falls, Grampians National Park

Southern Australian coastline

students have helped to make a 3km walk through some rough terrain. The walk takes approx. 2 hours and strong footware is needed. The park and lighthouse are easily reached by a scenic road skirting high, sheer cliffs around Nelson Bay, past the popular surfing beach at Yellow Rock. Also in the park is a unique stand of soap mallee. The lighthouse is sometimes open to the public and a fine view of Lawrence Rocks, a submerged extinct volcano, can be obtained from the top of the 129 steps.

On the opposite headland is Cape Bridgewater, home of the 'Petrified Forest', a tangle of wierd tree forms fashioned by wind and water from the old root systems of the native scrub. The enormity of the rugged coastline can be experienced from cliff walks with the powerful ocean pounding the rocks below, and occasionally shooting up through blowholes.

FESTIVALS:
The Portland Festival, Fishing Contest and Rodeo are all held in January.

FACILITIES:
Lawn bowls, croquet, golf, horse riding, tennis and aquatic sports.

OUTLYING ATTRACTIONS:
HEYWOOD, 25km north, is the centre of a sawmill and timber industry. Reasonable roads permit you to explore fern gullies and hardwood forests. The unique Bower Bird Museum at 'The Trees' has 200 collections in 30 rooms, plus 1000 floral arrangements.

HAMILTON, 60km north of Heywood, is the centre of rich wool and beef cattle country. Its Art Gallery, which is part of the Civic Centre and Town Hall complex, houses a vast collection bequeathed by Herbert Buchanan, as well as ceramics from ancient China.

MACARTHUR, 34km south of Hamilton, and 11km south of Byaduk Caves is also within easy reach of Mt. Napier and its volcanic surrounds. Only a few kilometres south-west of Macarthur is the Mt. Eccles National Park in which is found Lake Surprise, which is fed by underground rivers.

NELSON, 70km to the west of Portland, is a picturesque fishing hamlet at the mouth of the Glenelg River. It is a popular resort and there are numerous bushwalks in the area. A regular boat service takes tourists to the Margaret Rose Caves which are open daily for inspection. The caves also may be reached by road from the Princes Highway at Rennick.

SHEPPARTON – Pop. 28,373

LOCATION:
In the Lower Goulburn River Valley in northern central part of Victoria, 182km north of Melbourne.

CLIMATE:

Shepparton gets more sunshine than Perth, and the government has given grants for solar energy projects in the area.

CHARACTERISTICS:

Shepparton is the major city of the Goulburn Valley, which is one of the food bowls of the nation. The area produces enormous quantities of fruit, vegetables and dairy products, as well as cereal crops, grapes, wine, beef, wool and lamb.

HOW TO GET THERE:

BUS. Ansett Pioneer's, Deluxe's and Greyhound's Melbourne/ Brisbane via Toowoomba service stops at Shepparton.
RAIL. To/from Melbourne with a bus connection to Cobram and Tocumwal, from where you can connect to Sydney.
CAR. From Melbourne take the Hume Highway to near Seymour, and then the Goulburn Valley Highway to Shepparton; from Sydney take the Hume Highway to Benalla, and then the Midland Highway.

TOURIST INFORMATION:

Shepparton Tourist Information Centre, Victoria Lake Wyndham St., Ph (058) 21 5023.

ACCOMMODATION:

Sherbourne Motor Inn, 109 Wyndham St., Ph 21 3355 – RO $44-60 double; The Overlander Motel, Benalla Rd., Ph 21 5622 – RO $38-48 double; Victoria Lake Caravan Park, Wyndham Street, Ph 21 5431; Shepparton Golf Club Motel, Golf Links Drive, Ph 21 2155 – RO $37 double; Four Corners Motel, Goulburn Valley Hwy, Congupna 9km from Shepparton, Ph 29 9404 – B&LtB $30-40 double; Terminus Hotel, 212 High St., Ph 21 2147 – B&B $36.50-44.50 double; Victoria Hotel, Wyndham & Freyers St., Ph 21 9955 – RO $26-40 double;

EATING OUT:

There is a diversity of fine food in Shepparton whether it is for a quick family snack, or for a romantic candle lit dinner. Daiquiris in High Street has a contemporary decor that's hard to miss, and features a deli for quick lunches at the front and a restaurant at the rear. In the front, lunches cost round $5-8, and in the rear three courses average $20; For a good family meal try the Texas T Steak House, 114 Wyndham St. You can eat in or take away; The Emily Jane Restaurant has a cocktail bar and features a jazz or cabaret band on Saturday nights. The Mexican Passport is a mexican family restaurant at 29 Nixon St., and the food is mild enough for the kids but can be spiced up by add Salsa (hot sauce), which is provided on the tables; The Red Gum Inn, 302 High St. features reasonable prices and fresh seafood and steaks; Cellar 47, High Street, is a classy licensed restaurant and is really a cellar. For a quick snack try one of the coffee shops in the

Wyndham Mall. The Taiwan Restaurant at the City Walk Complex, 302 Wyndham Street is a BYO Chinese and European family restaurant. For warm friendly service drop into the Pine Lodge Hotel, Benalla Rd., Shepparton East. The Hotel Terminus, High Street has a Bistro which is open for lunches and dinners 6 days a week and serves cottage fare. Then there's the RSL Club, 88 Wyndham St which serves lunches and evening meals on most days. If you don't feel like going out they you can dial-a-pizza from Dino's Pizza, Shop 2 Centrepoint, Cnr. Wyndham & Vaughan Sts., Ph 22 2477 – open Mon-Wed noon-midnight, Thursday Noon-1am, Fri & Sat, Noon-2am and Sun noon-midnight.

POINTS OF INTEREST:

The Civic Centre which houses the town hall, art gallery, theatre and municipal centre is one of the most outstanding in any rural city in Australia. It was designed by architecture students from the University of Melbourne. The Art Gallery has Australian paintings, graphics, Australian and Japanese ceramics and is open Mon-Fri 1pm-5pm & Sun 2pm-5pm.

Visit the Telecom Tower in Fraser Street, which has an observation room 30m above street level, for a magnificent view over the whole irrigated plains of the district – open 8.30-5.30pm.

The Shepparton International Village, Parkside Drive, has displays by the Spinners and Weavers Guild, the Aboriginal Keeping Place Museum, the Japanese Folk Art Museum, the Dutch Windmill, the Greek Building and the paddle steamer, the Alexander Arbuthnot. It is free except for the P.S. Alexander Arbuthnot.

Shepparton is Victoria's orchard centre for pears, apricots, peaches and apples, and a tour of Shepparton Preserving Company's cannery (the largest in the southern hemisphere) is recommended – 10am or 2pm weekdays. The fruit picking season is January to April, but if you are interested in some casual work you will have to start looking in December.

At Apex Park you can test your puzzle solving prowess when you try to find your way out of the maze.

Redbyrne Potteries, Old Dookie Road, Ph 21 2753, is open daily 9am-5pm and has highly crafted functional studio pottery.

Lake Victoria at the southern entrance to the city, is a 20 ha stretch of water which is the city's boating and yachting centre.

Radio Australia has a powerful transmitter station 6km from Shepparton.

The Dookie State Agricultural College is 33km east of Shepparton.

The John A. Douglas Collection, 8 Victoria St., Ph 21 3858 for an appointment – gratis. It features stone artefacts from 38 countries and islands, Chinese pottery from the goldfields era, militaria, Zulu beadwork and American Indian artefacts. The Estrada Museum, 69 Newton Street has a similar collection and is open daily, by appointment.

FESTIVALS:

The annual Festival is held in September. The Agricultural Show is held in October.

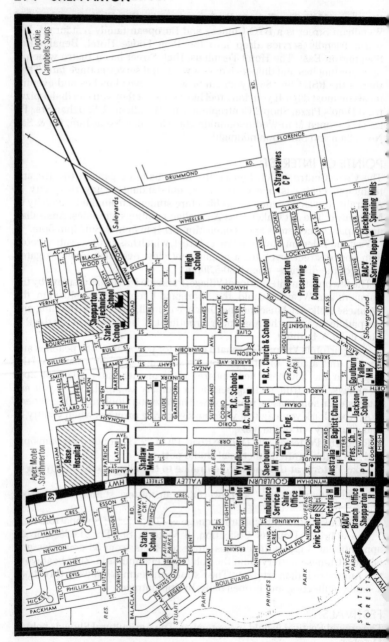

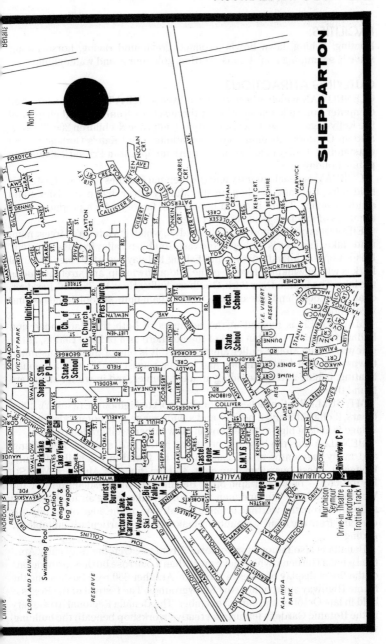

SHEPPARTON

FACILITIES:

Boating, fishing, lawn bowls, croquet, greyhound racing, horse racing, squash, swimming pool, tennis, trotting, golf course and water skiing.

OUTLYING ATTRACTIONS:

GLENROWAN which is best known as 'Ned's (Kelly) Town', has a life sized computer controlled simulation of three scenes from the final chapter of the Kelly saga – open 9am-5pm daily – Adults 50c & children 20c. There is also an Outdoor Museum – cost 20c adults – and Kate's Cottage has an outstanding display of local craft – open 9am-5pm Mon-Fri and 9.30am-6pm public holidays.

COBRAM is peach country and the biennial Peaches'n Cream Festival is held here. Cobram, nestling on the Murray River, has good fishing and sandy beaches. There is also a boomerang factory which produces large numbers of machine made boomerangs.

EILDON is on the shores of Lake Eildon, which is Victoria's largest man-made lake. The lake is the key to the vast Goulburn Valley irrigation system. It is a popular inland boating and fishing holiday resort. Fraser National Park is within walking distance of the Eildon township, and stretches along the lake. The Eildon Deer Park, Goulburn Valley Hwy, Ph 73 2236, has deer, quail, peacocks and pheasants – open 10am-6pm school holidays and weekends.

MANSFIELD is located at the terminus of both the Maroondah and Midland Highways, within 3km of the northern arm of Lake Eildon, at the gateway to the Mount Buller alpine resort. It is one of the few Australian towns that has both summer and winter tourist trade. It is a popular boating, fishing and horse riding area in summer, and in winter skiers are found there.

MT. BULLER is the closest major ski resort to Melbourne (245km). It has 6 bars, 2 chairlifts and 8 pomas, and a wide range of accommodation. The village is 1809m high at the end of an all-weather, well-graded road.

BENALLA was the base of operations in the 1870's for the Kelly Gang, and many mementos of the gang are to be found in the Kelly Museum, Bridge St., West, open 9am-5pm daily, and the Pioneers' Museum, Mair St., Ph 62 2061, – open Sun 2pm-5pm. Benalla has the headquarters of the Victorian Gliding Club, and men and women take to the air in gliders and sailplanes from the wartime training aerodrome on the edge of the city. Air currents from the nearby mountains make the area particularly suitable for gliding.

Benalla is also famous for its Roses. From late October until early April the Benalla Gardens, which have more than 1,500 rose bushes, provide one of the finest display of roses in the State. Another 650 rose bushes line the Hume Highway approaching the Showgrounds. The festival of the Roses is held in late October and early November. The Benalla Regional Art Gallery in the Botanic Gardens features a creative workshop beneath the building, where spinners, potters and painters work – open 11am-5pm weekdays and

10am-5pm Sat. The Manuka Art & Craft Gallery, Bridge St., is open Thurs-Fri 11am-4pm and 10am-12 Sats.

SEYMOUR is at the junction of the Goulburn and Hume Highways. It is a busy commercial, industrial and agricultural centre, strategically located to serve a rural and military community. Puckapunyal Army Camp, Australia's largest, is only a few kilometres south of Seymour.

WARRNAMBOOL – Pop. 22,500

LOCATION:
On the coast 263km west of Melbourne where the Princes Highway meets the Great Ocean Road.

CLIMATE:
Average Temperatures: January max. 23 deg. C – min. 13 deg. C.; July max. 14 deg. C.- min. 6 deg C; Average annual rainfall 726mm; Average hours of sunshine: summer 8; autumn 4; winter 3; spring 5; wettest 6 months May-October.

CHARACTERISTICS:
Warrnambool was a popular with the old whalers and sealers as they could repair their boats and process their catches on its wide beaches. Due to reduced hunting, Warrnambool is now visited each year by a herd of the rare Southern Right whales, and a viewing platform has been erected at Logan's Beach to enable visitors to obtain a better view of the whales which usually remain in the area for several weeks.

HOW TO GET THERE:
AIR. Kendell Airlines have flights to/from Portland – Melbourne three times daily and then bus.
BUS. Greyhound stops at Warrnambool on its Melbourne/Adelaide coastal route and there is a local bus to Port Fairy.
RAIL. On the Melbourne/Geelong route. Trip takes three and a half hours and there are two services daily.
CAR. From Melbourne, travel to Geelong and then take the Princes Highway if you are in a hurry, but if you have more time then take one of Australia's really beautiful roads, the Great Ocean Road which follows the coast and passes through Lorne. Warrnambool is 264km from Melbourne via the Princes Highway, 211km from Mt. Gambier and 654km from Adelaide.

TOURIST INFORMATION:
600 Raglan Parade (Princes Highway), Ph (055) 64 9837 – open 7 days – free 15 minute audio-visual of the city & district attractions.

ACCOMMODATION:

21 motels, 4 hotels, 7 caravan parks, numerous holiday flats and dormority accommodation:

Some names and addresses: Mid City Motor Inn, 525 Raglan Pde, Ph 62 3866 – RO $46 double; Raglan Motor Inn, 376 Raglan Pde., PH 62 8511 – RO $38-48 double; Caledonian Hotel, 112 Fair St., Ph 62 2170 – B&Lt.B $24 double; Warrnambool Hotel, Cnr. Koroit & Kelper Sts., Ph 62 2377 – RO $27 double; Ocean Beach Village Caravan Park, Pertobe Rd., Ph 62 3582 – sites $8-11 – on site vans $19-30 double; Warrnambool Surf-Side Parks, Pertobe Rd., Ph 62 3284 – site $7-10; Flying Horse Inn Caravan Park, Princes Hwy, Ph 62 1131 – site $5.50-9 double – on site vans $17-$29 – cabins $22-$34; There is a Youth Hostel 28km west, at 8 Cox St., Port Fairy, Ph 68 1547 – $6.75 ppn.

EATING OUT:

Specialist, quality restaurants, head the list but there is no shortage of cosy cafes, pubs serving counter meals and tasty take-aways. There are more than 60 places.

POINTS OF INTEREST.

At Flagstaff Hill Maritime Village you can relive the romance of the glorious days of sail at the reconstruction of the early Port of Warrnambool. Incorporated in the complex are old coastal fortifications built when Australians feared invasion by the Russians in the 1880's. There are sailmakers, shipwrights and ship's chandlers in the village. Among the relics on display there is the Loch Ard peacock an 1851 Minton porcelian statue, which was washed up (still in its packing case) in Loch Ard Gorge after a shipwreck.

Lake Pertobe Park has causeways, walking tracks, and a well-equiped Adventure Playground behind the surf beach of Lady Bay.

Fletcher Jones Gardens are a colourful advocate for Victoria's claim as the Garden State of Australia. Thousands of visitors come each year to see these gardens.

Tours of the Woollen Mills can be arranged – see the Tourist Information Office.

The Regional Performing Arts Centre is a modern style building situated in landscaped grounds in the heart of the business and restaurant district. It has three main venues suitable for stage presentations, conventions, dinners, cabarets, exhibitions, lectures, classes and meetings. Check the daily newspapers for programmes.

The Warrnambool Regional Art Gallery, 214 Timor Street, has a permanent collection of 19th and 20th century Australian and European paintings, watercolours and graphics – open 2pm-5pm daily – ph 62 5178.

Tower Hill State Game Reserve 14km from Warrbambool, is the remains of a volcano whose crater walls collapsed inwards during its dying stages 6000 years ago and blocked the 3km wide crater, which later filled with water. There is a sealed road which leads to the main island from where bushwalks radiate. There is also a natural history centre open from 8.30am-

4.30pm daily.

Hopkins Falls, 15km from Warrnambool, near Wangoom, is where thousands of tiny eels (elvers) make their way up the falls to the quiet waters beyond, to grow to maturity before returning to the sea to breed.

Warrnambool also has a mystery! There have been several reported sightings of the wreck of a mahogany ship in the windswept sandhills just north of the city. The last reported sighting of it was in 1880 and several artefacts have been found in the area. It is said that it foundered 400 years ago with a complement of Dutch and Spanish sailors. If it were true then it would mean that Europeans set foot on Australian soil long before Captain Cook. In 1980 the City Council formed a Mahogany Ship Committee to compile all the information known, which is then being fed into a computer in an endeavour to locate the wreck.

FACILITIES:

Boating, lawn bowls, croquet, fishing, golf, horse racing, greyhound racing, horse riding, rowing, sailing, roller skating, fitness centres, squash, surfing, swimming pool, beaches, tennis, discos, movies, speedway, ten pin bowling, and water skiing.

FESTIVALS:

Grand Annual Steeplechase is held in May.

OUTLYING ATTRACTIONS:

PORT FAIRY, 29km from Warrnambool, is a fishing-village with charm, where brighly painted boats tie up at the jetty with their catches of lobster and crab. The tall Norfolk Island pines were planted by the old whalers. Port Fairy has many old buildings some of which date back to the 1840's. The local Historical Society has a booklet guide for visitors which describes some of the historical buildings and their architecture. There is a large aquarium. It is also one of the few places where lobster pots are still made in the traditional way with cane. There is a mutton bird colony on Griffiths Island at the entrance to the port and there is a seal colony on Lady Julia Percy Island, but it is only accessible by large boats in the hands of skilled sailors.

Of course, the most spectacular scenery in the district is found in PORT CAMPBELL NATIONAL PARK. The continual breaking of the waves have battered the soft limestone cliffs, turning them into sea-sculptures, grottoes and gorges. The most famous of these are the Twelve Apostles – a row of enormous stone pillars in the midst of the hostile world of the sea. There are many more similar 'works of art' such as London Bridge. Most of the attractions cannot be seen clearly from the Great Ocean Road so it is necessary to turn off the main road and drive to the many sign-posted lookouts to see them.

LORNE, is at the other end of the Great Ocean Road 218km from Warrnambool and less than 2 hours drive from Melbourne. Although Lonre is famous as a beautiful beach resort, it is also a town for other seasons.

There are many waterfalls in the Otway Ranges which can be reached either by road or along walking tracks. Today, little can be seen of the devastation caused by the Ash Wednesday bushfires.

FLINDERS ○

PORT AUGUSTA ●

WHYALLA ●

RENMARK ●

TANUNDA
BAROSSA VALLEY ○

ADELAIDE ●

COONAWARRA WINERIES ○

MOUNT GAMBIER ●

SOUTH AUSTRALIA

ADELAIDE – Pop. 950,000

LOCATION:
Adelaide is situated on a narrow plain bounded on the west by the the waters of St. Vincent Gulf and, on the east, by the rising slopes of the picturesque Mount Lofty Ranges. Distance from: Sydney 1,196km;Melbourne 660km; Canberra 988km; Brisbane 1,967km and Perth 2,216km.

CLIMATE:
Adelaide has a mediterranean type climate with warm dry summers and cool winters. Average annual rainfall is 530mm which generally falls between May and August. Average Temperatures: January max. 30 deg.C – min. 16 deg. C; July max. 15 deg. C – min. 7 deg. C. Water temperature: January 19 deg. C; July 14 deg. C.

CHARACTERISTICS:
Colonel Light planned Adelaide to be a city of broad streets and handsome terraces. He dotted it with spacious squares and bounded it on all four sides with a broad band of natural parkland. To-day it is a vibrant, sophisticated city enjoying the fruits of Col. Light's planning.

HOW TO GET THERE:
AIR. From any of the other capital cities with Ansett or Australian Airlines. Australian Airlines and Ansett also fly to/from Alice Springs, Gold Coast and Launceston. Kendell Airlines fly to/from Melbourne, Broken Hill, Ceduna, Port Lincoln, Streaky Bay and Whyalla. Murray Valley Airlines fly to/from Broken Hill, Mildura and Renmark. Lloyd Air Airlines fly to/from Kangaroo Island, Port Lincoln, Whyalla and Olympic Dam. O'Connors Air Services fly to/from Mt. Gambier

BUS. Ansett Pioneer, Greyhound, Deluxe or VIP from other capitals.

RAIL. On the Indian Pacific from Sydney or Perth. From Melbourne, you can have an overnight ride in the Overland and awaken to spectacular views of the beautiful Mount Lofty Ranges.

CAR. National highways converge on Adelaide from the east, west and north. From the eastern states there are numerous possible routes. The coastal road from Melbourne enters South Australia through the forest and lakeland of the south-eastern part of the state and provides the chance to explore the wilderness of the Coorong and its prolific birdlife as well as winding through some old-world fishing villages on the way. The main overland route from Sydney crosses in to South Australia at Mildura and runs through the citrus and wine-producing area of South Australia. From the west the completely sealed Eyre Highway provides safe motoring from Perth across the Nullarbor Plain. An alternate route follows the Great Australian Bight where cliffs drop dramitcally to the sea below. The cliffs are the largest stretch of unbroken cliffs in the world. From the north, the

Stuart Highway is the main thoroughfare but there are still some sections which are unsealed and subject to flood damage and which become impassable after heavy rains. If you are planning to drive along this highway, it would be a good idea to get the pamphlet 'Outback Motoring' from one of the Automobile Associations.

TOURIST INFORMATION:

South Australian Travel Centre, 18 King William Street, Ph (08) 212 1644.

ACCOMMODATION:

Adelaide has a range of accommodation to suit every budget. For full details contact the Travel Centre.

A few names and addresses:

Budget: YMCA, 76 Flinders St., Ph. 2243 1611 – $12 single and $18 twin; Youth Hostel, 290 Giles St., Ph 223 6007. Fees must be paid in full with bookings $6.50 single; Levi Park Caravan & Camping Area, Landsdowne Tce., Ph 44 2209 – sites $6.50 – onsite vans $19-21 double; Alton Private Hotel, 260 South Terrace, Ph 223 3416 – BB $15 single. Kiwi Lodge Private Hotel, 266 Hindley St., Ph 51 2671 – $50;B&Lt.B $31.50 double; Kings Head Hotel, 357 King William St., Ph 51 556

Premier: Hilton International, 2323 Victoria St., Ph 217 0711 – RO $115 - $170 double; Adelaide Travelodge, 208 South Tce., Ph 112 1744 – RO $89 double;

Moderate: Princes Lodge Motel, 73 Lefeve Tce., North Adelaide, Ph 267 5566 – RO $28-B&B $45-double.

Accommodation Central Guide – Adelaide offers a free accommodation reservation service for hotel, motel, serviced apartments and townhouses in the city, suburbs and country for one or a group – ph (08) 274 122, Telex 82 770, 70 Glen Osmond Rd., Parkside, 5063.

EATING OUT:

If you want some take-away to eat in one of the parks then start looking around Hindmarsh Square; If you prefer to eat in a reasonably priced restaurant then try Hindley Street. You can usually find main courses for $5-7.e.g. Chinatown in the basement at No. 33 or Water Hole Down Under at No. 142. Cafe Michael, 236 Rundle St., Ph 223 3519 serves seafood from $2.50 – open 7 days; The Mezes BYO Greek Cafe, 287 Rundle St. serves home-style Greek dishes. The Newmarket Hotel, 1 North Terrace, Ph 211 8533 is open for lunch and dinner daily.

LOCAL TRANSPORT:

All metropolitan buses leave from the main city shopping areas and the State Transport Authority (STA) buses run to the outer suburbs of Elizabeth and Salisbury in the north-east and beyond Reynella and into the Fleurieu Peninsula region in the south. Services also connect most suburbs and most of the Adelaide Hill towns to Adelaide. Buses run from 6am to 11.30pm from Monday to Saturday and from 9am to 10.30pm Sundays. Metropolitan fares are divided into sections and Zones – travel within one zone costs 70c and two zones $1 or three zones $1.40 – this covers unlimited travel for up to two hours. Between 9am & 3pm the $1.40 fare drops down to $1 & the $1 to 70c. There is also a Day Tripper ticket available for $4 and is valid for unlimited travel for 2 adults and 2 children under 15 – for all enquiries Ph 210 100. Country buses leave from the Central Bus Station in Franklin St. There is one tram line to Glenelg from Victoria Square. All country and interstate trains leave from the Adelaide Rail Passenger Terminal, Keswick. Suburban trains depart from Adelaide Railway Station, North Terrace. Taxis: United 223 3111; Suburban 211 8888; and Amalgamated 223 333. Car Hire: Koala Car Rentals hire mopeds as well as the latest model cars – 39 Burbridge Rd., Mile End; Hire a Hack Car Rental, 219 Belair Rd., Torrens Park; Budget, Ph 223 1400.

POINTS OF INTEREST.

Victoria Square is the centre of the city and has some noted examples of early Adelaide architecture including the Treasury Building, St. Francis Xavier's Cathedral, the Magistrates Court House and Supreme Court House. The Victoria Square Fountain was designed by Adelaide sculpturer, John Dowie, and has as its theme three of South Australia's rivers – the Torrens, Onkaparinga and the Murray.

For a quick tour of the city start at Beehive Corner, Adelaide's busiest corner and most famous meeting place. Don't forget to look at the date on top of the beehive. Walk along Rundle Mall, a unique pedestrian thoroughfare, shaded by leafy trees, dotted by picturesque fruit and flower stalls and frequented by buskers of every kind. The city's major department stores, boutiques, cinemas and restaurants are all within a few minutes walk of each other. At Renaissance Tower take the glass lift to the top to enjoy a magnificient view of the city and Mall.

Turn into Pulteney Street and you will see Ruthven Mansions, Adelaide's oldest appartment block built in 1911 and recently renovated. Just along the street is Scot's Church built in 1850. Turn right into North Terrace, one of the world's most beautiful boulevards. Walk along to Ayre's House the office of the National Trust. This beautiful bluestone house was the residence of a former State Premier – open Tues-Fri 10am-5pm Sat & Sun 2-4pm. Cross North Terrace and wander through the Botanic Gardens which were established in 1855. Go back along North Terrace past the hospital, and you will see the University of Adelaide with its castle-like Bonython Hall. The next important building you will come to is the Art Gallery of SA which has an outstanding collection of Australian and European paintings and Asian ceramics – open daily (except Mon) 10am-5pm. Then there is the South Australian Museum with exhibits of fossils, animals and minerals as well as exhibits on Egypt and the Pacific – open Mon-Saturday 10am-5pm (closed Wed morning) & Sundays 2-5pm. The State Library of South Australia and the National War Memorial are further along North Terrace. There is a path from the war memorial to Government House part of which dates back to 1839. The Houses of Parliament are found on the cnr. North Terrace and King William Street which is 42m wide!. They are impressive marble and granite buildings and may be inspected Mon-Fri 10am-noon and 2-4pm. The Adelaide Town Hall, King William Street was built in 16th century Renaissance style. Adelaide has Australia's only political history museum, which is housed in the restored Legislative Council building of the old Parliament House. The Museum features an audio visual presentation which is a 100 minute journey through history – open Mon-Fri 10am-5pm and Saturday and Sunday from 1.30-5pm. The Holy Trinity Church in North Terrace is SA's oldest Church. It was built in 1838 and rebuilt in 1888. There are guided tours at noon on Mondays and Thursdays and at 4pm on Fridays.

One of Adelaide's most outstanding buildings is the Adelaide Festival Theatre complex in King William Road, Ph 51 0121. There are guided tours of the centre Mon-Friday on the hour from 10am-4pm and Sat at 10.30am, 11.30am, 2pm & 3.30pm. The tours last about 45min and cost $2. Just near the theatre in Elder Park is where the Popeye Motor Launches leave for Adelaide Zoo (open 9.30am-5pm daily) and the weir. The launches depart on the hour from 11am-3pm. If you prefer to do your own thing, then you could hire a paddle boat from Captain Jolley's also in Elder Park – open 11am-3pm.

Adelaide has many galleries and we list just a few of them: The Gallery of Aboriginal Art, 26-28 Currie St., Ph 212 2171 – open Mon-Thurs 9am-5.30pm, Friday 9am-9pm, Saturday 9am-12 noon and Sundays 10.30am-4pm; The Jam Factory Craft Centre has displays of handmade glass, ceramics, leather, wood and textiles produced by leading craftspeople – open Mon-Fri 9am-5pm, Sat 10am-5pm and Sundays 2-5pm; The Contemporary Art Gallery, 14 Porter Street, Parkside, has changing exhibitions – Ph 272 2682 for details and opening times.

Those seeking entertainment of a slightly less highbrow nature should head for Hindley Street where there are bars, restaurants, night-clubs and brash revues.

The Adelaide Casino, North Terrace, Ph 212 2811 has more than 98 gaming tables including roulette, black jack, two-up, craps, baccarat etc. It is open from 10am to 4am daily and has five bars and two restuarants.

The Adelaide Grand Prix is held in late October or November each year and the track is laid out on the city streets immediately east of the city centre.

At West Beach Airport, 9km east of the city, is a small museum which displays the Vickers Vimy Bomber in which four men set off in 1919 from England to fly to Australia. The trip took 28 days!

A trip to Adelaide would not be complete without a ride on the tram to Glenelg. The trip takes approximately 20 min. and is definitely worthwhile even if the beach is rather crowded in summer. On the foreshore (between the Jetty and Magic Mountain) is Bay World which has 200,000 shells and 12 large tanks containing marine life. At Glenelg North's Patawalonga Boat Haven, Adelphi Tce, is the reconstructed HMS Buffalo. It is a unique nautical museum and seafood restaurant. The museum displays extracts from the logbook, sketches and photographs which tell the story of the original ship's voyage from Portsmouth to Holdfast Bay in 1836. The restaurant has a new lunch menu – two courses and coffee for $18 per person.

Hallett Cove, 18km from Adelaide has attracted worldwide scientific interest as no other site offers a more comprehensive picture of the evolution of landforms. The National Parks & Wildlife Service in Adelaide has leaflets explaining the formations seen on the self-guiding walks. Picnicking is allowed in the park but there are no facilities.

FESTIVALS:

The most famous is the Adelaide Festival held biennially in even numbered years. This is recognised as Australia's most famous festival of the arts. Leading dance, opera, ballet and drama companies as well as internationally renowned orchestras, chamber groups, singers, actors, writers and directors converge on Adelaide during this time. In alternate years the Come Out Festival, a childrens' arts festival is timed to coincide with the holidays after the first school term of the year. It features theatre, dance and opera written for children and performed by children.

Wine Festivals: Perhaps the most famous is the Barossa Valley's Vintage Festival which is held biennally in the week after Easter in odd numbered years. At McLaren Vale in the Southern Vales a Wine Bushing Festival is held in October. Other cultural groups hold festivals throughout the year: the Germans have their Schuetzenfest at Hahndorf every January; the Cornish Kernewek Lowender celebrates the Cousin Jack & Jenny Festival in Moonta, Kadina and Wallaroo to name a few. Port Lincoln has its Tunarama Festival to mark the importance of its tuna fishing industry.

Burra recalls its heyday with a Copper Festival; the citrus rich Riverland has a Harvest Festival and Wilolunga an Almond Blossom Festival and for something unusual head for Mount Compass for the Mount Compass Cup, a cow race.

FACILITIES:

There are two 18 hole golf courses, both of which can be entered off Strangways Terrace. There is a 50m indoor heated swimming pool at Adelaide Aquatic Centre, Fitzroy Tce., North Adelaide and open daily. All the usual sporting and recreational facilities that you would expect in a big city, can be found in Adelaide.

OUTLYING ATTRACTIONS:

THE ADELAIDE HILLS are renowned for their breathtaking beauty and can easily be reached by bus or car from the city. Small villages are dotted through the hills which change colour depending on the season. The countryside is varied and the roads pass cool waterfalls, bubbling creeks, gorges, ravines, lush green pastures, fields of wildflowers and cherry orchards and almond groves. Old country pubs offer hearty country fare and blazing log fires in winter. Some popular picnic spots are Belair, Parra Wirra, Lenswood Recreation Park, the Torrens Gorge and Cleland Conser-

Hindley Street, Adelaide

Karlsburg Winery, Barossa Valley

vation Park where there are numerous walking tracks. There are a series of hostels in the Adelaide Hills extending from Kersbrook in the north to Inman Valley in the south. Using these hostels and other accommodation (camping or hotel), it is possible to walk over 200km on a walking holiday lasting approx. 10-14 days. Contact the Adelaide YHA Office for further details.

Some of the more interesting towns in the 'Hills' are:

ALDGATE, 19km from Adelaide, with its quaint pump, garden-lined main street, olde worlde shops and shaded lanes. The village is a picture in autumn when the trees turn colour.

BIRDWOOD, 44km from Adelaide, was originally named 'Blumberg' but the name was changed during World War I. Its most famous landmark is the Birdwood Mill which was built in 1852. The mill has been converted into a tourist complex incorporating the National Motor Museum, Technology and Applied Science Museum, demonstration areas, craft shops and a picnic ground. Bridgewater, 22km from Adelaide, also has an old mill, the Old Lion Mill on the Mount Barker Road. The mill was originally driven by water, then by steam, gas and electricity. On selected Sundays each month from May to October, the Australian Railway Historical Society operates a steam train from Adelaide to Bridgewater and return. The Sir Malcolm Barclay-Harvey pulls the pre-World War One carriages through magnificient scenery but bookings are essential – contact the SA Travel Centre.

GUMERACHA has the biggest Rocking Horse in the World (18.3m high) at the Toy Factory, Ph 389 1085. From the top you can view the whole of the Gumeracha Valley.

HAHNDORF, 28km from Adelaide, is one place that you simply must visit. It is the oldest surviving German settlement in Australia. It was founded in 1838. The immigrants have retained much of their culture and tradition and visitors to-day can enjoy the same type of food, music and dances as when the Germans first arrived. It is difficult to mention all the interesting buildings in the town as there are so many. It is much better just to wander through the town and see for yourself. The town really comes to life in early January when the Schuetzenfest is held. On this day there is something for all the family, stalls, train and pony rides, merry-go-rounds, German folk dancing, German beers and food such as spit-roasted pork and traditional German sausages and pastries. The associated rifle shoot is for members of the German Association who compete for silver trophies. The profit from this popular festival goes to chosen charities.

CARRICK HILL at Springfield in the Adelaide Hills (7km from the city) is an English-style house set in 100 acres of sculptured park and provides delightful walks and spectacular views of the city. The house contains one of the finest collections of art, silver, pewter and old English oak furniture in Australia – open Wed-Sun 10am-5pm – closed for lunch betwwen 12.30 & 1.30.

The ADELAIDE PLAINS wineries are only 30 mins drive north of the city but are frequently neglected by tourists speeding past on their way to the

Adelaide

AIRLINES
Cathay Pacific **G13**
Singapore Airlines **G11**
Ansett **G11**
TAA **G11**
Qantas **G12**
British Airways **G12**

RAILWAYS
Adelaide **E11**

SERVICES
GPO **G14**
Law Courts **G16**
SA Tourist Bureau **H12**
Royal Adel. Hosp. **K12**
Children's Hosp. **G6**
Police HQ **H16**
RAA **H14**
State Library **H11**
Town Hall **G14**
YMCA **I14**
YWCA **K17**
Central Bus Station **F15**
Central Market **F16**
Glenelg Tram terminus **F16**
Victoria Park Racecourse **N16**

SIGHTSEEING
Museum **I11**
University **J12**
SA Institute **J12**
St Francis **H15**
St Peters **F7**
Festival Theatre **G10**

HISTORIC INTEREST
SA Art Gallery **I11**
Parliament House **F11**
Ayers House **K12**
Edmund Wright House **F13**
Constitutional Museum **E11**
Botanic Gardens **M10**

PARKING
Currie Street **G13**
Gawler Place **H13**
Grenfell Street **I13**
John Martins **I12**
Light Square **D13**

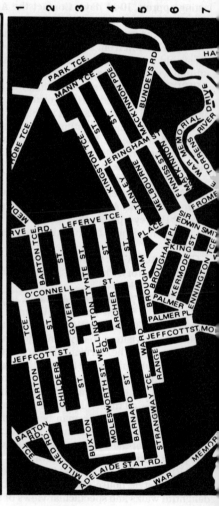

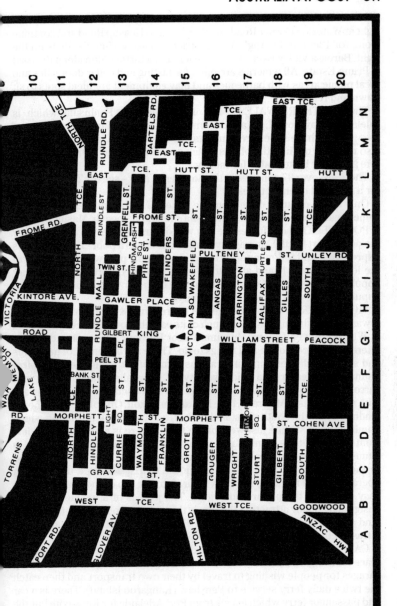

Barossa or Clare Valleys. Just travel north along Port Wakefield Rd., turn right at Waterloo Corner Road and then left into Heaslip Road and continue along for 12km to the Angle Vale District. Anglesey Wine Estate is on the right, Barossa Valley Estates is on the left and a further 8km along the road is Primo Estate. All wineries are open for tasting and cellar door sales and local picnic areas with barbeques and play equipment are ideal spots to sit down and relax.

The SOUTHERN VALES, part of the Fleurieu Peninsula which is Adelaide's playground, are another important wine producing area. Most of the wineries have superb restaurants but if you look a bit harder you will also discover quaint little places which specialise in traditional homestyle fare and offer better value for money.

There are over 37 wineries in the Southern Vales – see the T ourist Office for a map and opening times.

Only a few minutes drive from the wineries is the southern coast with some great beaches including Australia's first nude beach, Maslin Beach.

PORT ELLIOTT on Horseshoe Bay was originally selected as the site for the ocean port for the Murray River trade but it was a poor choice as it was unprotected and following several shipwrecks, the port was transferred to the lee of Granite Island at Victor Harbour. To-day, Port Elliott is a very popular tourist resort. At the western edge of the town is Boomer Beach, a popular venue with the surfing fraternity.

VICTOR HARBOUR is the largest of the resort towns on Horseshoe Bay. It was an old whaling base and much of its early history has been preserved at Whalers Haven Colony Museum. Victor Harbour has an abundance of interesting places to see and things to do. There are a number of museums and several galleries depicting various forms of art while the Urrimbirra Fauna Park features a wide variety of Australian fauna in natural surroundings with a nocturnal house. A newer attraction is Greenhills Park with waterslides, BMX track, bike hire and mini golf. One of the best known landmarks on the south coast is the Bluff, a natural rock formation which dominates the skyline just west of the town. There is a magnificient view from the top but the climb is rather demanding. A visit to Granite Island is a must. It has been a whaling station and an overseas port. It is connected to the mainland by a causeway and in the tourist season a tractor-train operates to and from the island. A chairlift to the top of the island enables easy access to the picturesque views. The jetty is of a unique screwpile design. The major attraction though, is the nightly exodus from the seas to land of the Fairy Penguins. Victor Harbour has all the usual tourist infrastructure one would expect of a popular resort.

CAPE JERVIS, 109km from Adelaide, is mostly known as a jumping off place for Kangaroo Island. There is a bus service from Adelaide and lock-up garages for people wishing to travel by their own transport and then catch the twice daily ferry service to Penshaw (Kangaroo Island). There is a car and passenger ferry which leaves from Port Adelaide for Kingscote but the trip takes six and half hours.

KANGAROO ISLAND has become a popular resort for those who want to 'get away from it all'. The main towns are Kingscote and Penshaw where the fairy penguins promenade on the foreshore at night. Sea lions frolic on the beach at Seal Bay. At one end of the island is Flinders Chase National Park which has 59,000 ha of wild, rugged, natural bushland. Visitors can view the hundreds of species of native plants, birds and mammals in their natural habitat. The focal point of the area is Rocky River Homestead Ranger Headquarters where tame wildlife continually seek handouts from the picnickers nearby. There is a sheltered enclosure with a gas barbeque and it is surrounded by a fence to keep the animals out. MURRAY BRIDGE, an hour's drive from Adelaide at the end of the Freeway is a delightful town on the Murray. A Paddlewheel steamer operates from there and you can take a trip along the Murray. Then there is Puzzle Park which is an irresistable challenge for maze masters. It is a 4.5km network of tangled passageways which takes from 40-60mins to complete. It is Australia's largest maze and is made from 10,000m of timber. As well as the maze there are giant size chess and draught sets and playground as well as an aquarium.

FLINDERS RANGES

LOCATION:
The foothills of the range start at the northern end of St. Vincent's Gulf and stretch north for approx. 800km into the dry outback region.

CLIMATE:
Semi-arid climate which leads to dry-country vegetation including salt-bush and light timber. In spring the area is alive with wild flowers, making it an ideal time to visit.

CHARACTERISTICS:
Granite mountain ranges with towering peaks, razor backed quartzite ridges, slashed by precipitious gorges, and creeks with cool deep waterholes framed by stately gums. The whole area is an artist's or photographer's delight. The colours and shadows change continually depending upon the time of day and the season of the year.

HOW TO GET THERE:
AIR. Dennan fly from Port Augusta to Leigh Creek and Marree, and the mail run to Innamincka, Birdsville, and Boula. Lloyd Airlines fly to/from Olympic Dam. There are also airports at Hawker and Balcanoona near Arkaroola.
BUS. Stateliner have a service to Wilpena Pound on Fridays returning on Sunday. The trip takes six hours. They also have a service to Quora, Hawker, Parachilna to Arkaroola.
CAR. From Port Augusta take Highway No. 47 to Hawker. From there it's

a sealed road to Wilpena Pound. From there to Blinman and on to Arkaroola its gravel.

TOURIST INFORMATION:

Flinders Ranges National Park, Phone (086) 48 0001.

ACCOMMODATION:

Quorn: Criterion Hotel/Motel, 20 Railway Tce., Ph (086) 48 6018 – B&LtB $25 double (hotel); The Mill Motel, 2 Railway Tce., Ph 48 6016 – B&LtB $41 double; Austral Hotel/Motel, 16 Railway Tce., Ph 48 6016 – RO $24 double (hotel) – RO $35 (motel); Grand Junction Hotel/Motel, Ph 48 6025 RO $27-29 double; Quorn Caravan Park, Ph 48 6031 – sites $4.50 double – on site vans $18-22 double. Hawker: Outback Motel, Wilpena Rd., Ph 489 1111 – RO $42 double; Hawker Hotel/Motel, Fourth St., Ph 48 9195 – RO $25 double (hotel) – $42-46 double (motel); Caravan Park, sites $4 double. Wilpena: Wilpena Motel, Ph (086) 48 0004 – B&LtB $60 double; Camping & Caravan Park, Ph (086) 48 0004 – sites $4.50 double; Rawnsley Park, Wilpena Road, Ph (086) 48 0008 – sites $7 double – on site vans $18-20 – cabins $22-25. Blinman: North Blinman Hotel, Ph Trunks 2K, B&B $40 double. Marree: Great Northern Hotel, Ph (086) 75 8344 – B&B $16 double – Marree Caravan Park, Ph 75 8371. Arakaroola, Mawson Lodge Motel, Ph (08) 21 21366 – RO $55 double; Greenwood Lodge Motel, Ph 21 21366 – RO $44; Arkaroola-Mt Painter Sanctuary Resort – sites $5.

EATING OUT:

Most of the hotels and motels have restaurants and the general stores and petrol stations usually sell take-away food.

POINTS OF INTEREST:

Quorn has four big hotels which dominate the other buildings in the long main street, and reflect the town's former importance as a railway junction. Nowadays, the only railway sounds are when an old steam train runs to the Pichi Richi Pass and back, a 25km trip. Only a short distance from town are the Wankerie Falls, Warren, Buckaringa and Middle Gorges. 14.4km south of the town is Mt. Brown 900m, the highest point in the area. Nearer town are Devil's Peak and Dutchman's Stern both of which are richly coloured and have walking trails to the summit. Quorn has retained much of its old world charater and the Mill, built in 1878 as a flour mill, has been restored and now houses a restaurant, gallery and museum. There are two other art galleries containing excellent displays of Flinders Ranges landscapes. Four wheel drive tours of the area can be arranged at Quorn, for those who would like to get off the beaten track and haven't the experience, or the resources to head off on their own.

Hawker, which flourished during the wheat rush years, has survived because all roads to the northern Flinders go through Hawker. Ruins of wheat farms dot the landscape, and testify to the times when flour milled at Hawker supplied properties as far away as Birdsville. The railway station, once a focal point of the now abandoned north-south line, features some unique architecture, and is a National Trust classified building. South of Hawker there are Aboriginal Rock Paintings and a rock shelter on a spur of the Yappala Range, adjacent to Yourambulla Peak and the ruins of Kanyaka Homesteads.

Wilpena Pound, 54km north of Hawker, is probably the best known feature of the Flinders Ranges. It is an oval bowl 16km long and 10km wide surrounded by high quartzite cliffs. The only route into the Pound is over Sliding Rock along the edge of Wilpena Creek. Aboriginal legend has it that the rim is formed by the bodies of two serpents. Enough rain falls on the higher walls of the range to keep the inner gorges and valleys green for at least part of the year making it an oasis in the dry heart of Central Australia. Handsome red rivergums line the watercourses. The whole of the Pound has been grazed at some time – some parts as recently as 1970. Sheep have removed most of the saltbush, and the plants which flower gaily each spring are mostly introduced weeds. Nevertheless, in most people's eyes, this does not detract from the beauty and majesty of this oasis. There are several walking tracks from Wilpena to gorges and parks. These range from easy to difficult, taking from an hour to a day. The walking track to the top of St. Mary's Peak (1164m) the highest point in the range, is a whole day's walk, but the view from the top is worth it. The walk should only be attempted after checking with the ranger, and only if you are fit. For those who haven't the time, the fitness or the inclination to attempt it, scenic flights are available (bookings at the motel). Tours are available from Wilpena to Aroona Valley-Bunyeroo Gorge, Sacred Canyon, Wilka-Wilina Gorge and Brachina Gorge.

Blinman, 60km from Wilpena, was once a booming copper mining town and some of the old mine machinery can still be seen. There is one hotel, a general store and a glassed-in swimming pool! The road to the east leads to Mount Chambers Gorge, through Eugunda Valley to Wirrealpa Homestead. A full day should be allowed to explore the gorge with its rock carvings. Mount Chambers offers a magnificent panorama of Lake Frome and the Flinders Ranges from Mt. Painter to Wilpena. There is a camping area. From Blinman the road west towards Parachilna on the Stuart Highway, takes you through the beautiful Parachilna Gorge. The Angorichina Hostel is on this road. A feature of this area is the nearby Blinman Pools which are fed by a permanent spring which flows even in the heat of summer.

Beltana on the road to Leigh Creek, was one of the major camel breeding stations of the far north. This old railway township has been gazetted an historical reserve, and its buildings are now being restored. The railway station houses a museum, general store and bottle shop; the police station, repeater station, bush hospital and Smith of Dunesk Mission are all being repaired. A free guide to the town is available at the railway station.

Leigh Creek South is 13km south of the original township and has excellent, modern facilities. The brown coal from Leigh Creek is used to fire the furnaces which produce the State's electricity at Port Augusta. During school holidays tours of the mine are available.

Further north is Marree, 694km from Adelaide. It is a small service centre for the surrounding pastoral area. It is the start or finish, of the infamous Birdsville Track. A journey along 'the Track' should only be undertaken after careful preparation and consultation with local authorities.

Arkaroola, in the northern Flinders Ranages, can be reached by turning off the road between Marree and Leigh Creek at Copley, and heading to Balcanoona. Arkaroola has airconditioned motels, bunkhouses and a caravan park. This remote resort is surrounded by majestic scenery. There are spectacular gorges enhanced by crystal pools. The area abounds with Aboriginal carvings and there are hot mineral springs at Paralana Springs. There is a spectacular Ridge Top Tour which would make even a mountain goat shudder.

MT. GAMBIER – Pop. 20,000

LOCATION:
451km south east of Adelaide on the slopes of an extinct volcano.

CHARACTERISTICS:
The volcano has three craters, the main one containing the Blue Lake which is famous for its mysterious change of colour from grey to rich blue each November, and back to grey again by March the following year. As a consequence, Mt. Gambier is known as the Blue Lake City.

HOW TO GET THERE:
AIR. O'Connor Air Services and Kendell Airlines have daily flights to/from Adelaide and Melbourne.
BUS. Greyhound stops at Mt. Gambier on its Adelaide/Melbourne coastal route and Ansett Pioneer have a Melbourne/Mt. Gambier/Naracoorte service. There is also a local bus service connecting Meningie/ Kingston/Mt. Gambier which travels via Bordertown at weekends.
RAIL. There is a regular service betwwen Adelaide and Mt. Gambier via Naracoorte and Bordertown.
CAR. Along the Princess Highway from Melbourne (438km) and 451km from Adelaide.

TOURIST INFORMATION:
Castertonm Road, Mt. Gambier, Ph (087) 25 1576 – open seven days.

ACCOMMODATION:
Hospitality Inn, Jubilee Highway, Ph 25 5122 – RO $47-50 double; Mid-City Motel, 7 Helen St., Ph 25 7277 – B&LtB $35 double; Mt. Gambier Motel, 115 Penola Rd., Ph 25 5800 – B&LtB $39-44 double; Central Caravan Park, 6 Krummel St., 25 4427 – site $6 double – on site vans $17-20 double; Jubilee

Caravan Park, Jubilee Hwy East, Ph 25 5109 – sites $7-9 double – cabins $25-35 double; Kalganyi Caravan Park, Cnr. Penola & Bishops Roads, Ph 25 1364 – sites $6 double – on site vans $16-18 double – cabins $20 double; the YMCA, 33 Percy St., Ph 25 6999 has accommodation for both men and women and charges $10 ppn.

EATING OUT:

Hospitality Inn Licensed Restaurant and Cocktail Bar is centrally located, Ph 25 5122; The Mt. Gambier Co-op, Commercial St. West, Ph 25 6744, has a tourist complex and the restaurant serves devonshire teas and lunches.

POINTS OF INTEREST:

The 197m deep Blue Lake is the premier tourist attraction but there are also three lakes in the secondary Valley Lake crater, but these remain the same colour all through the year. There are lookouts on the crater rim, and blowholes which allowed volcanic steam to escape are at Devils Punchbowl and on the lip of Valley Lake crater. The high point of the rim is crowned with a tower to mark 100 years of settlement. An oblisk stands near where the poet Adam Lindsay Gordon made a famous leap on horseback over a fence on to a narrow ledge overlooking the lake.

Many of the town's buildings have the distinctive colour of the local limestone, which is soft enough to be quarried with a saw and hardens to a rich creamy tone. The oldest building still standing is an old Convent which was erected in 1857 and is now used as a business house. The two-storey Court House, Commercial Mill, St. Martin's Lutheran and Christ Church Anglican Churches and the South Australian and Mt. Gambier Hotels are all of 1860's vintage. Behind the pink dolomite town hall is Cavern Garden, an open cave covered with flowers beds and, in season, is ablaze with roses.

The Cave Gardens in the centre of town have been built around a cave which provided the first water supply point for early settlers. It makes for an unusual garden and is flood lit at night.

Umpherston Cave to the east of the city, is situated in beautifully laid out grounds and is a popular barbeque/picnic place. Steep stairs lead down into the cave where a number of seats surround a gas barbecue.

The Mt. Gambier Co-operative Dairy Products factory in Commercial Street West, has a viewing gallery and audiovisual display as well as tastings and a restaurant.

The State Sawmill in Casterton Road, Ph 25 2237 is open for inspection at 9.45am Tues and Thurs. It is the largest sawmill of its kind in Australia and produces board products and treated round products.

The Mt. Gambier Stone Quarry, Cafpirco Road, Ph 39 9212 is open for inspection. Unique coraline limestone blocks, which are used to build houses etc. are mined here – open 7.30am-4pm Mon-Friday.

At the Turning Point, Commercial Street, you can see a wood turner at work as he fashions radiata pine products – open seven days a week – Ph 25 3270.

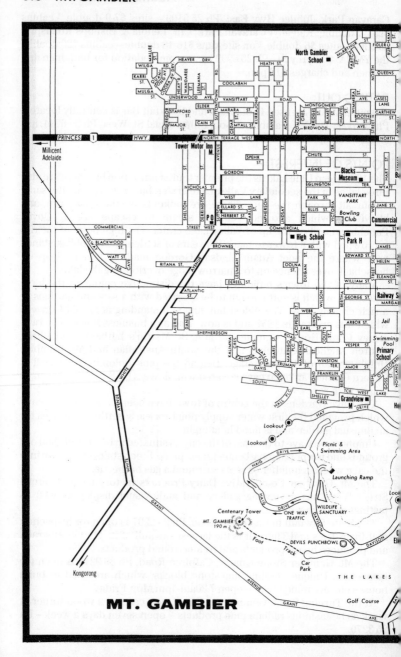

MT. GAMBIER

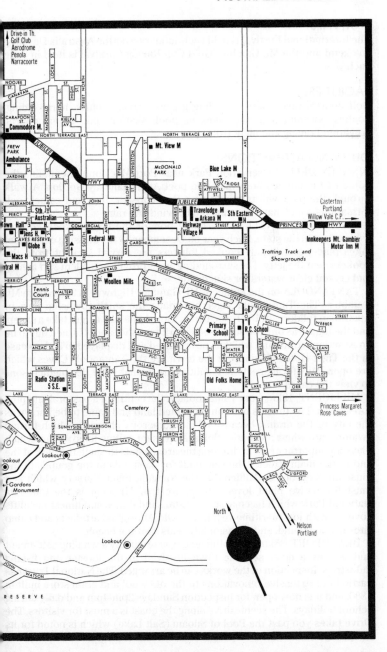

FESTIVALS:

The International Festival is held each January over the Australia Day long weekend and the Mt. Gambier Gold Cup Racing Carnival is held in June each year.

FACILITIES:

Golf course, race course, bowling greens, squash courts, horse riding, boating, swimming in the lakes or pool, skating rink, tennis courts, greyhound racing and night trotting.

OUTLYING ATTRACTIONS:

DINGLEY DELL Conservation Park near Port MacDonnell contains the home of the famous horseman and poet Adam Lindsay Gordon. A walk through the park will take you past the dinosaur, frog and camel rock formations which have been carved by wind and rain.

PORT MACDONNELL is the home port of the largest Rock Lobster fishing fleet in the state. Each year on December 28 the blessing of the fleet takes place, and freshly cooked lobsters are served straight from the cookers near the jetty. The surrounding areas provide excellent surf fishing and crystal clear waters for skin diving.

TANTANOOLA on the Millicent/Mt. Gambier Highway is 21km from Mt. Gambier. The Tantanoola Tiger has made the small township part of Australian folklore. In 1899 a local man thought he saw a tiger take a sheep, and the hunt was on! The supposed culprit was shot and it turned out to be an Assyrian wolfhound which is now stuffed and displayed in a glass case in the Tiger Hotel! 3.5km from the town are the Tantanoola Caves which are open daily for inspection. Facilities are available for disabled persons to view the caves.

MILLICENT, 19km from Tantanoola, is the centre of a pastoral and pine forest area. The town is built on reclaimed land and came to be known as the city of the drains, because of the numerous channels which turned swamps into wheat and barley fields. A pleasant willow-lined stream which plays an important part in draining the area, winds through the park at the end of the main street. A bicycle built for 35 stands in the gounds of the museum. 8km before Millicent is the Nangula Plant Nursery which is a must for native plant lovers. 13km west of Millicent is the Canunda National Park which has massive coastal sand dunes and limestone cliffs covered with low maritime vegetation. Old Aboriginal artefacts and camp sites may be found, and occasionally seals visit the beach.

BEACHPORT, 35km from Millicent, was originally a whaling settlement and is now a quiet sea-side town involved in the lobster and fishing industries. Inspection of the works can be arranged. The National Trust has carried out extensive renovations to the old wool and grain store built in 1880, and it is now open for inspection Sundays 2pm-4pm and daily during school holidays. The scenic drive along the coast is a must for visitors. The Drive takes you past the Pool of Siloam (Salt Lake) which is noted for its buoyancy.

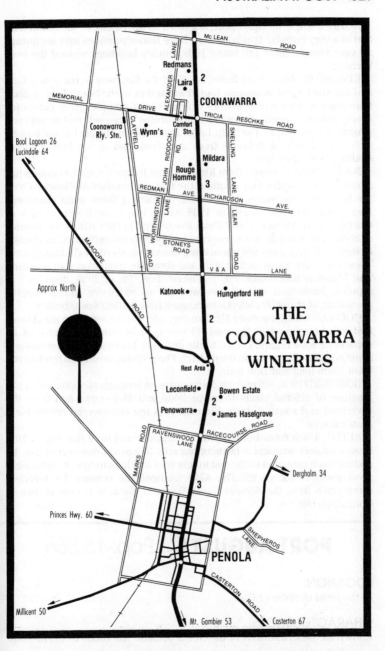

THE
COONAWARRA
WINERIES

Approx North

Bool Lagoon 26
Lucindale 64

Princes Hwy. 60

Millicent 50

Mt. Gambier 53

Casterton 67

Dergholm 34

PENOLA

McLEAN ROAD
Redmans
Laira
COONAWARRA
TRICIA RESCHKE ROAD
Comfort Stn.
Wynn's
Coonawarra Rly. Stn.
Mildara
Rouge Homme
REDMAN AVE.
RICHARDSON AVE.
STONEYS ROAD
V & A LANE
Katnook
Hungerford Hill
Rest Area
Leconfield
Bowen Estate
Penowarra
James Haselgrove
RAVENSWOOD LANE
RACECOURSE ROAD
SHEPHERDS LANE
CASTERTON ROAD
MEMORIAL DRIVE
ALEXANDER LANE
CLAYFIELD
JOHN RIDDOCH RD.
SNELLING LANE
LEAR ROAD
WORTHINGTON LANE
MARKS ROAD
MAAOOPE ROAD

ROBE, 50km from Beachport, is known as the Centre of the South East and is a very popular holiday resort. Lake Butler provides safe anchorage all year round. There are many 19th century buildings around the boat harbour.

KINGSTON, 44km from Robe, is called the Gateway to the South East and has the largest manmade tourist attraction in the South East, a giant fibre-glass lobster which towers over a tourist complex, that caters for every tourists' needs (souvenirs, theatrette, licensed restaurant and educational displays). The Cafe Jaffa Lighthouse in Marine Parade is open daily during school holidays from 2pm-5pm, and at weekends during summer from 2pm-5pm.

NARACOORTE, 100km from Kingston and 102km from Mt. Gambier has a large cave complex 8km south of the town. It consists of Blanche Cave, the first cave discovered in the area, containing three main chambers; Alexandra Cave discovered in 1908 which has some fine examples of marine fossils; Victoria Fossil Cave, discovered in 1894 which has a series of chambers and galleries connected by low narrow excavated walkways. In this cave, scientists are uncovering ossuary finds of world importance. These caves are a spectacular sight and should be a must on your itinerary. The Museum and Snake Pit, 1 Jenkins Tce., Ph 62 2059, displays live reptiles, birds and animals, as well as an extensive indoor display consisting of about 30 collections ranging from butterflies to bullets.

COONAWARRA, between Mt. Gambier and Narracoorte, is a small town that has blossomed in the past 30 years, to become the centre of an expanding wine region, known for its dry reds. There are ten wineries and some additional growers in the district. The growing area is a stretch of red loam 13km long and 1km wide.

BORDERTOWN, 80km from Naracoorte, is strategically situated at the junction of arterial roads from Adelaide and Melbourne and from the Riverland and south-western Victoria. It is the commercial centre for a pastoral area.

KEITH, 45km from Bordertown, struggled along until the Ninety Mile Desert project wrought a farming miracle. Scientists discovered that by adding trace elements to the soil in this area and irrigating it, it could yield good pastures for sheep. The AMP financed the scheme for returned servicemen from the Second World War and the area is now known as Coonalpyn Downs.

PORT AUGUSTA – Pop. 15,566

LOCATION:
At the head of Spencer Gulf.

CHARACTERISTICS:
Known as the Crossroads of the North because the roads from Adelaide

the Flinders Ranges, Alice Springs, Perth and Whyalla all intersect there.

HOW TO GET THERE:

AIR. Augusta Airways to/from Adelaide twice daily weekdays. Dennan fly to Leigh Creek, Marree and the mail run to Innamincka, Birdsville and Boula.

BUS. Ansett Pioneer, Greyhound and Deluxe all stop here on their Adelaide/Perth and Adelaide/Darwin Routes. Stateliner service the Eyre Peninsula from Adelaide.

RAIL. On the Indian Pacific route, the Ghan leaves from here for Alice Springs, and there is a regular service to Adelaide.

CAR. On the Eyre Highway 339km from Adelaide and 2439km from Perth.

TOURIST INFORMATION:

Corporation Office, Commercial Rd., Ph (086) 42 3555.

ACCOMMODATION:

Acacia Ridge Motel, 33 Stokes Tce., Ph 42 3377 – RO $38-$44 double; Augusta Westside, 3 Loudon Rd., Ph 42 2488 – RO $38 double, Poinsettia Motel, 24 Burgoyne St., Ph 42 2856 – RO $35 double; Port Augusta East Motel, National Highway One, Ph 42 2555 – RO $30 double; Flinders Hotel/ Motel, 39 Commercial Rd., Ph 42 2544 – RO $36 double; Myoora Motel, 5 Hackett St., Ph 42 3622 – RO $38 double; Northern Gateway Inn, Jervois St., Ph 42 2944 -RO $35-40 double; Pampas Motel, Stirling Rd., Ph 42 3795 – $35 double; Pt. Augusta Hi-Way One Motel, Ph 42 2755 – RO $38-52 double; Fauna Caravan Park, 33 Stokes Tce., Ph 42 2974 – sites $6 double, on site vans $16-20 double and cabins $25-30; Shoreline Caravan Park, 2km from P.O., Ph 42 2964 – sites $5-6.50 double – on-site vans $16-22 double – cabins $16-22 double; Stirling North Caravan Park, Brook St., Ph 43 6357 – site $4.50 double.

EATING OUT:

BP Westside, Main Road, Ph 42 2906 has a restaurant and take-away.

POINTS OF INTEREST:

The Thomas Playford Power Station supplies about a third of the state's power and uses brown coal from Leigh Creek. There are tours at 10am, 11am & 1pm. This is an important railway junction (the Indian Pacific and the Ghan) and there are large railway workshops here, which you can tour at 2pm Mon-Frid.

The Curdnatta Art & Pottery Gallery is found in the first railway station. There are other old buildings which include the Greenbush Gaol from 1869, the old town hall, the Grante and Homestead Park pioneer museum which also includes a railway museum on the corner of Elsie and Jaycee Sts.

OUTLYING ATTRACTIONS:

ANDAMOOKA, 287km north of Port Augusta, was once part of a vast inland sea. To-day is is famous for its opals. There is a hotel/motel, guesthouse and camping area. Meals are available from the hotel/motel, guest house and the Tuckerbox Restaurant. The Opal Gleam dugout home can be inspected. One of the local landmarks is Duke's Bottle Home built from discarded beer bottles. A matrified plesiosaur measuring 9m has been found in the diggings.

COOBER PEDY, 610km north of Port Augusta, on the Adelaide Darwin road, has a lunar-like landscape as a result of years of 'noddling' for opal. Most of the town's population is engaged in mining activities, and live in underground 'dug outs' which give protection from wind, dust, heat and flies. Coober Pedy is Australia's largest opal producing centre. You can camp above ground or underground at the Umoona Mine. There is a youth hostel and a hotel/motel. There are several galleries and a desalination plant, Crocodile Harry's Dugout and underground churches and a museum.

PORT PIRIE is 95 km south of Port Augusta and 223km from Adelaide. In 1889 three smelters were built near Port Pirie to refine the ore being railed from Broken Hill. To-day it is the largest lead smelter in the world, and produces lead, zinc, gold, cadmium, antimony and copper by-products and sulphuric acid. Lead is SA biggest single-produced export income earner. Conducted tours of the smelting works are available Mon-Fri at 2pm. Pt. Pirie has picturesque parks within its city area that are ideal for picnics. The Old Customs House and Railway Museum Complex house an exhibition of local history alongside which stands the 'Port Pirie' train.

PETERBOROUGH, 162km from Port Augusta and 243km from Adelaide, is currently one of only two centres in the world where three different rail gauges come together. Incorporated in the town's rail system is a Bogie Exchange which is one of only two in the State. The Steamtown Peterborough Railway Preservation Society officially commenced operations in 1981 almost 100 years after the first railway reached Peterborough. The Society runs steam passenger trains at specified times on the narrow gauge line from Peterborough to Orroroo, and the view enjoyed by passengers is one that shouldn't be missed. Timetables for this tourist attraction are readily available in town.

BURRA, 156km from Adelaide, nestles in the Bald Hills. It was here that copper was discovered in 1845. The mines closed down in 1877 but the era of the mining days has been preserved in the unique old buildings around Paxton Square, which resembles a Cornish mining village. There are many other old buildings including a museum, original miner's dugouts and century old churches featuring magnificient stonework and stained glass. Breaker Morant was filmed in the hills around, and Redruth Gaol was used to portray Fort Edwards in the film.

CLARE, 135km from Adelaide, has been made famous through its wines. There are 16 wineries in the valley and most are open for cellar sales and tastings – for full details and opening times see the SA Tourist Office. The visitor would be hard pressed to find signs of the devastating Ash Wednesday 1983 bushfires which swept through the valley. The Valley holds an Easter Wine Festival which is held bi-ennially in years of even

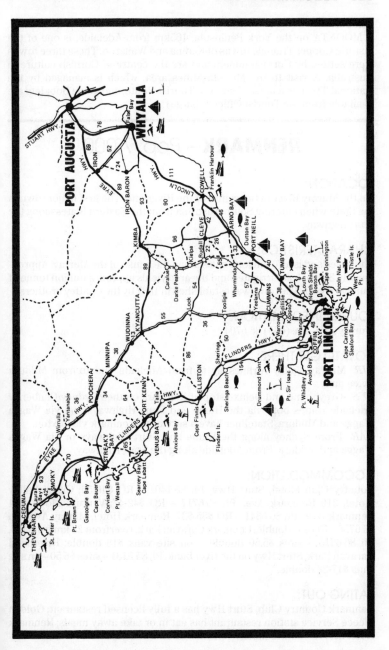

number.

MOONTA on the York Peninsula, 165km from Adelaide, is one of the historic Copper Triangle towns of Kadina and Wallaroo. These three towns were settled by Cornish miners and are the centre of Cornish culture in Australia. A visit to the Moonta Mines area, which is managed by the National Trust, is a must. There is a Tourist Route, and guide booklets are available from the Tourist Office (charge)

RENMARK – Pop. 7,000

LOCATION:
On the Murray River in the centre of the Riverland. The first major town in the State when entering South Australia from the Eastern States along the Sturt highway.

CHARACTERISTICS:
The Riverland is a 70 km long oasis along the banks of the Murray. Approximately 30,000 h are irrigated and the area yields approx. 2 million tonne of fruit each year. The town was established in 1887 by the Chaffey brothers.

TOURIST INFORMATION:
Murray Ave., Ph. (085) 86 6704

HOW TO GET THERE:
AIR. Murray Valley Airlines fly to/from Adelaide and to/from Mildura twice daily.
BUS. Greyhound and Deluxe stop at Renmark on their Sydney/Canberra/Adelaide routes both via the Hume and Sturt Highways and via Wagga Wagga and Mildura. Stateliner have a service to Renmark via Loxton.
CAR. From Sydney along the Hume and Sturt Highways or via Wagga Wagga and Mildura. From Adelaide along the Sturt Highway.

ACCOMMODATION:
Country Club Motel, Sturt Hwy, Ph 85 1401 – RO $46-56; Citrus Valley Motel, 210 Renmark Ave., Ph 86 6717 – RO $42-47; Ventura Motel, 234 Renmark Ave., Ph 86 6841 – RO $35-$37. Renmark Hotel, Murray Ave., Ph 86 6755 – RO $30 double. Renmark Caravan Park, riverfront 22 km from PO, Ph 86 6315 – sites $5.50 double – on site vans $18 double; Riverbend Caravan Park, Sturt Hwy on the river bank, Ph 85 5131 – sites $6.50 – on site vans $17-23 double.

EATING OUT:
Renmark Country Club, Sturt Hwy has a fully licensed restaurant; Golden Fleece Service station restaurant has eat in or take away meals; Renmark Hotel serves counter meals.

POINTS OF INTEREST:

The most historically significant building is Olivewood, built in the style of a Canadian log cabin in 1887 by the Chaffey brothers who pioneered irrigation in Australia.

The Renmark Hotel is a community owned hotel which has given much to charity and development projects.

The Paddle Steamer 'Industry' is now a museum moored adjacent to the town. There are several art galleries including the Ozone Gallery and the Frank Harding Folklore gallery.

Bredl's Reptile Park and Zoo has one of the largest collections of live reptiles in Australia.

FESTIVALS:

The Orange Week festival lasts nine days and is held in the first week of the Spring school holidays (September).

FACILITIES:

Golf course, bowling club, tennis courts, 50 metre pool, squash courts,

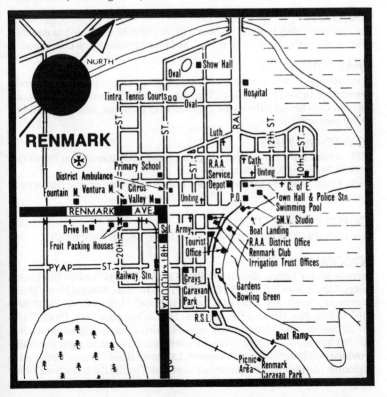

rollerskating rink, volleyball and basketball courts. Boating and fishing are popular.

OUTLYING ATTRACTIONS:

BERRI, 18km from Renmark is the industrial centre of the region. Well known because of its fruit juice factory. Tours are conducted daily – 9.30am, 10.30am, 2pm, 3.30pm Monday to Friday.

BLANCHETOWN, only 134 km from Adelaide. Fishing and water skiing centre.

LOXTON, 238 km from Adelaide and 38 km from Renmark. Possesses an Historical village and well known for its stone fruits and vineyards.

WAIKERIE, 175 km from Adelaide and 80 km from Renmark, has Australia's largest citrus packing house. Popular among gliding enthusiasts and fishermen and boating enthusiasts.

TANUNDA – Pop. 2,621

LOCATION:
The Barossa Valley is about an hour's drive north of Adelaide but could be a valley along the Rhine in Germany, as far as appearance is concerned.

CHARACTERISTICS:
A picturesque region with quiet villages, rolling hills, neat vineyards, and a German air. In 1842 Pastor Kavel lead a group of Lutherans to the valley and they not only brought their vine cuttings with them but ,also their building techniques and culture.

HOW TO GET THERE:
BUS. Ansett Pioneer, Greyhound, Deluxe and Stateliner stop at Nurioopta on their Brisbane/Adelaide route.
CAR. From Adelaide take the Stuart Highway to Gawler, the Gateway to the valley.

TOURIST INFORMATION:
Barossa Valley Vintage Festival Office, Murray St., Ph (085) 63 2707.

ACCOMMODATION:
Barossa Motor Lodge, Murray St., Ph 63 2988 – RO $44 double; Blickinstal Motel, Rifle Range Rd., Ph 63 2716 – B&B $45 double; Weintal Hotel/Motel, Murray St., Ph 63 2303 – RO $43; Tanunda Hotel, 51 Murray St., Ph 63 2030 – RO $35 double; Barossa House Guest House, Baroosa Hwy, Ph 62 2716 – $37-39 double; YHA at Kersbrook on the Chain of Ponds-Williamstown Rd., Ph (08) 389 3185 – $4 ppn – can be used as a base for touring the valley provided you have your own transport. Langmeil Road Caravan Park – sites $4 double (no phone) and Tanunda Caravan & Tourist Park, Barossa Valley Hwy, Ph 63 2784 – sites $8 double – onsite vans $18-22 double At Nurioopta

there is accommodation for 6 persons at the privately run Jan Matthew, Bunkhaus Hostel 1km from town. It is essential to phone ahead to ensure accommodation. The number is (085) 62 2260 – phone before 9am or in the evening – $6.50.

EATING OUT:
The Tanunda Hotel is renowned for fine counter meals served from 12-2pm & 6-8pm daily in the Public Bar, Lounge or Beer Garden – for a la carte try their dining room; the Heinemann Park Family Restaurant serves home cooked German and Australian meals at reasonable prices Ph 63 2151; for afternoon tea or a light meal try the Zinfandel Tea Rooms, 58 Murray Street, Ph 63 2822 or Anna's Konditorei, 82c Murray Street in Tanunda Arcade, Ph 63 3473; Die Galerie Restaurant has fine food and wine and a dinner dance on Saturday nights – 66 Murray St., Ph 63 2788 – open seven days; for something different try the Barossa Junction Restaurant Railway Museum at Tanunda North where you can dine in railway carriages of yesteryear decorated with memorabilia.

POINTS OF INTEREST:
Tanunda has beautiful historical bluestone buildings, tiny German cottages and the spires of the lovely German Churches. It is one of the oldest towns in the Barossa. It is the traditional German centre of the Valley, and Barossa Deutsche (a form of German traditionally spoken in the Barossa Valley) is still spoken by many of the older residents. It is widely referred to as one of the most attractive towns in Australia, and is noted for the civic pride shown by the local residents. This is reflected in the general apppearance of the township area – well maintained house properties, sealed streets, concrete footpaths and the high standard of public amenities.

The first common, Zeigenmarkt (Goat Square) is ringed with cottages straight out of the past, with the old water pump and tank still standing there. Its design shows how the marketplace operated.

The old post and telegraph office was saved from demolition and is now a museum.

The church was the most important building to the early settlers in the Barossa Valley, and Tanunda has three beautiful churches: Langmeil built in 1888 with a monument to Pastor Kavel, St. Johns built in 1868 with its lifesized wooden statues, Tabor built in 1849 with three bells in its 26m tower.

Tanunda has long been recognized as the centre of brass banding in Australia and competitions, held in late October or early November, attract bands from all parts of Australia and overseas.

The twin complex of Storybook Cottage, featuring a miniature world behind the little green door, and Whacky Wood, with its Aussie style fun and games, is a popular place for the whole family. As is Barossa Kiddy Park which has rides, games, picnic grounds, kiosk etc. and is open daily 10.30-5.30pm.

The Barossa Motor Museum has vintage and veteran cars, trucks etc. and is open 10am-4pm every day except Tuesdays.

Tanunda Wineries: Basedows, Bernkastel, Chateau Tanunda, Chateau Rosevale, Hoffmann's North Para, Krondorf and Veritas. Most of the wineries are open daily for tastings and cellar door sales.

FACILITIES:

Tanunda has fine sporting facilities including a German-style skittle alley. There is also a golf course, lawn bowls, swimming pool and tennis courts.

FESTIVALS:

The Barossa Vintage Festival is held in odd-numbered years during March or April. It starts on Easter Monday. An Essenfest (Eating Festival) is held in March. The Brass Band Contest is held in late October or early November and the annual Agricultural Show is held in March.

OUTLYING ATTRACTIONS:

GAWLER, 41km from Adelaide at the junction of the North and South Para Rivers, is the western gateway to the Barossa Valley. It has many beautiful Victorian buildings which have been faithfully preserved. A feature of Gawler's sporting calendar is the world renowned 3 day equestrian event, the West End Horse Trials, which is held every June long weekend.

LYNDOCH, 55km from Adelaide, is one of the oldest towns in South Australia. The Holy Trinity Church is worth looking at, as is the museum located just outside town, as it has a collection of Dresden China and Porcelain. Wineries: Chateau Yaldara, Chattertons, Das Alte Weinhause, Karlsburg, Karrawirra, Wards Gateway Cells and Wilsford. Chateau Yaldara was built in the ruins of a 19th century winery and flour mill. It is built along the lines of a European chateau and filled with art treasures – phone (085) 24 4200 for tour times.

ANGASTON, 79km from Adelaide, is set high in the ranges and is sometimes referred to as the 'Crown of the Valley'. It is an historic village with many beautiful homes and cottages. The Collingrove homestead, on the outskirts of the town, was built in 1853 for John Howard Angas. Lindsay Park, another historic property, built in 1847 for George Fife Angas, is now the home of Lindsay Park Stud one of Australia's most successful thoroughbred breeding complexes. The whole town may be viewed from the lookout on top of Mengler's Hill. Angaston is the home of a thriving fruit industry, with both glaced and dried fruits being produced. Half of all dried cut fruit produced in Australia is packed by Angas Park Fruit Company. Wineries: Saltram and Yalumba. Yalumba is built of blue marble with a clock town and surrounded by attractive gardens. Keyneton only has one remaining winery, Henschke's which was planted in 1847. It is open for tasings and sales.

SPRINGTON is the site of the famous Herbig Family Tree, a large, hollow red gum which was home for Friedrich and Caroline Herbig and their children from 1858 to 1860.

NURIOOTPA, 73km from Adelaide, is the commercial centre of the

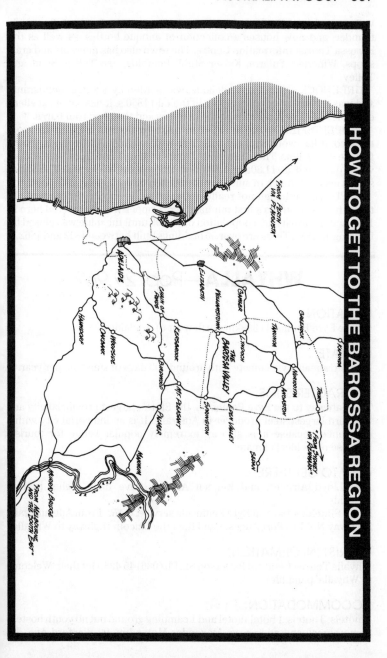

HOW TO GET TO THE BAROSSA REGION

Valley. Coulthard House in Main Street was once the home of the town's founder, and now houses a collection of antique bottles, as well as the Barossa Tourist Information Centre. The town also has many art and craft shops. Wineries: Yularra, Kaiser Stuhl, Penfolds, and Tolley, Scott and Tolley.

GREENOCK, 66km from Adelaide, was settled by Scottish immigrants and was the site of copper mining in the mid 1850's. It has some excellent examples of early Australian stone cottages and thatched roof barns.

SEPPELTSFIELD was founded in 1851 by Joseph Seppelt to grow tobacco. It has wonderful old buildings with magnificent grounds, which feature date palms. There are guided tours at 1am, 11am, 1pm, 1pm & 3pm week days and at 11.30am, 1.30pm & 2.30pm on weekends. The kiosk serves a superb lunch of spit roasted chicken or pork daily.

KAPUNDA, although not really in the valley, is another interesting old town. It was Australia's first mining town. Copper was discovered here in 1842 and the town had a population of 10,000 until the mine was closed by flooding, in 1888. There are over 50 buildings built between 1842 and 1862.

WHYALLA – Pop. 29,962

LOCATION:
On the Eyre Peninsula 398km north west of Adelaide.

CLIMATE:
Mediterranean style climate with around 300 days of sunshine per year.

CHARACTERISTICS:
The Gateway to the Eyre Peninsula, the State's largest provincial city and the third largest steel producer in Australia. It is an industrial city with a difference because it is also an extremely popular venue for tourists because of its ideal climate.

HOW TO GET THERE:
AIR. Lloyd Airlines, and Kendell Airlines have daily flights to/from Adelaide.
BUS. Stateliner have an Eyre Peninsula service. *CAR.* From Adelaide take Highway No. 1 to Port Augusta and then the Lincoln Highway to Whyalla.

TOURIST INFORMATION:
Whyalla Tourist Centre, 3 Patterson St., Ph (086) 45 428. Get their 'Welcome to Whyalla' pamphlet.

ACCOMMODATION:
4 motels, 3 hotels, 1 hotel/motel and 1 camping ground but no youth hostel. Some names and addresses: Alexander Motor Inn, 99 Playford Ave., Ph

45 9488 – RO $44; Airport Whyalla Motel, Lincoln Hwy, Ph 45 21232 – RO $32; Foreshore Motel, Watson Tce., Ph 45 8877 – RO $42; Spencer Hotel, Forsyth St., Ph 45 8411 – RO $28 double; Sundowner Hotel/Motel, Cowell Rd., Ph 45 7688; Bayview Hotel, 13 Forsyth St.., Ph 45 8544 – RO $28 double; Eyre Hotel, Cnr.Playford Ave. & Elliott St., Ph 45 7188 – RO $30 double; Whyalla Hotel, Darling Tce., Ph 45 7411 – RO $28 double; Whyalla Foreshore Caravan Park, Broadbent Tce., Ph 45 7474 – site only $6 double – on site caravans $14.50-$18 double; cabins $20-26; Whyalla Airport Caravan Park, Malaquana Rd., Whyalla Stuart, Ph 45 9357 – sites $6 – onsite vans $12 double.

EATING OUT:
The Foreshore Motel right on the beach has a fully licensed restaurant.

POINTS OF INTEREST:
B.H.P. has played a major part in Whyalla's development. With the discovery of iron ore in the Iron Knob area in the late 1890's, a tramway was built to Hummock Hill (Whyalla) to enable the rapid transfer of ore from the quarries to barges, and across the gulf to the smelters at Port Pirie. In 1938 it was decided to build a blast furnace at Whyalla closer to the iron ore source and this, coupled with the building of the shipyards and a deep water harbour brought prosperity to the town. In 1958 B.H.P. began building a steelworks, and in 1961 Whyalla was proclaimed a city. The shipyards were closed down in the 1970's leading to much unemployment.

A visit to Whyalla would not be complete without a tour of the steelworks. Tours are conducted by BHP at 9.30 on weekdays. Closed footwear must be worn.

The Mt. Laura Homestead in Ekblom St., a National Trust Museum, was built in 1922 as part of a grazing station, and now displays many items of historical interest relating to the city's early history – open Sundays & public holidays from 2-4pm.

Studio 41, Cnr. Wood & Donaldston Tce., Ph 45 8367 has the largest craft gallery on the Eyre Peninsula – open Mon-Fri 9am-5.30pm, Sats 9am-5pm & 2-5pm Sun.

Whyalla's foreshore has a caravan park, picnic ground and a small zoo. The arid salbush plains near the airport are occupied by a wildlife park including a reptile house and a walk-through aviary.

FESTIVALS:
The Tunarama Festival marks the start of the tuna season in Port Lincoln and is held on the long weekend in January. The Whyalla show is held in August.

FACILITIES:
Whyalla has good shopping centres throughout the city and there are cabarets, discos, floorshows, theatre, cinema etc. Of course, there is good fishing, boating, and swimming, as well as tennis, golf, lawn bowls, croquet

and squash.

OUTLYING ATTRACTIONS:

The coast to the south is a succession of serene villages and resorts set on crescent-shaped bays with charming names like Tumby Bay, Arno Bay and Lucky Bay. The beaches are long and deserted, broken by low, occasional headlands. The whole area affords good fishing. The coastline changes dramatically past Port Lincoln and the gentle bays change to tall, broken cliffs with the Southern Ocean pounding at their base.

COWELL is a sleepy village on the sheltered Franklin Harbour which is more like a large lagoon as it has an area of almost 50 sq km, but its entrance is only 100m wide! It is a safe fishing and boating resort with night crabbing in the shallows a special attraction. Australa's only jade is mined at nearby Mt. Geraghty. It is brought to the factory in Second Street where it is cut and polished. Visitors are welcome to watch the large diamond saws cutting the stone. There is also an historical museum in the old Post Office.

PORT LINCOLN, 270km south of Whyalla, is a popular tourist resort and home port of a large tuna fishing fleet. It lies on Boston Bay which is ideal for sailing, swimming, water-skiing, fishing and skin-diving. It was first settled in 1834 and has many old buildings, including the Lincoln Hotel in Tasman Terrace which first opened for business in 1840. Building on the Old Mill in Dorset Place commenced in 1846 but was never completed presumably due to poor harvests. It is now a small pioneer museum. There are several other buildings of interest, and the Tourist Office in Tasman Tce., Ph (086) 82 3255, can give you further information. For a delicious feed of strawberries & ice cream visit the Strawberry Farm at Little Swamp 7km from town, and then wander through the attached Fauna & Pioneer Park to see the kangaroos, koalas, deer and parrots. A 'must' on your visit to Port Lincoln is a trip to the southern-most tip of Eyre Peninsula as it has some of the most rugged scenery in Australia. As it is a Conservation Area, a permit must first be obtained from the Pt. Lincoln Tourist Office. The Park is 32km south of Port Lincoln and the 15km Whalers Way takes you to the old Sleaford Whaling Station at Fishery Bay. It is a drive you will long remember.

It is possible to drive along Flinders Way along the western side of Eyres Peninsula and rejoin the Eyre Highway at Ceduna. This road is rather quiet as it only goes through one or two service towns and fishing centres.

The area in the centre of the peninsula is rather flat with a string of salt lakes near the tip and gives way to waving fields of wheat and barley further north.

INDEX to locations of Places of Interest and Activity

APPLES CAN BE SEEN AROUND
Bridgetown – WA
Bright – Vic
Bunbury – WA
Huonville – Huon Valley – Tas
Orange – NSW
Renmark – SA
Shepparton – Vic
Stanthorpe – Qld

AUTUMN LEAVES CAN BE SEEN AROUND
Adelaide Hills – SA
Armidale – NSW
Bowral – NSW
Bright – Vic
Maldon – Vic
New Norfolk – Derwent Valley – Tas
Tumut – NSW

BANANA PLANTATIONS CAN BE SEEN AROUND
Carnarvon – WA
Coffs Harbour – NSW

CITRUS TREES CAN BE SEEN AROUND
Berri – SA
Gayendah – Qld
Helidon – Qld
Mildura – Vic

DAIRY CATTLE CAN BE SEEN AROUND
Bateman's Bay – NSW
Bega – NSW
Casino – NSW
Echuca – Vic
Kapunda – SA

Kyabram – Goulburn Valley – Vic
Maleny – Qld
Mt. Lofty Ranges – SA
Murray Bridge – SA
Nowra – NSW
Omeo – Vic
Port Elliott – SA
Scottsdale – Tas
St. Helens – Tas
Stanley – Tas
Traralgon – Latrobe Valley – Vic
Wedderburn – Vic
Wynyard – Tas

FAIRY PENGUINS CAN BE SEEN AT
Kangaroo Island – SA (also Sea Lions)
Penguin – Tas
Phillip Island – Tas
Rockingham – WA

FOSSICKING – GOLD PANNING
Alice Spings – Harts Range – NT
Andamooka – SA
Ararat – Vic
Ballarat – Vic
Beechworth – Vic
Bendigo – Vic
Bingara – NSW
Braidwood – NSW
Broken Hill – NSW
Buchan – Vic
Chinchilla – Qld
Cloncurry – Qld
Coober Pedy – SA
Cowell – SA
Glen Innes – NSW
Gulgong – NSW
Hill End – NSW

SURFING
Batesman's Bay – NSW
Bicheno – Tas
Byron Bay – NSW
Coffs Harbour – NSW
Gold Coast – Qld
Kangaroo Island – SA
Kingscliff – NSW
Lakes Entrance – Vic
Mandurah – WA
Melbourne – Vic
Nambucca Heads – NSW
Newcastle – NSW
Noosa – Qld
Port Elliott – SA
Sydney – NSW
Wollongong – NSW

TRAMS STILL RUN IN
Adelaide – SA
Melbourne – Vic

TURTLE ROOKERIES
Bundaberg – Mon Repos
Beach – Qld
Heron Island – Qld

WHEAT AND BARLEY FARMS CAN BE SEEN AROUND
Ararat – Vic
Ballarat – Vic
Bendigo – Vic
Emerald – Qld
Eyre Peninsula – SA
Hyden – WA
Kapunda – SA
Merredin – WA
Millicent – SA
Moonta – SA
New Norcia – WA
Toowoomba – Darling Downs – Qld
Wedderburn – Vic

WILD FLOWERS CAN BE SEEN
Christmas Bells Plain – South of
Pt. Macquarie – NSW
Flinders Ranges – SA

Grampians – Vic
Snowy Mountains – NSW/Vic
Stirling Ranges – WA
You Yangs – near Geelong – Vic
Near Geraldton – WA

WINE GROWING AREAS
Adelaide Plains – SA
Ararat Area – Vic
Avon Valley – WA
Barossa Valley – SA
Clare Valley – SA
Coonawarra – SA
Denmark – WA
Echuca – Vic
Glenrowan – Vic
Hunter Valley – Cessnock – NSW
Margaret River – WA
McLaren Vale – SA
Mildura – Vic
Mt. Barker – WA
Mudgee Area – NSW
Renmark – SA
Rutherglen – Vic
Seymour – Vic
Southern Vales – SA
Stanthorpe – Qld
Swan Valley – WA
Yanchep – WA
Yarra Glen – Vic

INDEX